Fourth Edition

THE POLITICS OF GLOBAL ECONOMIC RELATIONS

Robert S. Walters
University of Pittsburgh

David H. Blake
Southern Methodist University

PRENTICE HALL, Englewood Cliffs, New Jersey 07632

Library of Congress Cataloging-in-Publication Data

Walters, Robert S.
    The politics of global economic relations / Robert S. Walters,
David H. Blake. -- 4th ed.
        p.   cm.
    Authors' names in reverse order on previous eds.
    Includes bibliographical references and index.
    ISBN 0-13-682394-7
    1. International economic relations.   I. Blake, David H.
    II. Title.
    HF1411.B6   1992
    337--dc20   91-25961
                                                               CIP

Editorial/production supervision and
    interior design: Shelly Kupperman
Cover design: Ben Santora
Prepress Buyer: Kelly Behr
Manufacturing Buyer: Mary Ann Gloriande
Acquisitions Editor: Karen Horton
Editorial Assistant: Dolores Mars

To SCOTT, CLAIRE, DAVID, JENNIFER, and KIMBERLY

Printed in the United States of America
10 9 8 7 6 5 4 3 2

ISBN   0-13-682394-7

PRENTICE-HALL INTERNATIONAL (UK) LIMITED, *London*
PRENTICE-HALL OF AUSTRALIA PTY. LIMITED, *Sydney*
PRENTICE-HALL CANADA INC., *Toronto*
PRENTICE-HALL HISPANOAMERICANA, S.A., *Mexico*
PRENTICE-HALL OF INDIA PRIVATE LIMITED, *New Delhi*
PRENTICE-HALL OF JAPAN, INC., *Tokyo*
SIMON & SCHUSTER ASIA PTE. LTD., *Singapore*
EDITORA PRENTICE-HALL DO BRASIL, LTDA., *Rio de Janeiro*

CONTENTS

PREFACE

It has been fifteen years since the first edition of this book appeared. The analytical and topical foci used to organize this survey of the politics of international economic relations continue to serve us well. Readers familiar with the volume will see the same structure here as in earlier editions. Crises, altered trends, and new preoccupations in political-economic relations have required us, however, to change much of the content with the appearance of each new edition. The fourth edition is certainly no exception.

It seems to have become commonplace recently for events of major proportions to catch decision makers and analysts of international political and economic affairs off guard, only to have them later appear quite understandable in terms of forces known to be present all along. Yet, if we fully understood these forces, we should not be so shocked by developments as they unfold. It has been a period to humble serious analysts of international relations, ourselves among them.

Problems of policy coordination among the major economies in managing currency alignments during October 1987 precipitated the worst stock market crash in half a century. A decade witnessing an astounding economic performance by the United States has left it with trade and fiscal deficits that defy politically acceptable solutions. Together, they have made the management of United States domestic economic policy more vulnerable than ever to international economic developments. Japan replaced the United States as the world's largest creditor. There were fears in the United States that it was losing its technological and economic leadership to Japan and the European Economic Community on course to the creation of a single internal market in 1992. Mikhail Gorbachev unleashed reforms in the USSR and East Europe that resulted in the loss of Soviet control over East Europe and the overthrow of Communist regimes throughout the region. These developments seemed to have ended the Cold War on the West's terms and to have launched a process to reintegrate these nations with the global economy. At the same time, however, they have rekindled ethnic and nationality conflicts as well as challenges to political legitimacy that threaten the stability of countries in the region, including the Soviet Union itself. After bold experimentation during the 1980s with economic reforms going well beyond those of Communist states before, China shocked the world with its repression of students demanding democracy in June 1989. The likely course of its political and economic ties with the West have been less clear since. The world lurched into a war with Iraq during 1991 in an effort to evict it from its stunning occupation of Kuwait— marking the third time since 1973 that war and oil markets were linked in the Middle East. The United States' role in the war underlined its unique capacity to project political, economic, and military power relative to other major states in the international system—the USSR, Germany, and Japan. These developments and many others are discussed in this new edition of *The Politics of Global Economic Relations*. They are embedded in the more enduring features of the international political economy surveyed in the earlier editions.

The fourth edition also marks a change in the division of labor between the authors. David Blake assumed a new position as Dean of the Edwin L. Cox School of Business at Southern Methodist University during this revision. He contributed the chapter on multinational firms. Robert Walters assumed responsibility for the other chapters in the volume. Both of us hope the responsibilities of deaning at SMU will become routinized in a fashion that permits Dave to resume a greater role in future revisions. Our collaboration on subjects related to this book has kept us close personal friends as well as colleagues for twenty years.

We wish to thank, once again, all of the students and faculty who continue to find this volume relevant to their work. This is particularly gratifying in light of the greater knowledge all of them have about international political economy compared to our readers in 1976—and in light of the abundant materials now available on the subject matter.

R.S.W. and D.H.B.

Introduction: Economic Transactions and World Politics

Since the early 1970s we have been undergoing a key transition in American foreign policy that in some respects is even more profound than the dramatic foreign policy moves made by the United States immediately following World War II. The Bretton Woods system, membership in the United Nations, the Truman Doctrine, Marshall aid, NATO, and the construction of a complex of alliance systems ringing the Communist world are commonly viewed as evidence of that turning point in United States history when we abandoned our tradition of isolationism (however different its face in different parts of the globe). Through these instruments the United States was seen as having moved into a series of multilateral commitments that saddled it with tremendous responsibilities abroad and circumscribed American freedom of action in ways that the United States has found unacceptable in the past. But the United States since the 1970s has confronted a series of foreign economic challenges that are resulting in even more constraints on its freedom of action than did the agreements in the 1940s.

As an isolationist, the United States could maximize freedom of action in its international relations (economic and political) by avoiding formal commitments; this was a basic theme, for example, in opposition to American membership in the League of Nations. Following World War II, when the United States did bind itself by numerous multilateral commitments in the economic and political spheres, it did so from a clearly preeminent position and, thus, was able in substantial measure to shape the various agreements to conform to American interests. The postwar multilateral agreements were typically of a sort that committed all member states to abide by specified global norms of liberal economic behavior, which, while ensuring benefits for these countries, also underlined American preem-

1

inence. Global norms of economic liberalism reflected American political-economic philosophy and policy preferences. These commitments had the net effect of ensuring America's freedom of action in the globe rather than circumscribing it.

In more recent decades, however, the United States has had to reformulate its foreign economic and political relations to take into account new global realities. America has moved from virtual self-sufficiency in energy to extensive reliance on oil imports. Europe, through the creation of the Common Market, has transformed itself from a junior partner of America to a giant economic rival/partner. Plans for eliminating all remaining barriers to a single market among the twelve member states of the Common Market in 1992 underscore a renewed momentum toward European economic integration, posing a significant challenge/opportunity for American international economic leadership. Japan's economic miracle and vigorous promotion of exports now threaten the vitality of key industries (such as automobiles, steel, and semiconductors) and hundreds of thousands of jobs in the United States. In numerous rapidly growing economic fields such as telecommunications, computers, ceramics, fiber optics, superconductivity, and biogenetics, the Japanese are also threatening American supremacy in commercial applications of new process and product technologies. In the 1980s Japan's international financial position came to parallel its trade strength, replacing the United States as the world's largest creditor. Newly industrializing countries in Asia and Latin America have assumed an important position in the international economy as trading partners/competitors with the United States. As leading international debtors, less developed states occupy an important role affecting international financial stability and the health of some heavily exposed U.S. banks. The world's confidence in the dollar waxes and wanes in an era of flexible exchange rates. The United States now relies on attracting foreign capital to sustain investment and to finance its huge federal budget deficits. Its domestic economic policy and politics are driven intermittently by the imperatives of managing foreign capital flows and the exchange rate of the dollar in ways only dimly appreciated by most Americans. These and other developments have combined to produce an evolution toward a new global economic and political order in which American preeminence must either decline or be retained at substantially escalated domestic and international costs.

The political significance of global economic relations goes well beyond this contemporary transition in the international position of the United States. The increased sensitivity in economic interdependence among virtually all states compels us to assess the political implications of international economic transactions everywhere. Even if economic transactions between states have grown at a slower rate than have economic transactions within them,[1] the volume and speed with which economic

---

[1] See K. Deutsch and A. Eckstein, "National Industrialization and the Declining Share of the International Economic Sector, 1890–1959," *World Politics*, 13, no. 2 (January 1961), 267–99; and K. Waltz, "The Myth of National Interdependence," in *The International Corporation*, ed. C. Kindleberger (Cambridge, Mass.: M.I.T. Press, 1970), p. 208.

resources can now be transferred between states places tremendous economic and political strains upon them. For example, modern communications and the management capabilities of giant international banks and corporations, which command assets greater than the gross national products of most states, allow massive capital transfers in response to disparities in the market conditions (interest rates, growth rates, wage levels, and so on) and the political milieus of various states.[2] Long-term investments by these economic actors and the movement of their liquid assets in international monetary markets can undermine domestic economic and political programs and produce severe conflicts between states. Indeed, some observers of these banks and corporations have argued that they may ultimately undermine the contemporary nation-state system itself.[3]

Analysts of world politics develop conceptual frameworks to address international challenges they perceive to be of overriding importance. Almost without exception, American specialists in international politics for the two decades following World War II saw the Cold War and the defense of the non-Communist world as the primary focus of U.S. foreign relations. As a consequence, they relied heavily upon paradigms in which security and power relations among states were deemed central to world politics. The dominant paradigm (political realism) led to a focus upon states as sole or primary actors in world politics,[4] and except insofar as economic instruments (such as aid and trade) were employed directly in power struggles between states, the distribution of benefits from domestic and international economic relations were seen as lying outside the boundaries of international politics.[5] Within this analytical tradition, international economic transactions such as trade and monetary affairs were typically looked upon as essentially nonpolitical relationships. They were seen as being managed, in the non-Communist world at least, according to politically neutral, technical criteria and administered by functionally specific ("nonpolitical") international organizations such as the General Agreement on Tariffs and Trade and the International Monetary Fund. The study of such affairs was left to international economists, international lawyers, and students of international organizations—most of whom neglected to analyze the larger significance of such transactions (and of international economic organizations themselves) in world politics.

In short, the conceptual frameworks used most frequently by American analysts of world politics in the early postwar period tended to relegate economic relationships to the margins of inquiry; the interrelationships between domestic and international politics were seldom examined systematically; and actors other than states received scant attention in studies of

[2]For an elaboration of the sensitivity of international economic interdependence and its substantive implications, see Richard Cooper, "Economic Interdependence and Foreign Policy in the Seventies," *World Politics*, 24, no. 2 (January 1972), 159–81. See also Chapter 7 of this book.

[3]See Frank Tannenbaum, "The Survival of the Fittest," *Columbia Journal of World Business*, 3, no. 2 (March–April, 1968), pp. 13–20.

[4]See Hans Morgenthau, *Politics Among Nations*, 4th ed. (New York: Knopf, 1967).

[5]Ibid., pp. 25–26.

international politics. Marxist analyses dealing explicitly with interests and relationships neglected in the dominant analytical tradition of American scholarship on international politics were virtually ignored.

Changes in international economic relations confronting American decision makers over the past two decades have prompted numerous efforts at reconceptualizing relations in ways that capture international political-economic behavior better than the power and security focus of political realism. Such paradigms place economics alongside of military security as questions of "high politics." Multinational firms, international banks, trans-national policy networks of like-minded technocrats, international economic institutions, and economic classes are analyzed in addition to states as key actors in international relations. The logic of markets uniting countries in a global division of labor competes with the logic of the power and security dilemma in ordering relations within and among states.[6]

Despite the richness of these efforts at conceptualization, no single paradigm has assumed a position of orthodoxy in the 1970s and 1980s approximating that enjoyed in the United States by political realism during the quarter century following World War II. No attempt to fill the gap will be made in this volume. Instead, our aim is to describe more richly and explain more adequately the political significance of various relationships by contrasting assumptional bases that underlie alternative views of political and economic behavior. The chapters that follow examine the major substantive areas of trade, monetary relations, foreign investment, aid, technology transfers, alternative economic strategies for poor states, and the formulation of foreign economic policy in the United States. Each of these areas, and the interdependencies among them, will be described in terms of how they affect political relations among rich states as well as how they affect relations between rich and poor states. In addition, we will examine how various conceptual frameworks lead to alternative conclusions about which policies are most appropriate for resolving conflicts of interest among states and other actors.

Without attempting to force all analyses of global economic relations into one or the other of the following schools of thought, the major clash in description, explanation, prediction, and policy prescription relating to these problems over the years has been between those analysts and decision makers subscribing to the assumptions of classical liberal economic thought and those subscribing to the assumptions of what Americans refer to as

---

[6]See, particularly, Robert Keohane and Joseph Nye, *Power and Interdependence* (Boston: Little, Brown, 1977); Robert Keohane, *After Hegemony* (Princeton: Princeton University Press, 1984); Edward Morse, *Modernization and the Transformation of International Relations* (New York: Free Press, 1976); Peter Katzenstein, ed., *Between Power and Plenty* (Madison: University of Wisconsin Press, 1978); Stephen Krasner, ed., *International Regimes* (Ithaca: Cornell University Press, 1983); Robert Gilpin, *War and Change in World Politics* (Cambridge: Cambridge University Press, 1981) and *The Political Economy of International Relations* (Princeton: Princeton University Press, 1987); Immanuel Wallerstein, *The Modern World System* (New York: Academic Press, 1976) and *The Capitalist World Economy* (Cambridge: Cambridge University Press, 1979); Robert Cox, *Production, Power and World Order* (New York: Columbia University Press, 1987); and Susan Strange, *States and Markets* (New York: Basil Blackwell, 1988).

radical thought.[7] The classical liberal economic approach is evident in the works of numerous analysts[8] as well as in the basic contemporary foreign economic policy orientations of the United States and other governments of advanced industrial societies in the West. They are evident as well in the policy orientations of key international economic institutions such as the General Agreement on Tariffs and Trade, the International Monetary Fund, and the International Bank for Reconstruction and Development. Examples of radical thought can be found in the works of Cold War revisionists, analysts of contemporary American imperialism, neo-Marxian political economists, world systems theorists, and *dependencia* theories of Latin American relations in a capitalist international system.[9]

Although there are many differences of opinion among the decision-makers and scholars within each of these two general schools of thought, there are nevertheless certain basic assumptions that are shared widely by the adherents of each school; these assumptions distinguish clearly the two orientations. In particular, there are important differences between the two schools' basic assessments of the primary values underlying actions taken by decision makers on behalf of states, the distribution of benefits from international economic relations, the degree and patterns of conflict inherent in international economic relations, and the location of the major obstacles to the achievement of national economic aspirations. Taken together, these assumptional differences produce such contrary understandings of the purposes, payoffs, and processes characterizing international

[7]The term *radical* as used here comes from Marxist economists in the United States who, themselves, took the name during the late 1960s in the Radical Union of Political Economists. Throughout this volume *radical* connotes a disparate body of classical and neo-Marxist observers as well as derivative work such as that found in world systems analysis.

[8]Harry Johnson, *Economic Policies Toward Less Developed Countries* (Washington, D.C.: The Brookings Institution, 1967); "The Link That Chains," *Foreign Policy*, No. 8 (Fall 1972), 113–19; and "The Multinational Corporations as an Agency of Economic Development: Some Explanatory Observations," in *The Widening Gap*, ed. Barbara Ward (New York: Columbia University Press, 1971), pp. 242–52. See also, Richard Cooper, *The Economics of Interdependence* (New York: McGraw-Hill, 1968); Leland Yeager, with David Tuerck, *Foreign Trade and U.S. Policy* (New York: Praeger, 1976); Robert Lawrence, *Can America Compete?* (Washington, D.C.: The Brookings Institution, 1984), and, with Robert Litan, *Saving Free Trade* (Washington, D.C.: The Brookings Institution, 1986); and Richard Cooper, *Economic Policy in an Interdependent World* (Cambridge: M.I.T. Press, 1986).

[9]William Appleman Williams, *The Tragedy of American Diplomacy* (New York: Dell, 1959); David Horowitz, *The Free World Colossus* (New York: Hill and Wang, 1971); Gabriel Kolko, *The Limits of Power* (New York: Harper & Row, 1972); Harry Magdoff, *The Age of Imperialism* (New York: Monthly Review Press, 1969); Susanne Bodenheimer, "Dependency and Imperialism: The Roots of Latin American Underdevelopment," in *Readings in U.S. Imperialism*, eds. K. T. Fann and D. C. Hodges (Boston: Porter Sargent, 1971), pp. 155–82; André Gunder-Frank, "Sociology of Development and Underdevelopment of Sociology," in *Dependence and Underdevelopment*, eds. J. Cockcroft, A. G. Frank, and D. Johnson (Garden City, N.Y.: Doubleday, 1972), pp. 321–98; Johan Galtung, "A Structural Theory of Imperialism," *Journal of Peace Research*, 8, no. 2 (1971), 81–117; Fernando Cardoso, with Enzo Faletto, *Dependency and Development in Latin America* (Berkeley: University of California Press, 1979); Arghiri Emmanuel, *Unequal Exchange: A Study of the Imperialism of Trade* (New York: Monthly Review Press, 1972); Samir Amin, *Accumulation on a World Scale: A Critique of the Theory of Development*, 2 vols. (New York: Monthly Review Press, 1974); and Immanuel Wallerstein, *The Modern World System, The Modern World System II*, and *The Modern World System III* (New York: Academic Press, 1976, 1980, and 1989).

political-economic relations that one wonders if we are examining the same world. Some of the central tenets of these two analytical traditions are summarized in Table 1-1.

Adherents of classical liberal economic thought tend to see the focus of states' economic policies as the maximization of economic growth and efficiency. The basic value determining policy choice in regard to economic issues before the state should be the optimal allocation of resources for national growth in the context of a global economy that operates in accordance with the norms of liberal economic principles. Success or failure is usually stated in terms of aggregate measures of economic performance such as the level and growth of GNP, trade, investment, per capita income.

In this context, global as well as national economic growth and efficiency dictate that all states open themselves to foreign goods and capital and that they specialize in the production of those goods in which they possess a comparative advantage. The division of labor (distribution of production) resulting among firms and countries around the world is understood to be the outcome of market forces which should be permitted to operate unencumbered by political interference—except when it is necessary to correct market failures such as restraints on competition and the provision of public goods like defense. Existing international economic relationships are viewed as mutually beneficial, even if the distribution of benefits among states is not completely symmetrical.

To the extent that existing international relationships do not enhance growth and the efficient allocation of resources, this view blames the unwillingness of decision makers within states to pursue rational liberal economic policies. In other words, to the extent that the global economy as a whole, and individual states' policies, conform to classical liberal economic principles, *all* states' growth and economic efficiency will be maximized. Of course, world production will be maximized also.

Inherent in this positive-sum view of international economic relationships is minimal conflict of interest between states. For the adherents of classical liberal economic thought, policy prescription is universalist: No basic differentiation is made among policy prescriptions appropriate for different types of national actors (large or small, rich or poor). The formal rules of behavior in international economic relations, and the policies of international economic institutions enforcing these rules, such as the IMF, are seen as politically neutral among all states.

Liberal economic analysts are prone to see a world composed of sovereign, autonomous states enjoying equal economic opportunity (though not equality of economic condition) in an open international system. All states are understood to possess considerable autonomy and decisional latitude in critical choices about their domestic and foreign economic policies. Resource allocation in economic exchange within and between states should be determined principally by market mechanisms. To the extent that market mechanisms generate socially unacceptable inequalities, the state's function is to ameliorate them through redistribution programs. States should be very wary of intruding on market mechanisms, for they are the key to efficiency for all economic transactions, in the view of liberal analysts.

TABLE 1-1   Central Tenets of Liberal Economic and Radical Thought

BASIC PREMISE	LIBERAL ECONOMIC THOUGHT	RADICAL THOUGHT
1. Primary value being pursued by states	Maximum aggregate economic growth in national and global economies	Maximum national economic growth consistent with capacity for national self-determination and with equitable distribution of income within and between states
2. Distribution of benefits from global economic relations conducted according to liberal principles	Mutual benefit if not symmetrical distribution; positive-sum	Clearly asymmetrical distribution in favor of owners of capital and rich states; zero-sum
3. Degree of conflict *inherent* in global economic relations conducted according to liberal principles	Minimal; tendency toward equilibrium	Very great; tendency toward disequilibrium and recurrent crises
4. Persistent cleavages *inherent* in global economic relations conducted in accordance with liberal principles	None	Cleavages between rich states and poor states; cleavages between industrial-financial elites and labor within all capitalist economies
5. Major obstacle to achievement of national economic aspirations	Irrational state policies	Capitalist rules of behavior governing international economic relations
6. Overall result of activities of international economic institutions	Provision of infrastructure advantageous to all states in conduct of international economic relations	Provision of infrastructure for perpetuating dominance by rich, Western states and owners of capital
7. Characterization of existing international political system	Sovereign, autonomous states with considerable decisional latitude on economic policies	Hierarchically organized system of dominant and subordinate states; autonomy and meaningful decisional latitude on economic policy for dominant states only
8. Preferred means of resource allocation	Market mechanisms	State-administered terms of exchange
9. Relationship between economics and politics	Economics should be separated from politics	Economics determine politics

Liberal political-economists see highly developed, modern nations (and economic sectors within nations) existing alongside of underdeveloped, backward nations (and economic sectors within nations). The former are closely integrated with one another and owe their vitality to dense linkages with international markets. They are characterized by sociocultural-economic-political systems that are, among other things, highly differentiated by function, progressive, formally institutionalized, and achievement-oriented. The latter are seen as relatively isolated from other segments of the national economy and from world markets—for example, Appalachia in the United States. They are characterized by sociocultural-economic-political systems that are much less functionally differentiated, traditional, organized more by extended kinship patterns than formal institutions, and ascriptively rather than achievement-oriented.[10]

Political modernization and economic development, according to liberals, involves a diffusion of production techniques and modern forms of sociocultural-economic-political organization from the developed countries (sectors) to the backward countries (sectors) through integration into world markets—which order society by their internal logic and push all economic activity toward greater efficiency. As relative isolation from centers of modern political and economic activity explains backwardness, greater integration with such centers spurs modernization and rapid economic growth.

Liberals see less developed countries today as facing essentially the same challenges that countries in Europe and North America did in the nineteenth century. Indeed, they have certain "advantages of backwardness"—through linkages with highly developed states possible in today's world markets, less developed countries can telescope the development process by borrowing capital, technology, and production processes from international economic leaders. Liberals view backwardness and underdevelopment as an original state or condition in which all societies began. Modernization and development is a process which all states can someday experience. The societies that start the journey today or tomorrow can expedite it by emulating those that undertook it earlier.

The assumptional bases of radical thought are vastly different from those underlying the liberals' world view. Although growth and economic efficiency are seen as priority goals of states, national self-determination and equitable income distribution are just as crucial. Indeed, these last two goals would be ranked above economic growth by most radicals if, in the short run, the choice has to be made. The radical analyst tends to see income equality and the capacity for economic and political self-determination among poor states, at least, as incompatible with integration into the existing global economy, which operates in accordance with the norms of classical liberal economic thought. A poor state's open acceptance of foreign goods and capital, along with its specialization in the production

[10]For more extensive treatments of liberal and neo-Marxist development models, see J. Samuel and Arturo Valenzuela, "Modernization and Dependency: Alternative Perspectives in the Study of Latin American Underdevelopment," *Comparative Politics*, 10 (July 1978), pp. 535–57; R. Chilcote and J. Edelstein, *Latin America: Struggle with Dependency and Beyond* (Cambridge: Schenkman, 1974), pp. 1–87; and Gilpin, *The Political Economy of International Relations*, pp. 65–117, 263–88.

of those goods in which it enjoys a comparative advantage in modern world markets, condemns it to supplying raw materials and low-value-added manufactured goods (goods manufactured with relatively low capital and technology inputs), leaving it in a perpetually secondary and dependent position in relation to the leading economies. Liberal international economic relations affords fundamentally unequal economic units (states, firms) equal access to markets and resources around the globe. While appearing to be a system offering fair competition, the rules of liberal economic relations favor highly advanced commercial and financial enterprises based in modern states at the center or core of the global economy.

The benefits of such international economic relations between rich and poor states are distributed asymmetrically, in favor of the rich. This continued asymmetry in the distribution of benefits forms a basically exploitative relationship between dominant and dependent states that is seen by adherents of radical thought as the explanation for the existence and the widening of the gap between rich and poor countries. Hence, in a fundamental sense the major obstacle to the achievement of the national aspirations of poor states (most states in the world) is seen to be the nature of the international economic system itself, rather than the policies of individual poor states. Even if a poor state does formulate economic policy in accordance with classical liberal economic thought, the asymmetrical distribution of benefits in its international economic relations will condemn it to perpetual poverty, foreign penetration, and continued dependence upon rich states.

Great conflicts of interest between states are inherent in this basically zero-sum view of international economic relations. Policy prescription is not universalist. Policies appropriate for rich states in the center of the global economy are not appropriate for poor states in the periphery. Classical liberal economic thought is viewed by radical thinkers as compatible with the interests of rich states but not with those of poor states. The existing international economic system is not politically neutral, as the classical liberal economists argue. The policies of all the key international economic institutions and the distribution of benefits from most public and private economic transactions inherently favor rich states, ensuring their dominance in global economic and political relations.

Radical economic analysts visualize a hierarchically organized world with dependent, subordinate states relegated to the periphery of the international economy dominated by the leading capitalist states at its core. Only the latter possess autonomy in critical choices about their domestic and foreign economic policies. States in the periphery of the global economy must accept their place in an international division of labor imposed upon them by the leading capitalist states. Market mechanisms allocating resources in international and domestic economic exchange reinforce political, social, and economic inequalities that radical analysts find abhorrent. They seek an active role for the state in managing markets to introduce a greater measure of equity in domestic and foreign economic relations.

Contemporary neo-Marxists, such as *dependencia* and world systems theorists, have a very different sense of how world markets influence modernization and economic development from the "dual economy" view of liberals outlined above. The former do not attribute backwardness of countries (or of sectors within a domestic economy) to isolation from world markets, as do liberals. Quite the contrary, they understand the world market as creating a single division of labor closely linking advanced and backward sectors in the economies of core and periphery states. Markets simultaneously produce poverty and wealth. Development and underdevelopment are two faces of the market process. Advanced states expropriate the resources and capital surpluses of the politically and economically weak through exploitative terms of economic exchange (in trade, finance, and investment) they impose in world markets.

To neo-Marxists, closer integration of less developed countries with the advanced industrial states through international markets operating on liberal economic principles will further distort and stifle their modernization and development. Such growth as occurs will take the form of dependent development—development in the periphery states conditioned by (derivative of) decisions and political-economic interests of private finance and governments in the core states and implemented by dependent elements of society within less developed countries closely associated with these elites in the core states.[11]

In the view of neo-Marxists, less developed countries today face very different challenges of economic development from countries that industrialized early. They cannot modernize by emulating the liberal economic policies of today's rich states. Today's backward economies must overcome extensive penetration of their domestic political-economic systems by foreign economic interests and governments which siphon off economic surpluses needed for growth and development. That can be accomplished only by escaping from their unfavorable position in the international division of labor imposed by market forces in the liberal global economy.

Quite obviously, the analysts and decision makers who employ these alternative sets of primary assumptions will differ greatly in their assessment of, say, multinational corporations and in their prescriptions for the treatment of multinationals by nations, acting individually and in concert. The profound cleavage in their basic premises leads adherents of the two schools of thought to talk past each other in analyzing specific economic issues, such as multinational corporations. To the classical liberal, for example, foreign investment appears mutually beneficial; to the radical, it is exploitative. Analysts from both schools seldom examine the appropriateness of the different assumptional bases from which their perceptions and policy prescriptions flow. In the absence of this examination, political conflict over economic issues is exacerbated. The typical analyst or decision maker within each school of thought simply sees no necessity to question seriously the assumptions underlying one's own stance on the issue and continues to propose policies that are seen as harmful in their incidence or intent by adherents of the other analytical tradition.

The clash between these two schools of thought not only has important substantive implications for international relations; it also affords an op-

---

[11]See, for example, Peter Evans, *Dependent Development: The Alliance of Multinational, State and Local Capital in Brazil* (Princeton: Princeton University Press, 1979).

portunity to analyze the political implications of various dimensions of global economic relations. In the following chapters, we will refer frequently to these alternative perspectives, and we will develop them more fully in specific contexts.

Despite the centrality of the liberal-radical "dialogue" in international diplomacy and political economic analysis, it is by no means sufficient in itself to address all aspects of such a complex subject matter. For example, mercantilist thought also enjoys considerable prominence in examining contemporary political economic behavior.[12] Mercantilists see politics as determining economics. Economic relations are to be understood in terms of competition for the distribution of wealth and power among states, as distinct from the individual and global welfare maximization stressed by liberal economists or the class competition emphasized by radical economists. They view liberal economic policies as a function of the distribution of power in the international system and the position of a nation's industries in the global division of labor—thus, a liberal international economic order is most likely to emerge when hegemonial states like the United States since World War II and Britain in the nineteenth century are in the politically and economically advantageous position to press for it and to underwrite it. Mercantilists see liberal economics as an instrument sometimes useful to advance national interests, rather than an abstract, universal guide to rational policy or an inevitable outgrowth of capitalist social-economic systems. In the analysis of market-oriented political-economic systems, mercantilists argue that the state routinely plays a far more active role in the economy than liberal economists understand and a role more independent of leading industrial and financial interests than radical economists understand.[13] Accordingly, mercantilists explain contemporary conflicts over trade and industrial policies among the United States and its leading economic partners as a struggle by governments to secure a favorable position in an evolving international division of labor with immense implications for national power. In assessing international monetary relations they stress the implications of alterations in the position of the dollar for the exercise of U.S. economic and political power.

Contemporary mercantilist thought sees world markets operating over the long run to redistribute wealth and power among nations, generating cycles of ascendency and decline of great powers.[14] During periods when a hegemonic state enjoys competitive advantages in production pro-

[12]Notable examples include Robert Gilpin, *U.S. Power and the Multinational Corporation* (New York: Basic Books, 1975) and *War and Change in World Politics* (Cambridge: Cambridge University Press, 1981); Stephen Krasner, *Defending the National Interest* (Princeton: Princeton University Press, 1978) and "State Power and the Structure of International Trade," *World Politics*, 28, no. 2 (April 1976), pp. 317–47; John Zysman and Stephen Cohen, *The Mercantilist Challenge to the Liberal International Trade Order*, Study Prepared for the Joint Economic Committee, 97th Cong., 2nd Sess., December 1982, and *Manufacturing Matters* (New York: Basic Books, 1987).

[13]Krasner, *Defending the National Interest.*

[14]Gilpin, *War and Change in World Politics*; Paul Kennedy, *The Rise and Fall of the Great Powers* (New York: Random House, 1987). Recent critiques of these structural explanations of hegemonic cycles include Joseph Nye, *Bound to Lead* (New York: Basic Books, 1990) and Henry Nau, *The Myth of America's Decline* (New York: Oxford University Press, 1990).

cesses, availability of capital, technological innovation, managerial skills, and so forth, an open international economy allows it to reap great economic and political rewards. However, over time the very openness of the international economy it promotes as a hegemonic state accelerates the diffusion of these sources of its economic preeminence to other states emerging as rival powers. The hegemonic state seldom grows the most rapidly in the international order it underwrites—Germany and the United States grew faster than Great Britain in the nineteenth century, and Japan and Germany have grown more rapidly than the United States since 1945. Open world markets for a time help consolidate the wealth and power of a hegemonic state. Yet, they operate over the long run to erode the margin of that state's wealth and power relative to other countries. When that realization sets in, declining hegemonic states can be expected to retreat from their commitment to a liberal economic order. Such analysts explain increasing U.S. economic nationalism and international economic instability since the 1970s in these terms.

In these and other instances mercantilists offer very different insights than those yielded by liberal and radical economic analyses. Mercantilist observations of international economic behavior will be utilized in addition to liberal and radical views when appropriate.

Our essential objective in this volume is to clarify major political problems associated with international economic relations rather than to offer specific solutions to them; the latter can be done intelligently only after the problems themselves are understood better. There is really a great deal at stake in the success of this enterprise, toward which this volume is only a beginning. We live in an era of international relations during which political conflicts are widely perceived to be centered on economic issues. Yet, political scientists labor with underdeveloped substantive and conceptual tools for analyzing such behavior. By the same token, liberal economists who dominate American economic scholarship are ill-equipped to evaluate systematically the political forces shaping, and the political implications of, their prescriptions for "rational" economic policies in a era of highly politicized global economic relations.

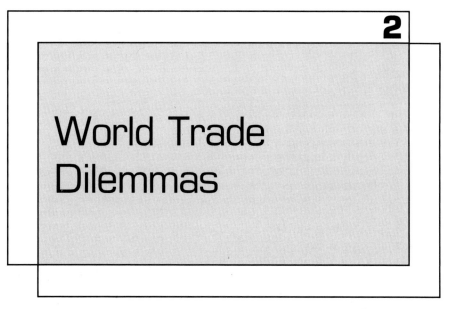

World Trade Dilemmas

There is no area of international economic activity that demonstrates more clearly than trade relations the general thrust of the remarks in Chapter 1. During the past decade, trade issues have figured prominently in political controversies between less developed countries and rich states, between East and West, and among the United States, Europe, and Japan. U.S. trade now amounts to almost 18 percent of its GNP compared with about 10 percent in 1960. Yet, at a time when America's trade is becoming increasingly important to its overall economic well-being, its loss of economic preeminence relative to that during the immediate postwar period makes it more difficult for the United States to shape international trade in conformity with its particular economic and political interests. Before examining trade issues of contemporary political importance, we need to look at certain basic characteristics of the global trade order as it has evolved since World War II.

THE POSTWAR ECONOMIC ORDER

Following World War II the Western states, under vigorous American leadership, were most anxious to construct an international economic order within which trade would flourish. In particular, efforts were devoted to avoiding the explicitly competitive "beggar-thy-neighbor" foreign economic policies that characterized international commerce during the 1930s.

> Intensive economic nationalism marked the . . . decade. Exports were forced; imports were curtailed. All the weapons of commercial warfare were brought into play; currencies were depreciated, exports were subsidized, tariffs raised,

13

exchanges controlled, quotas imposed, and discrimination practiced through preferential systems and barter deals. Each nation sought to sell much and buy little. A vicious spiral of restrictionism produced a further deterioration in world trade.[1]

These policies contributed not only to a deterioration of world trade, but also to global economic depression. Trade and monetary policies emerged as primary instruments used by major states to reinforce a division of the world into tightly knit political-economic regions, which in turn helped to contribute to the outbreak of World War II. In light of the consequences of the foreign economic policies characteristic of the 1930s, the need to encourage relatively free international movement of goods and capital was felt widely to be essential for world peace as well as for global prosperity.

It was toward the ends of peace and prosperity that the major Western states created the General Agreement on Tariffs and Trade (GATT) in 1947. GATT is a legally binding codification of rules for the conduct of trade among its member states. This institution, located in Geneva, Switzerland, has also provided the international infrastructure and the locus for all the major multilateral tariff-reduction negotiations since World War II. Its general goal is to maximize growth in world trade and the global economy through a reduction in trade barriers pursued on a nondiscriminatory basis.

GATT seeks to promote trade in ways that avoid "beggar-thy-neighbor" policies or the creation of highly competitive regional economic blocks of the sort characterizing the 1930s. Protection of domestic industry is to be carried out to the greatest extent possible through tariff duties, as opposed to other trade barriers such as quotas, controls on the use of foreign exchange, and so forth. (Quotas and other non-tariff barriers to trade that persist are to be applied in a nondiscriminatory manner and for limited periods of time.) The general level of tariff protection is to be reduced through successive multilateral negotiations. The progressive lowering of tariffs under these circumstances is expected to stimulate international trade and production. Tariff reductions are to be implemented in a non-discriminatory fashion in accordance with the "most-favored-nation" (MFN) principle. Accordingly, any state in GATT is assured that its goods will enter the markets of all GATT members at rates of duty no less favorable than those applied to similar products of any other country. The MFN principle is designed to accelerate the pace of tariff reductions and trade growth throughout the world as well as to avoid the creation of new preferential trade blocs protected by discriminatory tariff barriers, except under conditions specified in the General Agreement.[2]

The last point reflects the most significant contribution of GATT to the promotion of international economic order. The General Agreement establishes international norms of responsible trade policy against which the national trade policies of its member states can be evaluated. In cases where a national policy is found to be inconsistent with GATT principles,

---

[1]Clair Wilcox, *A Charter for World Trade* (New York: Macmillan, 1949), pp. 8–9.
[2]See The *General Agreement on Tariffs and Trade*, Article XXIV.

there are established procedures to settle grievances in a manner designed to minimize further restrictions of international trade. During the 1930s the absence of a permanent international institution with these functions undoubtedly contributed to the escalation of discriminatory trade policies during that period and to the more general deterioration in economic and political relations among states. Thus, GATT's primary utility has been to introduce a form of permanent international oversight and accountability for commercial policies that, prior to its existence, were viewed as exclusively national prerogatives.

GATT was complemented by the creation in 1944 of the International Monetary Fund (IMF), which was designed to promote the stability and liberalization of international monetary transactions.[3] The goals of GATT would have been impossible to achieve without both an adequate global supply of foreign exchange and provisions for capital mobility to finance trade flows. Through the IMF, states became internationally accountable for their monetary policies in varying degrees. These two institutions, along with the International Bank for Reconstruction and Development (IBRD),[4] became the foundation for multilateral efforts to prevent the political and economic consequences of economic nationalism that preceded World War II.

The United States provided the driving force for the construction of this postwar international economic order. It did so not only for the reasons discussed in the preceding paragraphs, but also because the United States was in a peculiarly advantageous position to benefit from international economic transactions conducted in accordance with the norms established by GATT and the IMF. Immediately following the war, with the economies of most countries in a state of devastation and disarray, the United States was in a commanding position as a source of global credit and exports. An international economic order based on the principles of free movement of goods and capital served perfectly America's domestic and foreign economic interests and capabilities. Such an economic order was an effective means of allowing the United States to penetrate the trade preference systems, especially Britain's sterling area, from which it had been excluded prior to the war.[5] The economic and political preeminence of the United States during the 1940s and 1950s assured the creation of an international economic order that reflected American interests, however sensible such an economic order might also be, from the perspective of liberal thought, for maximizing world trade flows, global prosperity, and peace.

The framers of GATT would look with considerable pride upon the evolution of world trade and production within the context of the economic order established following World War II. The original GATT membership

---

[3]The IMF and the political implications of international monetary transactions will be examined in Chapter 3.

[4]The IBRD is the dominant multilateral aid agency. Multilateral aid is discussed in Chapter 5.

[5]For an elaboration of this point, see Robert Gilpin, "The Politics of Transnational Economic Relations," in *Transnational Relations and World Politics*, eds. Robert Keohane and Joseph Nye (Cambridge, Mass.: Harvard University Press, 1971), pp. 57–59.

of twenty-three states has climbed to one hundred. Tariffs on dutiable industrial goods have been reduced through seven rounds of GATT negotiations (the last concluded in 1979) to an average level in 1987 of just 2.9 percent for Japan, 4.3 percent for the United States, and 4.7 percent for the ten members of the European Economic Community.[6] This represents a substantial reduction of tariffs. Tariff levels in the United States, for example, averaged 60 percent in 1934 and 25 percent in 1945 prior to the GATT's creation. Partly as a consequence of the liberal trade order developed under the auspices of GATT, world exports since 1950 have grown twentyfold in value (ninefold by volume) while world production has grown tenfold in value (fivefold by volume)—see Figure 2-1. On the basis of these aggregate indicators, it appears that the lessons of the 1930s have been learned; international oversight of national foreign economic policies has been successful in promoting production and in curtailing the excesses of economic nationalism with its negative economic and political consequences.

As remarkable as these developments in world trade may be, they, nevertheless, present a misleading picture of the extent to which trade issues have been defused as a source of tension in international relations. International institutional arrangements in trade and monetary policy have facilitated rapid growth in world trade, but the benefits have not been distributed symmetrically across products and geographical regions. Trade problems have reemerged as questions of high politics among all variety of states. That is, trade issues are once again occupying the attention of presidents and prime ministers as priority problems of foreign and domestic politics. These issues contribute significantly to the overall tone of states' foreign relations and to the success of domestic economic policies. They are too important to be treated as essentially technical problems to be handled by nonpolitical experts. We will examine trade policy as foreign policy in two contexts: (1) relations among advanced industrial states and (2) relations between these states and poor countries.

TRADE ISSUES AMONG ADVANCED INDUSTRIAL STATES

Trade issues have played a central role in the political dialogue between less developed countries and rich states throughout the period since World War II. Only since the 1960s, however, have trade issues among non-Communist, advanced industrial states reemerged as particularly important political problems. Several factors have contributed to this turn of events after a period of some fifteen or twenty years following the creation of GATT, a period during which trade issues among these states were effec-

---

[6]Gary Saxonhouse, "The Micro- and Macroeconomics of Foreign Sales to Japan," in *Trade Policies in the 1980s*, ed. William Cline (Washington, D.C.: Institute for International Economics, 1983), p. 260; "Japan Trade Barriers Called Mainly Cultural," *The New York Times*, April 4, 1985, p. 31.

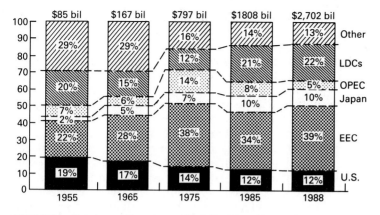

FIGURE 2-1   Exports as a Percentage of World Total (excluding USSR)

Source: International Monetary Fund, *Financial Statistics Yearbook, 1979* (Washington, D.C.: IMF, 1979), pp. 63–65; International Monetary Fund, *Financial Statistics*, XLII, no. 6 (June 1989), pp. 76–78.

tively depoliticized—that is, "discussed and resolved in their own realm . . . without intruding into high policy."[7]

As long as the United States had no economic peer in the non-Communist world and as long as the Cold War was perceived as the most salient problem in international politics, economic relations among Western states were not a predominant source of political tension. A shared perception of threat from the Communist world made advanced industrial states in the West relatively content to defer to Washington for security policy. The primacy of security concerns and the obvious dependence of Western states upon the United States in this area inhibited them from adopting trade, investment, and monetary policies wholly at odds with American interests. In any event, as long as other Western states were critically in need of American capital and production to reestablish their economic health, there was little incentive to challenge directly the postwar economic order that provided both. For its part, the United States was quite willing to tolerate departures by Western European states and Japan from GATT and IMF norms of nondiscrimination in foreign trade and monetary policies as long as such policies were deemed instrumental for the containment of communism and as long as they posed minimal threats to American economic interests at home and abroad. These conditions prevailed in substantial measure into the 1960s. They were conducive to an essentially constructive, though not always harmonious, approach to trade, investment, and monetary relations among advanced industrial states outside the Communist world.

As limited détente between the superpowers gradually superseded their intense Cold War postures in the 1960s and 1970s, intra-Western conflicts of interest previously subordinated to the dictates of alliance cohesion began to emerge. Conflicts arose over strategic and conventional de-

[7]Richard Cooper, "Trade Policy Is Foreign Policy," *Foreign Policy*, No. 9 (Winter 1972–1973), p. 19.

fense policy (France's demands for an independent nuclear force and the withdrawal of its armed forces from NATO command) as well as over U.S. conduct of the Vietnam war. Also, during the 1960s Japan and Western Europe became strong enough economically to act in accordance with new political and economic interests that they defined apart from the United States. A substantial reduction in the perception of threat from the Communist world made advanced industrial states in the West less prone to subordinate their particular interests to those of the United States in an effort to preserve Western unity. Whereas earlier all these states were desperately in need of American capital and exports, by the 1960s they were large exporters in their own right and had accumulated excess dollars as foreign exchange reserves. Thus, they were less dependent upon the United States and, indeed, were able to compete effectively against an increasing number of American goods in the U.S. market, their home markets, and around the world. American automakers, steelmakers, and producers of electronic consumer goods used to dominate world markets. During the 1970s and 1980s import competition from European, Japanese, Latin American, and Asian producers of these and other manufactured products threatened major U.S. industries. In 1971 the emergence of the first U.S. trade deficit in the twentieth century (followed by two decades in which its trade balance continued to deteriorate—see Figure 2-2) marked a watershed in America's foreign economic relations and introduced a

FIGURE 2-2 U.S., EEC, and Japan Trade Balances ($ billion)

Source: International Monetary Fund, *International Financial Statistics*, June 1989, pp. 76–79. International Monetary Fund, *International Financial Statistics Yearbook*. (Washington, D.C.: IMF, 1990), p. 14.

epoch of turmoil in the international economic order. U.S. trade and monetary policies took on a decidedly more nationalistic cast. The United States more frequently exploited its position as the world's largest import market and the top international currency to bargain hard with its major allies in Europe and Asia for changing policies harmful to American economic interests. It less consistently shaped its own economic policies to underwrite the costs of maintaining an open international economic order.

When the Europeans and Japanese were strong enough to pose a serious threat to American economic interests, less competitive American industries and organized labor mounted increased pressure for protection. As a result of these changes in the domestic and international environment, the United States became much less willing than it was previously to tolerate departures by European states and Japan from GATT and IMF norms for national trade and monetary policies, such as discriminatory regional trade ties and the maintenance of significant barriers to imports and investments from the United States. For their part, the advanced industrial states in the West pointed to protectionist American policies (such as demands for "voluntary" export controls on the part of others, import surcharges, currency devaluations, and a reluctance to undertake internal adjustment measures appropriate to manage its chronic balance-of-payments deficits) as evidence of American departures from GATT and IMF principles.

In short, evolution in the Cold War and the economic resurgence of Western Europe and Japan combined to place a severe strain on cohesion among the leading industrial economies. The United States in 1990 remained the largest economy in the world by a wide margin. But its declining shares of world exports and international reserves (see Figures 2-1 and 2-3), since the 1950s mean that the United States finds itself in a much less commanding position relative to its major economic partners than was the case during the formative years of the GATT, IMF, and other key inter-

FIGURE 2-3   International Reserves as a Percentage of World Total

Source: International Monetary Fund, *International Financial Statistics Yearbook, 1984* (Washington, D.C.: IMF, 1984); International Monetary Fund, *International Financial Statistics*, XLII, no. 6 (June 1989), pp. 49–51.

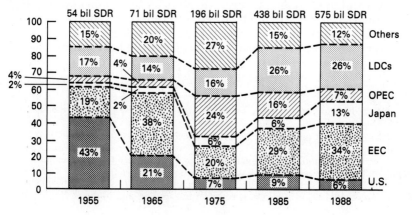

national economic organizations. The present international political and economic problems among the Western states are in a fundamental sense a result of this profound structural alteration in the international economy. These new economic realities will make it much more difficult for the United States to place its formative stamp on new global political-economic relations.

The advanced industrial states account for two thirds of world trade.[8] Their trade relations with each other have a decisive impact on the prospects for increased trade and economic growth throughout the globe. It is imperative, therefore, that trade disputes arising among them be kept within manageable bounds. Rather than attempting to survey all of the major conflicts that have threatened to disrupt trade relations among advanced industrial states over the years, let us examine a number of enduring behavioral traits and political and institutional characteristics that are likely to condition efforts to manage trade for the remainder of the twentieth century. Monetary and investment relations have so much importance in their own right that they will be examined separately in subsequent chapters, but it is important to remember in any discussion of trade issues that all these phenomena are closely interrelated.

Neomercantilism

One characteristic feature of the advanced industrial states' trade policies throughout the postwar period, notwithstanding GATT, has been the persistence of a neomercantilist trade orientation. This orientation manifests itself in numerous ways and is the source of major trade conflicts of contemporary importance. Neomercantilism is a trade policy whereby a state seeks to maintain a balance-of-trade surplus and to promote domestic production and employment by reducing imports, stimulating home production, and promoting exports.[9] The attractions of this policy for any single state are obvious. But, by the very nature of trade balances, a state can gain a trade surplus only when other states run a trade deficit. It is evident, therefore, that all states cannot successfully implement neomercantilist policies simultaneously.

Similarly, promoting domestic production at the expense of imports necessarily forces foreign producers to absorb production and employment losses. States that feel themselves victim to others' neomercantilist policies are seldom passive about it. The United States, the European Economic Community (EEC),[10] and Japan have been engaged over recent decades in

---

[8]International Monetary Fund, *Direction of Trade Statistics Yearbook, 1984* (Washington, D.C.: IMF, 1984), p. 6.

[9]Harold Malmgren, "Coming Trade Wars?" *Foreign Policy*, No. 1 (Winter 1970–1971), p. 120.

[10]The EEC, or Common Market, is comprised of twelve states. France, West Germany, Italy, Belgium, the Netherlands, and Luxembourg were the original six members at its creation in 1956. Britain, Ireland, and Denmark joined in 1973. Greece became a member in 1981. Spain and Portugal joined in 1986. East Germany became a member in 1990. In international trade agreements these countries negotiate as a single unit represented by the European commission of the EEC in Brussels. It is the largest trading unit in the world.

protracted neomercantilist conflicts of varying intensity. Their competitive performance as reflected in overall trade balances since 1975 is summarized in Figure 2-2 on page 18.

Neomercantilism on the part of states in the European Economic Community is reflected in a variety of trade agreements limiting imports in sensitive industries such as textiles, steel, automobiles, and electronics, as well as in heavy state subsidies to European producers of goods confronting global surplus capacity (most notably steel). Particularly noteworthy is its Common Agricultural Policy (CAP). The CAP has been described by American officials as "the ultimate in mercantilism: decrease in imports, stimulation of home production to substitute for imports, and increase in exports."[11] The CAP since its introduction in the 1960s protects inefficient European farmers and stimulates high-cost domestic agricultural production within the Common Market by placing variable duties on agricultural imports. In the absence of production controls, the policy has generated agricultural surpluses in Europe that are priced too high to compete freely in international agricultural markets. Accordingly, revenues derived from the agricultural import duties are used to subsidize EEC agricultural exports to world markets that the Europeans would otherwise be unable to penetrate.[12] American trade officials and farmers are bitterly opposed to the CAP because far more efficient U.S. agricultural producers are being denied their full export potential not only in Europe but also in third markets captured by subsidized EEC exports. This is an especially sensitive issue in the face of America's trade deficit. To deal with the problem, U.S. officials have tried to make alterations of the CAP a priority item in GATT negotiations with the EEC—without concrete success to date. The United States also responded in 1985 with its own agricultural export subsidies program designed to recapture markets lost to the EEC in recent years, especially in the Middle East and North Africa.[13] Neomercantilist conflicts over agricultural trade have been a persistent source of tension between the United States and the EEC for several decades. In the mid-1980s agricultural subsidies in all of the advanced industrial nations had assumed staggering proportions. The Organization for Economic Cooperation and Development (OECD) estimated agricultural support programs in these states were costing consumers and taxpayers about $185 billion a year in 1984–1986.[14] The budget of the CAP in 1987 was $27 billion, representing almost two thirds of the EEC's total budget.[15] The financial burden of agricultural support on all Western states prompted renewed initiatives by American trade negotiators in the Uruguay round of GATT talks to commit

[11]Malmgren, "Coming Trade Wars?" p. 121.

[12]See Kathleen Patterson, "Keeping Them Happy Down on the Farm," *Foreign Policy*, No. 36 (Fall 1979), p. 64.

[13]"EEC: Farm Trade War," *The Economist*, May 25, 1985, pp. 54–55; "U.S. Helps Grain Sale to Algeria," *The New York Times*, June 15, 1985, pp. 27, 42.

[14]Peter Winglee, "Agricultural Trade Policies of Industrial Countries," *Finance and Development*, March 1989, p. 9.

[15]*U.S. Economic Report of the President, 1989* (Washington, D.C.: GPO, January 1989), p. 175.

all countries to gradually eliminate subsidies and open agricultural markets. So contentious is the issue, however, that disputes between the United States and the EEC over agricultural policies affecting trade forced an extension of negotiations in the Uruguay round beyond their scheduled conclusion in December 1990.

Additional trade controversy has attended efforts of states in the EEC to protect and to subsidize traditional manufacturing industries like steel or to promote high-growth industries deemed vital to international competitiveness in the future, such as telecommunications. At various times the governments of Britain, Belgium, France, Italy, and Germany (in the Saar) have extended massive subsidies to steel firms enabling them to continue operations, maintain employment, and expand exports despite being uncompetitive in world markets burdened with surplus capacity. American steelmakers, while exaggerating unfair practices abroad as the source of their own difficulties, cite these subsidies and the practice of dumping as major causes of steel import surges in the United States that have threatened the viability of the U.S. industry and eliminated hundreds of thousands of steel jobs in America over the past decade.[16] Demands for protection of the U.S. market on these grounds have generated protracted trade conflicts between the EEC and the United States. They have been contained in recent years only by a series of unstable, ad hoc, bilateral agreements governing European exports of specified steel products to the United States for discrete time periods. For example, the United States and the EEC negotiated an agreement for the period 1982–1985 limiting European exports of ten categories of carbon steel to 5.46 percent of the American market. This was followed in 1983 by the imposition of quotas on EEC exports of specialty steel to the United States and in 1985 by still another agreement confining European exports of steel pipes and tubes (not covered in the carbon steel agreement) to 7.6 percent of the U.S. market through 1986.[17] Steel trade agreements with the EEC were folded into the comprehensive voluntary restraint agreements the United States instituted in 1984 to limit steel imports from twenty-nine countries to no more than 21 percent of the U.S. market for five years.[18] President Bush extended this program for an additional two and one-half years in the fall of 1989. The proliferation of such agreements in steel and other sectors makes a mockery of U.S. and EEC commitments to the liberal multilateral trade system administered by GATT.

National efforts such as these to maintain production, jobs, and exports in defiance of market forces are classic instances of neomercantilist

---

[16]See Robert Walters, "The U.S. Steel Industry: National Policies and International Trade," in *The Emerging International Economic Order*, eds. H. Jacobsen and D. Sidjanski (Beverly Hills, Calif.: Sage, 1982), pp. 101–27: Ingo Walter, "Structural Adjustment and Trade Policy in the International Steel Industry," in *Trade Policy in the 1980s*, ed. W. Cline (Washington, D.C.: Institute for International Economics, 1983), pp. 483–525.

[17]"Trans-Atlantic Trade: How Is It Faring?" *Europe*, March–April 1985, pp. 12–14.

[18]For a description of U.S. steel trade and the 1984 voluntary restraint agreements, see Robert Walters, *U.S. Negotiation of Voluntary Restraint Agreements in Steel, 1984: Domestic Sources of International Economic Diplomacy*, Graduate School of Public and International Affairs, PEW Initiative in Diplomatic Training, University of Pittsburgh, 1987.

challenges to the liberal international trade order. So, too, are some European efforts in high technology industries. The EEC, for example, is attempting to position European telecommunications firms more favorably in relation to their U.S. and Japanese competitors through the ESPRIT program (European Strategic Program for Research and Development in Information Technology) and additional joint research efforts such as RACE (Research and Development in Advanced Communications Technology).[19] European market interventions in basic manufacturing industries such as steel affect the United States primarily in terms of import penetration, whereas promotion of high technology industries by European governments threatens highly competitive U.S. exports. In both instances the implications for national trade balances and domestic economic prosperity introduce a source of great political tension in trans-Atlantic relations.

Plans being developed by the EEC commission for creating a single European internal market of 320 million people in 1992 are raising new challenges in U.S. foreign trade and economic relations with the Common Market. Despite great progress toward economic integration of the member states in the EEC over the past thirty years, numerous non-tariff barriers remain to prevent free movement of capital, goods, and services within the Common Market—for example, border delays, differences in industrial/labor standards and regulations, incompatible national controls over important sectors such as finance and telecommunications, discriminatory government procurement practices, separate currencies and monetary policies, and so forth. EEC actions to remedy these and other barriers to a single market have important trade implications for the United States and other countries, even though their exact dimensions will not be clear until reforms are implemented in the 1990s. Setting new, uniform standards for telecommunications in the EEC, for example, will have a decisive impact on market shares in computing and various telecommunications services where U.S. and Japanese firms presently enjoy a very strong competitive position in Europe. Uncertainty about how new policies in the EEC will affect access by foreign firms to the new single European market after 1992 was already stimulating increased direct foreign investment in Europe by American and Japanese firms in 1989.[20]

Across the Pacific, Japan has experienced a remarkable economic resurgence since World War II that has catapulted it past the USSR as the second largest national economy in the world after the United States. In 1971, Japan surpassed West Germany as the world's leading exporter of industrial goods. Over the past decade it has operated with global trade balances that are the envy of all industrialized states (see Figure 2-2). Japan

[19]Michel Carpentier, "Toward a New Kind of Community: ESPRIT Program on Information Technology Represents Europe-Wide Industrial Policy," *Europe*, May–June 1984, pp. 28–29. Jonathan Todd, "Europe Launches New High-Tech Project," *Europe*, June 1988, pp. 32–33.

[20]For a concise summary of the EEC plans for a single market in 1992 and issues they raise for the United States, see U.S. Department of State, Bureau of Public Affairs, *The European Community's Program for a Single Market in 1992*, Western Europe Regional Brief. Washington, D.C.: November 1988.

is renowned for its extraordinary success in penetrating EEC and U.S. markets in electronic consumer goods, optics, steel, automobiles, numeric machine tools, semiconductors, and a host of additional manufactured products. At the same time, even highly competitive American producers of high technology products such as semiconductors, computers, and tele-con.munications find much smaller market shares in the rapidly growing domestic Japanese economy than they obtain in world markets generally. Overall, the share of manufactured products as a proportion of Japan's total imports through the mid-1980s was less than half that of all other industrialized states[21] (although its imports of manufactured goods increased substantially after 1986).[22] The United States ran bilateral trade deficits of $49 billion to $60 billion with Japan during 1986–1990 (accounting for approximately 40 percent of its overall trade deficits in that period), despite the imposition of quotas or voluntary export restraints on Japanese shipments of steel, televisions, textiles, motorcycles, and automobiles over the years. Approximately 40 percent of Japan's exports to the EEC are covered by export restraint agreements, yet the European Community trade deficit with Japan was $20 billion in 1987, double the figure in 1984.[23] These developments reflect vigorous pursuit of neomercantilist trade policies by Japan in the view of observers in Europe and the United States. American and European sentiment in the 1980s for protection against "unfair" Japanese competition was running higher than anytime during the postwar period.

Foreign critics attribute Japan's economic growth and trading success to a complex array of neomercantilist policies. Industries counted upon to lead Japanese economic growth (shipbuilding, steel, autos, consumer electronics, robotics, semiconductors, telecommunications, computers, biogenetics, fiber optics, and so on) have been nurtured behind highly protectionist trade barriers and restrictions on inward directed foreign investment until they achieve economies of scale and attain world class competitiveness. Then formal trade and investment restrictions are dropped. Still remaining, however, are numerous non-tariff barriers to imports including quotas, customs procedures, standards and testing requirements, complex and inefficient distribution networks, and an innate cultural preference for traditional Japanese suppliers and products that hamper the ability of foreign suppliers to penetrate Japanese markets even with competitively priced products. In addition, the Ministry of Trade and Industry (MITI) catalyzes cooperation between the government and business communities to secure financing, rationalizes industrial structures, stimulates research and development for commercially applicable products and product technologies, and subsidizes exports of industries vital to the Japanese economy. Lack of consumer credit and tax incentives help give Japan the highest savings rate in the industrialized world. The savings generated make available a large stock of capital at low rates of interest enabling Japanese firms to obtain investment funds at a fraction of the capital costs facing, say, Amer-

---

[21]Saxonhouse, "Micro- and Macroeconomics of Foreign Sales to Japan," p. 266.

[22]Japan Economic Institute, *JEI Reports*, No. 16B (April 21, 1989), p. 4.

[23]Ibid., No. 37A (September 30, 1988), p. 20.

ican firms.[24] The Japanese financial system also allows the government to steer capital toward particular sectors of the economy in ways not possible in the United States.[25] Finally, until 1985 an undervalued exchange rate for the yen and restrictions on foreign participation in Japanese financial markets are viewed as instrumental in Japan's commercial success.

These practices are cited repeatedly by private and public officials in the United States and Europe as evidence of a neomercantilist assault by Japan on the liberal international economic order that enabled it to achieve its economic miracle. They provide the rationalization for imposing American and EEC restrictions on Japanese imports. Yet many economists and specialists on Japan argue that the significance of MITI, Japanese industrial policies, and high levels of trade protection have been exaggerated as explanations of Japan's economic success.[26] MITI's powers over the Japanese economy were greatest during the postwar recovery when it exercised control over foreign exchange, then in short supply. High levels of trade protection were reduced dramatically during the 1960s. If industrial policies and trade barriers were important to Japan's economic success, their contribution was greatest in the 1950s and 1960s. Indeed, Japanese tariff levels in the 1980s are below those of the United States and Europe. Japan retains import quotas on only five industrial products (coal briquettes and four types of leather goods), and Japan's non-tariff barriers are not notably more restrictive than those imposed by the United States and Europe.[27] If Japan removed all tariff and non-tariff barriers that are the subject of American complaints, and at the same time eliminated all voluntary restraints limiting its exports to the United States, it would appear that Japan's bilateral trade surplus with the United States would increase rather than diminish.[28] The success of the Japanese in world markets seems to be attributable primarily to a combination of factors, including an exceptionally well-qualified labor force, the entrepreneurial skill of its business leaders, a highly competitive and rapidly growing domestic market remote from its major trading partners, a high domestic savings rate, an undervalued exchange rate for the yen, and successful application of product and process technologies in industries in which the Japanese were until recently catching up.

[24]Edson Spencer, "Japan: Stimulus or Scapegoat?" *Foreign Affairs*, 62, no. 1 (Fall 1983), pp. 124–125.

[25]John Zysman, *Governments, Markets and Growth* (Ithaca: Cornell University Press, 1983), pp. 233–81. For a survey of Japanese industrial and trade policies, see Ira Magaziner and Thomas Hout, *Japanese Industrial Policy* (Berkeley: Institute of International Studies, University of California, 1980); and Chalmers Johnson, *MITI and the Japanese Miracle* (Stanford: Stanford University Press, 1982).

[26]Philip Trezise, "Industrial Policy Is Not the Major Reason for Japan's Success," *The Brookings Review*, Spring 1983, pp. 13–18; Jimmy Wheeler et al., *Japanese Industrial Development Policies in the 1980s: Implications for U.S. Trade and Investment* (Croton-on-Hudson, N.Y.: Hudson Institute, 1982); Ed Lincoln, *Japan's Industrial Policies: What Are They, Do They Matter and Are They Different from Those in the United States?* (Washington, D.C.: Japan Economic Institute of America, 1984).

[27]Saxonhouse, "Micro- and Macroeconomics of Foreign Sales to Japan," pp. 260–61.

[28]Ibid., p. 264.

Whatever the causes, Japan's aggregate trade surpluses with Europe and the United States are creating great political and economic tensions among the advanced industrial states. These tensions become especially acute when Japanese import surges are linked to financial, employment, and production crises facing important industries abroad, such as those that occurred in the U.S. automobile industry between 1980 and 1983. American automobile firms lost $6 billion during 1980–1981 and laid off more than 200,000 employees, while Japanese auto imports surged to capture 21 percent of the U.S. market. Vigorous public and private pressures in the United States led to the negotiation of voluntary export quotas limiting Japanese auto imports to 1.68 million units a year from 1981 to 1984 and 1.85 million units from 1984 to 1985. The spectacular recovery of the American automobile industry in 1984 and 1985 was attributed to a combination of strong U.S. economic growth and these limits on Japanese auto imports, which allowed U.S. firms to recapture a larger share of the market. The protectionist sentiment unleashed in the United States by Japanese automobile imports in the late 1970s and early 1980s convinced several Japanese automakers (Honda, Nissan, Toyota, and Toyo Kogyo) to locate production facilities in the United States as a hedge against the possible erection of additional trade barriers in the future. Semiconductors superseded automobiles as the most salient irritant in U.S.–Japanese trade relations during the second half of the decade. In 1986, U.S. trade officials found that the Japanese had been dumping 64K RAM chips to expand their share of the American market, while U.S. semiconductor manufacturers had been able to capture only about 10 percent of the Japanese market (compared to several times that figure in world markets). The two states sought to control this trade conflict through a bilateral agreement in 1986 to raise prices of Japanese chips in world markets and to expand the market share of U.S. chips in the domestic Japanese economy. When the agreement seemed to be failing, the Reagan administration imposed import duties of 100 percent on $300 million worth of selected Japanese exports to the United States in 1987.

Sectoral trade crises in the steel, automobile, semiconductor, agriculture, construction, and other industries (superimposed on large bilateral trade imbalances) provoked a seemingly unending series of political economic conflicts between the two leading Western economies over the course of the 1980s. Indeed, this pattern gave rise to the conviction among some influential American observers that Japan should be understood as a predatory economic giant that must be contained rather than a partner that can be accommodated within an open trade system.[29]

In an effort to break the pattern of lurching from one sectoral trade crisis to another and to develop an alternative to contentious "Super 301" provisions introduced to U.S. trade law in 1988 (to be discussed below), U.S. and Japanese trade officials undertook a Structural Impediments Iniative (SII) to discuss underlying structural and policy problems each saw

[29]See James Fallows, "Containing Japan," *The Atlantic Monthly*, May 1989, pp. 40–54; Clyde Prestowitz, *Trading Places* (New York: Basic Books, 1988); and Karel van Wolferen, *The Enigma of Japanese Power* (New York: Knopf, 1989).

as underpinning its trade imbalances with the other. In these talks the United States focused on such things as land taxes skewing land use in Japan, low public-works spending, its distribution system and price mechanisms impeding imports, savings and investment patterns, and exclusionary business practices embedded in Japanese industry structures. The Japanese focused on the U.S. budget deficit, low U.S. savings rates, and the short-term business horizon of American businesses. In 1990 the two states agreed upon actions they would undertake in these and other areas.[30] The agreement marks a new focus in formal negotiations on broader political-economic factors affecting bilateral trade between the United States and Japan, but it will be some years before there is any real sense of how this will actually influence trade balances. Few observers expect the SII will defuse their trade conflicts.

As the 1990s commenced, there were signs that the United States would take a tougher stance on Japanese trade. By standing aside from the agricultural subsidies issues that led to the collapse of negotiations in the Uruguay round, Japan was seen by U.S. trade officials as failing to become a force for trade liberalization. By its low profile and grudging economic contributions to coalition efforts in the Gulf War of 1991, Japan was criticized in the United States for being unwilling to assume a broader international role commensurate with its economic position—a role the Japanese often say they see for themselves. Failure of larger political tests such as these has further eroded U.S. tolerance of questionable Japanese trade practices—especially in the face of large U.S. trade and fiscal deficits and rapid increases in Japan's direct foreign investment.

Despite its posture as the world's leading proponent of free trade, the United States has embraced neomercantilist trade policies along with Europe and Japan. The preferred American instrumentality for reducing imports and stimulating domestic production in industries facing stiff import competition has been the negotiation of "voluntary export restraints." The United States offers the largest market in the world to foreign producers. This gives it extraordinary bargaining leverage in international trade negotiations. It has repeatedly prevailed upon foreign producers of goods threatening the vitality of economically important and politically potent American industries to "voluntarily" restrain the level of their exports to the U.S. market. In return, U.S. negotiators agree to head off more restrictive administrative and legislative measures that would otherwise be introduced to limit exports of interest to foreign producers. The approach, while protectionist, has the benefit of leaving the United States in formal compliance with its GATT commitments, since the United States is not itself introducing new trade barriers—other states are "voluntarily" reducing their exports. The most notable recent examples of this policy are the Japanese auto export restraints and the steel export restraints of twenty-nine countries outlined above; however, these are but two instances of a long series of similar arrangements covering shoes, electronic consumer

[30]See "U.S., Japan Reach SII Agreement," *Congressional Quarterly,* June 30, 1990, p. 2040; "U.S. and Japan Set Accord to Rectify Trade Imbalances: Fundamentals Attacked," *The New York Times,* June 29, 1990, pp. A1, C2.

goods, textiles, and other products over the years. Orderly marketing arrangements such as the Multifiber Agreement governing trade in textiles and apparel, as well as the introduction of formal quota restrictions such as in specialty steels are additional means by which the United States limits import penetration. It has been estimated that 45 percent of America's imports of manufactured imports are subject to major non-tariff barriers.[31]

We have noted American criticism of European and Japanese government intervention to promote their key industries competing with U.S. producers. These industrial policies are viewed by U.S. officials as unfair, neomercantilist trade practices that displace American production, jobs, and exports. Yet, U.S. defense and space programs have stimulated developments in process and product technologies, as well as economies of scale that have been important in helping establish and maintain American semiconductor, computer, air-frame, and telecommunications firms as world leaders since World War II. Government loan guarantees in excess of $1 billion were made available to the Chrysler Corporation between 1979 and 1983 to avoid its collapse. The Department of Defense has provided half of the funding for SEMATECH, a consortium of leading American semiconductor firms whose goal is to develop new process technologies for the manufacture of semiconductors. This government support of the semiconductor industry is felt to be necessary for the United States to retain an indigenous production capability vital to the nation's future competitiveness and defense. Since the surprising discovery of high temperature superconductivity (HTS) by IBM scientists in 1986, public funding in the United States to stimulate commercialization and defense applications of HTS technology has been second to none.[32] At the end of the decade the Defense Department was also spearheading government efforts to help American firms catch up with their Japanese and European rivals in the development of high-definition television. To foreign observers the United States is no less inclined toward its own forms of government intervention to promote American production, employment, and exports than are European states or Japan.

The United States has engaged in more comprehensive efforts to alter its international trade balance on occasions when its trade and payments positions deteriorate seriously. When in 1971 the value of American imports exceeded its exports for the first time in the twentieth century, the United States resorted to a temporary 10 percent import surcharge and ultimately negotiated a revaluation of its major trading partners' currencies to the advantage of American producers. Unprecedented trade deficits during the mid-1980s—$170 billion in 1987—prompted renewed congressional interest in such blatantly neomercantilist remedies as the

---

[31]"Japan Trade Barriers Called Mainly Cultural," *The New York Times*, April 4, 1985, p. 31.

[32]Robert Walters and Ellis Krauss, "Science, Technology, and Economic Competitiveness: U.S. and Japanese Efforts to Commercialize High Temperature Superconductivity," paper delivered at the Thirtieth Annual Convention of the International Studies Association, London, April 1, 1989.

imposition of a steep import surtax[33] and the introduction of reciprocity legislation designed to raise U.S. trade barriers, unless states abroad lower their obstacles to American producers.[34] While neither of these bills became U.S. trade law, they reflected mounting domestic hostility to a liberal U.S. trade policy that strongly influenced the contours of the Omnibus Trade and Competitiveness Act of 1988 governing contemporary American trade policy (to be discussed below).

The EEC, Japan, and the United States together account for half of world trade. They all employ a variety of neomercantilist trade policies. Each justifies its own departures from GATT norms in this regard by pointing to the abuses of others. This growing counterpoint to the liberal trade order among the world's leading economies gathers strength in periods of stagnation or decline in the global economy (such as the mid–1970s and early 1980s) and in the presence of great disjunctures in international trade and payments equilibria (such as the oil crises in the 1970s and the U.S. trade deficits in the mid-1980s).

Neomercantilist behavior in the postwar trade system suggests that there are clear limits to the liberal world view of international economic relations, even for explaining relations among the leading market economies in GATT. International trade is, at best, partially understandable as a quest for global and individual welfare through the maximization of economic efficiency and the free flow of goods and services across national boundaries—however desirable that may be in theory. The mercantilist world view[35] is invaluable for helping us to understand that trade policies are inevitably bound up with considerations of national power and prestige. All states employ vigorous government policies in attempts to position their nations' industries favorably in the international division of labor and to manipulate their trade and payments balances. Liberal economists validly point out the mutual gains obtainable through international trade. Mercantilists just as validly cite zero-sum qualities of competition between states that will forever inhibit complete attainment of the goals of free trade and intermittently threaten to precipitate trade wars.

Trade and the Domestic Economy: Inflation and Unemployment

It is increasingly difficult to separate domestic economic performance from international economic relations. Trade balances and trade policies have important impacts on inflation and employment in the domestic economy of even large countries like the United States. As a general rule of thumb, it is estimated that approximately 24,000 American jobs are lost for each $1 billion in the U.S. trade deficit. This means that the U.S. trade deficit of $123 billion in 1984 contributed to the loss of almost 3 million

[33]"Import Tax Sought to Resolve Trade Imbalance," *Congressional Quarterly*, April 13, 1985, pp. 669–71.

[34]"Many Trade Weapons U.S. Can Use," *The New York Times*, April 5, 1985, p. 38.

[35]See Chapter 1, p. 11.

jobs in the American economy at a time when over 7 percent of the labor force was unemployed.[36] The U.S. trade deficit during the mid-1980s was widely cited as a leading cause of unemployment and a primary restraint on higher levels of domestic economic growth. At the same time, imports play an important role in reducing inflation by increasing the supply of goods in the economy and providing price discipline on domestic manufacturers. During the period 1983–1986 U.S. inflation dropped to an average of 3.8 percent from its average level of 8.3 percent during 1980–1982.[37] The tremendous surge in imports by the United States after 1982 was a major factor in controlling the rise of consumer prices (see the U.S. trade deficit in Figure 2-2).

Such connections between international trade, employment, and inflation pose difficult challenges to policy makers. Import restrictions often seem imperative to protect industries and jobs threatened by foreign producers, but they exact a high price from the consumer. For example, it has been estimated that the trade restraints on Japanese autos in the early 1980s raised the price of Japanese cars entering the United States by $1,000 and the price of American-produced autos by $400. Trade restrictions did, indeed, save approximately 46,000 jobs. But the cost to the American consumer in the form of higher car prices amounted to nearly $160,000 per job saved.[38] In 1980 a family of four in the United States paid over $1,000 a year for the protection of various American industries from import competition.[39]

Trade policies can be used to combat inflation as well as to protect domestic production and jobs. Lowering import barriers makes greater supplies of goods available to consumers and threatens domestic producers that raise prices with a loss of their share of the market to foreign competitors. In 1973–1974, when many industrialized countries were confronted with double-digit inflation for the first time in the postwar period, the United States, Japan, Australia, and Canada each unilaterally cut some of their tariffs.[40] When beef prices in the United States soared 35 percent in 1978, President Carter reduced barriers to beef imports in an effort to offset domestic shortages creating the price escalation.

In these instances trade policy to combat domestic inflation involved further liberalizing and expanding world trade. Yet, states have also experimented with export controls to curtail inflation by cutting off foreign demand on nationally produced goods, thus, increasing supplies available for domestic consumption. In 1973 the United States invoked temporary

[36]"How Import Rise Affects U.S.," *The New York Times*, February 1, 1985, p. 35.

[37]*World Economic Outlook, 1985* (Washington, D.C.: IMF, 1985), p. 212.

[38]Robert W. Crandall, "Import Quotas and the Automobile Industry: The Costs of Protectionism," *The Brookings Review*, Summer 1984, p. 16.

[39]Michael Munger and Kathleen Rehbein, "The High Cost of Protectionism," *Europe*, May–June 1984, p. 10.

[40]C. Fred Bergsten and William Cline, "Trade Policy in the 1980s: An Overview," in *Trade Policy in the 1980s*, ed. W. Cline, p. 92.

controls on wheat, soybeans, metal scrap, and timber toward this end.[41] Its major trading partners, particularly Japan, were heavily dependent on the United States for these vital goods. Indeed, shortly after the imposition of export controls on soybeans, U.S. Treasury Secretary Shultz visited Japan. While there, he was a guest at a seventeen-course Japanese dinner in which every dish contained some soybean ingredient. "I got the message," he said.[42] Ironically, Japan itself later imposed unilateral export restrictions on fertilizer and petroleum-based intermediate goods to cope with its own inflation problems. Such trade policies carry with them as great a potential for global trade disruptions and political conflict as neomercantilist actions.

The relative salience of unemployment and inflation as preoccupations of economic policy varies over time and across countries; but, since the 1970s advanced industrial states have commonly confronted unemployment levels and rates of inflation well above the levels they found politically and economically acceptable throughout the 1950s and 1960s. Inflation and unemployment in the industrial states averaged less than 4 percent between 1960 and 1972. During the period 1977–1986 these countries confronted average inflation and unemployment rates of 6.5 percent and 7 percent respectively.[43] The challenge of managing trade conflicts among the leading states is heightened immeasurably as the pressures of stagflation mount in their domestic economies.

Protectionist Domestic Political Forces

These structural conditions give rise to strong domestic political pressures on the part of producers, organized labor, and consumers for their governments to erect various trade barriers. Domestic political considerations make constructive trade alternatives difficult to achieve, no matter how enlightened statesmen might wish to be in their attempts to avoid a resurgence of economic nationalism. Whereas the economies of advanced industrial states may in the aggregate be better off in the absence of protectionist trade policies, those particular interests hurt by liberal trade policies (such as textile, steel, and automobile manufacturers in the United States) bring extraordinary protectionist pressure to bear on their governments. For example, during the presidential campaign of 1968, Nixon's southern strategy dictated a firm pledge to protect the southern textile industry from strong Japanese import competition. This campaign commitment was honored by President Nixon and underlaid his administration's hard and bitter negotiations with Japan to curtail sharply Japanese

---

[41]A domestic wage and price freeze was in effect at the time to combat inflation. Had there been no export controls, further domestic shortages would have resulted from additional agricultural production being exported abroad where higher prices could be obtained. Also it should be noted that we are addressing the issue of export embargos for the express purpose of affecting domestic price levels, *not* export embargos for political reasons such as those directed at the Soviet Union in 1980.

[42]Mary Locke and Hans Binnedijk, "GATT Talks Begin," *European Community*, No. 170 (November 1973), p. 16.

[43]*World Economic Outlook, 1985*, pp. 209, 212.

exports of textile goods to the United States. Even if the costs of trade protection are high for society as a whole, those costs are typically broadly diffused and hard to identify. Meanwhile, the benefits from protection in the form of increased earnings, production and jobs are concentrated and self-evident to organized interests lobbying for relief from import competition.

Ever since the conclusion of the Kennedy round of GATT negotiations in 1967, Congress has been bombarded with a host of minor and major bills calling for trade protection. Demands in the late 1960s were made for import restrictions on a wide variety of products, liberalized procedures for claiming injury from imports, more vigorous and prompt relief from imports that are dumped or subsidized, and more extensive financial aid to firms, regions, and workers disadvantaged by import competition. The most salient of these legislative initiatives were the Trade Act of 1970 (the Mills Bill) and the Foreign Trade and Investment Act of 1972 (the Burke-Hartke Bill). The Burke-Hartke Bill, for example, called for a sweeping imposition of import quotas to confine present and future imports to that share of the American market for which they accounted during the 1965–1969 period. Only strong pressure from the executive branch prevented either the Mills or Burke-Hartke bills from coming to a vote in Congress. Passage of either bill would have provoked strong retaliation from our major trade partners.

The Nixon administration initiated legislation committing America to a seventh round of multilateral trade negotiations in GATT (the Tokyo round), notwithstanding evidence of substantial domestic opposition to further reductions in trade barriers. The legislation was, however, more sensitive to protectionist sentiment than were previous authorizations for trade negotiations. The Trade Act of 1974 passed by Congress made it easier for industries to obtain a finding of import injury from the government. Relief, in the form of either new import barriers or adjustment assistance to firms and workers, no longer required that injury from imports be linked to earlier trade concessions by the United States. Also, relief can be obtained when imports are found to be "a substantial cause" of serious injury, rather than "the major cause," as under previous trade law.

Initiatives from the private sector and Congress for trade protection have continued unabated through the 1980s. In the late 1970s the U.S. International Trade Commission dealt with about fifty cases a year seeking relief from imports under U.S. trade law. By 1983 and 1984 it was acting on approximately 200 cases a year. During the first half of the decade about 700 bills a year were introduced in the Congress seeking various types of trade protection.[44]

These efforts culminated in passage of the Omnibus Trade and Competitiveness Act of 1988 which presently guides American trade policy. The

[44]"Protecting America's Free Trade," *The Economist*, March 2, 1985, p. 81. For an astute analysis of increased U.S. protectionism in the 1980s as an attempt by Congress to protect itself from political pressure rather than to protect industry from foreign imports, see I. M. Destler, "Protecting Congress or Protecting Trade," *Foreign Policy*, No. 62 (Spring 1986), pp. 3–23.

law basically reaffirms the U.S. commitment to free trade while introducing some controversial new mechanisms to pressure other states, especially those enjoying large bilateral export surpluses in trade with the United States, to eliminate what American trade officials identify as "unfair" trade practices. Under the so-called Super 301 provisions of the law, American trade officials were required in 1989 and 1990 to list "priority" countries that persistently treat American exports unfairly. Being cited as a "priority" country triggered up to eighteen months of bilateral negotiations with the United States, by which time an agreement was to be reached to remove "unfair" barriers to American exporters within three years. Should the barriers remain, the law required American retaliation that could impose tariffs of up to 100 percent on selected imports from that state.[45] In the first year of the law's application, Japan, Brazil, and India were designated priority countries.[46]

The Super 301 process was almost unanimously viewed abroad as a clear violation of the GATT. Under its provisions U.S. trade officials *unilaterally* defined unfair trade and *unilaterally* determined the appropriateness of the accused countries' responses to American complaints. The negotiations which took place were conducted within the shadow of a clear threat of severe sanctions by the United States. The GATT prohibits unilaterally imposed increases in tariffs as prescribed under Super 301.[47] U.S. trade officials argued that the Super 301 negotiations' purpose was to give other states greater incentive to open their markets. They expressed every intension of expanding free and fair trade through the process, pointing out that the United States has not yet imposed any tariff increases under its provisions.

The Bush administration must strike a compromise between strong neomercantilist pressures from Congress and America's multilateral trade obligations under the GATT. Trade negotiators are attempting to "square the circle" by satisfying domestic forces advocating greater economic nationalism in U.S. trade policy by means of aggressive diplomacy with its major trading partners, ostensibly driven by a desire to expand free trade. The Super 301 provisions of U.S. trade law introduced an element of brinkmanship in the international trade system. Taiwan and South Korea did remove some barriers to trade sought by the United States in a successful effort to avoid being designated priority countries under the Super 301 statute in 1989. Sufficient progress was made in negotiations with Japan and Brazil that they were removed from the priority list in 1990, leaving only India exposed to retaliation by the United States under the Super 301 process.

These and other developments in recent years clearly indicate that domestic political support for liberal trade policy has declined markedly

[45]"U.S. Feeling Pressure to Cite Japan on Trade," *The New York Times*, April 24, 1989, p. 26.

[46]"Japan, India, Brazil Cited for Import Barriers," *Congressional Quarterly*, May 27, 1989, pp. 1242–43.

[47]"U.S. Target of Criticism at GATT. Its Threat of Trade Sanctions Against 3 Nations Assailed," *The New York Times*, June 22, 1989, p. 23.

in the United States since the late 1960s. Most significantly, organized labor has moved from its keystone position among domestic interests supporting free trade to a highly protectionist position. The AFL-CIO, for example, placed its full weight behind the Burke-Hartke Bill and most subsequent neomercantilist legislation. Speaking in 1977, George Meany addressed the subject of trade policy in the following terms:

> Foreign trade is the guerrilla warfare of economics—and right now the United States is being ambushed. . . . Free trade is a joke and myth. And a government trade policy predicated on old ideas of free trade is worse than a joke—it is a prescription for disaster. The answer is fair trade, do unto others as they do to us—barrier for barrier—closed door for closed door.[48]

It should be noted that organized labor as a whole, and the AFL-CIO in particular, overrepresents those segments of the American labor force in traditional manufacturing industries that are most threatened by imports. Most underrepresented are workers in the services sector and high-technology industries that gain from liberal trade policies. For example, "workers in the service industries account for almost 70 percent of the total labor force, but only about 40 percent of the membership of the AFL-CIO. Traditional manufacturing industries such as textiles and steel, make up almost three times as great a share of AFL-CIO membership as they do of the total labor force."[49] These facts help to explain why organized labor has become so avidly protectionist. Its membership is bearing the brunt of the structural adjustment being forced on the American economy by the increased competitiveness of traditional manufacturing industries located abroad. Note in this regard that, only two years after the American automobile industry was threatened severely by Japanese imports in 1979, the United Auto Workers (long-time advocates of free trade) moved toward reintegration with the AFL-CIO and its protectionist stance on trade. Seventy-five percent of the products manufactured in the United States now face significant import competition compared to 25 percent two decades ago.[50]

The erosion in domestic political support that can be mobilized for liberal trade policies will make it considerably more difficult for the United States to promote liberal trade in the coming years than at any time since World War II. Yet, the U.S. economy as a whole continues to have a tremendous stake in an open international trade order. Approximately one out of every six U.S. jobs in manufacturing and one out of every three acres of U.S. farmland are producing for export abroad.

---

[48]Copyright ©1977 by The New York Times Company. *The New York Times*, December 9, 1977, p. 5. Reprinted by permission.

[49]Fred Bergsten, *Toward a New International Economic Order: Selected Papers of C. Fred Bergsten, 1972–1974* (Lexington, Mass.: Lexington Books, 1975), p. 475. See also, pp. 476–478 for more specific data on this issue.

[50]U.S. House of Representatives, Industrial Competitiveness Act, Committee on Banking, Finance, and Urban Affairs, 98th Cong., 2nd Sess. (Washington, D.C.: GPO, 1984), p. 25.

It is also important to realize there are strong internal political pressures that make it difficult for America's major trading partners to move toward more liberal trade policies. For example, a goal of the United States in its trade relations with the European Common Market has been to secure a major alteration in the community's Common Agricultural Policy in favor of reliance upon cheaper American agricultural supplies.[51] But such a move by the EEC would fly in the face of strong domestic pressure by European farmers for protection, and it would go to the heart of a political agreement holding the Common Market together. The CAP was the quid pro quo that France, as the Common Market's leading agricultural producer, secured for its willingness to open itself up to more efficient industrial producers within the EEC, such as Germany. Many observers feel there could be no Common Market without the CAP. This is a prime example of how political pressures *within* the EEC are likely to frustrate the growth of trade and development of smoother political relations *between* Europe and the United States. Similarly, most of the quotas remaining as a symbol of Japan's formal protectionism apply to farm products (such as rice). These will be very difficult to remove despite intensified American pressure, because rural areas provide a critical constituency for the ruling Liberal Democratic Party in Japan.

The Crises in Multilateral Institutions

The internal and external forces prompting protectionist trade policies in the major industrial states pose significant new challenges for effective multilateral management of contemporary trade relations. Unlike previous negotiations, the Tokyo round of GATT negotiations completed in 1979 seemed to be driven less by the conviction that further reductions in trade barriers would assure dramatic new gains in trade flows and economic growth than a fear that failure to maintain the momentum toward a more liberal, nondiscriminatory trade order would unleash a series of highly protectionist moves.[52]

The challenge now facing states is that the General Agreement on Tariffs and Trade is unable to contribute much more to world trade growth merely by performing the tasks it has done so well in the past. It succeeded admirably in reducing the level of tariff protection for industrial trade among its member states. These tariffs are now sufficiently low that nontariff barriers such as government procurement regulations, quota restrictions, export restraint agreements, and various national standards (safety, pollution, health, services, and so on) are relatively more important than are tariffs as barriers to trade. Hence, advanced industrial states are entering a period of diminishing returns from tariff reductions among them-

---

[51]Ironically, by unilaterally initiating its embargo on grain exports in 1973 to fight inflation, the United States gave the EEC its strongest argument *against* relying upon cheaper American agricultural imports for its food needs.

[52]For an excellent account of the GATT and the Tokyo round of trade negotiations, see Gilbert Winham, *International Trade and the Tokyo Round Negotiation* (Princeton: Princeton University Press, 1986).

selves focused on industrial goods. Further tariff cuts will unleash intense domestic pressures for protectionism; yet, because tariff levels are already low for most industrial goods, the growth in world trade from further tariff cuts on these products is likely to be less dramatic than in the past.

The eighth, Uruguay, round of GATT negotiations began in 1986 and was scheduled for completion in 1990. U.S. priorities in the conduct of these talks reflect new thrusts in the trade agenda for industrial states. Further tariff cuts are certainly being sought, but the focus is on a number of other, more troublesome policies.[53]

Great pressure is being brought by the United States to bring agriculture within the scope of GATT provisions. As we noted previously, all the advanced industrial states maintain support programs that distort agricultural trade. The United States is pressing for multilateral commitments to eliminate agricultural subsidies and to treat agricultural trade like trade in industrial goods.

American officials are also attacking the trade-distorting effects of direct foreign investment practices. Countries stipulating domestic content and other performance requirements on the operations of multinational firms are forcing important shifts in the location of production and jobs. Through such practices Latin American states like Brazil and Mexico have captured a greater share of automobile related manufacturing in recent decades, for example. U.S. negotiators in the Uruguay round are attempting to bring the trade-distorting effects of such policies under the purview of the GATT. As with agriculture, this represents a significant expansion of GATT's purview. The GATT was premised on the notion that trade was conducted between arms-length buyers and sellers in world markets. Yet, multinational firms account for a large portion of world trade—approximately 35 percent of U.S. exports consist of sales of U.S. parent firms to their subsidiaries abroad. Effective management of international trade will require greater scrutiny of intra-corporate transfers as well as states' efforts to steer them to national advantage. The GATT must take more explicit account of the rapid internationalization of production since its creation.

Opening trade in services has been a third area of major interest to the United States in the Uruguay round. The GATT was designed to deal with international exchange of goods, not services. Over the decades, services have come to assume a very large role in the economies of advanced industrial states. Approximately 70 percent of the U.S. labor force is employed in the service sector, for example. Moreover, about 20 percent of world trade and perhaps a quarter of U.S. exports now take the form of services—construction, banking, informatics, transportation, investment, insurance, and so forth. A major effort is now being undertaken in the GATT to codify and make transparent barriers to trade in services with a view toward negotiating nondiscriminatory access of services across national

---

[53]For an assessment of issues before the GATT in the mid–1980s, see C. Michael Aho and Jonathan Aronson, *Trade Talks: America Better Listen* (New York: Council on Foreign Relations, 1985).

boundaries. Opening markets in these areas raises great sensitivities among nations since control of key service sectors such as finance and telecommunications have traditionally been jealously guarded national prerogatives.

Non-tariff barriers to trade (NTBs) are now perhaps as much as ten times more restrictive of international trade than tariffs. Such trade barriers placing foreign competitors at a disadvantage relative to domestic producers take innumerable forms:

- High taxes on automobiles with large engine displacements and cumbersome safety and pollution inspection procedures for autos exported to Japan have helped indigenous automakers retain high market shares.
- Sending all Japanese VCRs through a tiny customs inspection station in France sharply curtailed their penetration of the French market.
- Regulations for minimum nitrogen content in fertilizers consistent with only Belgian fertilizer manufacturing limited imports to the Belgian market.
- Government standards for switching and other components in telecommunications systems have been used in Europe and Japan to exclude strong U.S. firms like IBM, Motorola, and AT&T.
- Health standards on beef have long been used to protect the American beef industry from its Argentine competitors.
- Government procurement practices typically favor national over foreign suppliers regardless of price and performance differences.
- Voluntary export restraints and formal market sharing agreements have been used by the EEC and the United States, especially to protect their auto, steel, footwear, textile, apparel, machine tools, semiconductor, and consumer electronics industries.

The GATT estimates that there are now more than 250 such agreements in place[54] affecting almost half of advanced industrial states' trade. These mechanisms have been particularly important in restricting exports from newly industrializing countries in Asia and Latin America. All of them have been negotiated outside of the GATT safeguards framework to avoid giving affected countries legal grounds for retaliation. Supporters of liberal trade systems argue that action must be taken soon to absorb and modify these agreements within GATT mechanisms before they undermine the postwar mutilateral trade order.

In a word, the outstanding trade issues among the major economic powers in the West are concentrated in precisely those policy areas in which nations have shown the least interest in agreeing to international oversight by GATT, or in those policy areas that GATT was never designed to tackle. What seems to be required, therefore, is the negotiation of a widely accepted, enforceable system of new rules for these new issues, somewhat like those already developed by GATT for tariffs on industrial goods.

There are major problems with successful negotiation of these sorts of issues presently dominating the multilateral trade agenda, besides their intrinsic complexity. The focus on agriculture, services, investment, and

[54]"GATT Weighs Rules on Aiding Industries," *The New York Times*, June 28, 1989, p. 26.

NTBs in the GATT represents the trade-distorting effects of *domestic* policies and the need for greater international accountability in dealing with them. Such international agreements are necessarily far more intrusive on national practices than traditional agreements on tariff reductions. Moreover, addressing such problems means arriving at internationally acceptable norms for safeguarding and subsidizing industries deemed crucial to nations' social, political, and economic interests. Questions about the proper role of governments in shaping domestic economic structure, therefore, arise alongside questions of acceptable trade levels as matters of international trade diplomacy. Structural economic concerns create far more contentious bargaining between states than bargaining about trade expansion by reducing tariff levels with calculable economic effects.

Several additional considerations make rapid progress on significant international trade reform particularly difficult at the present time. At the same time that existing GATT arrangements for the regulation of trade are recognized as being inadequate to cope with current trade problems, international mechanisms for handling monetary relations among countries are also proving inadequate. Since the end of the Bretton Woods monetary system in 1971, for example, fluctuating exchange rates have greatly complicated trade relations. Appreciation of the dollar 65 percent against other major currencies between 1980 and 1984 was responsible for half of the U.S. trade deficits in 1984 and 1985.[55] Effective management of trade will require greater coordination of trade and monetary policies at national and international levels than has been possible in the past.

In early postwar negotiations on trade and monetary relations, the United States was in such a commanding economic and political position relative to its negotiating partners that it was able to secure agreements on trade (GATT) and monetary affairs (IMF) that were substantially in accord with American preferences. The present negotiations find Europe and Japan as major economic powers alongside the United States, even if the United States is still the strongest single economic power in the world. Thus, the United States cannot expect to emerge from contemporary and future trade and monetary negotiations with agreements that conform perfectly with American preferences. More important, this current distribution of economic and political power among advanced industrial states is likely to make a truly significant final agreement very difficult to achieve at all. The Europeans and the Japanese are now strong enough to challenge American leadership in the construction of a new economic order, but at the same time they are too weak and divided to replace U.S. leadership in the global political economy. This situation makes the challenge of constructing new trade and monetary orders more formidable to the United States and the world than the challenges of the 1940s.

The existence of these various pressures for the reemergence of economic nationalism among advanced industrial states has led to the fear that the future may bring an international trade order characterized by highly competitive regional trade blocs led by the United States, the EEC, and

---

[55]*Economic Report of the President, 1985*, p. 103.

Japan.[56] The prospects for such a development are enhanced by the fact that multilateral institutions (such as GATT, the Organization for Economic Cooperation and Development, and the International Monetary Fund), long serving as guardians of the principle of nondiscrimination in international economic exchange, seem increasingly less able to produce conformity with this goal. Indeed, they as often appear to legitimize new forms of protectionism by advanced industrial states as to administer an open trade order.[57] Of course, this disarray in multilateral institutions is a reflection of an erosion of consensus among the leading industrial states on the norms that should govern the international trade order.

American negotiation of bilateral free trade pacts with Israel and Canada during the Reagan administration might be considered confirmation of regionalist trends challenging universalist trade principles. For example, the Canada–U.S. agreement which went into effect January 1, 1989, will eliminate all duties on their bilateral trade by 1998. President Bush in 1991 invited Canada to join the United States and Mexico in opening talks to create a North American Free Trade Zone encompassing 360 million people with an annual output of $6 trillion. The United States defends such agreements and negotiations as evidence of its commitment to advancing free trade wherever it finds willing partners. Others view the pacts as thinly veiled threats to develop its own trade block as a counterpoint to the GATT order, if the rest of the GATT membership is unwilling to further advance the multilateral trade system through successful completion of the Uruguay round on U.S. terms.

The harmonization of trade policies among advanced industrial states will be a formidable task indeed. These nations must cope simultaneously with neomercantilism, global inflation, domestic pressures for protectionism, alterations in the relative economic strength of states, and the emergence of new problems in international economic relations with which existing international economic institutions are ill equipped to deal. These factors constitute general parameters that condition any efforts to construct a new global trade order. Their existence need not prevent progress toward that goal, however. These forces are clearly evident to decision makers within all advanced industrial states. At least in a general way, all recognize the danger that excessive economic nationalism poses for the maintenance, much less the growth, of their national prosperities. The acute oil crises of 1973 and 1979 as well as the international debt crises of the 1980s reinforced the fact that their national economies are increasingly interdependent. They amply demonstrated that even the largest powers are incapable

[56]For empirical evidence of the existence of such trends already, see D. Calleo and B. Rowland, *America and the World Political Economy* (Bloomington: Indiana University Press, 1973), pp. 123–24. See also Ernest H. Preeg, *Economic Blocs and U.S. Foreign Policy*, National Planning Association Report No. 135 (Washington, D.C.: NPA, 1974).

[57]See Susan Strange, "The Management of Surplus Capacity: Or How Does Theory Stand Up to Protectionism 1970s Style?" *International Organization*, 33, no. 3 (Summer 1979), p. 330. Strange focuses her attention on textile, steel, and shipbuilding production and trade. Developments in the automobile sector and many others would also conform to her observations.

of externalizing their economic problems by means of unilateral actions harmful to others. Thus, the salience of the threats to global economic prosperity posed by aggressive trade and monetary policies insensitive to the needs of others may provide the momentum necessary for constructive multilateral efforts to establish a new, more resilient framework for the promotion of orderly trade and monetary relations. Indeed, the habits of multilateral consultations and the mechanisms of economic organizations made a major contribution to international economic peacekeeping during the 1970s. Virtually all states were buffeted by a series of international economic shocks unprecedented since World War II—grain shortages, oil price increases, high rates of inflation, and economic stagnation. Even with their imperfections, the present international economic institutions succeeded well enough in these crises to help prevent nations from slipping back to the beggar-thy-neighbor policies of the 1930s.

TRADE AND LESS DEVELOPED COUNTRIES

Export earnings account for 75 percent of less developed countries' foreign exchange resources, clearly dwarfing foreign aid, commercial borrowing, and private investment as alternative sources of foreign exchange. It is not surprising that trade issues have long figured prominently in the political dialogue between less developed states and the advanced industrial states with which they conduct two thirds of their trade. In particular, less developed countries share a profound sense of frustration with the international trade order developed after World War II. This frustration stems from a number of substantive trade practices and institutional characteristics of GATT that, in their view, combine to inhibit the development of their economies and relegate them to a secondary status in the global economy.

Less developed countries are particularly sensitive to the tariff structures of most advanced industrial states. As we noted earlier, successive rounds of negotiations under GATT's auspices have reduced the average level of tariffs on dutiable manufactured and semimanufactured products to less than 5 percent. But the manufactured and semimanufactured products of particular export interest to less developed countries (such as textiles and semiprocessed metal or wood products) typically face tariff levels of two to four times this average, and tariffs on these items have frequently been ignored altogether in GATT negotiations. In addition, agricultural commodities face a variety of trade barriers—quantitative restrictions, tariff, health, environmental regulations, and so forth—that are designed to protect the agricultural sector in advanced industrial states.

These explicit barriers to less developed countries' exports are supplemented by more subtle aspects of tariff structures in advanced industrial states. For example, tariff protection typically increases by stages of production, thereby presenting greater barriers to processed commodities than to raw materials in their unprocessed state. Unprocessed wood from Indonesia enters Japan with no tarriff, compared to a 30 percent tariff on its plywood.[58] On average, tariff rates in the major OECD countries are 1.6 percent for raw materials, 6.3 percent for semifinished manufactures, and 7.1 percent for finished manufactures. Moreover, *effective* tariff protection is actually at much higher levels than *nominal* tariff rates would indicate.[59] Tariff rates are also typically higher for the more easily produced consumer goods than for capital goods.

These cascading tariff structures and other trade policies of advanced industrial states impose particularly severe barriers to goods that less developed countries are most capable of producing for export—agricultural goods, semiprocessed commodities, and labor-intensive consumer goods.[60] Capital goods and industrial products that face the lowest tariff barriers in world trade are traditionally the exports of rich states.

Less developed countries also complain that, when they are capable of penetrating these barriers, advanced industrial states, responding to domestic political pressures, erect new ones to protect inefficient domestic producers. In this regard, less developed countries refer frequently to the increased protectionism imposed by advanced industrial states in textiles, clothing, footwear, steel, and assembly of electronic consumer goods; economic sectors in which less developed countries are coming to possess a competitive advantage and that are suffering a decline in mature economies.

Less developed countries argue, further, that certain institutional characteristics of GATT contributed to the emergence of these trade practices and made it difficult for them to secure trade reforms commensurate with their needs. The most-favored-nation principle is one of the problems they see in GATT, notwithstanding the fact that its existence has meant that tariff reductions negotiated among advanced industrial states have lowered trade barriers to exports of less developed countries as well. Their main objection to the MFN principle is that it inhibits rich states from granting preferential treatment to less developed countries' exports of manufactured goods as a spur to their development efforts.

> There are no industrial products of importance that are not produced for export by some developed country. Therefore, no country can now eliminate tariffs on manufactured goods for the benefit of the developing industries of poorer countries without simultaneously opening its markets to unrestrained competition from developed countries [because of the MFN prin-

---

[58]Brewster Grace, "UNCTAD VII," *University Field Staff International (USFI) Reports,* No. 16, 1987, p. 5.

[59]To illustrate this fact, let us assume that copper ore faces no tariff protection whereas refined copper faces a tariff of 10 percent. Let us also assume that refining a unit of copper ore raises its value from 75 cents to $1. The 10 percent tariff (10 cents) on the refined copper applies to the $1 price, not just to the 25 cents of value added by the refining process. Thus, the *effective protection* on refined copper is 40 percent (the 10 cent tariff divided by the 25 cent value added by refining), not the 10 percent nominal tariff rate.

[60]For an excellent discussion of the obstacles to less developed countries' exports, see Harry Johnson, *Economic Policies Toward Less Developed Countries* (Washington, D.C.: The Brookings Institution, 1967), Chap. III.

ciple]. It is this problem that has given rise to the demands of less developed countries that the most-favored-nation clause [of GATT] be suspended in their behalf.[61]

The bargaining principle of reciprocity underlying all tariff reduction negotiations is another characteristic of GATT long criticized by less developed countries. Poor states feel that they are placed at a disadvantage by the necessity to offer rich states an equivalent tariff concession for every tariff reduction they receive from them. They argue that reciprocity is equitable when applied to negotiations among states at approximately the same stage of economic development, but in negotiations between industrialized and less developed states, reciprocity (as with the MFN principle and the whole philosophy of the existing world trade order, for that matter) is a call for equal competition among fundamentally unequal economic units. Supporters of less developed countries argue that the reciprocity principle has made it difficult for these states to participate actively in GATT negotiations, and this in turn helps to account for the fact that tariffs remain high on industrial products of particular export interest to them:

> The developing countries of course have had no bargaining power, politically or economically. The rule of reciprocity has required them to give a matching concession, but clearly they are not in a position to give any. While over the past fifteen years, tariffs on industrial products of interest to industrial nations have been gradually brought down, those on products of interest to developing countries have remained at a high level.[62]

Less developed countries' criticism of the MFN principle and reciprocity are symptomatic of a more general charge they level at the GATT. They view it as a club created by advanced industrial states and managed in accordance with their primary interests. The norms guiding trade policy, the nature of trade negotiations, and the principal dimensions of progress in expanding world trade all reflect this fact. In the view of less developed states, these characteristics of GATT account for the continued existence of major barriers they face in their exports of agricultural products, mineral resources, semimanufactures, and industrial goods they are capable of producing. Less developed countries' exports have grown despite these features of the international trade system dominated by Western states—see Figure 2.4. However, their share of world trade was less in 1987 (25 percent) than in 1950 (31 percent),[63] notwithstanding the dramatic export performance of oil exporting states during the period 1973–1980 and the recent

---

[61]John W. Evans, "The General Agreement on Tariffs and Trade," in *The Global Partnership*, eds. R. Gardner and M. Millikan (New York: Praeger, 1968), pp. 92–93.

[62]Ambassador K. B. Lall of India, cited in John Evans, "The General Agreement on Tariffs and Trade," p. 76. Evans goes on to argue, however, that rich states have, in fact, extended tariff reductions to less developed countries without demanding equivalent concessions.

[63]*IMF Survey*, July 25, 1988, p. 252.

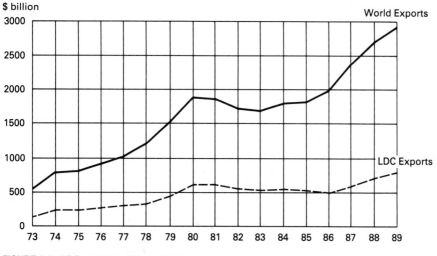

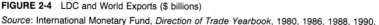

FIGURE 2-4   LDC and World Exports ($ billions)
Source: International Monetary Fund, *Direction of Trade Yearbook*, 1980, 1986, 1988, 1990.

trade success of Newly Industrializing Countries (NICs).[64] A widespread fear exists within less developed countries that participation in the liberal international trade order is not allowing them to keep up, much less catch up, with the advanced industrial states (see Figure 2-4).

There is no shortage of either alternative conceptualizations of the basic trade challenges facing less developed countries or of policy prescriptions purporting to deal with these challenges. Not surprisingly, the proponents of liberal economic thought and the representatives of radical thought suggest starkly different courses of action on the part of various states to meet the trade needs of less developed countries. Let us examine these briefly, as well as the prescriptions of Raul Prebish, the noted Argentinian economist and international politician, who more than any other person provided coherence for the Third World's demands of rich states in trade and financial matters since World War II.

The Liberal Economic Explanation and Prescription

From the perspective of liberal economic thought, the basic problem facing less developed countries is the extent to which national trade policies of rich and poor states continue to depart from the ideal of free trade. Policy prescriptions focus upon the need for all states to return to the underlying spirit of GATT. This requires that both rich and poor states abandon their policy of negotiating waivers from conformity with free trade

[64]These are a handful of less developed countries in Latin America and Asia experiencing rapid industrial growth and great success in exporting manufactured goods to advanced industrial states. Such countries include Argentina, Brazil, Chile, Mexico, Hong Kong, South Korea, Singapore, and Taiwan.

principles to protect relatively inefficient domestic production. Having created GATT and provided its leadership, advanced industrial states should bring their actual trade policies into line with their liberal trade rhetoric. They are called upon to remove the remaining barriers to trade among themselves and especially those particularly high barriers facing the goods that less developed countries produce for export. Moreover, advanced industrial states should accommodate structural shifts in international production and trade which give some newly industrializing countries a comparative advantage in the production and export of numerous manufactured goods (shoes, steel, shipbuilding, consumer electronics, and so forth) rather than resist these market forces with trade protection. South Korean steelmakers, for example, operate modern production facilities combining the very latest in technology with labor costs that are a fraction of those in Japan, Europe, and the United States. For their part, less developed countries are called upon to liberalize their own national trade policies, which, based on the protection of infant industries and import substitution, are often more protectionist than those of advanced industrial states. In 1989, Brazil maintained an average tariff level of 34 percent, with some as high as 85 percent.[65] Liberal economists feel that less developed countries can facilitate the modernization process by exposing their domestic producers to external competition through the encouragement of trade and foreign investment. If rich and poor states were to follow these policies, the argument runs, global production would be maximized and trade could make a maximum contribution to the development of poor states.[66]

There are substantial questions concerning the political efficacy of policy prescriptions for trade and development advanced by liberal economists. This is the case even for decision makers who are basically committed to the tenets of free trade, because (1) all organized interests within their societies do not embrace free trade as a concept, and (2) those who do, tend to abandon the concept when, in the short run, it adversely affects their particular jobs, industry, region, or nation. Inefficient producers that would be hurt by the removal of existing trade barriers, whether within rich or poor states, will mount strong political opposition to policy prescriptions for further trade liberalization, notwithstanding the impact that their action will have on the national economy or the global economy. They will repeatedly marshal the argument that the national economy will benefit from continued protection of its relatively inefficient enterprises, since jobs are thereby preserved at home and the nation is able to enjoy the security of maintaining an indigenous productive capacity in the affected economic sector.

We have seen how the complexity of the issues and the nature of domestic opposition to free trade will make it difficult for advanced industrial states to make great strides toward further liberalization of trade

---

[65]Elizabeth Wehr, "U.S. Plies Uncharted Waters in Effort to Open Markets," *Congressional Quarterly*, May 20, 1989, p. 1172.

[66]For a discussion along these lines, see Harry Johnson, *Economic Policies Toward Less Developed Countries*, pp. 47, 130. See also Richard Cooper, "Third World Tariff Tangle," *Foreign Policy*, No. 4 (Fall 1971), pp. 35–50.

policies during the coming years. In addition, less developed countries will find liberalization of national trade policies of the sort prescribed here very difficult to achieve. Less developed countries typically feel unable to compete on an equal footing with producers of advanced industrial states within their own economies, much less in international markets. The apprehensions of the less developed states must be overcome if they are to implement the policies prescribed by liberal economists. This is unlikely to occur on a broad scale since exposing one's economy to competition through trade and foreign investment is seen by important political elements within countries throughout the Third World as leading inevitably to foreign penetration and further loss of control over their economic and political destinies. Whatever the aggregate economic results, any leader of a less developed country who today embraces liberal economic policy prescriptions does so at the risk of generating substantial domestic political opposition by economic and political nationalists who are acutely sensitive to injustices stemming from various forms of political and market dominance that advanced industrial states have exercised over less developed countries.

The Prebisch Explanation and Prescription

In his writings as an economist, and through his activities as head of the Economic Commission for Latin America and later as the first secretary-general of the United Nations Conference on Trade and Development (UNCTAD), Raul Prebisch mobilized considerable political support from less developed countries for an alternative conceptualization of these states' trade difficulties. Liberal economists attribute less developed countries' trade problems to the unwillingness of rich and poor states to adopt national trade policies consistent with the principles of a liberal trade order embodied in the General Agreement on Tariffs and Trade. Prebisch agreed that less developed states would be better off if barriers to their exports were removed, by rich states in particular; however, the actual implementation of free trade would not get to the heart of their trade and development problem. Prebisch argued that, even in a world of free trade, the benefits will be reaped disproportionately by advanced industrial states as a consequence of structural differences between countries at different stages of development.

The structural problem of central importance to less developed countries, according to Prebisch, is a long-term decline in the terms of trade for the exchange of commodities for industrial products; that is, the value of primary products has declined relative to the value of manufactured products in world trade. Price trends during the 1980s for primary products (excluding oil) and for manufactured goods are shown in Figure 2-5. Since less developed countries typically are large exporters of primary products (such products constitute roughly 75 percent of their exports) and must import most industrial goods, they find themselves having to export ever larger amounts of primary products to earn the foreign exchange necessary to purchase the same volume of manufactured imports from year to year.

A number of factors are cited to account for the decline in the terms of trade between less developed states and advanced industrial states. Cru-

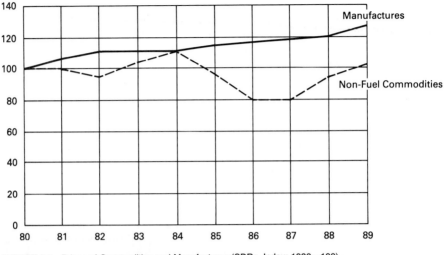

FIGURE 2-5   Prices of Commodities and Manufactures (SDRs, Index: 1980 = 100)
Source: IMF Survey, July 24, 1989, p. 238.

cial among them, according to Prebisch, is the fact that productivity advances in advanced industrial states lead to wage and other input cost increases that keep prices constant or rising. In contrast, in less developed countries productivity advances do not lead to wage increases and/or constant prices because of disguised unemployment and weak labor organizations. Instead, they lead to price declines that are passed on to the consumers—located predominantly in rich states.[67]

Additional factors involve the relatively lower income elasticity of demand for primary products, as compared with manufactures. This means, for example, that forces operate to dampen increases in demand for primary products as income increases: Food expenditure as a percentage of income declines, and primary products as a percentage of total factor inputs needed to produce industrial goods decline. These forces, along with the development of synthetic substitutes, serve to depress demand and prices for primary products in world trade relative to manufactured goods, for which demand and expenditures increase as a proportion of income as income increases.

All these factors are seen by Prebisch and most other advocates for less developed countries as evidence of a structural bias in world trade that relegates producers of primary products to a permanent second-class status in the global economy, even if all barriers to free trade were to be removed. Of course, numerous restrictions on trade continue to exist in fact, and as we have seen they make it particularly difficult for less developed countries to transform themselves from exporters of primary products to exporters

[67]See Albert O. Hirschman, "Ideologies of Economic Development in Latin America," in *Latin American Issues* (New York: Twentieth Century Fund, 1961), pp. 14–15. Hirschman provides a concise overall summary of Prebisch's economic philosophy.

of manufactured and semiprocessed goods as a means of overcoming the problem posed by the terms of trade.

This conceptualization of the manner in which less developed countries are denied their fair share of trade benefits is quite at odds with classical liberal economic theory. Not surprisingly, Prebisch and his followers find the liberal policy prescription for free trade a deficient solution to the trade and development problems of poor states. Instead, they call for comprehensive reforms of the international economic order designed to eradicate the structural inequalities that produce disproportionate gains from trade for rich states and to compensate poor states for any remaining inequalities. Such a program would require advanced industrial states to facilitate the expansion of less developed countries' exports of manufactured and semimanufactured goods. It would also include numerous commodity agreements covering primary product exports of particular importance to less developed countries. These agreements between major exporters and importers would be designed to ensure access to the markets of rich states as well as to stabilize world market prices for specific commodities at levels assuring poor states both a larger income and smaller annual fluctuations in revenues. To the extent that such agreements in commodity and industrial trade fail to arrest the decline in the terms of trade between less developed and industrial states, the former insist that a compensatory finance scheme be established by which industrial states would return capital to less developed countries in the form of grants or low-interest loans. This capital flow should be in amounts at least equal to the "excess" in revenues industrial states receive as a consequence of any further declines in the terms of trade.

Prebisch argued that trade reforms cannot and should not be accomplished primarily by reciprocal tariff cuts of the GATT variety between rich and poor states. Rather, he summoned the rich states unilaterally to extend preferential treatment to less developed countries for their exports of manufactures and semimanufactures. Such a move would help to arrest the decline in the terms of trade between center and periphery states while facilitating industrialization crucial to the latter's rapid development.[68]

Quite obviously, Prebisch and his advocates do not want a return to the spirit underlying GATT. Indeed, they want to create a new economic order—one that recognizes the special needs of less developed countries and that affords them a greater share of the benefits from the conduct of trade than could be expected even in a world of free trade. Trade in accordance with GATT principles is viewed as a means of exploiting poor states and denying them the opportunity of industrializing rather than as a means of enhancing the welfare of all states. Consistent with this orientation, less developed countries pushed hard for the establishment of the United Nations Conference on Trade and Development (UNCTAD) in 1964, with Raul Prebisch as its first secretary-general. UNCTAD is the

---

[68]For a more complete account of Prebisch's economic analysis and policy prescription, see *Towards a New Trade Policy for Development*, report by the Secretary-General of the United Nations Conference on Trade and Development (Raul Prebisch), E/CONF. 46/3 (New York: United Nations, 1964).

institutional expression of Prebisch's conceptualization of the global economy and the less developed states' role in it. It was created to challenge GATT both philosophically and institutionally as the central multilateral arena for world trade relations.[69]

Through UNCTAD and other bilateral and multilateral channels, the less developed countries have sought to secure a variety of structural reforms of world trade toward the ends specified by Prebisch. They have been notably successful in challenging liberal economic principles as a guide to north-south trade. However, they have achieved very limited results in translating trade reforms into financial and economic transfers from rich to poor states on a significant scale.

The generalized system of preferences. In the early 1970s, after years of negotiations within UNCTAD, the less developed countries were successful in obtaining a Generalized System of Preferences (GSP) from rich states. Some nineteen advanced industrial states agreed to eliminate tariffs unilaterally for ten years (renewed during the 1980s for a second decade) on manufactured and semimanufactured goods exported by less developed countries. These tariff concessions were applicable to the trade of some 140 less developed countries, seeking to stimulate their industrialization and to improve the competitiveness of their exports in world markets relative to like goods exported from more advanced economies. In 1990, GSP utilization reached $60 billion.[70]

The GSP constitutes a departure from the most-favored-nation principle and the practice of reciprocity underlying GATT—the poor states were not asked to offer tariff concessions in return for those granted by the advanced industrial states. The advanced industrial states have placed a variety of limitations on their GSP programs to minimize domestic economic disruptions and protectionist demands. European states, for example, imposed quota-ceilings on goods imported from less developed countries under the GSP; above a specified level of imports LDC goods would not be accorded preferential treatment. The United States has excluded, altogether, particular types of imports from eligibility under its GSP—textiles and apparel, certain footwear, electronic, steel, and glass products. It also denies GSP treatment for any less developed country's product that amounted to 50 percent of total U.S. imports of that good or that exceeded a value of $88 million per year (in 1989).[71] Some additional political conditions exclude from the U.S. program those Communist states not members of the GATT or the IMF, members of OPEC, and less de-

[69]For a comprehensive description and assessment of UNCTAD as an institution from an advocate's viewpoint, see Branislav Gosovic, *UNCTAD: Conflict and Compromise* (Leiden: A. W. Sitjhoff-Leiden, 1972). See also, R. S. Walters, "International Organizations and Political Communication," *International Organization*, 25, no. 4 (Autumn 1971), pp. 818–35.

[70]*UNCTAD Bulletin*, No. 9 (May–June 1991), 3.

[71]U.S. Department of State, Bureau of Public Affairs, "Generalized System of Preferences," *GIST*, August 1988, p. 2. The $88 million ceiling was for 1989. It is indexed to the growth rate of the U.S. economy and was raised about $6 million per year during the mid–1980s.

veloped countries which run afoul of American policies on illegal drugs, terrorism, and workers' rights.[72]

The Generalized System of Preferences is most significant as a symbol of the advanced industrialized states' willingness to depart from cherished principles of liberal trade philosophy (MFN and reciprocity) on behalf of less developed countries under carefully defined and circumscribed conditions. Limitations placed upon it by the industrial states have inhibited the GSP from becoming a major stimulus to the industrialization and exports of less developed countries. In 1988 the United States imported $18.4 billion in goods from less developed countries under the GSP program. But this amounted to only 19 percent of American imports from less developed countries, excluding OPEC. Over the course of the program the most industrialized of the LDCs (Taiwan, South Korea, Hong Kong, Mexico, and Brazil) have captured the lion's share of the benefits. In recent years the United States has tried to steer its GSP benefits toward poorer LDCs by graduating from the program countries that reach a level of economic development and competitiveness so that they no longer need preferences to compete in the U.S. market. In 1989 Hong Kong, South Korea, Singapore, and Taiwan were declared ineligible for the program on these grounds.

The United States' GSP program is now operative until 1993 without additional congressional action. Less developed countries are looking for further relaxation of the constraints now limiting the potential of the GSP, but such changes are unlikely. Advanced industrialized states are increasingly concerned about the political and economic consequences of losing domestic manufacturing output to the Third World producers. Rather than liberalizing the GSP program, the United States is reemphasizing elements of reciprocity and stressing the need for LDCs with higher per capita incomes to "graduate" from the GSP arrangements to treatment on a most-avored-nation basis.

The integrated commodity program. Ninety-three less developed countries relied on commodities (crops or minerals) other than oil for more than 50 percent of their total export earnings in the early 1980s.[73] Commodity trade is, accordingly, an overriding preoccupation of most LDCs. They are concerned both about declines in the terms of trade between the prices of their commodities relative to the prices of manufactured goods (see Figure 2-5) and abrupt fluctuations in commodity price levels. Both problems dramatically affect the foreign exchange earnings of less developed countries relying heavily on exports of one or a few primary products. At a time when Zambia, for example, relied on copper for 94 percent of its export earnings in the 1970s, copper prices on the world market plunged to $1,290 per ton at the end of 1974 from a peak of $3,034 per ton just eight months before. This price drop for copper, combined with a contin-

---

[72]Ibid.

[73]*UNCTAD Statistical Pocket Book* (New York: UNCTAD, 1984), p. 40.

ued rise in the prices of industrial goods on world markets, forced a reduction in the volume of Zambia's imports by 45 percent and a 15 percent decline in its Gross Domestic Product between 1974 and 1975.[74] Mexico, which relied on oil for 80 percent of its export earnings in 1985, experienced a similar catastrophe when oil prices dropped to under half of their level of the previous year. Its export earnings dropped 27 percent that year, from $22 billion to $16 billion, creating both domestic political-economic turmoil and a severe problem in servicing its international debt. No industrialized states face such economic uncertainty as a result of price movements in world markets.

Less developed countries capitalized upon the demonstration effect of OPEC, high commodity prices, and fears of raw materials supply interruptions among advanced industrial states after the oil crisis of 1973 to press vigorously for commodity agreements during the 1970s. Their efforts were concentrated on securing implementation of an Integrated Program for Commodities (IPC) proposed by UNCTAD. The IPC represents a bold departure from the isolated efforts in past years to control both the price fluctuations and the average price levels of commodities through agreements between major exporters and importers negotiated on a case-by-case basis. It involves a comprehensive effort to forge commodity agreements for eighteen primary products that account for approximately 75 percent of less developed countries' exports of agricultural and mineral commodities. Ten of these eighteen commodities were identified as suitable for stockpiling[75] and, thus, lend themselves to the creation of buffer stocks as a means of influencing the market when it approaches the floor and ceiling prices established through individual commodity agreements.[76] The IPC calls for the creation of a common international fund through contributions from commodity importers and exporters. The Common Fund would presumably make it easier to finance any buffer stock arrangements that might emerge as a component of a commodity agreement negotiated under the auspices of the IPC. In addition, the IPC envisions the adoption of various measures to develop markets for raw materials, stimulate local processing of commodities in LDCs, and encourage economic diversification of LDCs heavily dependent upon commodity trade.

The IPC in the 1970s was more than an attempt to manage commodity markets. Progress in negotiations on the IPC was taken as symbolic of the seriousness advanced industrial states attached to less developed countries'

---

[74]Willy Brandt, *North-South: Program for Survival* (Cambridge: M.I.T. Press, 1980) p. 145.

[75]The commodities are cocoa, coffee, copper, cotton and cotton yarns, hard fibers and products, jute and jute products, rubber, sugar, tea, and tin. A buffer stock facility is a stockpile of a commodity managed under the auspices of an international commodity agreement. The stockpile is used for the purpose of controlling prices of that commodity traded in world markets.

[76]When approaching the floor price, the buffer stock manager would enter the market to purchase the product and strengthen prices; when approaching the ceiling price, the buffer stock manager would enter the market to sell quantities of the product to reduce prices.

demands for a new international economic order.[77] The high water mark of efforts to implement the Integrated Program for Commodities occurred between 1976 and 1980, culminating in an agreement among rich and poor states in UNCTAD to establish a Common Fund of $400 million to finance buffer stocks in association with commodity agreements. A second account of $350 million was also to be established to promote new commodity markets and economic diversification of LDCs.[78] Both would begin operations upon ratification of the agreement by ninety states, representing two thirds of the capital contributions. While attracting much attention at the time, the funding agreements fell considerably short of the $3 billion to $6 billion sought by the less developed countries for these purposes.

Developments in the international economy during the 1980s made it impossible for less developed countries to consolidate these gains. A global recession of the early 1980s produced a precipitous decline in commodity prices to their lowest level in over thirty-five years (see Figure 2-5). Even OPEC states found it impossible to maintain oil prices. Indeed, the viability of OPEC itself came into question.[79] The pressures on advanced industrial states for reform of commodity trade were, thus, eroded. It took until 1989 to secure commitments from enough states to actually establish the Common Fund. Only five international commodity agreements were in effect in 1985 covering coffee, cocoa, tin, sugar, and rubber. Of these only the last was a product of the IPC process; and the agreements on cocoa and sugar were not successful in achieving their price objectives.[80] UNCTAD studies and negotiations on copper, jute, sisal, cotton, and tropical timber have failed to produce formal commodity agreements to date.

The major Western powers, and the United States in particular, remain highly skeptical of the Integrated Program for Commodities, although they have participated in the negotiations in recognition of the importance attached to them by all less developed countries and by the OPEC states. American officials remain convinced that only in rare circumstances should negotiated commodity agreements replace traditional market mechanisms governing commodity trade. To the extent that commodity agreements are explored, the United States still prefers to do it on a case-by-case basis. American officials are wary of universal formulations, such as the IPC emphasis on buffer stocks, which they do not think will work as hoped for by the less developed countries. The aim of any commodity agreement entered into by the United States is likely to be stabili-

---

[77]The new international economic order is discussed in Chapter 7. For an analysis of the IPC negotiations in UNCTAD, see R. Rothstein, "Regime Creation by a Coalition of the Weak: Lessons from the NIEO and the Integrated Program for Commodities," *International Organization*, 28, no. 3 (September 1984), pp. 307–28.

[78]"A Fund for the Future," *UNCTAD Monthly Bulletin*, No. 165 (September 1980), pp. 3–6.

[79]OPEC and oil constitute a unique phenomenon in the political economy of commodity trade—see Chapter 7.

[80]"Markets Test Commodity Agreements' Ability to Meet Objectives of Price Stabilization," *IMF Survey*, December 10, 1984, p. 370.

zation of fluctuations in price levels, not an increase of the price level above market trends for the product. That would increase inflationary pressure and discourage inefficient producers from diversification. American analysts, moreover, view as a fallacy the notion that less developed countries as a group actually benefit from a comprehensive program of commodity agreements stabilizing and raising the prices of primary products in world markets. Many advanced industrial states including the United States, Canada, Australia, and South Africa are major commodity exporters, and less developed states import many primary products. Less developed countries account for only 32 percent of the world's nonoil commodity exports,[81] and they possess approximately 45 percent of the world's known reserves of nonfuel minerals.[82] Thus, the potential effects of the IPC are very complex and would not necessarily reduce the gap between rich and poor states. "In most cases, selected industrial countries would benefit as much or more from price increases in nonfuel minerals than would the less developed countries."[83]

For these reasons the United States was not among the 103 countries that ratified the agreement to create the Common Fund when it went into effect in 1989, and the prospects of *comprehensive* implementation of UNCTAD's Integrated Commodity Program are slim. On the other hand, the mere participation of the United States and all other advanced industrial states in IPC negotiations since 1975 represents a major change in their behavior and significant concessions in principle. Perhaps the IPC can provide a framework for future efforts to stabilize international commodity trade of importance to less developed countries should developments in world markets once again give advanced industrial states an incentive to negotiate as was the case in the 1970s.

Compensatory financing. A third component of Prebisch's philosophy involves financial transfers from advanced industrial states to less developed countries through grants or low-interest loans to make up for shortfalls in the export earnings of less developed countries that arise for reasons substantially beyond their control. These may result from a decline in the terms of trade, crop failures in agricultural raw materials, or decreased demand for raw materials exported from less developed countries because of recessions in advanced industrial nations. This compensatory finance would supplement, not replace, traditional forms of bilateral and multilateral economic assistance to poor nations. Compensatory finance is a means of dealing with the *effects* of shortfalls in export earnings, notwithstanding reforms such as the Generalized System of Preferences and the Integrated Program for Commodities designed to deal with the *causes* of the shortfalls. The goal of compensatory finance is to guarantee export earnings, not to administer commodity prices. As such, it is more popular

[81]*World Economic Outlook, 1985* (Washington, D.C.: IMF, 1985), p. 137.

[82]Dennis Pirages, *The New Context for International Relations: Global Ecopolitics* (North Scituate, Mass.: Duxbury Press, 1978), p. 170.

[83]Ibid.

than commodity agreements in countries such as the United States that are reluctant to interfere with market mechanisms presently governing commodity trade.

Two compensatory finance schemes are presently in operation. The International Monetary Fund (IMF) introduced a compensatory finance facility in 1963, which was expanded and whose terms governing access have been liberalized in 1976. It is available to all IMF members although it is designed primarily for the less developed states. It can be used when a country finds itself with a balance-of-payments deficit due to reductions in its overall export earnings for reasons substantially beyond its control. This IMF facility has grown steadily since 1975 and is, of course, relied upon most heavily during periods of declining terms of trade for commodity exporters, such as 1980–1985. During the period 1980–1986, sixty-nine less developed countries drew $8.3 billion from the IMF compensatory finance facility, of which $3.5 billion was borrowed in 1983 alone.[84] In August 1988 a Compensatory and Contingency Financing Facility (CCFF) was established by the Fund to replace and enhance its previous facility. It retains the basic features of the earlier compensatory finance scheme, to finance temporary export shortfalls, while supplementing it with financing for excesses in import costs resulting from factors beyond the member state's control and for helping members to maintain IMF-supported adjustment programs in the face of adverse external shocks[85]—such as oil price increases associated with Iraq's invasion of Kuwait in 1990.

A second compensatory financing scheme, STABEX, has been a component of the three Lomé Conventions governing economic relations between the European Economic Community and sixty-five less developed African, Caribbean, and Pacific (ACP) states since 1975. The STABEX scheme involves the extension of grants or interest-free loans to ACP states when their export earnings from any of several dozen primary products specified in the Convention fall more than a certain percentage below their average export receipts for the previous three years in trade with the EEC. The STABEX facility was funded at $650 million for the period 1985–1990.[86] The terms of financial assistance under STABEX are more favorable to LDCs than those for the IMF facility. However, the IMF facility is much larger and applies to the overall export earnings of any less developed country in the IMF—regardless of the products traded or the direction of trade. STABEX involves just those LDCs that are parties to the Lomé Convention, and it is concerned only with export earnings from specified commodities to the twelve member states of the European Economic Com-

[84]"UNCTAD Makes a Contribution to IMF Comprehensive Review of Its Compensatory Finance Facility," *UNCTAD Bulletin*, No. 236 (October 1987), p. 13; "Use of Fund Resources Escalated in 1982/83," *IMF Survey*, September 19, 1983, p. 284.

[85]R. Pownall and B. Stuart, "The IMF's Compensatory and Contingency Financing Facility," *Finance and Development*, December 1988, pp. 9–11.

[86]"The EEC and 65 Developing Countries Agree to New Pact on Trade and Aid," *IMF Survey*, February 4, 1985, p. 40.

munity.[87] A new facility, COMPEX, has been added by the EEC for least developed countries not signatories to the latest Lomé III agreement. While it functions in a manner very similar to STABEX, it is less than one-tenth the size.

The less developed countries are understandably disappoined in the present international trade system and are frustrated over the limited progress in reforming the world trade order. Nevertheless, there has been a fundamental alteration of the principles underlying trade between less developed states and the Western powers. To these accomplishments should be added the explicit recognition given throughout the Tokyo round that the GATT principals of nondiscrimination and reciprocity would be relaxed on behalf of less developed countries.[88] The ideas that Prebisch popularized and politicized constitute the agenda for contemporary commercial relations between rich and poor states in a variety of negotiating forums. That, itself, is a substantial accomplishment on behalf of less developed countries, even if resource transfers through these trade reforms are far less than initial expectations or current needs.

Further progress toward implementation of Prebisch's concept of an international trade order that benefits less developed countries is, nevertheless, likely to be very slow. The policy prescriptions outlined by Prebisch and his followers to benefit poor states place the burden of international structural reform primarily on the shoulders of advanced industrial states. In advanced industrial states relevant decision makers typically think in terms of liberal economic principles. Liberal economists view the critical assumptions of Prebisch's economic theory (such as the terms of trade arguments) with great skepticism.[89] Thus, successful implementation of the

---

[87]For an excellent, brief summary of these compensatory finance facilities as well as of the Generalized System of Preferences and the Integrated Program for Commodities, see Guy Erb, *Negotiations on Two Fronts: Manufactures and Commodities*, Development Paper No. 25 (Washington, D.C.: Overseas Development Council, March 1978). See also, *UNCTAD Bulletin*, No. 211 (April 1985), 1–4; and John Ravenhill, "STABEX and Commodity Producers," *International Organization*, 38, no. 3 (Summer 1984), pp. 537–74.

[88]See Stephen Krasner, "The Tokyo Round," *International Studies Quarterly*, 23, no. 4 (December 1979), p. 524.

[89]Classical liberal economists are skeptical of the terms of trade arguments advanced by Prebisch and others. They note that the magnitude, and indeed the direction, of the terms of trade between primary products and manufactured goods vary greatly from commodity to commodity, depending upon the base years chosen from which to measure price trends. Basing calculations on prices prevailing in the early 1950s or early 1970s, for example, reveal sharp declines in the terms of trade for commodity exporters because those base periods reflect extraordinarily high commodity prices relative to those for industrial goods. The choice of other years as a base period would yield very different results. Also, while commodity exports have virtually the same characteristics today as they did years ago, manufactured goods embody significant qualitative improvements over the years. The properties of natural rubber, for instance are the same today as they were in the 1950s, but automobile tires may get four times the mileage as they did in the 1950s. Therefore, it may be appropriate that prices for rubber (or other primary products) have not increased as rapidly as for tires (or other manufactured products).

Notwithstanding the controversy over the terms of trade among economists, most advocates for less developed countries believe the Prebisch position to be valid. It constitutes

Prebisch program to meet the trade and development problems of poor states depends upon unilateral concessions by advanced industrial states, whose decision makers are not predisposed to accept the philosophical underpinning that gives rise to demands for these concessions.

Differences in economic philosophy are only part of the problem. More important is the lack of a sense of community among center and periphery states that is strong enough to trigger a substantial redistribution of income through commodity agreements, aid programs, preference agreements, and the like that are adequate to meet the development needs of poor states. At the heart of any effective income redistribution program is a prior sense of political and social community. Prebisch's program for a comprehensive structural reform in the global economy depends upon a sense of community *between* rich and poor states that is every bit as strong as that existing *within* advanced industrial states with a long tradition of national unity. This sense of community between rich and poor states simply does not exist at present.

Evidence of this fact, and still another obstacle to implementing Prebisch's policy, is the domestic opposition within the major advanced industrial states to unilateral concessions on the order of those demanded by Prebisch. Protectionist forces within all advanced industrial states are likely to prevent a resource transfer to poor states from ever approaching the scale contemplated by Prebisch and less developed countries in their demands for a generalized system of preferences, an integrated program for commodities, and expanded compensatory finance. This is particularly true when advanced industrial states are preoccupied with substantial economic problems of their own such as slow economic growth, budget deficits, trade deficits, unemployment, or inflation.

The politicial obstacles to the implementation of Prebisch's proposals are not confined to advanced industrial states. Less developed states, for example, must act together in pressing demands for structural reforms in the international economic order that are consistent with Prebisch's philosophy. Since commodity agreements, tariff preferences, aid programs, and other means of transferring resources to less developed countries are very uneven in the benefits they confer on different states, there is increasing difficulty in maintaining political cohesion among them in their negotiations with core states on structural international economic reform. The economic problems and prospects of Chad bear little resemblance to those of South Korea, for instance. In the absence of a united front by less developed countries, it is unlikely that advanced industrial states will find it necessary to extend concessions along these lines.

---

the assumptional base underlying virtually all their political and economic assessments of world trade.

For a summary of views attacking Prebisch's terms of trade arguments, see A. S. Friedeberg, *The United Nations Conference on Trade and Development* (Rotterdam: Rotterdam University Press, 1970), pp. 46–61.

The Radical Explanation and Prescription

The radical view of the trade and development problems faced by poor states has some things in common with Prebisch's orientation, but in other respects it differs sharply. Radical analysts in rich and poor states share with Prebisch the conviction that the free trade prescription in the liberal economic tradition will not generate modernization and economic development in less developed countries. They embrace Prebisch's argument about the decline in the terms of trade and view the conduct of trade between Western states and less developed countries in accordance with GATT principles as an exploitative relationship.

In spite of these similarities with the Prebisch conceptualization of the global economy, the radical view goes well beyond Prebisch in its assessment of how profoundly the structural arrangements *among* and *within* states are at odds with the developmental possibilities and capacity for autonomy of poor states. Consequently, radicals differ greatly with Prebisch on what solutions are appropriate to achieve the basic political and economic interests of states in the periphery of the global economy.

Prebisch views inequities in international economic relations between rich and poor states as having evolved gradually out of certain structural characteristics of exchanges between states at different stages of economic development. As we have seen, his prescription to remove these inequities focuses upon comprehensive reform of the norms governing international economic relations. In essence, this means reliance upon policy changes by advanced industrial states designed to redistribute income to less developed countries. Prebisch feels that this can be accomplished through multilateral negotiations between less developed countries and advanced industrial states if the former maintain a unified position in applying sustained political pressure for precisely defined alterations in the conduct of trade and other forms of international economic exchange. Since 1964, UNCTAD and the United Nations have been the primary locus of this effort.

Radicals see the poverty of poor states as a consequence of a capitalist (imperialist) international political economy in which periphery states are held subordinate politically and economically to Western states. The global political economy based on the norms of liberal economic philosophy is very effective in assuring advanced industrial states access to cheap raw materials and cheap labor as well as to new markets for capital investments and exports. These characteristics of the international political economy are the key to understanding both the poverty of the Third World and the prosperity of Western countries, the United States in particular. The development of center states and the underdevelopment of periphery states are both "outcomes of the same historical process: the global expansion of capitalism."[90]

Western states are able to continue this exploitative relationship with less developed countries because of their power in world markets and their

---

[90]Suzanne Bodenheimer, "Dependency and Imperialism: The Roots of Latin American Underdevelopment," in *Readings in U.S. Imperialism*, eds. K. T. Fann and D. Hodges (Boston: Porter Sargent, 1971), p. 160.

control of the key international institutions that establish norms for international transfer of goods and capital. In addition, these governments buttress the leadership position of a small economic and political elite (client class), present in most poor states, whose source of domestic power derives from the maintenance of close external ties with the political and economic elites of advanced industrial (capitalist) states. This client class is viewed by radicals as a junior partner to elites in center states. Such a class benefits handsomely from its position in the international capitalist system, even though the country it dominates may remain economically underdeveloped.

Given these perceptions, it is easy to understand the radicals' criticism of both the liberal economists' and Prebisch's prescriptions for dealing with the trade and development problems of poor states. The liberal prescription of free movement of goods and capital among states is to the radicals merely a blatant effort by advanced industrial states to penetrate and further denationalize the political and economic systems of less developed countries. Prebisch's prescriptions appear very naïve to radical thinkers. Western states are not going to redistribute income to poor states to remedy inequalities in the benefits derived in international economic exchange. To do so would mean an end to the exploitative relationships that they created (consciously or unconsciously) and upon which their continued prosperity depends. In radical thought, multilateral negotiations of the sort Prebisch suggests hold no promise. The international economic institutions that define the post–World War II economic order (GATT, IMF, IBRD) are firmly controlled by Western (capitalist) states. Indeed, these agencies constitute the machinery through which rich states exploit less developed countries. Radicals also see little progress resulting from negotiations in an international institution such as UNCTAD, even though it ostensibly represents the interests of poor states. Not only will Western states refuse to agree to any critical reforms demanded by less developed countries in such a forum but also, since the leaders of most less developed countries depend so thoroughly on Western ties for their economic and political survival, they will not even pose demands that would threaten the dominant position of advanced industrial states in the global economy.

For poor states to secure autonomy of economic and political action or to escape from the economic exploitation that has condemned them to poverty, they must interrupt the existing linkages between center and periphery states. Among the radicals there is general agreement that this can be accomplished only by replacing capitalism with a socialist political-economic order. New Left advocates in the United States tend to focus their attention on the need for the emergence of socialism in the United States and in other center states. Only then will the rich states be predisposed toward a redistribution of income to less developed countries and the erection of a new, nonexploitative global economic order based on socialist principles of exchange. Moreover, the external support critical for continued control by present-day political and economic elites in less developed countries would be withdrawn by socialist governments in rich states. Hence, from this perspective the emergence of socialism in Western states would be necessary and sufficient to remove the primary local and international obstacles to the development of poor states. *Dependencia* theorists in Latin America, on the other hand, tend to focus their attention on socialist revolutions in periphery states, revolutions that would remove present domestic political-economic elites and clear the way for an interruption of the existing ties between poor states and the capitalist global economy that produces their poverty. Mutually beneficial international economic ties could then be constructed among the less developed countries themselves. Hence, radical solutions to the trade and development problems of poor states stress revolution (not necessarily violent). It is dramatically different from the partnership in development envisioned in either the classical liberal or Prebisch approaches. While at odds with each other, these two orientations are similar in that they call upon rich and poor states merely to alter existing foreign economic policies, or for the former to implement relatively modest reforms in trade and the larger international economic order for the sake of the LDCs.[91]

A number of questions arise regarding the political efficacy of the radicals' policy prescriptions. The program of the New Left in the United States depends essentially on the transformation of the United States and other Western states from capitalist to socialist systems. There is very little evidence to suggest that such a transformation is likely to occur, at least in the near future. But even if it were likely to occur, careful scrutiny would have to be given to the categorical assertion that less developed countries will be incomparably better off in dealing with a socialist West and a socialist United States than with the same states under capitalist systems. Whether Western states are socialist or capitalist, less developed countries will be engaged in economic exchanges with economic and military giants. Throughout history, the largest economic and military powers have defined their relationships with lesser powers in a manner that lesser powers typically view as exploitation. This situation is likely to repeat itself even in a world of socialist states.[92] Soviet relations with the People's Democracies of Eastern Europe provide some evidence on this point. From the perspective of the 1990s, socialism is in retreat rather than an effective model of development.

The emphasis of the *dependencia* theorists upon socialist revolutions in the periphery states raises another basic problem. In most instances, if a state or states in the periphery of the global economy achieve a socialist revolution, their need for foreign capital, technology, and markets will still exist. Unless the advanced industrial states also abandon capitalism, the new socialist state or states in the periphery will still have to operate within a capitalist global economy. Even if the character of its linkages with the

---

[91]For examples of the radical perspective on trade, see Arghiri Emmanuel, *Unequal Exchange: A Study of the Imperialism of Trade* (New York: Monthly Review Press, 1972); and Harry Magdoff, *The Age of Imperialism* (New York: Monthly Review Press, 1969).

[92]This discussion of the radical interpretation of global economic relations between rich and poor states has purposefully been couched in terms larger than the trade issue. The basic dynamics described here can be applied to other forms of economic exchange besides trade, such as aid, private investment, and monetary relations.

international economy is altered drastically by a socialist revolution at home, the state in the periphery will in all probability find that the alternative to dependency is not autonomy; rather, at best it will be a new form of interdependence, one that still sets severe constraints on domestic economic and political programs.

Summary

The profound differences among the liberal, Prebisch, and radical interpretations of the contemporary trade and economic challenges facing less developed states are summarized in Figure 2-6. Each school of thought identifies a different fundamental obstacle inhibiting the economic performance of poor states. Each school of thought, accordingly, identifies a different focal point for concerted action appropriate to alter the condition of less developed states.

Liberal analysts and decision makers attribute the source of poor states' problems in trade to departures in the foreign economic policies of rich and poor states from the liberal economic principles embodied in the GATT and IMF statutes. They are likely to place primary emphasis on bringing the foreign economic policies of less developed and advanced industrial states into conformity with liberal trade principles that, in their view, serve appropriately as the norms for economic relations in the post–World War II era. Doing so will mean acceptance of some structural shifts in the domestic economies of both poor and rich states.

Prebisch and his followers attribute the primary sources of the poor states' trade problems to inequities of the market system and of liberal principles governing foreign economic exchange. They are likely to place primary emphasis on redefining these liberal norms governing international economic exchange to give particular advantages to less developed states relative to advanced industrial states. For example, they would like to see UNCTAD's philosophy replace the GATT philosophy as the linchpin of the international trade order. The burden of adjusting to new norms governing world trade would necessarily fall primarily on the advanced industrial states whose foreign economic policies toward poor states must change dramatically. Implementing these reforms would mean some structural shifts in the domestic economies of rich and poor states, as well as some alteration of the foreign economic policies of less developed states.

Radical analysts take a more holistic approach to problem definition and proposed reforms than do liberal analysts or Prebisch. All activities at the domestic and international levels are interrelated inextricably. Radical doctrine insists that nothing can be left the same if the development prospects of poor states are to improve markedly. These analysts place primary emphasis on a radical alteration of the domestic economic and social structures of all advanced industrial and less developed countries. Capitalism must be replaced by socialism. This domestic transformation would necessarily produce drastic shifts, as well, in the foreign economic policies of rich and poor states and in the norms governing international economic exchange.

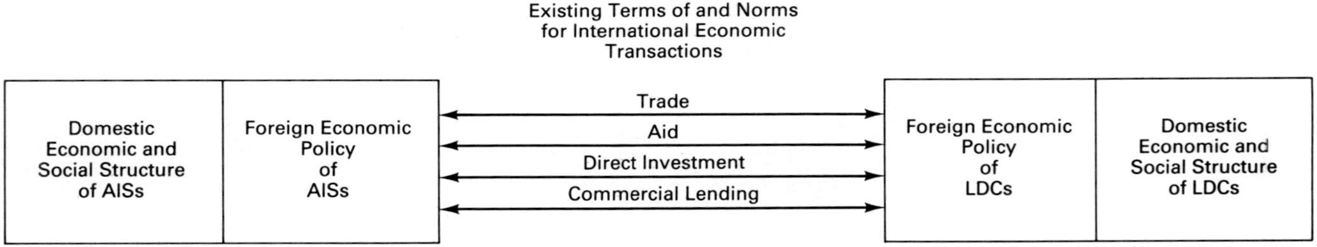

Existing Terms of and Norms
for International Economic
Transactions

Domestic Economic and Social Structure of AISs	Foreign Economic Policy of AISs		Foreign Economic Policy of LDCs	Domestic Economic and Social Structure of LDCs

Trade
Aid
Direct Investment
Commercial Lending

Analytical Approach	First Order Problems and Efforts at Reform	Second Order Problems and Efforts at Reform	Third Order Problems and Efforts at Reform
Liberal	Foreign economic policies of LDCs Foreign economic policies of AISs	Domestic economic and social structures of LDCs Domestic economic and social structures of AISs	Existing terms of and norms for international economic transactions
Prebisch	Terms of and norms for international economic transactions Foreign economic policies of AISs	Foreign economic policies of LDCs	Domestic economic and social structures of AISs Domestic economic and social structures of LDCs
Radical	Domestic economic and social structures of LDCs Domestic economic and social structures of AISs	Terms of and norms for international economic transactions Foreign economic policies of LDCs Foreign economic policies of AISs	

FIGURE 2-6 Emphases for Reform in Trade and Other Economic Relations Between Advanced Industrial States (AISs) and Less Developed Countries (LDCs)

CONCLUSION

We have attempted to outline the way in which prescriptions for reforms in trade between states in the center and states in the periphery of the global economy follow logically from the assumptions that liberals, Prebisch, and radicals make about the nature of international economic exchange. Serious questions arise concerning the prospects for conducting trade completely in accord with the desires of advocates of each school of thought. The questions raised about each approach need not be seen as a cause of despair. No serious analyst truly expects global economic and political relations as complex as trade to lend themselves to solutions that are totally consistent with a single school of thought, particularly in an era when even the most powerful state in the world finds it increasingly difficult to mobilize international and domestic support for policies consistent with the school of thought it has long championed. Rather, the questions we have raised point to the need for decision makers and analysts of the various persuasions discussed to recognize the political, attitudinal, and structural realities that make their policy proposals difficult to implement. More fundamentally, these questions point to the need for decision makers and analysts to reexamine the basic assumptions that generate logically compelling, yet often unworkable, policy prescriptions.

To the extent that this reexamination of assumptions occurs, particularly within governments, workable solutions to the trade and development problems facing less developed countries may be generated. If it does not occur, political discourse among states at different levels of economic development will continue to produce conflicts as to which is the most appropriate, if unattainable, utopia within which to conduct economic exchange.

It is unlikely that significant progress in trade reform on behalf of less developed countries will take place in the 1990s as a result of global negotiations (comprehensive in issue coverage and countries included). The less developed countries remain as convinced today as they were in the 1970s that improvement in their trade and development prospects depends upon international trade reform. But their bargaining position has eroded over the past decade. Strident, ideologically based demands that maintained unity among some 140 LDCs proved moderately successful in challenging existing liberal trade principles. On the other hand, the political appeal of such an approach has diminished since it yielded few substantive economic gains for Third World countries. Skyrocketing commodity prices and the cutting edge provided by OPEC for joint LDC bargaining with Western states during the 1970s gave way to commodity price declines and OPEC impotence after 1980. The advanced industrial states have little inclination to negotiate major concessions with less developed countries as a whole under these circumstances. Indeed, the UNCTAD VII conference held in 1987 was notable for the avoidance of confrontation between less developed countries and Western states along traditional North-South lines. Issues of international economic reform were cast in ways that lent themselves to quieter, more technocratic problem solving that could be continued within the frameworks of other key international economic institutions like GATT, IMF, and IBRD. This marks an important shift away from the less compromising, strident, ideologically based negotiations that characterized most earlier plenary meetings of UNCTAD. Much of the credit for this shift was given to UNCTAD's new secretary-general at the time, Kenneth Dadzie.[93]

Countries in the Third World are positioned very differently in relation to their trade and development prospects, as well as their relations with the leading states in the global economy. Oil exporting states with small populations and large oil reserves, like Kuwait and Saudi Arabia, have accumulated immense financial reserves, have undertaken major transformations of their economies, and are important players in international trade and investment. Other oil exporting states, like Mexico, face serious debt problems and domestic political turmoil. The newly industrializing countries of Asia have demonstrated great success in sustaining rapid economic growth, attracting foreign capital, and penetrating the domestic markets of advanced industrial states with exports of an expanding variety of manufactured goods. The APC states have privileged trade and aid relationships with the EEC, as do Caribbean states with the United States and certain Asian states with Japan. At the same time, most countries in Africa, Asia, and Latin America remain in dire economic straits. It is unrealistic to expect any comprehensive negotiations to meet the practical economic needs of states in such disparate political and economic situations. Instead, we are likely to see more meaningful trade relations between LDCs and advanced industrial states developed through an expanded array of bilateral and regional arrangements with decidedly different agendas and bargaining strengths.

At the end of the 1980s, the newly industrializing states were the focus of the Western states' trade diplomacy with the Third World. The advanced industrial states will threaten to reduce access to their markets unless the newly industrializing countries with the most rapidly growing markets in the world open their domestic markets much more than they have to date. The pressure will be especially acute on the Asian states running large trade surpluses with advanced industrial states. We have seen this in U.S. implementation of the Super 301 provisions of its new trade law. Another salient set of trade issues revolved around the necessity of heavily indebted countries in Latin America and Africa being assured greater access to markets in the West in order for them to earn sufficient foreign exchange to service their international financial obligations.

Liberal economic principles may not guide economic relations between less developed countries and advanced industrial states in the future. It seems reasonable to expect increased reliance on negotiating sectoral market share agreements, for example. Yet, it is clear that states in the periphery and the core of the global economy have a mutual interest in expanding trade with each other. Less developed countries purchase one

---

[93]For a general summary of UNCTAD VII, see Grace, "UNCTAD VII."

third of U.S. and Japanese exports.[94] That gives the leading industrial states a great incentive to help promote the LDCs' development and enhance their import capacity. Even if the style and structure of bargaining between rich and poor states has changed over the past decade, trade negotiations will not diminish in importance to either.

[94]International Monetary Fund, *Direction of Trade Statistics Yearbook, 1988*, (Washington, D.C.: IMF, 1988), p. 56.

3

The Global Monetary Order: Interdependence and Dominance

The political-economic links among states through international economic relations as well as the links between domestic and foreign economic policy are nowhere more evident than in balance-of-payments adjustments and the conduct of international monetary relations. Balance-of-payments policies and international monetary relations involve highly technical economic decisions that carry with them extremely important domestic and foreign political implications. We will discuss the technical aspects of these relations only in the depth required to appreciate some of the political connotations of international financial interdependencies.

BALANCE-OF-PAYMENTS ADJUSTMENT ALTERNATIVES

A country's balance of payments consists of a comparison of the sum of all payments the state and its residents made to foreigners with the total of all receipts obtained from abroad by the state and its residents during the same year. Any expenditures or movement of finances abroad contributes to a country's payments deficit. Any purchases by foreigners or movement of finances into the country contributes to a payments surplus. Most states seek to achieve a balance-of-payments surplus or equilibrium (financial outflows equal to inflows). Components of a country's balance-of-payments position include the gamut of public and private financial transactions across national boundaries—trade (exports and imports), services (shipping, insurance, banking fees, consulting, and so on), direct investment portfolio investment (stocks, bonds, and so forth), tourism, and government expenditures abroad (military personnel and bases, diplomatic personnel and support, economic and military aid, and the like).

Countries that persistently find themselves with a significant payments imbalance must find ways to restore a position of financial equilibrium. Those with payments surpluses feel fewer pressures for adjustment as they are, after all, in the enviable position of earning more than they spend in international economic transactions. Typically, deficit countries are under much more urgent pressure to adjust their payments position, because they seldom enjoy the luxury of being able to "live beyond their means" for years on end.

There are three basic types of mechanisms available to states for adjusting their deficit payments position: internal adjustment measures, external adjustment measures, and access to liquidity (loans or financial reserves). The adjustment mechanism, or combination of mechanisms, chosen has important political-economic impacts at home and abroad.

Internal adjustment measures include any policies designed to decrease a country's purchases abroad by reducing domestic and foreign expenditures of the state and its residents. This might involve such policies as raising interest rates and taxes to reduce the level of spending by businesses and individuals, as well as reducing government expenditures by curtailing publicly financed programs at home and abroad. These "deflationary" policies place less disposable income in the hands of individuals, businesses, and government agencies for domestic and foreign purchases. As a result, a country's balance of payments should theoretically, improve through a reduction in its imports, foreign investment, travel abroad, foreign aid, military and diplomatic presence abroad, and the like. All variety of expenditures contributing to a country's payments deficit should contract.

Obviously, internal measures are adopted at considerable economic and political costs to the country (or elements of society within it). Deflation closes businesses and throws people out of work. Cutting government programs means sacrificing certain domestic and foreign policy goals. Should a nation sacrifice social policy by reducing unemployment compensation, social security payments, and aid to education? Should a nation sacrifice security by reducing defense expenditures, foreign economic and military aid, and military, economic, and political presence abroad? The choices are difficult. Restoration of a balance-of-payments equilibrium is seen typically as an economic problem. But the determination of where to cut and upon whom the impact of the cut falls are political decisions at the core.

Internal measures place the burdens of adjustment primarily upon the citizens, business enterprises, and the government of the state adopting them. This is not to say, however, that such measures are without impacts abroad. Deflation in the United States, for example, reduces economic growth and production in states abroad by virtue of America's importance as a market in world commerce. A reduction of American defense expenditures and foreign aid affects not only our own security but also the security and development of numerous states around the world.

External adjustment measures are designed explicitly to restore equilibrium to a country with payments deficits by altering directly the terms of exchange for foreign economic transactions. New tariffs or quotas might be introduced to limit imports. Tax incentives might be extended to domestic firms expanding their exports. Financial controls may be applied to reduce the outward flow of direct and portfolio investments. Companies with foreign operations might be encouraged to accelerate the repatriation of profits from their foreign subsidiaries. A country might devalue its currency—reduce the value of its currency relative to foreign currencies. This discourages purchases of foreign goods, services, and capital because everything abroad will cost more to its citizens. It simultaneously encourages foreigners to purchase goods, services, and capital in the country devaluing, because all will be cheaper to foreigners. Policies such as these have the effect of reducing financial outflows and increasing financial inflows to the nation confronted with balance-of-payments deficits.

External measures place the burdens of adjustment primarily upon citizens, enterprises, and governments abroad rather than upon the country seeking to restore its balance of payments to equilibrium. However, these measures are likely to increase domestic inflation and favor inefficient domestic producers at the expense of more internationally competitive enterprises at home and abroad. External adjustment measures disrupt international economic exchange and, characteristically, invite retaliation from states whose domestic and foreign economic interests are harmed.

States with access to financial assets (liquidity) in the form of gold holdings, accumulated reserves of foreign exchange from past balance-of-payments surpluses, or in a position to secure loans from international banks or other states can finance their payments deficits without resort to stringent internal or external adjustment measures. Very few states are in a position to handle a chronic deficit position for a sustained period in this manner. They rapidly exhaust their accumulated international financial reserves as well as their credit worthiness from major lending institutions. Financing balance-of-payments deficits through liquidity is usually suitable only in the short run. Chronic payments deficits must be dealt with through some combination of internal and external adjustments.

The relationship among the three alternative methods has been illustrated most clearly by Richard Cooper through the device of a triangle (see Figure 3-1), the points of the triangle representing internal measures, external measures, and access to liberal liquidity. Most analysts and decision makers want states to "avoid extreme forms of each of the three categories of action."[1] Public officials and analysts differ, however, over where they would prefer to see states with a balance-of-payments deficit positioned in terms of trade-offs among the three methods of adjustment available. Bankers and finance ministers insist typically upon the need for discipline and rely upon external and internal adjustment measures to eliminate the root causes of a state's payments deficits. They desire to see states located away from the liberal liquidity position in the triangle—in other words, strict economic constraints should be placed on states seeking to finance their payments deficits.[2]

[1]Richard Cooper, *The Economics of Interdependence* (New York: McGraw-Hill, 1968), p. 19.

[2]Ibid.

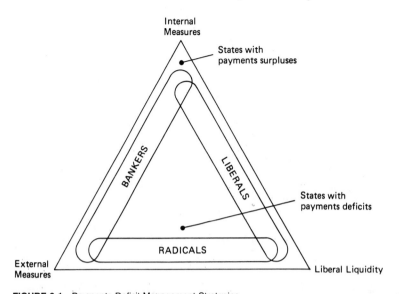

FIGURE 3-1   Payments Deficit Management Strategies
Source: Adapted from Richard N. Cooper, *The Economics of Interdependence* (New York: McGraw-Hill, 1968), p. 18.

Liberal economic analysts and decision makers insist upon avoiding policies that interrupt the free flow of goods, capital, and services across national boundaries. They desire to see states located away from the external measures position in the triangle. Radical economic analysts and decision makers insist upon states' prerogatives to pursue autonomous paths to development with social-economic policies assuring full employment and equity in income distribution. Not wanting to sacrifice these goals to achieve balance-of-payments equilibrium, they desire to see states located away from the internal measures position in the triangle. Decision makers of states enjoying balance-of-payments surpluses are prone to argue that states in deficit should rely primarily upon internal measures and assume the primary burdens of adjustment themselves. Decision makers of states confronting payments deficits, not surprisingly, are prone to argue for access to liberal liquidity with minimal conditions and rely upon external measures designed to force creditors and states with payments surpluses to share the burdens of adjustment with them.

In addition to identifying various schools of thought, the diagram also enables us to appreciate distinctions among the policy positions of various states over time. For example, with its massive financial reserves generated from oil exports, Saudi Arabia was able to operate very near the liquidity corner of the triangle when it faced a balance-of-payments deficit in 1985. For reasons we shall see shortly, the United States has enjoyed a unique capacity since World War II to operate near the liquidity extreme while remaining in a chronic payments deficit posture. During the 1930s virtually all nations were operating near the external measures position in the triangle while pursuing beggar-thy-neighbor foreign economic policies. During the 1920s, Britain operated near the internal measures extreme of the triangle—unemployment rates of over 10 percent were accepted for years to restore the pound sterling to its 1913 value and maintain it in relation to gold.[3]

THE BRETTON WOODS INTERNATIONAL MONETARY ORDER

Just as Western statesmen developed an international trade order after World War II with the creation of GATT, they institutionalized an international monetary order through the creation of the International Monetary Fund (IMF) at Bretton Woods, New Hampshire, in 1944. The liberal trade and monetary systems embodied in the two institutions under American leadership are closely related. A liberal international economic order requires the free flow of capital as well as goods. International trade cannot flourish in the presence of severe restrictions on international financial flows. Instability in the international monetary order and insufficient availability of credit were at the base of the trade decline, protectionism, and depression during the 1930s.[4] If countries with payments deficits resort systematically to external measures of adjustment, for example, the liberal trade order envisaged in GATT would collapse. Accordingly, the framers of the IMF attempted to create a postwar international monetary order that would prevent the excessive monetary and trade nationalism that destroyed the international economy in the 1930s.

The IMF provides loans to its member states to tide them over *temporary* balance-of-payments deficit problems. These loans provide an alternative to states imposing draconic internal or external adjustment measures that would disrupt their domestic economies, raise barriers to international trade, and invite retaliation by injured foreign economic interests. For states with *structural* rather than temporary payments problems, the IMF makes loans conditional upon the borrower's undertaking internal adjustment measures appropriate to restore it to a balance-of-payments equilibrium. These loans help to soften the impact of deflationary policies typically required in such circumstances, and at the same time are meant to enable states to retain liberal foreign economic policies.

In terms of the diagram of payments adjustment alternatives, the IMF was designed to move states away from the external measures location in the triangle (where most countries were positioned after the war) and toward a location closer to the internal measures position, through the incentive provided by IMF loans. The financing available through the IMF is more an inducement for adopting internal adjustment measures (always discomforting to a state) than a solution in and of itself for a payments deficit problem. Strict limits on borrowing from the IMF prevent extensive,

---

[3]Ibid., p. 26.

[4]Susan Strange makes a strong case that the international trade system is secondary to the international monetary system in "Protectionism and World Policies," *International Organization*, 39, no. 2 (Spring 1985), pp. 233–60.

persistent reliance upon its resources by member states with chronic payments deficits.

The capital pool of the IMF has grown from $8.8 billion in 1944 to approximately $196 billion, under the most recent quota increases agreed to in 1990.[5] Contributions to the pool are made by its member states (presently 152) in accordance with quotas assigned on the basis of countries' relative economic capabilities (as reflected in such indicators as size of GNP, volume of trade, and reserves holdings). The U.S. share of the total IMF quotas is 19.62 percent. One fourth of each country's quota is paid in gold, more recently foreign exchange, and the remainder in the member state's national currency. States are permitted to borrow foreign currencies from the IMF for the purpose of settling their international accounts in amounts up to 125 percent of their quota per year. The conditions imposed upon a nation borrowing from the IMF become increasingly stringent as that nation approaches the limits of its borrowing capacity. The IMF insists that countries seeking loans adopt internal (and sometimes external) measures under multilateral (IMF) supervision sufficient to restore it to a stable balance-of-payments equilibrium. The conditions giving rise to a nation's deficit position are to be corrected so it will not be necessary to reapproach the fund repeatedly in future years.

Voting power in the IMF is weighted roughly in proportion to nations' quotas. As the largest contributor to the IMF, the United States presently exercises just under 20 percent of the votes in IMF decision making. Quotas and voting power are adjusted through periodic reviews of the fund's capital needs and of alterations in the relative economic positions of its member states. In 1989, for example, Japan ranked only fifth in IMF quotas even though it had emerged over the course of the decade as the world's largest creditor and second largest economy. In the 1990 IMF quota review, Japan was ranked in second place, with Germany; each was assigned 6.1 percent of total quotas.

In addition to these liquidity (financing) and adjustment provisions of the IMF, the Bretton Woods monetary system envisioned a regime of easy convertibility among the currencies of states at stable exchange rates. As the dominant nation in the international economic system following World War II, the U.S. dollar became the centerpiece of the international monetary order. The dollar was valued at $35 per ounce of gold, and the United States committed itself to exchange its gold upon request for dollars held by central banks abroad at this stable exchange rate. Other countries joining the IMF, in turn, valued their currency at an appropriate exchange rate vis-à-vis the dollar. Members agreed to alter the exchange rate of their currency only when absolutely necessary to correct a fundamental disequilibrium in their balance of payments—and, even then, only upon prior consultation with other states through the IMF. It was felt that liberal international trade could thrive only if stable exchange rates enabled importers and exporters to make commitments for future trade transactions at predictable prices. Conversion of one national currency into another at predictable exchange rates was to be a routine matter.

[5]135.2 billion SDR, calculated at 1 SDR = $1.45.

The international monetary order evolved in a manner somewhat differently from the original concept that emerged at the Bretton Woods conference. The International Monetary Fund was little used during the first one and one-half decades of its existence. The major European powers and Japan found that the requirements of postwar reconstruction necessitated maintenance of stringent controls on their currency and foreign trade. They did not make their currencies widely convertible until 1958. Exchange rate alterations proved to be traumatic politically and economically under the Bretton Woods system. Devaluations were taken as indications of weakness and economic failure by states and, thus, were resisted. Exchange rates became more rigid than the founders of the IMF had anticipated. When states, nevertheless, were compelled by market forces to devalue their currencies, it was usually done without consultation with the IMF, because negotiations prior to the fact invited heavy speculation against the weakening currency in international money markets. Also, developments in connection with the U.S. dollar took monetary relations in unanticipated directions with tremendous political and economic consequences. The IMF evolved to accommodate these developments and has emerged over the years as perhaps the key international economic institution—but a very different one from that created in 1944, as we shall see.

THE CHANGING ROLE OF THE DOLLAR IN INTERNATIONAL MONETARY RELATIONS

Most international economic transactions—such as trade, investment, loans, and travel—involve the exchange of goods, services, land, and labor for some form of monetary compensation. Internationally acceptable currencies are therefore, required to conduct virtually any large-scale economic exchange across national boundaries. Such currencies (e.g., the U.S. dollar, British pound, German mark, French franc, Japanese yen, and Swiss franc) perform several basic functions in the international monetary system. We will focus on the dollar as the most important of the international currencies in the post–World War II era.

First, the dollar as an international currency serves as a medium of exchange. It is an acceptable form of payment to providers of goods and services in a wide array of countries. The dollar is used widely to finance trade and other economic relations between parties that do not even involve the United States; Italy, for example, may be asked to pay for its oil imports from Saudi Arabia with dollars, because dollars are more useful than are lira to the Saudi Arabians in their other foreign transactions. About 25 percent of world trade is financed in dollars, whereas the United States accounts for only a little over 10 percent of world trade. International currencies, unlike the currencies of most states, have purchasing power outside their own nation. This is so because they are easily convertible into other international currencies or gold, and their value in relation to other international currencies or gold remains comparatively stable.

Second, international currencies (and the dollar in particular) serve as a store of value, a reserve asset, that states can save for future purchases throughout the world. As long as there is general confidence that the dollar is widely acceptable as a medium of exchange with stable value, it is held willingly as a reserve asset by other states. Under the Bretton Woods system, the American promise to convert dollars held abroad into gold upon request made the dollar a reserve asset "as good as gold."

Finally, the dollar as an international currency serves as a unit of account—a widely understood standard by which to price international transactions. Thus, in international economic transactions, the prices or value of goods and services are frequently quoted in dollars, even if the exchange is not necessarily conducted in dollars. A recipient of foreign aid from the Soviet Union, for example, might announce the value of its economic aid package in dollars, even though the aid itself is disbursed in rubles. This occurs because the dollar is understood much more broadly as a unit of account in international economic relations than is the ruble. Within specific states, prices are denominated in their national currencies, but by and large, where international transactions are involved, the domestic currency price is converted at prevailing exchange rates and expressed in terms of an international currency, such as the dollar.

Although the pound, the mark, the yen, and a few other currencies also perform these three functions, the dollar since World War II has become the top international currency. It is relied upon to finance a greater variety of international economic transactions by a far greater number of states than is any other currency. The dollar, like the British pound in an earlier era, achieved top currency status by virtue of the dominant political and economic position in the international system the United States enjoyed after the war. Over a prolonged period of time, the dollar's role as top currency has had profound implications for the United States and for the international political economy.[6]

The top currency state has unparalleled opportunities for expanding its economic, political, and military presence abroad. Countries in need of foreign exchange are particularly interested in forging relations with the top currency state because this helps to bring the most universally accepted medium of exchange within grasp. Following World War II, for example, all variety of states clamored for exports to the United States, direct foreign investments from U.S. firms, American economic and military aid, and agreements for U.S. military base rights, among other things. They sought these things because they shared political-economic-security interests with America and also because such relations generated dollars for states with critical shortages of internationally acceptable currencies and reserves. Moreover, the universal utility of the top international currency as a medium of exchange gives the top currency nation the unique privilege of enjoying international support, or at least tolerance, for running persistent balance-of-payments deficits without having to adopt significant adjustment measures to restore a payments equilibrium. Deficits for the top currency state pump money into the international economy that can be used by other

---

[6]The discussion that follows on the implications of top currency status is based primarily upon the work of Susan Strange. See her illuminating piece, "The Politics of International Currencies," *World Politics*, 23, no. 2 (January 1971), pp. 215–31.

countries for international transactions. Thus, the top currency nation can enhance its economic-political-military posture abroad at levels of expenditures that exceed its international earnings for years on end—no other nation in the international system can behave in such a fashion. Charles de Gaulle pointed to this fact with frustration as America's "exorbitant privilege."

If the dominant state in the international system consciously seeks to pursue a policy of expansion and penetration abroad, having the top international currency immeasurably facilitates implementation of the policy. If the dominant state manifests no explicitly expansionist designs, having the top international currency will almost certainly draw it into an internationalist posture with vital political-economic stakes throughout the globe. Charges of self-aggrandizement and imperialism would seem to be an inevitable concomitant of occupying the top currency status in the international economy.

Years of occupying top currency status also make a country's decision makers prone to equate their state's national economic interests with the interests of the international economic system. An attack on the dollar is viewed instinctively by Americans as an attack on international economic stability. Given the roles played by the dollar in international economic exchange, this viewpoint is understandable. On the other hand, it fails to accord any legitimacy to other states' concerns that their own national economic interests are not always served best by American concepts of appropriate international monetary policy. It also fails to take account of the unique political and economic advantages that accrue to the United States by virtue of its top currency status—and the resentment this generates among states that must operate on a different and more strict standard of balance-of-payments discipline. The viewpoint leaves other countries with little legitimate basis, in the eyes of the top currency state, for challenging the dominant state's prescriptions for foreign monetary relations.

Susan Strange refers to this viewpoint as the "top currency syndrome." She has seen it manifested in the behavior of both Britain and the United States:

> The Top Currency state seems inclined to develop a strong political/economic ideology that asserts (a) that [its] domestic and international interests are coincident if not identical, and (b) that a prime aim of the state should be to persuade others that their national economic interests coincide with the maximum development and extension of the international economy. The Top Currency state characteristically does all it can to propagate this ideology and to use it to enlist the support of others for whatever measures of international cooperation and support it thinks are needed to protect, defend, and stabilize the international economic system . . . the opinions of foreigners who put national economic interest before the general welfare are regarded as simply unregenerate and perverse. Indeed, a high moral tone quickly creeps in, and what I would describe as the Top Currency syndrome is distinguished by an obstinate and to others inevitably an objectionable, tendency to self-righteousness.[7]

[7]Ibid., p. 229.

The syndrome helps us to understand the basis for profound political-economic clashes between the United States and other countries as the international monetary order has evolved since World War II.

Top currency status imposes great burdens on a state while affording it unique political-economic opportunities. As the major reserve asset and international medium of exchange, there are tremendous international and domestic pressures to maintain a stable value for the currency—even when altering its exchange rate might seem appropriate for the nation's economic competitiveness and payments equilibrium. Other states can undergo exchange rate alterations without generating the international turmoil that inevitably follows when the same policy is adopted by the top currency state. In short, the top currency state is denied (at least in a monetary system based upon fixed exchange rates) a useful economic policy instrument available to virtually all other states. The top currency state faces an additional burden since its currency is the vehicle for the bulk of international economic transactions—any financial shock or major imbalance emerging anywhere in the international economy affects the top currency state directly. It is extremely vulnerable to the transmission of economic shocks from abroad, notwithstanding its substantial economic capabilities. Largely for reasons such as these, neither West Germany nor Japan have been willing to let their currencies assume roles in international monetary relations proportionate to the position these states occupy currently in the global economy. Only the United States possesses the economic capacity and the political will to let its currency become the centerpiece of the international economy.

With these general characteristics of top currency status in mind, let us examine the dollar's performance and its impact upon international monetary relations since World War II.

The Dollar Ascendant

From 1947 to 1960 the United States, with the enthusiastic support of its major economic and political partners, managed the international monetary system through a calculated effort to run balance-of-payments deficits. The United States continued to export more goods than it imported, but it regularly spent more each year than it earned through trade—primarily as a result of foreign military and economic assistance (such as the Marshall Plan), expenditures connected with developing and maintaining bases abroad and an expansion of direct foreign investments by American firms.

The persistent American balance-of-payments deficits were welcomed internationally during this period for a variety of reasons. In 1947 the United States held 70 percent of the world's total official monetary gold stocks upon which nations relied principally at that time for their international reserve position. This was viewed by all international economic experts as a maldistribution of international reserves. It is said that international liquidity, like manure, works better when spread around than when accumulated in one place. By running balance-of-payments deficits, the United States helped other countries to acquire dollars that they could either hold on to or convert to gold from the United States at $35 an ounce.

Most countries chose the former since dollars were so useful as a medium of exchange for all variety of international economic transactions, since dollars could be converted to gold at any time, and since dollars could earn interest (unlike gold) while being retained as reserves. As new quantities of gold could not be produced to keep pace with the overall liquidity needs of a rapidly expanding international economy, dollars sent abroad through U.S. payments deficits provided the primary source for the necessary expansion and redistribution of international reserves. The U.S. deficits were regarded as a temporary, controllable phenomenon. They were a result of a policy choice by the United States with which its post–World War II allies concurred. Moreover, an export surplus each year underlined the inherent strength and international competitiveness of the American economy. There was a sustained demand for dollars in the international economy. The deficits in no way cast doubt upon the vitality of the American economy or the strength of the dollar as an international currency.

Of course, these deficits were also financing the establishment of a massive foreign presence by the United States through private investment, economic aid, and the maintenance of a system of military bases abroad. This posed few problems in U.S. relations with its major partners because they felt that their own economic, political, and security interests were served by these American actions. If American deficits were to cease, the allies reasoned, their own interests would be hurt.

For all these reasons there was broad international support for the United States' continuation of its balance-of-payments deficits through the 1950s. During this period the dollar established itself clearly as the linchpin of the international monetary system.

The Dollar in Question

International acceptance of persistent American balance-of-payments deficits and unbounded confidence in the dollar as an international currency gradually gave way to opposition and doubt during the 1960s. U.S. payments deficits had been widely acceptable abroad as long as (1) U.S. foreign policy and expenditures abroad were regarded as consistent with other countries' own sense of their political, economic, and security interests, and (2) there was general confidence in the strength of the American economy and the ultimate capacity of the United States to control its payments position. Confidence in the dollar as an international currency remained firm as long as it remained clear that dollars held abroad would be converted to gold upon request at $35 an ounce. Over the course of the 1960s serious questions arose in connection with all of these points, with potent effects on the functioning of the international monetary system and the dollar's role in it.

As the United States continued to run balance-of-payments deficits over the years and foreign governments willingly held on to dollars generated in this fashion, the amount of official dollar holdings abroad gradually approached, and then exceeded, the value of total American gold reserves. The foundation of the dollar's role as a reserve asset under the Bretton Woods monetary system was the American commitment to convert official dollar holdings abroad into gold upon request. Over the course of the 1960s it became clear that the United States was incapable of honoring *en masse* its gold conversion obligations. By 1971 official dollar holdings abroad exceeded U.S. gold stocks by over 300 percent.

During this period the "dollar overhang" problem was kept within manageable proportions by several forces. The American economy continued to remain internationally competitive, as evidenced by yearly export surpluses. International confidence in American economic strength was firm. Also, the United States successfully prevailed upon its major economic partners to continue to hold dollars without exercising their right of conversion to gold in the interest of international monetary and economic stability. The United States, for example, linked maintenance of its NATO troop strength in West Germany to the latter's refraining from converting its dollars into gold. By the 1960s the international monetary system revolved around the dollar as a medium of exchange and an international reserve unit. In 1965, for example, foreign exchange (mostly dollars) comprised $24 billion of the world's total reserves of $71 billion.[8] Whose interests would be served by an international stampede to convert dollars to gold? Such behavior on a massive scale would undermine the value of the dollar—not only harming the United States but also eroding the value of one third of the world's total international reserves. Realization of this fact led most states to refrain from exchanging their dollars for gold on a large scale, but the problem of the dollar overhang continued to worsen. Everyone, including U.S. officials, realized that international monetary and economic interests were no longer served by America's persistent balance-of-payments deficits. There was a widespread belief that the United States should bring its balance of payments back into equilibrium. Failure to restore the U.S. balance of payments to equilibrium would result sooner or later in a gold and dollar crisis.

Pressure for ending its deficits and altering the political-economic prerogatives enjoyed by the United States as the top currency state came from another quarter during the 1960s—Charles de Gaulle. De Gaulle's challenge was explicitly political, in contrast to the largely economic challenge of the dollar overhang.

As long as America's major political allies and economic partners saw fundamental congruence between their own interests and American foreign policy, there was relatively little criticism of U.S. deficits. American deficits permitted a more vigorous pursuit of foreign political, economic, and security goals of importance to Europeans as well as to Americans than would have been possible with U.S. payments discipline. When de Gaulle defined French interests in a way that diverged from U.S. policies, he also attacked the United States for its payments deficits and sought to convert dollars into gold in an attempt to force an alteration of America's international posture.

French interests and American foreign policy were increasingly at odds during the late 1950s and 1960s. The United States opposed French-

[8]International Monetary Fund, *1971 Annual Report* (Washington, D.C.: IMF, 1971), p. 19.

British occupation of the Suez Canal in 1956 and forced an embarrassing retreat. France also developed considerable doubts about the reliability of American nuclear guarantees. Beginning in the late 1950s, de Gaulle opened a severe conflict within the Western alliance over the issue of a greater French voice in Western strategic policy and, later, over the development of French nuclear capability independent of American or NATO controls. During the course of the 1960s, de Gaulle drew away from the United States' pro-Israeli position in the Middle East conflict and opposed U.S. policies in Vietnam. Along another dimension of policy, the French became wary of the massive influx of direct foreign investment by U.S.-based multinational firms operating in Europe. The French and European economies appeared to be threatened with progressive denationalization and subjugation to U.S. corporate giants.[9] For these as well as other reasons, de Gaulle no longer saw French interests as congruent with the United States' international security and foreign economic policies.

De Gaulle correctly linked America's capacity to pursue such an active international posture with its top currency status. The scope of American international involvement was enhanced by its capacity to run persistent balance-of-payments deficits without having to make internal or external adjustments to bring them under control. This constituted the "exorbitant privilege" of the United States as the top currency state. Its payments deficits expanded other nations' international reserves, permitting it to elude the pressures of living within its means. Alone among states, America could finance its foreign activities virtually through printing money.

This exorbitant privilege and a virtually limitless international expansion of U.S. political and economic influence could be curtailed if countries refused to hold those dollars pumped abroad through U.S. payments deficits. By holding dollars, other countries were underwriting U.S. foreign policy. If the United States were forced to finance its payments deficits through gold conversion, it would exhaust its reserves rapidly and be required, like other states, to restore a balance-of-payments equilibrium. The inevitable result would be an erosion of American public and private expenditures abroad—hence, a decline in U.S. international political and economic influence. De Gaulle demanded gold conversion for dollars held by France, and he launched a largely unsuccessful international campaign to have other countries do the same. Through attacking the dollar, de Gaulle was attempting to erode American hegemony.

The United States responded to de Gaulle's attack on the dollar in exactly the manner Susan Strange refers to as the "top currency syndrome." The French position was regarded in Washington as an attack not primarily on the dollar and U.S. foreign policy but, rather, a perverse assault upon global monetary and economic stability, which depended upon the strength of the dollar during the 1960s. The United States prevailed in this struggle with de Gaulle because most nations sought to avoid bringing the dollar overhang problem to a head and because few Western states were as disaffected with American leadership as was de Gaulle.

---

[9]See Chapter 4.

This episode illustrates forcefully the pursuit of national objectives through the instrument of international monetary policy. The economic-legal questions of dollar conversion to gold during the 1960s turned essentially on America's retaining top currency status and international political-economic hegemony.

The dollar overhang and the French challenge indicated that international political and economic conditions were changing rapidly during the 1960s. New conditions and new opposition would not permit the United States to run payments deficits without incurring substantial political and international economic costs. Yet a dilemma emerged. If the United States were to bring its deficits under control, the primary source of growth in world financial reserves would be eliminated and the international economy would be threatened with a shortage of liquidity. On the other hand, if U.S. deficits continued, the increasing excess of dollars abroad relative to U.S. gold stocks would produce a gold and dollar crisis.[10]

The international economy requires an adequate supply of financial reserves (liquidity) in the form of gold or international currencies. Shortages of reserves reduce global demand for the purchase of goods and services through international trade, inhibiting the growth of economic production in all nations. Continued growth of the global economy and the economic health of most states require an expansion of liquidity adequate to meet the increasing financial needs of expanding international economic transactions. By the 1960s, as we have seen, it became apparent that the United States should eliminate its payments deficits. But how would an expanding global economy's liquidity needs be met? Gold was simply not being mined in amounts sufficient to meet the liquidity requirements of the international economy and private gold consumption.

Monetary officials in 1969 agreed to the formation of a new, multilaterally controlled international reserve asset to be disbursed and administered in accordance with global economic needs under the auspices of the International Monetary Fund. The new reserve assets were called special drawing rights (SDRs). National financial authorities agreed to accept SDRs in addition to gold or international currencies to settle official financial accounts among their central banks. SDRs would be created by the IMF to supplement gold, dollars, and other international currencies during periods when the latter were not expanding sufficiently to satisfy the liquidity needs of the global economy. Approximately $9 billion worth of SDRs were created between 1969 and 1972 and disbursed to countries within the IMF in proportion to their IMF quotas. At the time of their creation, one SDR had the value of one dollar.

The creation of SDRs as a reserve asset seemed to offer the solution to several problems confronting the international monetary system in the 1960s. The United States could now eliminate its payments deficits without precipitating an international liquidity shortage. The SDR plan offered the prospect of liquidity expansion appropriate to the financial requirements

---

[10]This came to be called the "Triffin dilemma." Robert Triffin first identified the dilemma in the late 1950s. See his *Gold and the Dollar Crisis* (New Haven, Conn.: Yale University Press, 1961), pp. 3–14.

of the international economy. Neither the mining of gold nor the creation of dollar reserve assets through U.S. payments deficits bore a direct relationship to the liquidity requirements of international monetary relations. Equally significant, unlike the dollar or any other international currency, SDRs conferred no special political or economic privilege to a particular state. That was essential in their acceptability to finance officials throughout the world.

The 1960s ended with the dollar's role in the international monetary order being brought into question on economic and political grounds. Widespread confidence in the strength of the American economy and the innovative step of creating special drawing rights preserved the Bretton Woods system and delayed the ultimate challenge to the dollar as the top currency. As it turned out, the delay was brief.

The Gold-Dollar Crisis and the Demise of the Bretton Woods System

The United States ran a disastrous balance-of-payments deficit in 1971. Compared with "modest" deficits of $1.9 billion to $3.8 billion over the previous five years, the 1971 deficit soared to $10.6 billion.[11]

The most alarming aspect of the 1971 deficit, in addition to its size, was the fact that U.S. imports exceeded exports for the first time in the twentieth century. Most analysts attributed the emergence of the trade deficit to inflation unleashed in the late 1960s, when financing the war in Vietnam and uncurtailed domestic expenditures produced huge budget deficits in the United States. The pace of inflation, combined with an overvalued dollar relative to the German mark and Japanese yen, cut deeply into the ability of the U.S. economy to retain its overall international competitiveness.

Confidence in the dollar as an international currency had rested upon widespread confidence in the strength of the American economy as evidenced by its export surpluses. The 1971 deficit was alarming not only because its magnitude suggested the United States' inability to maintain control over its payments position but also because the 1971 trade deficit raised doubts about the vitality and strength of the U.S. economy. Against the backdrop of increasing international concern about the dollar in the 1960s, these developments threatened to unleash international monetary chaos. Confidence in the dollar was collapsing.

Rather than waiting for an international stampede to convert dollars held abroad into gold—an obligation that the United States clearly could not honor—the Nixon administration took the initiative in August 1971. The United States insisted that its major economic partners enjoying payment surpluses should assume a major share of the burdens of adjustment required to restore the United States to payments equilibrium, in return

---

[11]*International Economic Report of the President* (Washington, D.C.: GPO, March 1975), p. 137. For excellent analyses of U.S. monetary policy during this period, see Peter Odell, *U.S. International Monetary Policy: Markets, Power, and Ideas as Sources of Change* (Princeton: Princeton University Press, 1982), and Joanne Gowa, *Closing the Gold Window: Domestic Politics and the End of Bretton Woods* (Ithaca: Cornell University Press, 1983).

for past American actions on their behalf. These actions included postwar U.S. aid to Europe and Japan, as well as massive defense expenditures incurred by the United States, assumed to enhance the security of its major allies. In addition, among the major economies only the United States had maintained the value of its currency since World War II, thereby contributing stability to the international monetary order. Plainly, these factors had contributed to U.S. payments deficits and had benefited its allies. Therefore, the United States sought to force the strong European and Japanese economies to assume a major share of the burdens associated with ending U.S. deficits. In so doing the United States was abandoning its traditional position that the deficit country should bear the burdens of adjustment to restore payments equilibrium.

The United States insisted that the Japanese yen and German mark be revalued upward to assist the American trade balance; this would have the same effect as a dollar devaluation, except that its impact would be concentrated on those economies contributing the most to America's trade deficit in 1971. As a bargaining chip to promote the currency realignment, the United States imposed an across-the-board 10 percent surcharge on all imports. And to stanch the anticipated stampede of foreign central banks to convert their dollars into gold, the United States abruptly repudiated its commitment of twenty-five years to exchange gold for dollars. Finally, the United States called for intensive international negotiation on trade and monetary affairs, hoping to restore order and to strengthen the U.S. payments and trade position. These unilateral moves in August 1971 marked the demise of the Bretton Woods monetary order created in 1944 and opened a new, more volatile era of international monetary relations.

These actions provide a classic example of a strong state's relying heavily upon external adjustment measures to cope with its payments deficits. The Smithsonian Agreement in December 1971, involving the leading Western economies, formalized commitments to implement the basic elements of the unilateral U.S. demands for monetary and trade reform. The dollar was devalued approximately 10 percent relative to the mark, the yen, and gold. The United States rescinded its 10 percent surcharge on imports. Intensive efforts were started to reach multilateral agreement on new rules to ensure international monetary stability in the post–Bretton Woods era. In the meantime, states holding dollars as reserves, in response to earlier American appeals to refrain from converting them to gold, were stuck with the dollars—now worth less in settling their international accounts. Gold conversion was a relic of the past. An extraordinary display of American economic power, this would be the high-water mark of America's postwar, unilateral dominance over the international monetary system.

These dramatic changes in 1971 failed to restore equilibrium to the international monetary system or produce stability for the dollar. In February 1973 the United States found it necessary to devalue the dollar again and to abandon any commitments to maintain fixed exchange rates between the dollar and other major currencies. Exchange rates for the dollar and other major currencies would henceforth be allowed to fluctuate in accordance with supply and demand for particular international currencies in global monetary markets.

THE POST–BRETTON WOODS INTERNATIONAL MONETARY SYSTEM

International monetary relations now differ in important respects from the Bretton Woods system. They are less orderly and considerably less predictable. Even so, some basic characteristics of the contemporary international monetary system and their implications for political-economic relations are clear.

Flexible Exchange Rates

The most salient feature of the post–Bretton Woods system is, of course, the emergence of flexible exchange rates. Since 1973 the dollar has had no fixed value in relation to gold or to other currencies. Over the years this has resulted in some periods during which the dollar lost considerable value in relation to other currencies and in other periods when the dollar greatly appreciated in value. Over the course of the 1980s the dollar's value against the German mark, for example, appreciated from 1.8 marks/dollar in 1980 (one third below the dollar's level in 1973) to 2.9 marks/dollar in 1985, only to depreciate again to 1.5 marks/dollar by the end of 1990 (the lowest value of the dollar in relation to the mark since World War II). The fluctuations of the dollar against all foreign currencies since 1973 are summarized in Figure 3-2.

A complex array of factors determines the dollar's value in relation to other currencies. In general, the value of the dollar reflects perceptions by private and public economic officials throughout the world of the

FIGURE 3-2   The Changing Value of the Dollar, 1973–1990 (1973 = 100, trade weighted average,* adjusted by changes in consumer prices)

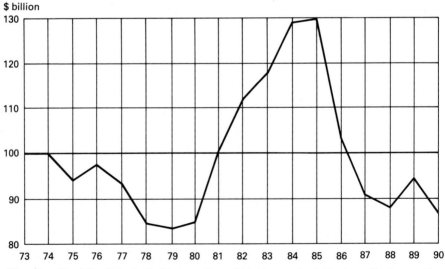

*The value of the dollar relative to all other currencies, weighted in proportion to the share of foreign countries in U.S. trade.

Source: Economic Report of the President, 1989 (Washington, D.C.: GPO, 1989), p. 431. Data for 1989 and 1990 from Ibid, 1991, p. 410.

strength of the American economy. This involves, as well, assessments of the appropriateness of U.S. domestic and foreign policies in comparison with assessments of the economic performance of other leading industrial states. Disparities in macroeconomic policies and economic performance such as price stability and growth prospects among the major states are the primary causes of fluctuations in exchange rates between their currencies over the medium term. These fluctuations are often exacerbated, however, by speculation in international money markets about the likely direction of currency values. There are times when exchange rates are driven more by psychology and speculation than by sound economic principles. Most analysts felt this was the case in early 1985, for example, when an already overvalued dollar was being pushed higher daily in international money markets.[12] Speculation, quite apart from indicators of underlying economic conditions, frequently determines exchange rates in the short term.

Economists and decision makers attach varying importance over time to particular economic conditions and policies that determine confidence in an economy and its currency. In the late 1970s the dollar's weakness was attributed primarily to large U.S. trade deficits—along with spiraling inflation, increased American oil import dependence on Middle East suppliers, and lack of confidence that the Carter administration's economic policies could deal effectively with these problems. In the mid-1980s American trade deficits were far worse than the late 1970s (see Figure 2-2), yet that did not dampen confidence in the American economy. The dollar remained strong in world foreign exchange markets. Economists now consider capital flows to be more decisive determinants than trade flows in assessing America's economic vitality and prospects, because of their greater magnitude and the speed with which capital flows can change direction. In 1984 and 1985, the dollar's value was buoyed by massive inflows of foreign capital in response to high interest rates, a favorable political environment for business, and confidence in U.S. economic growth. In late 1987, concern about substantially diminished inflows of foreign capital contributed to a fall in the value of the dollar. These shifts in fashion regarding the factors deemed most important for establishing confidence in a nation's economy greatly complicate our ability to explain and predict the movement of exchange rates. Like dramatic changes in the stock market, convincing explanations for alterations in currency values are usually ex post facto.

Ideally in a flexible exchange rate system, all states pursue their preferred domestic economic policy goals, and the exchange rates of their currencies in international economic relations will be allowed to find their own level in financial markets according to global supply and demand for different currencies. Problems emerge, however, when a country's currency is either grossly undervalued or overvalued. An undervalued currency typically improves a country's international competitiveness by making its exports of goods and services cheaper, making its imports more expensive, and attracting direct foreign investment into the national economy. But, it

---

[12]"Dollar's Strength Persists: Expectations Bolster Value, Analysts Say," *The New York Times*, February 19, 1985, p. 29.

also increases inflation by inhibiting import competition that imposes price restraint on domestic producers. An overvalued currency has the opposite effect. It is very harmful to the international competitiveness of national producers. Typically, this means a deterioration in the country's trade and payments balances as well as increased unemployment. On the other hand, an overvalued currency helps reduce inflation by inviting stiff import competition from foreign producers. These effects of overvaluation were clearly evident in the American economy of 1983–1985.

To prevent the disturbances that currency misalignments introduce into their domestic economies, states often try to "manage" their exchange rates by various means. When the British pound was at its lowest level relative to the dollar in early 1985, the British government raised interest rates four percentage points to attract foreign capital to London, thereby raising the value of its currency. Governments, acting alone or in concert, also intervene in international money markets (buying or selling large amounts of currency) in attempts to influence foreign exchange rates. The central banks of the seven largest Western states spent approximately $90 billion between January and October 1987 in a joint effort to defend the value of the dollar—an effort that ultimately failed after the stock market crash that October. Efforts at manipulating exchange rates among the major currencies through market interventions are problematic. Even massive interventions of several billion dollars a day by central banks cannot necessarily influence the world's money markets, where several hundred billion dollars are typically exchanged daily.[13] Such efforts enjoy success especially when markets are widely expected to move in a certain direction and are looking for signal or a catalyst to set them in motion. This was the case in the Plaza Accord of September 1985 when the finance ministers of the largest states announced their intention to intervene jointly in foreign exchange markets to lower a then highly overvalued dollar (the dramatic reaction of the market is reflected in Figure 3-2).

An important recent approach to managing exchange rates involves efforts at policy coordination among the leading economies. The major Western states attempted some coordination of their macroeconomic policies during the mid–1980s to stabilize international economic relations and dampen speculation causing volatility in international currency markets. Beyond interventions in money markets to help influence exchange rates in the short term, the G-7 states[14] sought to alter their domestic economic policies in ways that would correct large trade and payments disequilibriums driving foreign exchange markets over the medium term. In a series of meetings including the Plaza Agreements (September 1985), the Tokyo Economic Summit (July 1986), and the Louvre Agreements (February

---

[13]For a description and assessment of such intervention efforts, see "U.S. and Allies Show Ability to Influence Currency Levels," The New York Times, September 23, 1988, pp. 1, 32; "Signs of New Flexibility in U.S. Dollar Policy," The New York Times, May 22, 1989, p. 26.

[14]G-7, the Group of 7, refers to the seven largest economies in the West (the United States, Japan, West Germany, France, Britain, Italy, and Canada). Their finance ministers and central bank heads meet frequently to discuss and develop policies to stabilize international financial relations.

1987), the United States, Japan, and West Germany reached a general understanding about the direction of their respective economic policies. Running immense trade surpluses, the Japanese and West Germans were to stimulate their domestic economies by tax cuts and maintaining low interest rates relative to the United States. This would help reduce their trade surpluses and American trade deficits. In addition, their maintaining low interest rates would help the United States continue to attract foreign capital, upon which it had become dependent for financing the immense federal budget deficits that skyrocketed under the Reagan administration and which transformed the United States into the world's largest debtor. For its part, the United States was to reduce its unprecedented budget and trade deficits, calling into question its economic stewardship and threatening to undermine confidence in the dollar.[15]

The combination of market interventions to shore up the dollar and the promise of effective policy coordination among the major Western states succeeded in producing a "soft landing" for the dollar in 1987. But U.S. domestic economic health and the stability of the dollar in international currency markets came to depend more than ever on maintaining the dollar's value through effective multilateral cooperation. Flexible exchange rates have made it increasingly difficult for the United States to follow its traditional practice of subordinating international economic policies to its domestic economic policies and maintaining American autonomy from international monetary constraints.[16]

Stability of the dollar's exchange rate and continued flows of foreign capital to the United States assumed such centrality in 1987 that declines in either threatened both the American and international economies. Indeed, doubts about the dollar's value and the ability of the United States to attract foreign capital at prevailing interest rates were closely related to the stock market crash on October 19, 1987. August trade figures for the United States, released on October 15, revealed the second worst monthly trade deficit on record. They implied that a further devaluation of the dollar would be necessary to reduce the staggering U.S. trade deficit—a bad omen for continuation of foreign capital flows required to finance the federal budget deficit, as foreign investors would be receiving payments with dollars that were worth less. This bad economic news was followed on October 16–18 by statements of the Secretary of the Treasury James Baker on the eve of a trip to talk with West German officials, that the Louvre Agreements on policy coordination were unraveling—Germany was neither stimulating its economy fast enough nor lowering its interest rates enough to satisfy the United States. Secretary Baker implied that the United States might be forced to further devalue the dollar and to raise its own interest rates to meet the twin challenges of its trade deficit and the need to sustain foreign capital inflows in the absence of multilateral coopera-

---

[15]For a summary and analysis of these policy coordination efforts, see Yoichi Funabashi, *Managing the Dollar: From the Plaza to the Louvre* (Washington, D.C.: Institute for International Economics, 1988).

[16]Joanne Gowa, *Closing the Gold Window* (Ithaca: Cornell University Press, 1983).

tion.[17] The prospects of a declining dollar and higher interest rates to provide foreign investors with sufficient incentive to continue bringing funds into the United States helped trigger the Wall Street crash on October 19. Higher interest rates implied declining business opportunities in the United States, and financial instruments other than stocks promised higher returns for investors. A long-expected "correction" in an overvalued stock market turned into "Black Monday" on Wall Street when the Dow Jones dropped 23 percent as Secretary Baker arrived for his discussions in West Germany. The remainder of 1987 witnessed alarming reverberations in stock markets throughout the world and declines in the dollar below levels embodied in the Louvre Agreement.[18]

The dollar-stock market crisis of 1987 illustrates vividly the extent to which international economic considerations now influence the American economy. Public officials must balance the imperatives of attracting foreign capital to the United States through fiscal and monetary policy against the desire to satisfy domestic political demands for expanding business opportunities and high employment levels. In coming years, prudent foreign economic policy may well require higher taxes and interest rates, while domestic interests seek lower taxes and interest rates. The United States became so dependent upon foreign capital to finance its federal budget deficits during the 1980s that there will probably be times when domestic political interests in economic policy simply must yield to the necessities of maintaining the level of the dollar and assuring higher interest rates for investment in the United States than can be found abroad. Flexible exchange rates since 1973 have created a link between domestic and foreign economic policy that most Americans do not fully appreciate. The United States has lost much of its autonomy in domestic economic policy as a result of changes in the international monetary system and the role of the dollar within it.

A Diminished Role for Gold

Gold has occupied a less important position in the international monetary system after the United States abandoned its commitment to exchange dollars for gold at the official rate of $35 per ounce in 1971. Since then monetary authorities have sought to "demonetize" gold by letting it trade at market prices like most other commodities. The volume of gold held as international reserves has remained essentially stable since 1973. Indeed, both the United States and the International Monetary Fund auctioned off small portions of their gold holdings in the late 1970s. International mon-

[17]"U.S. Cautions Bonn That It May Force the Dollar Lower," *The New York Times*, October 16, 1987, pp. 1, 34. Of course, the United States had not delivered on its promises to reduce the trade and budget deficits either. Baker's criticisms of Germany should be understood as a bargaining position in association with his upcoming trip, not as an objective assessment of Germany's sole responsibility for undermining the policy coordination agreements.

[18]"Central Bankers Permit the Dollar to Slide Further," *The New York Times*, October 29, 1987, pp. 1, 37; "New Course, Fresh Risks," *The New York Times*, November 6, 1987, pp. 1, 33.

etary experts are trying to erode the anachronistic connection between gold and international money that was long ago accomplished in domestic monetary policy. Moreover, the USSR and the Republic of South Africa are the primary sources of newly mined gold entering the international monetary system. Diminishing the role of gold in international monetary relations reduces the influence that these two countries can potentially exercise over the global economy through their impact on the volume of gold reserves.

The price of gold has fluctuated under the post–Bretton Woods system just as exchange rates of the major currencies. Ordinarily, its value has increased dramatically during periods of great concern about the stability of international currencies, such as the dollar's decline in 1978–1980. The price of gold drops when there is general confidence in the strength of the dollar as the centerpiece of the international monetary system, such as occurred during the period between 1983 and 1985. In general, the movement of gold prices serves as a barometer of confidence in the international monetary order; the higher the confidence, the lower the gold price—and vice versa.

The Role of the Dollar and SDRs

Despite flexible exchange rates and the greater instability in currency values since 1973, foreign exchange (international currencies) still comprises the primary source of the world's international reserves. The dollar remains the top international currency by a substantial margin, accounting for about 63 percent of the foreign exchange held as reserves. The mark and the yen linger far behind the dollar in this role, accounting for only 16 percent and 7 percent of foreign exchange reserves, respectively.[19] The dollar's dominance as a reserve asset in the period since 1973 rests less on the world's continued confidence in U.S. economic policies and the intrinsic value of the dollar than on the fact that there is simply no practical alternative. No other economy is large enough to permit its currency to become so widely used as a vehicle financing international economic exchange. In 1969, for example, international speculation that the mark would appreciate was so great that it produced a 25 percent increase in Germany's money supply in a single week.[20] For reasons such as these, Japan, Germany, and other leading economies refuse to accept the burdens and the risks of allowing their currencies to challenge the dollar as the centerpiece of the international monetary order—to do so would risk losing all autonomy and control over their domestic economic policy. The United States remains in a class by itself in terms of international monetary relations by virtue of its immense economic size.

Whereas the dollar remains unchallenged as a medium of exchange and reserve asset, the SDR is assuming one important function previously

---

[19]"International Currencies: The Rise of the Deutsche Mark," *Finance and Development*, September 1990, p. 38.

[20]Richard Cooper, "A Monetary System for the Future," *Foreign Affairs*, 63, no. 1 (Fall 1984), p. 171.

performed by the top international currency—a preferred unit of account. This is the case despite the fact that SDRs amounted to less than 4 percent of international reserves other than gold held in 1989. The value of SDRs is presently a weighted mix of the world's five most important international currencies—the dollar, mark, yen, pound, and French franc. In a system of flexible exchange rates, the value of this "basket" of currencies fluctuates considerably less than the value of the dollar or any other single currency, because some currencies in the basket inevitably rise when others fall. For this reason the SDR has become a more stable unit of account than the dollar. Accordingly, the SDR is used increasingly for reporting economic statistics such as GNP, international loans, balance of payments, and so forth. By international convention air fares are established in SDRs. We might well see OPEC oil prices denominated in SDRs rather than dollars someday.

Monetary experts envision a possible evolution whereby the SDR could gradually displace the dollar, other national currencies, and gold as the centerpiece of the international monetary system.[21] That would require an unprecedented degree of political and economic cooperation among states, involving the transfer of considerable monetary power to a multi-national institution such as the IMF. It would also imply a considerable reduction in the political-economic power of the United States based on the present status of the dollar as the top international currency. But, to keep the possibility alive should circumstances warrant it, Western monetary officials are carefully guarding the integrity of the SDR as a reserve asset and doing everything possible to position it securely in contemporary international economic relations. SDRs are assuming far greater importance in the international monetary system than their present use in relation to dollars or gold would imply.

The Expansion of International Liquidity

There has been a great expansion of international liquidity in the international monetary system since the demise of the Bretton Woods system in 1971. International reserves rose from $129 billion in 1971 to more than $800 billion in 1989 (see Figure 3-3). The quantity of gold held as international reserves remained virtually steady throughout this period, but changes in the market price of gold have raised the total value of these reserve assets markedly. Continued U.S. payments deficits were responsible for most of the increase in the value of international reserves held in the form of foreign exchange.

In addition to increases in official holdings of international reserves, there has been an explosion of private bank lending to governments during the 1970s and 1980s, primarily through the growth of the Eurocurrency market. Eurocurrencies, approximately 67 percent in the form of dollars in 1988, are currencies deposited in and loaned by banks outside the country of those currencies. For example, dollars managed by banks in Europe

---

[21]Ibid., p. 183.

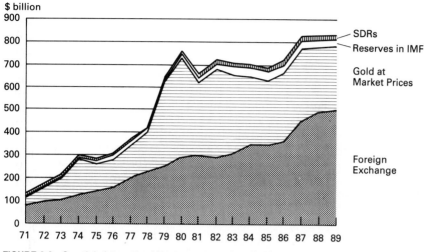

FIGURE 3-3 Growth in International Reserves, 1971–1989 ($ billions)

Source: International Monetary Fund, *International Financial Statistics*, June 1989, pp. 40, 41, 44, 50.

or European branches of U.S. banks are referred to as Eurodollars. German marks and Swiss francs held in banks outside Germany and Switzerland are referred to as Euromarks and Eurofrancs, respectively. The Eurocurrency market began in the late 1950s and has grown rapidly since then because banks trading in currencies outside their country of origin can escape the regulatory practices of national monetary authorities (such as minimal reserve requirements, interest rate limitations, and exchange controls). They are able to offer higher rates of interest to depositors and lower rates of interest to borrowers than those prevailing in domestic money markets, thus attracting immense deposits and large borrowers from all over the globe. The Eurocurrency market grew from $85 billion to $4,500 billion between 1971 and 1988. Advanced industrial states and less developed countries borrowed extensively in Eurocurrency markets to finance staggering current account deficits caused by oil price hikes and runaway inflation during the 1970s and early 1980s. The market played a central role in recycling "petrodollars" from OPEC states to oil-importing nations (rich and poor) with payments deficits—particularly in the years immediately following the abrupt oil price increases in 1973 and 1979.

The combination of massive increases in the value of gold, large U.S. payments deficits, and the availability of large amounts of credit in the Eurocurrency market enabled many states to finance their payments deficits without confronting the politically sensitive and economically painful discipline of implementing internal or external adjustment measures. This undoubtedly stimulated international trade and production during the 1970s, but it also postponed adjustment of serious payments imbalances that became all the more difficult to implement in the 1980s. This tremendous expansion in international liquidity, moreover, has constituted an important source of global inflation.

Summary

The international monetary system since 1971 makes the Bretton Woods system look tranquil and coherent by comparison. It is becoming more highly politicized as U.S. international financial vulnerabilities increase and as American dominance of the global economy erodes. American policies of devaluing the dollar to deal with trade deficits in the mid-1980s has sped the ascendancy of Japan's international economic role and broadened it.[22] Japanese firms have adjusted to the strong yen by rapidly expanding their direct foreign investment while Japan continues to run immense trade surpluses. Tokyo has emerged as a leading international money center, with Japanese banks accounting for nine of the top ten positions in global ratings by assets in 1987 (the only American bank in the top ten, Citicorp, was eighth in the rankings).[23] Japan replaced the United States as the world's leading creditor in 1987. Plans for further integration of the EEC in 1992 call for movement toward a common currency and development of a single monetary policy for the Community, vastly increasing Europe's strength as an actor in international financial relations. The United States must now bear a greater share of the burdens of adjustment as it copes with trade and payments imbalances than it has come to accept as "normal" by virtue of its top currency status for the past forty years. We should expect a long period of transition toward a more truly multilateral direction of international monetary relations that will be very problematic because of the absence of a consensus among important states on norms to guide international finance and on how to manage the political-economic consequences of an explosive growth in international banking. With international capital flows estimated at fifteen to twenty times the value of world trade in the 1980s, financial relations will assume ever greater centrality in the domestic and foreign economic policy of all states in the years ahead.

DEVELOPING STATES AND MONETARY RELATIONS

Thus far, we have examined the nature of international monetary problems and their relationships to domestic and international politics by focusing on advanced industrial states, particularly the United States. Developing countries encounter a number of particularly serious difficulties in their attempts to interact with and adapt to the international monetary order. We need to consider briefly how the monetary problems of the advanced industrial states adversely affect the developing countries. Center state concerns about balance-of-payments deficits frequently result in policies

---

[22]See "U.S. Currency Policy Speeds Japan in Vast Economic Role," *The New York Times*, November 28, 1988, pp. 1, 34.

[23]"The Global Money Centers," *JEI Reports*, No. 14A (April 7, 1989), 6. For assessments of the challenges in regulating changing financial markets, see Joan Spero, "Guiding Global Finance," *Foreign Policy*, No. 73 (Winter 1988–89), 114–34; and Ethan Kapstein, "Resolving the Regulator's Dilemma: International Coordination of Banking Regulations," *International Organization*, 43, no. 2, (Spring 1989), 323–47.

that are detrimental to the interests of developing countries. To reduce a deficit, advanced industrial states may seek to erect barriers (external measures) against the import of goods from other countries. When they do this, the burdens fall heavily on the developing countries, since they often depend on the export of a relatively narrow range of commodity and manufactured goods for their foreign exchange earnings. We saw in the discussion of trade how the trade deficit of the United States and the overvalued dollar of the 1980s have stimulated domestic political pressure for protection across a wide array of manufacturing industries of substantial export importance to less developed countries—textiles, shoes, and steel, for example. Such policies of the United States and other industrial countries to deal with trade imbalances inhibit less developed countries' industrialization efforts and their capacity to service foreign debts through export earnings.

Other center state policies might involve the establishment of restrictions on capital outflows for investment purposes. To the extent that a less developed country desires such capital to further industrialization, to tap natural resources, or to obtain needed capital and technology, it will perceive these restrictions as harmful. Similarly, balance-of-payments problems in center states may lead them to reduce foreign aid expenditures or to require that such funds be used to purchase goods from the donor country; either strategy is costly to developing countries. Thus, in trying to correct balance-of-payments deficits, advanced industrial states often adopt policies that are detrimental to the interests of the developing countries. There are few remedies for these states since they are frequently innocent bystanders to conflicts among and within the advanced industrial states.

Balance-of-payments adjustment problems and liquidity concerns are as important to developing countries as they are to center states. Indeed, most less developed countries have traditionally been confronted with chronic payments deficits and extraordinary liquidity needs. Fluctuation in the prices received for their commodity exports and extended periods of decline in their terms of trade lead to shortages and unpredictable foreign exchange earnings through exports. Yet their ambitious development programs require a sustained, high level of imports. It has become increasingly difficult for most less developed countries to finance the gap between their export receipts and import bills through reliance upon international reserves and development assistance from foreign governments and public international lending institutions such as the World Bank.

The International Monetary Fund was, of course, created for the purpose of providing loans to its member states facing payments deficits. Less developed countries have frequently relied upon the IMF, but they feel that IMF policies often ignore economic and political realities and place unwarranted burdens upon the less developed countries. Thus, they rely upon the fund only as a last resort.

In particular, less developed countries object to strict limits on the size of loans they can obtain from the IMF. Countries are normally limited to borrowing 125 percent of their quota, with longer-term stand-by agreements negotiated with the IMF sometimes permitting states to triple that figure. Since quotas are calculated upon states' overall economic size and capabilities, however, less developed countries typically have relatively small quotas—and, thus, small borrowing capacities in the IMF.

Also problematic are the economic policies typically imposed by the IMF upon less developed countries as conditions for access to substantial IMF loan packages. The IMF has been inclined to impose severe economic austerity programs upon less developed countries with serious payments deficits. These programs include stringent curtailment of public expenditures, restrictive fiscal and monetary policies, devaluation of the nation's currency, and removal of restrictions on the free flow of trade and foreign investment.

Less developed countries argue that the political and economic impacts of this standard IMF prescription are often catastrophic. Currency devaluation is often as likely to increase inflation and worsen a less developed country's balance of payments as it is to reduce its payments deficit. A large proportion of their imports, such as energy and intermediate and heavy industrial goods, cannot be obtained domestically and are essential for the economy—so reducing the volume of a less developed country's imports means undermining its economy in the short term. Rather than reducing imports, devaluation frequently increases the size of a less developed country's import bill by raising the cost of vital foreign goods. Also, most primary products (the chief exports of poor states) exhibit a price inelasticity of demand—that is, lower prices made available to foreign consumers by devaluation will not lead to a proportionate increase in the volume of purchases. The demand for coffee, for example, does not increase much when the price drops. The dilemma is that currency devaluation by less developed countries does not necessarily increase export revenues or reduce import expenditures in the manner expected by the IMF and liberal economists.

The deflationary policies imposed by the IMF often produce traumatic political upheavals in less developed countries, referred to as "IMF riot." Domestic chaos has confronted regimes in Turkey, Peru, Portugal, and Egypt during the 1970s in the wake of these governments' acceptance and implementation of austerity packages required for access to IMF loans. Over 700 people died in Egyptian riots prompted by IMF-imposed elimination of government food subsidies in 1976. Announcement by Venezuelan officials of austerity policies demanded by foreign creditors unleashed riots in 1989 in which dozens of people were killed and hundreds wounded before order was restored. Some countries such as Brazil, Tanzania, Jamaica, and Peru have found the conditions attached to IMF lending so objectionable economically, politically, and ideologically that they have broken off negotiations for desperately needed foreign loans on occasion. While most less developed countries have not gone this far, they all find the demands made by the IMF upon their domestic and foreign policies excessively one-sided and intrusive. Kenneth Dadzie, secretary-general of UNCTAD, for example, noted that "while the United States payment deficit is being tackled symmetrically by the developed market countries—i.e., 'through macro-economic policy [coordination] efforts on the part of surplus countries as well as the deficit country'—developing countries have been subject to the traditional asymmetrical approach which puts the burden of adjustment [exclusively] on deficit countries. This has been particularly evident as regards debt."[24]

The view of the IMF by less developed countries can, perhaps, be better understood by Americans if we were to contemplate what the IMF might well demand of the United States were it dependent upon the IMF for financing its balance-of-payments disequilibria. The Fund would have found federal budget deficits in excess of $150 billion a year and trade imbalances of $120 billion a year in the late 1980s completely unacceptable. To secure IMF funds the United States might well be told by foreign economic experts to slash government expenditures on social programs such as unemployment benefits, social security, food stamps, aid to education, and medicare as well as to severely curtail military spending. A significant tax increase might also be required to bring the budget deficit within acceptable bounds. A dollar devaluation would be in order, inviting higher levels of inflation which could be controlled by tightening the U.S. money supply and raising interest rates. The fact that the latter might wreak havoc on industries important to the overall vitality of the American economy would be viewed by IMF officials as a regrettable, but necessary, by-product of reestablishing a more sound future economic footing for the United States. The President's promises of no new taxes, protecting core social programs needed by the less well-off elements of the country, and his commitment to maintain U.S. defense would simply have to be abandoned in response to unavoidable external pressures from the IMF.[25] Anyone in the United States can imagine the likely congressional response and public reaction to such a set of demands placed upon the President from abroad. Less developed countries dependent upon IMF support are no less resentful of its intrusions upon their domestic and foreign economic policies than Americans would be.

Even though the conditions that the IMF attaches to its loans are resented by less developed countries and the magnitude of IMF loans is limited by their relatively small quotas, most less developed countries with severe payments problems wind up agreeing to an IMF loan package. This occurs not only because the need access to IMF resources but also because they find it impossible to obtain private bank loans and bilateral development assistance elsewhere until other creditors are assured by a less developed country's agreement with the IMF that they are good credit risks. In short, the IMF is not only a lender of last resort, but the international economic community's legitimizer of a state's credit worthiness for all variety of public and private sources of foreign capital.

Not surprisingly, less developed countries have long pressed for access to larger amounts of resources from the IMF on easier terms (lower interest rates, longer repayment periods, fewer conditions attached to their domestic and foreign economic policies). Over the past one and one-half decades, the IMF has responded by creating and expanding a number of special facilities of particular relevance to less developed countries' needs. In addition to the Compensatory and Contingency Fund Facility for un-

---

[24]UNCTAD, *Press Release*, TAD/INF/1960, September 19, 1988, p. 1.

[25]This scenario was adapted from *The New York Times*, October 24, 1983, p. A19.

anticipated export earnings declines or import increases (such as oil price increases for LDC importers during Iraq's invasion of Kuwait in 1990), these programs include the following: a Buffer Stock Financing Facility to help LDCs finance contributions to approved international buffer stocks as part of commodity agreements; an Extended Fund Facility to help overcome structural balance-of-payments maladjustments; and a Structural Adjustment Facility offering concessional terms to help the least developed countries finance macroeconomic and structural adjustment programs to meet protracted balance-of-payments problems.[26]

Beyond these specialized, supplementary facilities, less developed countries have sought to increase their access to Fund resources through enlargement of their quotas and implementation of a proposal to link new SDR allocations to increased development assistance for less developed countries. Since the mid-1970s IMF quotas have more than tripled, expanding the resources of the Fund to 135 billion SDR (approximately 196 billion). Less developed countries are able to borrow more as their quotas, like everyone else's, have been increased proportionately. Less developed countries as a group, however, still account for only about 30 percent of total IMF quotas.

The less developed countries have been far more frustrated in their efforts to link special drawing rights to their development aspirations. SDRs are created in accordance with international liquidity needs and are disbursed to members of the IMF in proportion to their quotas. Thus, less developed countries receive approximately only 30 percent of any new SDR allocations. For years less developed countries have pressed for a variety of proposals that would distribute new SDR allocations primarily to poor states—either directly or through an international lending agency such as IBRD. Because of the less developed countries' great need for imports, the newly granted reserves would finance increased purchases from the advanced states; these purchases would in turn contribute to the development objectives of the developing countries. Greater liquidity would be provided in the world monetary system, but instead of SDR reserves sitting more or less idle in rich countries with balance-of-payments surpluses, they would be working to provide needed goods and services in the poor countries—goods and services that would be obtained largely from the advanced industrial states of the West. SDRs would, in essence, be allocated to less developed countries with the expectation that they would be recycled to the advanced industrial states.[27]

Decision makers in advanced industrial states have remained very cool to such proposals. If SDRs are to have the possibility of emerging as the principal international reserve asset replacing existing international currencies, the international financial community must have complete confidence that SDR creation will be governed exclusively by liquidity requirements of the world economy viewed as a whole. Should SDRs be transformed into a new type of development assistance through these link

[26]"Supplement on the Fund," *IMF Survey*, September 1988, p. 2.

[27]For a brief overview of SDR link ideas, see "SDRs and Development, $10 Billion for Whom?" *Foreign Policy*, No. 8 (Fall 1972), pp. 102–28.

proposals, less developed countries would be expected to demand new SDR allocations in large quantities to meet their development aspirations. Yet there would frequently be occasions when further reserve creation would clearly be inappropriate in terms of liquidity requirements of the global economic system. In short, the SDR link would enhance the prospect of exacerbating global inflation by creating excessive amounts of liquidity, and it would politicize the SDRs in a fashion that could undermine their potential for emerging as the centerpiece for the international monetary system. Such fears were confirmed in 1980 when the finance ministers of twenty-four less developed countries called for the creation of an additional 56 billion SDRs over the period 1980–1986. Western monetary officials feared this would be highly inflationary.[28]

The complaints of less developed countries about the IMF extend beyond the limits upon and terms attached to their borrowing. They have sought a more potent role in the IMF's decision-making process. The Fund relies upon a weighted voting arrangement reflective of countries' quotas. Although less developed states comprise three fourths of the IMF membership, they hold only about one third of the votes. The United States alone has 19.1 percent of the votes in the IMF, and the five largest Western states together account for 42 percent of the votes in the Fund. Until well into the 1960s, moreover, the most important international monetary deliberations and decisions took place in the Group of Ten—a body meeting under the auspices of the Organization for Economic Cooperation and Development in Paris that performed a kind of executive function for the entire international monetary order, including the IMF. The Group of Ten was comprised of only the most important advanced industrial states, and less developed countries were seldom even consulted about deliberations conducted there.

Over the years the less developed countries have fought to enhance their voting power in the IMF and to move international monetary decision making into forums, including the IMF, where their power could be felt. Partially in response to these pressures, in combination with other events, the IMF has become a more central forum for key international monetary deliberations.[29] Less developed countries have also sought to politicize monetary questions and to enhance their bargaining position by raising monetary policy in UNCTAD and other U.N. institutions where they enjoy a voting majority.

The Debt of Less Developed Countries and International Monetary Challenges in the 1980s

Steadily frustrated by the IMF and the conduct of international monetary relations, the less developed countries were confronted with the need to finance rapidly expanding payments deficits following the sharp increase

---

[28]*The New York Times*, September 9, 1980, p. D8.

[29]Of course, this has not eliminated regular consultations among the advanced industrial states under the auspices of the OECD, G-7, and other institutions.

in the prices of their oil, food, and industrial goods imports after 1973. The current account deficits of non–oil-exporting less developed countries are shown in Figure 3-4. These deficits ballooned after the oil price hikes of 1973 and 1979. Without access to foreign loans, these countries would have found it necessary to curtail their imports and their development sharply—to their detriment and that of the advanced industrial states with large export markets in the Third World.

The poorest, less developed countries had to rely on foreign aid and borrow heavily from the IMF through both the regular credit and supplementary lending facilities outlined previously. The more rapidly industrializing, less developed states in Latin America and East Asia, by contrast, were able to borrow extensively from private banks operating in expanding Eurocurrency markets fueled by deposits from OPEC states with financial surpluses after 1973 and 1979. In this way credit-worthy less developed countries could finance continued development through private foreign loans without having to submit to politically and economically objectionable IMF conditionality. Officials in the advanced industrial states were happy to see this borrowing conducted through private banking channels because it reduced the need for publically financed loans to less developed countries. Private borrowing accounted for 43 percent of the less developed countries' outstanding foreign debt in 1980 compared to only 12 percent in 1970.[30] At the same time it permitted LDCs to sustain imports from advanced industrial states. This ability of less developed countries to finance development and imports through loans is estimated to have generated about 900,000 jobs a year in the advanced industrial states of OECD in each year between 1973 and 1977.

FIGURE 3-4   Current Account Deficits of Non–Oil-Exporting LDCs, 1973–1985 ($ billion)

Source: International Monetary Fund, *Finance and Development*, 17, no. 3 (September 1980), 7: International Monetary Fund, *World Economic Outlook*, April 1985, p. 239.

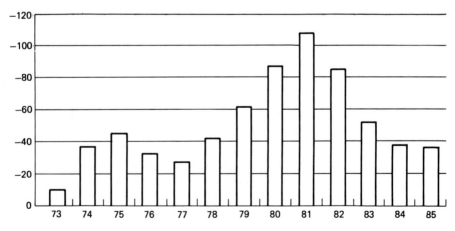

[30]International Bank for Reconstruction and Development, *World Development Report, 1981* (Washington, D.C.: IBRD, 1981), p. 57.

Although these arrangements were generally satisfactory to all parties through the 1970s, an international debt crises emerged in the early 1980s as the volume of loans and service payments continued to rise (see Figures 3-5 and 3-6). The debt service ratio (principal and interest payments as a percentage of exports) for all less developed countries increased from 16 percent in 1977 to over 20 percent in 1982. The more heavily indebted countries of Latin America faced a debt service ratio of 54 percent in 1982 (see Figure 3-6)—bringing into serious question the ability of these states to assume further debt obligations. Yet, they needed ever larger loans to sustain imports and economic growth and to repay past debts.

International conditions at the outset of the 1980s made it impossible for less developed countries to continue borrowing unabated in private financial markets. Interest rates on old and new loans suddenly skyrocketed to 18 percent in 1981 as banks around the world followed the lead of financial markets in the United States. Each one percent increase in interest rates added $4 billion annually to the interest payments of less developed countries at that time. Petrodollars were no longer pouring into Eurocurrency markets since the earnings of OPEC states plummeted during the early 1980s. Private banks found themselves overexposed to less developed country borrowers such as Brazil, Mexico, and Argentina that only a few years before were considered excellent clients. The governments of advanced industrial states began to fear that they would have to assume the financial risks of further loans to less developed countries that private markets had handled during the previous decade. With 40 percent of Latin

FIGURE 3-5   LDC Foreign Debt, 1981–1990 ($ billion)

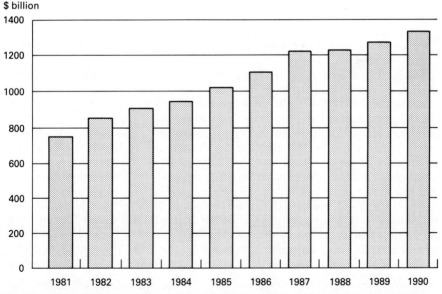

Source: International Monetary Fund, *World Economic Outlook, 1989*, p. 186. Data for 1990 from *IMF Survey*, February 4, 1991, p. 38.

FIGURE 3-6 LDC Debt Service (percent of exports)

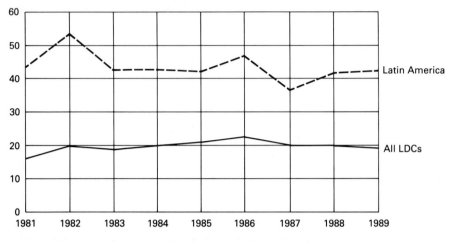

Source: International Monetary Fund, *World Economic Outlook, 1989*, p. 194.

America's outstanding foreign debt held by American banks, there was also fear that default by any of the large Latin American countries in trouble could threaten to unleash a crisis in the U.S. domestic banking system.

Forty-six multilateral renegotiations of private debt were arranged for less developed countries between 1980 and 1984, compared to only five between 1975 and 1979.[31] The IMF assumed a pivotal role in multilateral efforts to manage the international debt crisis. The banks refused to reschedule existing debts or to make new loans to troubled LDCs until the debtors negotiated stand-by agreements with the IMF and committed themselves to the type of austerity program typical of IMF conditionality. So, less developed countries in the 1980s found themselves driven to IMF-sanctioned domestic and foreign economic policies as a precondition for further borrowing in private financial markets that earlier allowed them to circumvent IMF oversight. In a new twist, the IMF frequently demanded that Western banks "involuntarily" extend further capital to less developed countries as a prerequisite for IMF loans and approval of the debtor's future credit worthiness. In this process the International Monetary Fund has emerged with an enhanced position in the bargaining between less developed countries and the private banking community in international financial markets.

Strategies to manage the international debt crisis have gone through three basic stages since the threat of Mexico's default on its foreign debt focused global attention to the issue in 1982. From 1982 to 1985 the emphasis was on strict austerity programs by the LDC debtors under IMF supervision as a precondition for further access to international borrowing.

---

[31]International Bank for Reconstruction and Development, *World Development Report, 1985* (Washington, D.C.: IBRD, 1985), p. 28.

New loans were necessary to honor renegotiated loan repayment schedules. Despite new loans, however, the LDC debtors turned into net *exporters* of capital to creditors in the advanced industrial states. Heavily indebted LDC's domestic political and economic programs were sacrificed to the imperative of meeting foreign debt service obligations. Less developed countries, especially in Latin America, sharply curtailed their imports and new investment to husband the financial resources required for their debt service. Indeed, so dramatic was the drop in Latin American economic growth and imports that U.S. shipments of manufactured goods to the region between 1981 and 1983 declined 38 percent, from $42 billion to $26 billion.[32] This was an important development for the United States at a time when its trade deficits were rapidly increasing.

This course of action offered no solution to the Third World debt problem. The size of the debt continued to mount (see Figure 3-5). Little progress was made to reduce the share of LDCs' exports devoted to servicing the debt (see Figure 3-6). Western banks' "voluntary" lending to less developed countries declined. The debts were merely being "rolled over" through extended repayment schedules, accompanied by "involuntary" loans so banks could continue to claim them as earning-assets rather than losses on their books. Meanwhile, development virtually ceased in the largest LDC debtors, concentrated in Latin America.

At the annual meeting of the IMF in the fall of 1985, U.S. Secretary of Treasury James Baker proposed a new "plan" which was to mark a shift in strategy for managing Third World debt for the period 1985–1988. It emphasized the need to supplement short-term austerity in the debtor states with long-term economic growth. As in the period before 1985, the Baker Plan called for less developed countries to restore discipline in their economies by increased reliance on market-oriented policies. In addition, however, commercial banks holding most of the LDC debt were asked to provide an extra $20 billion in loans over a three-year period to help finance the economic growth of LDCs in compliance with the plan. The IMF was encouraged to avoid over-emphasis on austerity programs in negotiating its agreements with the major debtors while still upholding its conditionality principles. The International Bank for Reconstruction and Development (IBRD) was asked to increase aid to the leading LDC debtors to help stimulate their growth in the face of their debt obligations. The United States and other advanced industrial countries were, for their part, to make larger contributions to the IBRD and otherwise increase concessionary public finance to cooperating countries in the Third World.

The Baker Plan constituted a major shift in policy for the United States, which had previously taken the position that the debt was a matter between the banks and their LDC clients. The burdens of managing the debt problem were broadened, in principle at least, to include the governments of the West and multilateral economic institutions beyond the IMF.

[32]International Monetary Fund, *Direction of Trade Statistics Yearbook, 1988* (Washington, D.C.: IMF, 1988), p. 407. For an overview of the debt crisis and the political burdens it imposes on LDCs, see Miles Kahler, ed., *The Politics of International Debt* (Ithaca: University of Cornell Press, 1986).

Yet, the Baker Plan was unable to deal effectively with the debt challenge. The banks, given no incentive to expand involuntary lending, never came forward with the additional capital Baker had envisioned. Despite its emphasis on growth, the heavily indebted less developed countries continued their economic decline. As in the earlier period, the debt continued to grow.

The Latin American economies, for example, were in a state of crisis. From net capital importers of $35 billion in 1980, they had become net capital exporters of $30 billion in 1988. The interest burden on Latin American states was much greater as a percentage of their GNP than the interest burden found politically and economically intolerable by Weimar Germany in 1929.[33] During the 1980s, the standard of living in these states declined to levels they had achieved ten to twenty years earlier. The case of Mexico was typical. The purchasing power of the average laborer in Mexico declined 50 percent between 1982 and 1988. The country had repaid $56 billion on its debt, net of new assistance, since 1982. Compliance with IMF austerity programs and cooperation under the Baker Plan had imposed such severe economic conditions on the Mexican population that the PRI, the party ruling the country unopposed for decades, could retain its power only by rigging the 1988 presidential election. The political fabric of the country was being torn apart by the burdens of servicing its foreign debt.[34]

Recognizing these developments and stimulated by the Venezuelan riots in March 1989 over austerity policies related to an IMF agreement, Nicholas Brady, President Bush's secretary of the Treasury, advanced a new strategy for coping with the debt problem. The Brady Plan was based on the heretofore abhorrent notion in the United States that ways must be found for the international community to support officially some reduction in the debt of the less developed countries. The economic decline and political instability faced by the fifteen largest LDC debtors came to be viewed by Western officials as insurmountable in the face of existing debt levels—even with good faith efforts at economic reform, such as in the case of Mexico. Debt relief had become a necessary, though not a sufficient, condition for economic growth. While still taking shape in 1989 and 1990, the Brady Plan envisioned a menu of choices for banks (including new lending, reducing principal, or reducing interest rates) and expanded possibilities for less developed states to purchase some portion of their outstanding private debt at discounted prices reflecting the value of their loans in secondary financial markets—approximately 30 percent to 40 percent of their face value at the time of the initial proposal. For example, LDCs might finance purchases of debt by issuing bonds to be guaranteed by the IMF, IBRD, and advanced industrial states. The less developed countries would pay off the bonds by agreeing to set aside, perhaps in an escrow

    [33]Carol Graham, "The Latin American Quagmire," *The Brookings Review*, 7, no. 2 (Spring 1989), p. 43.

    [34]For a picture of Mexico's debt quandary, see "Mexico Feels Squeeze of Years of Austerity," *The New York Times*, July 25, 1989, pp. 1, 42.

account with the IMF, a certain percentage of their export earnings each year.

Within months of the proposal the IMF and the IBRD were discussing debt-purchase guarantee funds of $25 billion. Japan was the first advanced industrial state to promise funds to the program in the spring of 1989.[35] Creditors were expected to prefer the likelihood of collecting on the bonds for a reduced LDC debt at full face value (guaranteed by the key international economic institutions and the leading Western states) to the risks of attempting to collect their immense, existing LDC loans at only a small fraction of their face value. Mexico was the first country to negotiate debt relief, approximately $35 billion, in the context of the Brady Plan.[36] As of 1990, additional agreements for debt reduction under the Brady proposals had been negotiated with Costa Rica, the Philippines, Venezuela, Morocco, and Chile. These agreements, while reducing debts owned to private banks, will increase LDC debt owed to multilateral financial institutions. They will also involve Japan, the United States, and European governments more deeply in managing the private commercial debt problems of less developed states.

The foreign debt of less developed countries will continue to be a prominant feature of the international financial landscape for the foreseeable future. Although the policies of less developed countries themselves will be important, periods of debt crisis are likely to yield to periods of quiet primarily as a function of developments in the global economy beyond the control of the LDCs. William Cline estimates that 80 percent of the $500 billion increase in the debt of nonoil developing countries from 1973 to 1982 was attributable to externalities confronting the LDCs—oil price increases, declines in the terms of trade, and increases in real interest rates prevailing in the financial markets of advanced industrial states.[37] Experience over the past decade suggests that managing the debt problem will require forging new, complex relationships among the international banking community, governments of rich and poor states, and multilateral financial institutions such as the International Monetary Fund. As the last resort, the banks can push the risks of exposure to Third World debtors upon their home governments, since public officials in industrialized states will employ any measures to prevent LDC debt problems from undermining the viability of their own domestic banking systems. Accordingly, it is unlikely that private markets will be relied upon to finance LDC debts with as little oversight from public officials in the leading industrial states as was the case during the 1970s.

[35]"Brady Signals Shift in Policy Toward Debt Reduction," *Congressional Quarterly*, March 11, 1989, pp. 510–13. See also, Jeffrey Sachs, "Making the Brady Plan Work," *Foreign Affairs*, 68, no. 3 (Summer 1989), pp. 87–104.

[36]"Japanese Banks, Government Part of Complex Mexican Debt Plan," *JEI Report*, February 9, 1990, pp. 1–3. The Brady Plan was developed jointly with Japan, and Japan has led all advanced industrial states in allocating funds for debt relief. This is a further indication of Japan's emerging leadership in international financial affairs, commensurate with its position as the world's leading net creditor.

[37]*IMF Survey*, January 7, 1985, p. 11.

THE RADICAL VIEW OF THE IMF

The conditions attached to IMF loans that require deflationary domestic economic policies, reduction of public expenditures (often designed to reduce income inequalities within society), and liberalization of international trade and investment policies expose the IMF to harsh criticism from radical analysts and decision makers. The acceptance of IMF policies sharply limits the options of less developed countries. They may be required to abandon socialist policies designed to reduce domestic income inequalities, or to protect local production from displacement by foreign imports or direct foreign investment, or to sever existing links with the international capitalist economy. The Fund, in the radical view, imposes capitalist domestic and foreign economic policies on borrowing states, thereby ensuring the dominance of the advanced market economies over the developing countries. The IMF's reliance upon traditional liberal economic advice, its rejection of noncapitalist policies, and its attempts to bind borrowing states to the current political-economic system (through their vulnerability and indebtedness) are all seen as evidence that the Fund serves as the handmaiden of dominant capitalist states. Harry Magdoff charges that "the very conditions which produce the necessity to borrow money are continuously reimposed by the pressures to pay back the loan and to pay the interest on these loans."[38] Another radical critic of the IMF writes that "IMF missions descend like vultures in the wake of right-wing coups in countries such as Ghana, Indonesia, and Brazil."[39] Moreover, "the discipline imposed by the IMF has often eliminated the need for direct military intervention in order to preserve a climate friendly towards foreign investment."[40]

The influence of the IMF is not limited to its ability to impose conservative policies on developing countries that seek to borrow from the Fund. Equally important, according to radical thought, is the central role the IMF occupies in the entire public and private credit system at the international level. If a deficit developing country seeks to obtain funds from the IMF but refuses the latter's advice or is otherwise denied a loan, then most of the other major sources of credit (including multinational institutions such as the World Bank, regional development organizations, bilateral government-to-government loans, and private sources of credit) also refuse to loan money to that country. The IMF acts somewhat as a central credit agency, then, setting the standard by which other sources of funds may be obtained. The radicals claim that it is no coincidence that President Allende of Chile was unable to find any loans after the IMF rejected his request for funds because of his unwillingness to accept IMF conditions. And they point out that in the wake of the military coup in September 1973 the IMF did indeed provide funds to a then more pliable

[38]Harry Magdoff, *The Age of Imperialism* (New York: Monthly Review Press, 1966), p. 98.

[39]Cheryl Payer, "The Perpetuation of Dependence: The IMF and the Third World," *Monthly Review*, 23, no. 4 (September 1971), p. 37.

[40]Ibid., p. 38.

Chile; what is more, this was followed by loans from other sources, both public and private.[41] In sum, the IMF is perceived by some to be the linchpin of the entire international monetary and economic order, which is designed to perpetuate capitalism and the subservience of developing states to the advanced industrial states. Events of the past two decades would only confirm the argument of Cheryl Payer in this regard that:

> The [international loan] system can be compared point by point with peonage on an individual scale. In the peonage, or debt slavery, system the worker is unable to use his nominal freedom to leave the service of his employer, because the latter supplies him with credit (for overpriced goods in the company store) necessary to supplement his meager wages. The aim of the employer-creditor-merchant is neither to collect the debt once and for all, nor to starve the employee to death, but rather to keep the laborer permanently indentured through his debt to the employer. The worker cannot run away, for other employers and the state recognize the legality of his debt; nor has he any hope of earning his freedom with his low wage.
>
> Precisely the same system operates on the international level. Nominally independent countries find their debts, and their continuing inability to finance current needs out of imports [sic], keep them tied by a tight leash to their creditors. The IMF [and IBRD] orders them, in effect, to continue laboring on the plantations, while it refuses to finance their efforts to set up in business for themselves. For these reasons the term "international debt slavery" is a perfectly accurate one to describe the reality of their situation.[42]

SUMMARY

We saw in the previous chapter how liberals, radicals, and advocates for less developed countries in the Prebisch tradition differ in their analyses of key problems and policy prescriptions for enhancing the Third World's trade and development prospects. Similar patterns are present in their assessments of international monetary relations. Liberal economists, reflected in U.S. and IMF policy positions, stress the need for less developed countries to concentrate on internal adjustment measures while opening their economies to market forces in foreign trade and investment. Their prescriptions focus on the need for alterations in the domestic and foreign policies of states with payments deficits. Consistent with the Prebisch approach, less developed countries analysts stress the need for changing the terms of, and norms for, international financial relations. They seek improved access to loans from the IMF and other sources as well as loans

---

[41]The same pattern applied in the case of Jamaica under leftist Prime Minister Michael Manley. His refusal to accept IMF terms of reduced public employment, budget cuts, and higher prices for desperately needed loans during 1980 led commercial banks to refuse extension of further credits until Jamaica resumed discussions with the Fund. Manley's electoral defeat by Edward Seaga, a staunch advocate of private enterprise, resulted in a prompt renegotiation of an IMF loan package and the resumption of private bank credits.

[42]Cheryl Payer, "The Perpetuation of Dependence: The IMF and the Third World," *Monthly Review*, 23, no. 4 (September 1971), p. 40.

with fewer strings. In a word, they seek to reform the international monetary order. Radical analysts deplore the less developed countries linkage with advanced capitalist states—a linkage that increases their dependence through indebtedness and vulnerability to center states. The IMF, of course, lies at the center of less developed countries dependency, in their view. As in the case of trade, radical analysts argue for a transformation of Western states and less developed countries to socialist political-economic systems that would truly revolutionize existing international financial relations.

4

The Multinational Corporation: Challenge to the International System

The multinational corporation is probably the most visible vehicle for the internationalization of the world economic system. As the economies of different nations have become increasingly linked and functionally integrated, the multinational corporation seems to have been the institution most able to adapt to a transnational style of operation. Certainly, they are more international in scope, perspective, and effectiveness than most governmental organizations. Indeed, multinational corporations are a major result of and a prime stimulus for furthering the number and complexity of transnational interactions and relationships.

The growth and presumed power of multinational corporations have focused attention on its consequences for domestic as well as international politics and economics. The activities of multinational corporations have led to extensive investigations and studies by such diverse groups as the U.S. Senate, the United Nations, the International Labor Organization, the World Council of Churches, and a large number of other governmental and nongovernmental agencies at national, regional, and international levels. Labor unions in the United States, Sweden, and the United Kingdom have charged their own multinationals with exporting jobs and have attempted to obtain government action to restrict the ease with which these corporations can invest abroad. In various host states, both U.S. and non-American multinational firms have been accused of economic imperialism, the fostering of intercountry competition, and the promulgation of insensitive and unsavory business practices. In sum, multinational corporations have become the most visible and the most attacked agents in the global economic system.

At the same time, nearly every country in the world actively pursues multinationals to invest in their countries with the competition frequently occupying front-page headlines. A major development has been the eagerness of many socialist and formerly socialist countries to open their economies to foreign investment. Foreign investment is seen as a way to obtain capital funds, technology, managerial know-how, and industrial and consumer products so desperately needed for economic development. A further change has been the emergence of successful multinational companies from a few of the developing countries. Companies in Korea, Taiwan, India, Brazil, Mexico and elsewhere have found great advantages in becoming international companies. Some compete successfully with firms from the advanced industrial states.

CHANGING PATTERNS OF DIRECT FOREIGN INVESTMENT

Multinational corporations or their predecessors have existed for a long time. For instance, in the fifteenth century the Fuggers, headquartered in Augsburg, created and managed financial houses, trading concerns, mining operations, and processing plants in many parts of Europe.[1] Companies such as Singer, Heinz, Unilever, Nestlé, and a number of others have been active direct foreign investors for most of this century. However, the rapid expansion of direct foreign investment during the last four decades has done much to accelerate the internationalization of production. This has attracted increased attention to the impact of multinational firms on the world's economy and the economies of individual countries.

The total book value of all direct foreign investment was approximately $598 billion in 1984.[2] This reflects a 279 percent increase in the value of the worldwide stock of foreign direct investment from $158 billion in 1971. Of the total amount of direct foreign investment in 1984, the U.S.-based multinational corporations accounted for 40 percent; European firms, 44 percent; Japanese, 6.3 percent; and Canadian, 5.3 percent. The predominance of American multinationals has declined as the Europeans and Japanese have increased their international activity as a result both of their new economic and political stature in the world and of the devaluations of the American dollar.[3] Table 4-1 indicates the relative change in

---

[1]A. W. Clausen, "The Internationalized Corporation: An Executive's View," *The Annals*, 403 (September 1972), 21.

[2]U.S. Department of Commerce, *International Direct Investment: Global Trends and the U.S. Role, 1988* (Washington, D.C.: International Trade Administration, November 1988), p. 87.

[3]An emerging phenomenon is the rise and growth of Third World multinationals from South Korea, Mexico, Taiwan, Hong Kong, the Philippines, India, and Brazil.

TABLE 4-1   Trends in the Direct Investment Abroad of Selected Countries, Selected Years, 1971–1984 (In percentages)

PARENT COUNTRY	1971	1976	1981	1984
United States	52.3%	47.6%	41.4%	40.0%
United Kingdom	15.0	11.2	11.9	14.3
Germany	4.6	6.9	8.3	7.7
Japan	2.8	6.7	6.7	6.3
Canada	4.1	3.9	4.7	5.3

Source: United Nations, Economic and Social Council, Commission on Transnational Corporations, *Transnational Corporations in World Development: A Re-examination, E/C 10/38* (New York: United Nations, March 1978), p. 236; U.S. Department of Commerce, International Trade Administration, *International Direct Investment, 1984*, August 1984, p. 7; and *International Direct Investment, 1988*, 1988, p. 87.

the international activity of selected source countries of multinational corporations.

American multinational firms have a profound impact on the ways in which the United States is linked to the world economy. Data in Table 4-2 indicate the large size and rapid growth of American direct investment abroad since 1950. However, these figures represent the cumulative book value of U.S. direct foreign investment. On an annual basis, the affiliates of U.S. companies abroad had sales of $1,195 billion in 1988.[4] This compares with U.S. exports for that year of $529.8 billion.[5] In the first half of the 1980s, though, the growth of U.S. direct foreign investment slowed considerably as a result of the 1981–1982 recession, the strength of the dollar, the increased expansion of host state regulations, and perhaps host state political instability.

The direction and composition of American direct investment have changed dramatically. As Table 4-3 shows, by 1970 Europe had become

TABLE 4-2   Total Stock of Direct Foreign Investment of U.S. Multinational Corporations, Selected Years, 1950–1990 ($ billions)

	1950	1960	1970	1980	1990
Direct foreign investment (Book value)	$11.8	$32.0	$78.1	$215.4	$421.5

Source: U.S. Congress, Senate Committee on Finance, *Implications of Multinational Firms for World Trade and Investment and for U.S. Trade and Labor*, 93rd Cong., 1st sess., 1973, p. 95; and U.S. Department of Commerce, *Survey of Current Business*, June 1991, p. 29.

[4]U.S. Department of Commerce, *U.S. Direct Investment Abroad, 1988* (Washington, D.C.: Bureau of Economic Analysis, July 1990), p. 7.

[5]This figure excludes exports of goods under U.S. military agency sales contracts.

TABLE 4-3 Geographic Breakdown of U.S. Direct Investment Abroad, Selected Years, 1950–1990 ($ billions and percentages)

	1950 Amount	1950 % of Total	1960 Amount	1960 % of Total	1970 Amount	1970 % of Total	1980 Amount	1980 % of Total	1990 Amount	1990 % of Total
Total developed areas	$ 5.7	48%	$19.6	61%	$53.2	68%	$157.1	74%	$312.2	74%
Canada	3.6	31	11.2	35	22.8	29	44.6	21	68.4	16
Europe	1.7	14	6.7	21	24.5	31	95.7	45	204.2	48
Others	0.4	3	1.7	5	5.9	8	16.8	8	39.6	9
Total less developed areas	4.4	37	10.9	34	21.3	27	52.7	25	105.7	25
Unallocated	1.7	14	1.5	5	3.6	5	3.7	2	3.6	1
Total	$11.8	99%	$32.0	100%	$78.1	100%	$213.5	100%	$421.5	100%

Source: U.S. Congress, Senate Committee on Finance, *Implications of Multinational Firms for World Trade and Investment and for U.S. Trade and Labor*, 93rd Cong., 1st sess., 1973, p. 72. The 1980 and 1985 figures are from the U.S. Department of Commerce, *Survey of Current Business*, August 1981, pp. 21–22; June 1986, p. 31; and June 1991, p. 29.

the most important area for the operations of American multinational corporations; Latin America and the developing countries have become relatively less important. This same pattern is descriptive of foreign investment from all capital-exporting countries.

At the same time, in the 1970s and 1980s, the size of the U.S. market, its political stability, and the more aggressive expansion of non-American enterprises led to a rapid inflow of foreign investment into the United States in spite of the high value of the dollar during part of this period. From 1973 to 1990, foreign direct investment in the United States increased from $20.5 billion to $403.7 billion.[6] There is already more direct foreign investment in the United States than in any other country. The leading sources of foreign direct investment in the United States, by country of origin, are the United Kingdom, Japan, the Netherlands, Canada, Germany, and Switzerland respectively, and these nations account for more than 80 percent of the total.[7]

The composition of U.S. investment abroad has also changed. During the 1960s and thereafter, American firms invested much more heavily in manufacturing facilities than in petroleum operations. By 1990, 40 percent of U.S. direct foreign investment was in manufacturing industries, compared with 35 percent in 1960. From 1960 to 1990, the share of investment in petroleum industries decreased from 43 percent to 14 percent. Investment in other sorts of economic activity, such as service industries and financial institutions, accounted for 46 percent of all American direct foreign investment by 1990.[8]

These figures convey several important points. First, American and non-American direct foreign investment and multinational corporations have expanded so rapidly within the last three decades that they now account for a major part of international economic activity. Furthermore, although they do have predecessors, their size and growth make them essentially a new international economic institution. Third, the patterns of international business activity are changing. Direct foreign investment, including that from the United States, is more likely to be a manufacturing or service industry located in other advanced industrial states than an extractive industry located in developing countries. Fourth, direct foreign investment is a global phenomenon with companies from advanced industrial states and developing countries investing across borders. The United States, the world's largest exporter of direct foreign investment, is also the largest recipient of such investment from other countries.

[6]U.S. Department of Commerce, *Survey of Current Business*, June 1991, p. 28.
[7]Ibid., p. 32.
[8]U.S. Department of Commerce, *Survey of Current Business*, June 1991, p. 29.

THE NATURE OF MULTINATIONAL CORPORATIONS AND DISTINCTIONS AMONG THEM

What is a multinational corporation? The definitions vary. Some are broad ("all firms—industrial, service, and financial—doing international business of all types, within a myriad of organizational structures"[9]); others are narrower, based on size, extensiveness of operations in foreign countries, type of business, and organizational structure and managerial orientation. The difficulty in arriving at a widely accepted definition is that various parties, such as government officials, international executives, and scholars, all have different interests and purposes in their analyses of multinational corporations. Consequently, their definitions vary. For instance, the Harvard Business School Multinational Enterprise Project was interested primarily in studying large international firms appearing in *Fortune*'s 500 with each firm having operations in no fewer than six different countries.[10] However, government officials in a developing country may be faced with unemployment resulting from the closure of a subsidiary of a rather small foreign-owned firm with operating facilities in only two or three countries. In this case, the international character of the corporation is as real and as disconcerting as if the corporation were among the one hundred largest manufacturing firms and had facilities in many areas of the world.

Our objective is to examine the political implications, both national and international, of these firms as important actors in the international arena. Consequently, a broad rather than a narrow definition seems more appropriate for our purposes—although finer distinctions will be drawn shortly. Multinational corporations are those economic enterprises—manufacturing, extractive, service, and financial—that are headquartered in one country and that pursue business activities in one or more foreign countries. We are concerned with direct investment that is central to the business of the firm—not portfolio investment. Using these criteria, there are well over 10,000 multinational corporations with the developing countries of India, South Korea, Taiwan, Singapore, and Brazil among others adding to the numbers from the advanced industrial states. These more than 10,000 firms have de facto control over 90,000 subsidiaries.[11]

Although this definition is useful for incorporating the many variations found in this class of actors, it is too broad to allow more precise statements of relationship and analysis. For instance, questions regarding the impact of multinational corporations on host states or the importance of foreign operations to corporations cannot be answered in the general terms we used earlier. Instead, distinctions must be made among different types of multinational enterprises to determine their effect on host states. To indicate the great diversity of multinational corporations, a number of important factors will be examined. The behavior, impact, and conse-

---

[9]U.S. Congress, Senate Committee on Finance, *Implications of Multinational Firms for World Trade and Investment and for U.S. Trade and Labor*, 93rd Cong., 1st sess., 1973, p. 83.

[10]Ibid., p. 83.

[11]U.S. Department of Commerce, *International Direct Investment*, 1988, p. 2.

quences of corporate activities will vary with the specific set of characteristics used to describe the enterprise.

Some multinational corporations are gigantic. Others are rather small. Some are household names like IBM and Coca-Cola. Others are small firms occupying special niche markets. Based on 1978 data, 16,761 affiliates of U.S. companies are estimated to be abroad.[12] Worldwide, it has been estimated that the largest 500 multinationals control about 80 percent of the subsidiaries and their production.[13] Even though these figures are approximate, they do suggest that, although there are many foreign subsidiaries that interact with host state governments, society, and culture, no more than several hundred of them—large and well-known firms—dominate American foreign investment activity. The size and consequent visibility of these American firms make them particularly important domestic and international economic actors. On the other hand, the many smaller and often less sophisticated firms may themselves act in a fashion that poisons the atmosphere for all foreign investment. In 1978 a small subsidiary of Raytheon in Belgium engaged in behavior that mobilized European unions and governments to press the Organization for Economic Cooperation and Development (OECD) to monitor general corporate adherence to its guidelines for multinational corporations. Moreover, the guidelines were incorporated into the national laws of Belgium and several other countries.

The size of a corporation's international component relative to its overall operations is another important distinguishing characteristic. For some firms, such as Pfizer and IBM, international (non-U.S.) activities may account for nearly 50 percent or more of their sales or profits, but for many other corporations international operations constitute a minor part of their business. Generally, it is likely that those firms whose international activities are quite large and critical will seek actively to secure a favorable environment for these activities in host and parent states and at regional and international levels. Foreign investment is fundamental and important to their business success, but such investment may be of marginal concern to other companies involved less internationally. However, the growing globalization of national economies and the internationalization of business activity have forced many companies to become international themselves in order to remain competitive. For many firms international operations are no longer just attractive opportunities but have become essential for their very survival at home as well as abroad.

A related factor serving to differentiate types of firms is the number of countries in which a firm's subsidiaries are located. The extent to which a specific firm's activities are located around the world may reflect its commitment to international business. It may also indicate a conscious effort to decentralize and thus make its international activities less vulnerable politically and economically. Firms with subsidiaries in only a few countries may just be beginning their international efforts, or they may

[12]U.S. Department of Commerce, *U.S. Direct Investment Abroad, 1987*, July 1990, Table 2.

[13]U.S. Department of Commerce, *International Direct Investment*, 1984, p. 2.

merely be doing business where critical natural resources can be found, or they may centralize production to serve business activities throughout the world. Simple conclusions cannot be drawn from the extent of a firm's activities throughout the world.

The nature of the corporation's business is a fourth type of distinction that must be made among multinational firms. A partial list of the different types of businesses conducted on an international scale is presented in Figure 4-1. There is frequently a significant difference between the behavior and impact of an extractive type of multinational corporation, that of a capital goods enterprise, and the activities of a consumer products manufacturing concern. From the perspective of the host state, the costs and benefits of each type of firm are quite different. For example, host states may tend to view direct foreign investment in extractive industries as more exploitative than investment in manufacturing,[14] but on the other hand, an extractive investment may generate vast amounts of capital for the host state while tapping expensive-to-mine natural resources. On issues such as employment, technological transfers, taxes and other revenues, and balance-of-payment matters, a host state's evaluation of a foreign firm varies with the specific character of the firm and also with its own set of values and national priorities. Even within the category of extractive industries, important differences exist in the relative bargaining strengths of firms in various industries, implying that there will be differences among the political and economic relations between host states and the multinationals.[15]

Another characteristic distinguishing multinational corporations is the

FIGURE 4-1   Types of Business Activities Pursued by Multinational Corporations

1. Extractive
   Petroleum (Exxon)
   Mining (Broken Hill Proprietary Co. Ltd.)
   Lumber (Weyerhaeuser)
2. Agriculture (H.J. Heinz)
3. Industrial
   Capital goods (Caterpillar Tractor)
   Intermediate goods (Ford)
   Consumer goods (Johnson & Johnson)
4. Service
   Transportation (American Airlines)
   Public utilities (GTE)
   Wholesaling and retailing (Sears)
   Tourism (Holiday Inns)
   Insurance (INA)
   Advertising (The Interpublic Group)
   Management services (McKinsey and Co.)
5. Financial Institutions
   Banking (Citicorp)
   Investing (Merrill Lynch)
6. Conglomerate (IT&T)

Note: The companies in parentheses are examples of the types of firms. However, many of these firms engage in numerous kinds of business activities and, thus, might be found in several of these categories.

[14]See the discussion of nationalization in Chapter 7.

[15]Raymond Vernon, *Sovereignty at Bay* (New York: Basic Books, 1971), Chap. 2.

pattern of ownership linking the parent firm with its subsidiaries. Multinational corporations may have wholly owned subsidiaries or they may share ownership, to varying degrees, with joint venture partners of different types. The host country partner of a majority- or minority-owned investment may vary widely. Three of the more likely partners are private entrepreneurs, individual stockholders, and host government or quasi-governmental agencies. There are a number of other types of possible partners in joint venture arrangements, but the main point is that corporate practices and objectives as well as the response of host state government officials and other interest groups may differ with the specific nature of the joint venture relationship. For example, some corporations may feel that a joint venture with a host state government agency may reduce the chances of nationalization,[16] but the price may be constant governmental meddling.

During the 1980s, there has been extensive cross-border purchasing of major companies. In the United States, such well-known firms as Pillsbury, CBS Records, Bloomingdale's, and Firestone Tire and Rubber Company have been purchased by non-American companies. In the reverse direction, Ford owns 25 percent of Mazda, and General Electric purchased a major Hungarian manufacturer of electrical goods.

Of the other factors that are useful in attempting to differentiate among types of multinational enterprises, two of the most important are organizational structure and managerial orientation. A number of schema have been developed by students of multinational corporations to describe these aspects of international firms, and although they differ in the terms they use, they are basically quite similar.[17] Several general types of organizational forms are examined in the paragraphs that follow, but it must be recognized that they are only archetypes; any specific firm is likely to incorporate attributes from more than one of these models. The value in making these distinctions is the help they provide in analyzing the relationship between the multinational and the host state.

The parent-dominant, subsidiary-subservient type of enterprise is organized in such a way as to ensure that its international activities enhance the efforts of the firm in its major market in the parent country. Organizationally, the international operations are subordinate to the objectives, standards, and actions of the domestic business of the headquarters. Similarly, management orientation is that of the parent company and parent country. As Howard Perlmutter[18] has termed it, management is *ethnocentric* regarding goals, frames of reference, perspectives, and nationality. The prevailing view in this type of organization is that what is good and appropriate for the parent firm is paramount, and the efforts of the foreign

---

[16]Stephen Kobrin has suggested that having a joint venture arrangement with a host government agency is not a safeguard against nationalization. Stephen J. Kobrin, "Foreign Enterprise and Forced Divestment in the LDCs," *International Organization*, 34 (Winter 1980), 65–80.

[17]See Howard V. Perlmutter, "The Tortuous Evolution of the Multinational Corporation," *Columbia Journal of World Business*, 3 (January–February 1969), 9–18.

[18]Ibid.

subsidiaries should support and supplement the business in the parent country. This type of enterprise tends to emphasize differences between the multinational corporation and the host state, for host state objectives, practices, and standards are clearly secondary to those developed by the parent company.

A second type of multinational enterprise structure and orientation can be likened to an international holding company in which the various subsidiaries operate with a high degree of autonomy. In this, the subsidiary-independent form of organization, the parent company has very little to do with either the goal-setting or operational phases of the subsidiaries' business. Local managers, most likely citizens of the host country, determine their own objectives, standards, and ways of doing things with little interference from or reference to the headquarters. In this type of arrangement, clashes between host states and the international enterprise are less likely to occur, since the subsidiaries are very similar to local firms. The international nature of the subsidiary-independent type of corporation is primarily in the area of ownership, not in the area of control.

The third type of multinational organization, the integrated international enterprise, is quite different from the other two in that the parent company's operations as well as the subsidiaries' are incorporated into an overall managerial effort. The enterprise is organized in such a fashion as to advance regional or global objectives and activities; no particular nationality, whether parent or host country, prevails. Instead, corporate goals, corporate standards of performance, and corporate practices dominate. Decentralization of management occurs but only within the framework of an integrated, centrally directed effort aimed at maximizing broad-scale corporate objectives. In this structure, the potential for clashes with state interests is great, but the source of such conflict comes from the truly international or a-national character of the firm, not, as in the first archetype, from its foreign, ethnocentric character. Interestingly, operations in the parent state have almost the same status as those in host states. They are judged in terms of their contributions to the overall objectives of the company. If production costs are too high and not competitive, the operation may be closed down and moved to another country where conditions are more favorable, or the product may be bought from a foreign manufacturer.

Increasingly, multinational enterprises are tending to take on the characteristics of this third type of organization. The more progressive and successful U.S. multinationals are consciously attempting to develop a worldwide approach to business, in terms of organization, management orientation, and the substance of their business activity. W. J. Barnholdt, vice president of Caterpillar Tractor Corporation, described this type of enterprise in a speech in the early 1970s:

> Caterpillar is owned by approximately 48,000 shareholders and our stock is traded on exchanges in the United States, France, England, Scotland, West Germany, Switzerland, and Belgium. We have 65,000 employees, 22 percent of whom work abroad. We are a multinational company, treating

foreign operators as co-equal with domestic, in both structure and policy, willing to allocate resources without regard to national frontiers.

We will one day become a transnational company—a multinational business managed and owned by people of different nationalities—through current programs aimed at developing more top managers of different national origins and greater ownership by investors outside the U.S. Thus, while we export from the U.S., our views as to transportation, markets, and product are worldwide. For example, there is no U.S.-made Caterpillar tractor. A Caterpillar product—wherever it is built—is just that—a Caterpillar product—graphic evidence that people of different national origins and political interest can achieve common objectives.[19]

While this sounded quite revolutionary in 1973, this is the goal of those companies that want to thrive in the current era of global competition.

What this means is that the activities of the enterprise are integrated on a regional or global scale. This type of firm is particularly sensitive to political and economic developments in various states and in the global economy, and through its worldwide orientation it seeks to capitalize on international economic interdependencies. Thus, for instance, capital needed for new investment or expansion is secured wherever the most favorable terms exist. Similarly, marketing strategies are integrated and coordinated in such a fashion as to take advantage of spillover advertising and similar markets. Of course, to the extent feasible, production is also integrated. Major breakthroughs in superconductivity were achieved in a small IBM research laboratory in Switzerland.

The international nature of production is illustrated by a map that depicts General Motors' "J" car global assembly lines and product sourcing (Figure 4-2).

Although most multinational corporations are variants of one of the three archetypes discussed, other ideal types have been suggested. One proposes the existence of a supranational corporation that is truly non-national in that its ownership, board of directors, management, and orientation are not dominated by one nationality. Such an enterprise would be chartered by, and pay taxes to, an international body on the order of a GATT or an IMF established precisely for this purpose.

Richard Robinson describes another type of organization, the transnational association, that a number of Japanese firms have adopted.[20] It is not like the forms of foreign investment already described, but it is a mechanism, he thinks, that might allow transnational business activity without severely threatening the sovereignty of states. Under this structure, the headquarters has little or no equity investment in the "subsidiaries" located in various countries. Instead, the "subsidiaries" are locally owned and managed, but they receive extensive managerial and technological assistance

---

[19]Quoted in *U.S. Multinationals: The Dimming of America,* a report prepared for the AFL-CIO Maritime Trades Department, Executive Board Meeting, February 15–16, 1973, p. 12.

[20]Richard Robinson, "Beyond the Multinational Corporation," in *International Business-Government Affairs,* ed. John Fayerweather (Cambridge, Mass.: Ballinger, 1973), pp. 17–26.

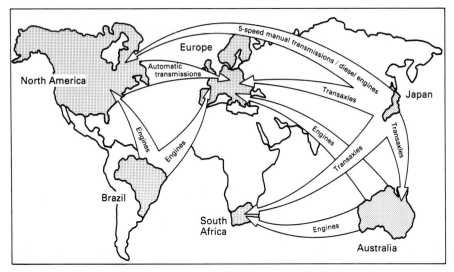

FIGURE 4-2   The J Car's Global Assembly Lines.
Source: *World Business Weekly*, September 14, 1981, p. 22. Reprinted with permission of the Financial Times of London.

from the headquarters. In addition, most or all of the production of the "subsidiaries" is sold contractually to the headquarters, which then serves in some cases as the assembler and, most important, as the international marketer and distributor for the association. The central headquarters still plays a dominant role in the integration of production and marketing, but its role as owner and as "subsidiary" manager is for the most part eliminated.

One cannot predict with certainty how foreign investment will evolve, but it is clear that a global perspective is necessary for competitive success. Further, as the international political economy becomes more open and interdependent, corporations of many types will organize to take advantage of expanded opportunities. Recently, there has been significant growth in strategic alliances among firms from different countries which join together to pursue specific markets with the enhanced technological, production, and marketing strength of the combined effort.

The wide variation among multinational corporations has been demonstrated in this discussion. However, the characteristics of different types of multinational corporations may appear in combination in a single corporation. For instance, the same firm may contain an extractive subsidiary that is wholly owned and that is treated in an ethnocentric fashion and a majority-owned subsidiary that is involved in the production of intermediate goods and that is linked closely with operations in other countries. Thus, it may be inappropriate to generalize from an overall pattern describing the enterprise as a whole to the specific cases of individual subsidiaries and vice versa. As a result, assessments or predictions about the nature of the relationships between the host country and the multinational corporation depend very much on the specific characteristics of the subsidiaries as well as of the corporation as a whole.

MOTIVATIONS FOR CORPORATE INTERNATIONAL EXPANSION

Both corporate apologists and radical critics agree that corporations expand internationally for sound economic and business reasons from the capitalist's self-interested point of view. Certainly these two groups differ as to the legitimacy of the capitalist perspective and, therefore, the impact of foreign investments. Despite this difference of opinion, both groups recognize a number of motivations for domestic firms to become international corporations. As we just indicated, however, distinctions need to be made among various types of multinational enterprises.

Extractive industries have traditionally been international in scope because they depend upon the location of fuel, mineral, or other raw material deposits. Consequently, even if domestic supplies exist, extractive firms must seek foreign sources of supply to supplement or substitute for domestic sites that are drying up or are too expensive to operate. Moreover, control over foreign resource supplies serves as a hedge against disruptions in supply or as a preemptive maneuver designed to deny existing or potential competitors access to the same source.

Manufacturing corporations establish foreign subsidiaries for quite different reasons. If the firm has obtained foreign markets through the export process, it is possible that increasing costs of production and transportation will lead the firm to serve these same markets more profitably through local manufacturing facilities. Establishing a local subsidiary also eases servicing problems and allows for greater adaptation of the product to local conditions and desires. The possibility of losing a market to either local or international competition also stimulates corporations to establish foreign subsidiaries, sometimes in anticipation of a future market developing. Also, investing in the parent country of an international competitor may cause the latter to redirect its energies away from international expansion to protect its home country market. This is one of the reasons why U.S. companies have been so insistent that they be allowed to operate freely within Japan. Furthermore, tariff and other trade barriers raise the cost of exporting to the protected market, and local subsidiaries constitute an effective mechanism to circumvent these barriers and maintain or increase market share. The European Common Market's external tariff was a major reason for the explosive growth of U.S. direct foreign investment in Europe in the 1960s. The fear of a similar situation in Europe as a result of 1992 is leading to an expansion of foreign investment in those countries in preparation for the more unified Common Market.

A quite different stimulus to establish manufacturing subsidiaries abroad is the practice by many states of offering substantial investment incentives that are designed explicitly to attract foreign investment to depressed areas. Tax holidays, cash grants, the training of a local work force, and the provision of land and buildings are a few of the many ways by which host countries attempt to draw foreign investors. Often, actual cash grants are made to foreign investors. Canada provided IBM with a $6 million nonrepayable grant for the purpose of establishing a large computer facility in a depressed area of Quebec. Volkswagen received a set of incentives amounting to $58 million from Pennsylvania's government to establish its assembly facility near Pittsburgh, a plant that has subsequently ceased production.

Such efforts are duplicated many times over by most of the countries of the world, and they serve to emphasize the fact that multinational corporations are often pulled into specific foreign investments by the actions of host governments. Similarly, host country requirements sometimes force foreign companies to invest locally. Local content requirements that insist that a certain percentage of the product be produced locally lead to direct investment as opposed to exports from the home country. This image is quite different from that of the corporation forcing itself upon an unwilling host state.

Furthermore, parent country policies may foster the development of foreign subsidiaries. For example, the U.S. government's tax credit and deferral policies stimulated massive investment abroad by American firms. In response to fuel and natural resource shortages, the Japanese government urged Japanese firms to find new sources of supplies in other countries.

Of course, many manufacturing concerns become international because of the existence of a substantial and growing overseas market, which offers excellent earnings prospects. The huge expansion of American investment in manufacturing in Europe during the 1960s reflected, among other things, the wealth, size, and stability of the market available in an economically healthy Europe. The attractiveness of the reduced trade barriers and the large market offered by the 1992 European Economic Community are critical to the expansion of foreign investment there. Conversely, the inconvertibility of the Soviet ruble has severely impeded international economic transactions, including foreign investment.

Additionally, the increasingly competitive and saturated markets at home have led dynamic firms to look to other countries as a place for new profit and growth opportunities, for the effective utilization of restive management talent in new and challenging areas, and for a method by which headquarters' overhead costs could be shared over a larger base. Raymond Vernon and his colleagues at Harvard summarized many of these motivations in the concept of the product cycle, wherein the firm facing a decline in its technological advantage in the parent country market essentially exports this advantage to foreign countries through the vehicle of foreign subsidiaries.[21]

These reasons for corporate international expansion do not suggest a conspiracy among capitalists to dominate the world. Rather, they suggest a rational response, from the capitalist perspective, to opportunities for the

---

[21]Vernon, *Sovereignty at Bay*, pp. 65–77.

pursuit of business activities in other countries and globally. Business executives as well as most radical critics would agree that the development of multinational corporations is a logical and rational step in the evolution of capitalism.[22] Indeed, some of the largest European-based multinationals like Renault have been fully or partially state-owned, indicating that the drive for foreign investment may be a phenomenon of business, not necessarily private capitalism.

The growth and development of the more highly integrated and managerially sophisticated multinational corporations are due to additional motivations. Business operations with a regional or global orientation can integrate, finance, produce, and market in a fashion that maximizes the ability of the firm to take advantage of different costs and investment climates around the world. New developments in communications and transportation systems and important improvements in management practices have greatly facilitated the task of managing these complex international enterprises.

For example, some American-based multinational firms have shifted production away from the well-organized labor force and the high production costs in the more developed countries to the developing countries. Much of the small appliance manufacturing of U.S. companies occurs in other countries, and VCRs are just not made in the United States. Similar developments are occurring in European and Japanese firms as they face rising labor and production costs in their home countries. Foreign manufacturing may be necessary to stay competitive on a worldwide basis. Interestingly, many of these firms are establishing investments in the United States to take advantage of reduced labor costs and to avoid U.S. barriers to imports. As the international economic system becomes more open, firms are taking advantage of opportunities throughout the world. For some companies, the perspective is not doing business abroad but rather how can we be most competitive by using the world as the base of our operations.

Corporations, banks, and other firms involved in service activities tend to expand overseas because of their need to provide services on an international scale to their multinational clients. U.S. banking, consulting, and advertising firms become international because their customers in the United States were multinational. Most assuredly, the reasoning goes, if one firm in a particular service sector failed to provide these necesssary facilities and processes for its clients, competitors would do so on the international level and might, in that fashion, eventually capture the huge domestic business of serving such firms. Again, the logic and reasonableness of the growth of multinational enterprises are inescapable if the basic premises of capitalism are accepted.

Radical critics, while recognizing this logic, do not accept the premises of capitalism as an appropriate basis for organizing the economy and society, at either the national or international levels. Thus, although the

---

[22]We have not examined, and will only mention here, the traditional Leninist argument that the expansion of foreign investment is the result of the need to find an outlet for surplus investment capital.

growth of multinational corporations may logically follow from capitalism, neo-Marxist critics focus on the social costs and economic exploitation of such firms, and of capitalism in general, for parent and host states as well as for the international system. They view the transcendence of capitalism, either in parent states or in host states (according to *dependencia* theorists) as the only sure way in which to control multinational corporations. On the other hand, classical liberal theorists typically stress that the benefits of direct foreign investment outweigh some of its admittedly negative aspects. They feel that the problems associated with foreign investment can be alleviated or eliminated through more sensitive state and corporate policies.

THE IMPACT OF THE MULTINATIONAL CORPORATION: SOURCE OF CONFLICT OR AGENT OF GROWTH?

Various domestic groups and policymakers within both parent and host states are likely to react differently to multinational corporations. Those with a particularly strong ideological commitment will see either great benefit or great harm resulting from the actions of these enterprises; most, however, will observe a mixture of effects, and policy debates and policy prescriptions will thereby reflect a mélange of promotion and restriction. Different postures that might be adopted by host and parent governments or by regional and international organizations will be examined in the paragraphs that follow, but before doing so, let us examine the complaints and praises stimulated by the existence of multinational enterprises.

Host States' Concerns

Countries, especially developing countries, that serve as hosts to extractive industries frequently charge the extractive subsidiary with "stealing" its precious natural resources—the petroleum, copper, bauxite, or whatever is deemed to be a national resource—and point to the significant profits being obtained from this source of national wealth by multinational enterprises. Furthermore, such firms often exist in enclave-type surroundings and have few meaningful links to the local economy. The product is exported; the management is foreign; the benefits accrue primarily to the foreign firm and foreign societies. Moreover, because of the importance of the natural resource, the foreign firm and the parent government are often thought to collaborate and sometimes interfere in order to protect the investment from local political and social disturbances. In sum, the allegation is that the large and wealthy foreign firm—supported by a powerful, and probably imperialistic, parent government—is exploiting a relatively weak, underdeveloped host state, which seeks to obtain a reasonable return on its natural resource while trying to maintain its national sovereignty and pride.

This somewhat exaggerated view of the negative aspects of international firms engaged in extractive operations is not nearly as appropriate for multinational manufacturing companies. Manufacturing firms are much more integrated with host state societies and economies. In many cases, the extractive operation seems to be almost a wholly foreign enterprise with the exception of local workers and the location of the facility. Foreign-owned manufacturing subsidiaries, in contrast, become very much a part of the local scene. For example, they are likely to have local business supporters as well as domestic business enemies. Often, the products are consumed locally, a situation that is aided by massive advertising campaigns designed to increase consumer awareness and a predisposition toward the product. The plants tend to be located in the more heavily settled areas of the country unlike the often isolated sites of extractive facilities. Frequently, they are major exporters of new technology. Generally speaking, manufacturing enterprises are more pervasive (though not necessarily more important) in the host state environment than are extractive operations. The charges leveled against such firms are particularly important because of the extent of international manufacturing, because of its growth, and because of the acute concern that has been expressed in advanced industrial states as well as in the developing countries.

Many host states fear that the size and wealth of multinational corporations, whether extractive or manufacturing, will dominate their economies. One frequently sees lists that rank states according to GNP and size of central government budgets in relation to sales figures of the largest multinational corporations.[23] Leading firms have sales figures larger than the GNPs of most states, even some that are industrialized. Such comparisons are designed to indicate the huge power of multinational corporations. Aggregate data of this sort do support fears that multinational corporations have the size and strength to dominate weaker states. But, in reality, such lists are deceptive. There is often an erroneous implication that General Motors, for example, would marshal all its resources to influence or overwhelm a state like Belgium.

A more specific concern is that, within a particular state, foreign investment may dominate the most profitable, the most technologically advanced, the most growth-oriented, and the economic trend-setting industries. Studies have shown that American multinationals tend to invest in the most profitable host state industries and then to be even more profitable than their local competitors. As a result, host states (even if highly industrialized) perceive that important segments of their economy are increasingly subject to the control of multinational companies rather than national firms.

In addition, some argue that, almost by definition, the control of multinational corporations resides in the hands of executives whose loyalties are to the foreign-based corporation and probably the parent country. Critical decisions are thought to be made at headquarters in foreign countries, which makes host country efforts to influence those decisions very difficult. The combination of foreign ownership and ultimately foreign management control leaves host country nationals feeling powerless to affect those decisions with substantial impact for the host state. This view

[23]An example of such a list can be found in Charles Kegley and Eugene Wittkopf, *World Politics: Trend and Transformation*, 2nd ed. (New York: St. Martin's Press, 1985), pp. 152–53.

is being advanced by many in the United States who see major U.S. communications firms and much valuable downtown real estate in key cities being purchased by foreign investors.

Host states at all levels of industrialization also fear that these circumstances will produce technological dependence upon the United States or other technologically active parent states, such as Japan. The charge is often made that the headquarters company and country will become technological innovators while the rest of the world becomes little more than technology consumers or technological colonies.[24] In the pharmaceutical, synthetic fiber, and chemical industries in Colombia, Constantine Vaitsos found that a mere 10 percent of the patent holders (all of which were multinational enterprises) owned 60 percent of all patents in these industries.[25] When this situation occurs, there is a fear that host state industry will be stunted and that the multinational corporation will be able to extract enormous profits through license fees and royalties. This process is advanced by the centralization of research and development activity in the parent state of most multinational enterprises and by the brain drain in terms either of the emigration of scientists to the United States or of their working for local subsidiaries of foreign firms.

Continuing with the technology theme, it is often alleged that multinational corporations charge exorbitant prices to host countries for technology that has already been developed and applied. Sometimes, it is claimed that these high prices are demanded for technology that is old and obsolete, but the company continues to reap profits at the expense of the host country. Another concern is that the technology transferred to the host country is "inappropriate." This usually means that the technology is too advanced, too expensive, and too capital-intensive for a country that desperately needs to find jobs for large numbers of unemployed and would thus need labor-intensive investment instead of capital-intensive facilities.[26]

All these factors combine to produce fears that multinational corporations will act in a fashion counter to what is perceived to be in the best interests of the host state. Failure to conform to national plans and the precedence of international or foreign business objectives over national political, economic, and social interests are especially galling and are very noticeable when committed by foreign firms.

The takeover of Chrysler-UK by Peugeot-Citroen in August 1978 created anxieties among the trade unions affected. The new owners made it clear that no ironclad guarantees of continued employment of the work force could be made, but, in addition, Peugeot appeared to be more interested in launching its new cars than in committing itself to the preservation of the U.K. facilities and jobs. Efforts by foreign airlines (KLM and British Airways) to buy a significant number of shares in the parent com-

---

[24]See Chapter 6 for a more comprehensive discussion of technological gaps in the international political economy.

[25]Constantine V. Vaitsos, "Patents Revisited," *The Journal of Development Studies*, 29 (1973), 12.

[26]The major issue of the transfer of technology will be discussed in greater length in Chapter 6.

panies of Northwest Airlines and United Airlines led to intervention by the U.S. Department of Transportation to prevent these purchases. These instances illustrate that sometimes multinational corporations act in ways that are considered inappropriate, clumsy, and alien by elements of the host state, including government officials.

Problems associated with controlling the activities of American multinational enterprises are heightened by the influence of the U.S. government (or any other parent state) over corporate policies. American antitrust policies may prevent a merger between the foreign subsidiary of an American firm and a host country enterprise, even when the merger is expressly desired by the host government. Provisions concerning trade with the enemy, which are applicable to the foreign subsidiaries as well as the headquarters of American firms, have prohibited trade with some Communist states. In 1968, for example, a Belgian subsidiary of an American multinational was prevented by the U.S. Treasury Department from exporting farm equipment to Cuba even though the contract had been signed by the Belgian national firm prior to its takeover by an American multinational. U.S.-imposed technology embargoes against the Soviet Union after the shooting down of a Korean airplane affected French subsidiaries of U.S. firms as well. There are many such instances. Host state resentment of these extraterritorial extensions of parent state policies are supplemented by fears that foreign subsidiaries may seek support from the government of the parent country in their disputes with the host state. The concerns of Latin American states in this regard are well-known.[27] In Asia, many countries have similar fears about Japanese foreign investments, and the French government has come to the aid of French firms in trouble with the governments of former French colonies in Africa. In addition, there is concern that multinational firms will engage in political meddling to establish a favorable investment climate. United Fruit in Guatemala, IT&T in Chile, and the corporate bribery cases in the late 1970s represent attempts by foreign firms to influence not only government policies but also the very structure of government in host countries.

Host governments are also interested in the impact of multinational corporations on their balance-of-payments position. Critics of these enterprises claim that they generally contribute to a deficit, in that they take more international currency out of the country than they bring in. It is sometimes claimed that negative items (repatriated earnings, charges for royalties, interest, licenses, and various management services, and expenses incurred by importing necessary equipment and component products) far outweigh positive items (the inflow of the new capital, savings resulting from import substitution, and earnings gained through exports) in the balance-of-payments accounts. Analyses of the impact of multinational corporations need to be conducted on a case-by-case basis, but in the aggregate critics can point to official U.S. government statistics showing that American

---

[27]Many Latin American countries have incorporated variants of the Calvo doctrine in their investment laws. This doctrine suggests that foreign enterprises cannot legally turn to their parent governments for protection since they are subject to the laws and legal procedures of the host state.

multinational enterprises make a substantial positive contribution to the parent country's balance of payments. For example, the Department of Commerce statistics for 1989 indicate that income from American direct investment abroad was $53.6 billion, whereas the outflow of capital funds was $31.7 billion.[28] This net positive contribution to the United States must, of course, be balanced by a negative effect on the payments position of some host states.[29]

One difficulty faced by host states in their dealings with multinational corporations involves the problem of obtaining accurate information about the firms' activities. Information disclosure about financial transactions, transfer pricing, payments for licenses and royalties, and profit earned is necessary for the development of policies by host countries, but often, because of corporate concern about secrecy and consolidated accounts, such information is not readily available. Consequently, there is the suspicion that multinationals are able to hide behind financial complexities and manipulations to avoid their fair share of taxes.

Depending upon their nature and pervasiveness, multinational manufacturing enterprises may also be accused of undermining the culture and national identity of host states. Jean-Jacques Servan-Schreiber's best seller, *The American Challenge*, was an early plea for Europeans to counteract this challenge so that European economic, political, technological, and cultural independence could be preserved. Periodically, similar concerns are expressed when foreign firms take over a visible domestic enterprise. To the extent that multinational firms threaten cultural identity, some host states will become quite concerned. Recently, takeovers of CBS Records and MCA by Japanese firms have raised the specter of Japanese control of major cultural institutions in the United States. Because of the many linkages between manufacturing subsidiaries and the host state society, the foreign agent-of-change nature of the enterprise may be considered quite threatening. The same effect is somewhat less likely for extractive industries since they rarely are as closely integrated into the host country environment.

Another factor that frightens host state governments, and particularly labor officials, is the mobility and flexibility of the corporation, as opposed to the immobility of the state and its work force. In certain instances, multinational enterprises must be able to leave states in which the investment climate has become less satisfactory, for whatever reason. As a result, states compete with one another by offering more attractive incentives to foreign industry, and companies can play one state against another in pursuit of the more ideal opportunity. An interesting example of this, involving the work force, occurred in Europe when a European multinational firm told its employees in the Netherlands that they would have to

[28]U.S. Department of Commerce, *Survey of Current Business*, August 1990, pp. 58, 59. Of course, the effects of the import and export activities of multinational corporations must also be considered for a more accurate perspective of their impact on balance-of-payments outcomes.

[29]For an interesting assessment of the negative balance-of-payments effects of multinational corporations in Latin America, see Ronald Muller, "Poverty Is the Product," *Foreign Policy*, No. 13 (Winter 1973–1974), 71–103.

operate on three shifts since that was the only way in which the unprofitable facility could be kept open. Furthermore, the Dutch workers were told that the workers in the German subsidiary, which was also liable to being closed down, were willing to accede to management's request. The same story, but in reverse, was related to the German employees in an attempt by management to use its internationalism to coerce its employees. There are no statistics regarding the ease with which multinational enterprises can and do shut down operations in one state in favor of operations in others, but the concern about this alleged mobility is certainly real. Moreover, this mobility illustrates how multinational corporations can take advantage of and indeed manipulate the sensitivity accompanying economic interdependency among states.

Multinational enterprises are often thought to be able to use their internationalism to avoid onerous government policies. Thus, worker safety precautions, pollution control regulations, and restrictions on drugs can be circumvented by an international enterprise by locating in countries where such concerns have not become part of governmental policy.

Many of the aforementioned causes for concern at the governmental level are shared by various economic, social, and political groups within the host state. Labor has been mentioned briefly, and its interest in these issues is obvious. In addition, segments of domestic business experience conflicts of interest with multinational enterprises. Multinational firms are fierce and often successful competitors with local firms for domestic and international markets. Their large size, huge managerial and financial resources, worldwide reputation, and product recognition often mean that multinational firms can literally overwhelm local corporations. Aside from marketing competition, domestic industries frequently face severe competition from multinational firms for skilled workers, research and development scientists, effective managers, and investment capital. The larger and more successful international enterprise can frequently offer higher wages to employees and provide more attractive research facilities for scientists, and it generally sets the pattern that domestic firms must follow. In the financial arena, domestic business interests must compete with the international firms for local capital. Where investment capital is scarce, foreign firms may be using local sources of capital to the exclusion and disadvantage of local enterprises. As Servan-Schreiber plaintively cries, "we pay them to buy us."[30]

Bifurcation of the national economy and the society is one result of this ability of foreign firms to attract scarce factors of production in the host state, a result that is especially likely in the developing countries. The better paid and more skilled employees of the multinational corporations are linked to the global economic system through their employers, but an increasingly wide gap exists between their life styles and orientations and those of their compatriots who are essentially untouched by the international economy. Consequently, the state develops in an uneven fashion. A small international-oriented elite coexists with a more backward and more

[30]Jean-Jacques Servan-Schreiber, *The American Challenge* (New York: Atheneum, 1968), p. 14.

parochial majority of the population. The Brazilian census of 1980, for example, reveals a pattern of income distribution clearly indicating that the country's rich are becoming richer—a development some attributed to the explosion of foreign investment in Brazil after the 1964 military coup. Specifically, between 1970 and 1980, that portion of the population earning at least twenty times the minimum wage increased from 0.4 percent to 1.6 percent; the share of total personal income earned by this group, however, increased nearly twelvefold, from 1.6 percent to 19.1 percent.

Multinational corporations are also criticized for the introduction and aggressive marketing of products that are not necessary for the primary tasks involved in modernization and development. Such efforts draw money from social, health, and educational necessities only to contribute it to the coffers of wealthy corporations. For example, there is the feeling that it is wasteful, indeed immoral, for destitute people to be urged to purchase such things as soft drinks instead of purchasing education, nutritious food, housing, and other fundamentals of life for their young.

These complaints apply to service industries as well as to manufacturing subsidiaries. Furthermore, they are voiced by elements of advanced industrial states as well as by the developing ones, whereas the fears associated with extractive firms seem more applicable to host states that are developing countries. Regardless, within this set of grievances, ample substance and opportunity exists for the development of conflict between multinational corporations and host states over the objectives, policies, and even the existence of these firms. Tensions have risen as host states increasingly insist upon their right to exert more control over foreign investment to increase their benefits and reduce their costs. Indeed, as will be discussed later in this chapter, host states have developed and implemented a wide variety of policies that address the issues raised here.

Overall, there seem to be three major sources of conflict provoked by the existence and actions of multinational corporations in host states. First, the international corporation is a foreign entity that behaves in a fashion that is unusual, different, or wrong from the host state's point of view. Second, the corporation is often perceived as an enterprise associated closely with a foreign country—the parent state—that is able to exert its influence on the host state through the mechanism of the corporation. Third, the multinational enterprise is an international entity able to take advantage of economic interdependencies among states without itself being subject to the rules and regulations of a comparable international agency. Consequently, conflict continues between the host states, which seek to determine and control the nature of their relations with multinationals, and the corporations, which desire stability, predictability, and freedom to pursue their business in a relatively unfettered manner.

Host States' Benefits

Although host states hold substantial fears of multinational corporations, almost all countries of the world not only accept these foreign enterprises but also actively seek to attract them through an extensive array of incentives. Thus, for most states, the benefits of these corporations are worth obtaining, particularly if the negative effects of their operation can be controlled.[31]

One of the more important benefits of multinational corporations for host countries is the mobilization and productive use of investment capital. The developing countries as well as certain regional and industrial sectors of the advanced industrial states often lack the capital to develop industries that tap natural resources, provide useful products, and generate employment and income. In such cases, the mobilization of investment capital, whether it involves a substantial amount of reinvested earnings of foreign subsidiaries or the actual transfer of funds from the parent country to the host country, accelerates industrialization that cannot take place without large infusions of capital. Singapore, Taiwan, Thailand, Malaysia, and South Korea are often cited as countries that have used foreign investment and trade policies to achieve industrialization, increased export activity, and a remarkable rise in per capita income.[32]

A number of states have taken advantage of the flexibility of multinational corporations to entice them into establishing facilities in depressed areas of a country. A study released in 1973 indicated that one third of the U.S. investment in the United Kingdom was located in officially designated development areas and had created about 150,000 jobs.[33] Multinational firms are frequently more responsive to these incentives than are indigenous corporations. For example, Behrman reports that from 1959 to 1966 Belgian incentives to locate companies in depressed regions attracted three foreign-owned firms for every Belgian firm.[34] Most of the states of the United States have established specific offices to woo potential foreign investors.

Furthermore, most countries are attracted by the employment that foreign investors generate. In the United Kingdom, for instance, American subsidiaries directly employ 817,000 persons.[35] Total employment of American subsidiaries in Latin America in 1988 was 1,214,000, compared with 830,000 persons in 1957.[36] In 1988, according to a Commerce Department study, affiliates of American-owned multinational corporations employed approximately 6.4 million persons in their foreign operations on sales of $1 trillion.[37] In 1988 affiliates of non-American multinationals employed

---

[31]For an excellent and ground-breaking discussion of why host countries welcome multinational corporations, see Jack N. Behrman, *National Interests and the Multinational Enterprise* (Englewood Cliffs, N.J.: Prentice-Hall, 1970), Chap. 2.

[32]This topic is addressed at greater length in Chapter 7.

[33]Economists Advisory Group, *United States Industry in Britain* (London: The Financial Times, 1973), p. 4.

[34]Behrman, *National Interests*, p. 20.

[35]*Survey of Current Business*, June 1990, p. 38.

[36]Herbert K. May, *The Contributions of U.S. Private Investment to Latin America's Growth* (New York: The Council for Latin America, 1970), p. 19; and U.S. Department of Commerce, *Survey of Current Business*, June 1990, p. 38.

[37]Obie G. Whechard, "U.S. Multinational Companies: Operations in 1987," *Survey of Current Business*, June 1989, p. 28.

3,160,000 in the United States.[38] Japanese firms employed 284,600 Americans in 1987.[39] Moreover, none of these figures includes the secondary employment by those firms that supply these foreign-owned subsidiaries or service their employees. A study by the Mexican government revealed that, between 1965 and 1970, foreign investment generated nearly four times as much employment as did Mexican companies, although this result is probably somewhat overstated given the acquisition of Mexican firms by foreign multinationals.[40]

Host states are concerned about the effect of multinational corporations on balance-of-payments accounts, and, as we have seen, charges of decapitalization are frequently leveled as the result of the disparity between capital inflows to the host states and the outflow of funds for dividends, royalties, and various other services. Raymond Vernon suggested in a study for the United Nations that this argument is inappropriate because it fails to account for the changes that foreign investment can produce in domestic output, changes that in turn often have significant positive effects on a country's balance of payments.[41]

In addition, the manufacturing subsidiaries of multinational enterprises may provide significant benefits to the host country in terms of import substitution and export promotion. The former refers to products that the host state once imported, therefore causing a drain on its balance of payments, but now produces domestically as a result of the foreign investment. Most available data seem to indicate that the subsidiaries of multinational corporations are more effective in exporting their products, especially manufactured products, than are domestic firms. In the United Kingdom, American subsidiaries in 1988 exported 30 percent of their total output. U.S. firms exported 79 percent of their output in Ireland, 58 percent in Switzerland, and 82 percent in Singapore. In contrast, U.S.–Japanese operations exported only 18 percent of their output.[42]

Although no generally accepted conclusion can be reached with regard to the ultimate effect of multinational corporations on a host country's balance-of-payments position, the studies by Vernon, May, and John Dunning all conclude that such enterprises probably contribute to a surplus rather than a deficit in the host country. It must be understood, however, that the impact varies according to the country and the specific type of investment.

States also actively court foreign investment because of the benefits received from the transfer of technology and managerial skills. Products and processes developed elsewhere in the multinational network of the corporation are rapidly dispersed throughout the firm, thereby benefiting

---

[38]Ned G. Howenstine, "U.S. Affiliates of Foreign Companies: 1987 Benchmark Survey Results," *Survey of Current Business*, July 1, 1989, p. 116.

[39]Ibid., p. 125.

[40]As reported in *Business Latin America*, August 6, 1975, p. 256.

[41]Raymond Vernon, *Restrictive Business Practices* (New York: United Nations, 1972), p. 20.

[42]U.S. Department of Commerce, *U.S. Direct Investment Abroad, 1988*, July 1990, Table 34.

those countries (both host and parent) that are the recipients of these innovations. The computer industry is a case in point. Although quantification of the benefits of technological transfer is difficult, John Dunning reports that in 1970–1971 American subsidiaries used both labor and capital more productively than British counterparts in thirty-five of thirty-nine industries he examined. This advantage was greatest in the capital-intensive and technologically leading industries.[43] A Mexican government study revealed that in 1970 worker productivity was on the average twice as high in foreign-owned subsidiaries than in Mexican-owned facilities. Moreover, between 1962 and 1970, production in foreign-owned firms increased at a rate 60 percent higher than that of locally owned firms.[44] The flow of technology, both scientific and managerial, directly affects customers and users, and this, in conjunction with managerial innovations, stimulates domestic enterprises to improve and modernize their products and procedures to remain competitive. Thus, a frequent side benefit of foreign investment may be a general upgrading of the industrial efforts of the host country.

Host states also appreciate the fact that multinational corporations generate significant amounts of taxable income, which the state can use for its own objectives. In 1988 taxes paid to host states by nonbank foreign subsidiaries of U.S. firms amounted to $31 billion. Of this amount 25 percent was paid to the developing countries.[45]

Although many journalistic, academic, and political commentaries emphasize the negative effects of multinational firms on host states, the actions of most host state governments to attract foreign investment indicate clearly that important segments within host states perceive significant benefits from the operations of these firms. The changes in East Europe, the Soviet Union, and China have led many of these countries to seek foreign investment to revitalize their economies, provide new technologies, and stimulate domestic production. Countries want to increase the benefits, yet reduce or control the costs of foreign investments. If multinational firms were purely exploitative in their activities, they would be denied access to most countries.

Parent States' Concerns

Until the early 1970s, it was generally assumed that multinational corporations could only be an asset to their parent countries. However, beginning in 1971 American labor, led by the AFL-CIO, mounted serious legislative challenges to U.S.-based multinationals, challenges that brought to the fore a series of accusations regarding the harm caused by these firms in the parent country. Essentially, labor charged that American international firms profited from their internationalism to the detriment of the American economy and work force. The United States as a whole is not

---

[43]Economists Advisory Group, *United States Industry in Britain*, p. 6.

[44]*Business Latin America*, August 6, 1975, p. 256.

[45]U.S. Department's of Commerce, *U.S. Direct Investment Abroad, 1988*, July 1990, p. 31.

benefiting from this internationalization of production and marketing; only the corporations are. These issues motivated U.S. labor's resistance to the free trade pact with Mexico.

Of paramount importance to labor, American jobs are being exported by multinational enterprises in a number of ways, according to labor leaders. Foreign markets once served by exports from the United States are now supplied by the foreign subsidiaries of U.S. corporations, with a consequent loss of jobs for Americans. Furthermore, some American multinationals, especially in the electrical and electronic appliance fields, have shut down operations in the United States and have opened up new but similar facilities in low-wage areas of the world. The products of these foreign plants are then imported for sale in the U.S. market. This is another case in which jobs seem to have been exported to take advantage of low wages and docile labor in other countries.

Third, labor contends that multinational corporations telescope the technological transfer process so that technology, often developed with the help of federal government funds, becomes available rapidly to other countries by way of local subsidiaries or licensing agreements. Consequently, export markets are lost and so too are important numbers of American jobs as the competitive edge of technology is lost.

The question of the employment effects of multinationals is difficult to evaluate definitively, and the more useful studies clearly specify the sets of assumptions that lead to different conclusions. For example, the Tariff Commission study estimates the impact on employment varying from 1.3 million jobs lost through 1970 to a net increase of 500,000 jobs. Robert Hawkins projected the impact to range from 660,000 U.S. jobs lost to a net gain of 240,000. Frieman and Frank found a net annual loss of 120,000 to 200,000 jobs, but a majority of the workers found new jobs in seven weeks.[46] Robert Stobough and his colleagues studied nine industries and concluded that multinationals created jobs but that many of the jobs created were in the white-collar and managerial areas whereas the jobs lost came from the blue-collar ranks.[47] Of course, these estimates of aggregate impacts on U.S. employment tend to mask the fact that dislocations do occur; people do lose jobs; and families do suffer.

Although American labor has been the labor group most concerned about the job export question, several European labor movements, including those in Germany, Sweden, and the United Kingdom, have expressed similar concerns. The revaluations of the German mark and the Japanese yen in the 1970s, along with rapidly rising wage rates in these and other industrial states, resulted in a shift of production of certain goods from those countries to low-wage countries. This process has continued. This may be acceptable as long as appreciable unemployment does not exist in the parent country, but if unemployment increases, as it did in the early

[46]These studies are reported in C. Fred Bergstern, Thomas Horst, and Theodore H. Moran, *American Multinationals and American Interests* (Washington, D.C.: The Brookings Institution, 1978), pp. 102–104.

[47]Robert B. Stobough, *U.S. Multinational Enterprises and the U.S. Economy* (Cambridge, Mass.: Harvard University Press, 1972).

1980s in Europe, domestic labor has reacted as the AFL-CIO did. The British labor movement expressed serious misgivings about the job export matter, and in Sweden one regulation requires a review of the effects of outward investment plans on domestic employment. The potential seriousness of the problem is illustrated by a comparison of wage rates in developed and developing countries. In 1989, the average hourly compensation for Canadian production workers was $14.72 and $17.58 in Germany. In Brazil, the average hourly compensation was only $1.72, and $2.32 in Mexico.[48] The potential for production shifts and job exports is obvious.

American multinational corporations are also accused by the AFL-CIO of adversely affecting the American balance of payments. Markets once served by exports are now serviced by foreign subsidiaries, causing a decline in earnings from exports. Moreover, importing electrical appliances, electronic consumer goods, textiles, cars, and other products from the foreign subsidiaries of American multinationals causes an actual outflow of American funds. In addition, the tax deferral provisions of the U.S. tax code enable corporations to retain earnings abroad and avoid U.S. taxation until the profits are actually repatriated. Consequently, profits that could return to the United States and contribute to a balance-of-payments surplus are instead reinvested in other countries. Finally, the actual outflow of dollars in the form of private investment capital is a drain on the balance of payments.

Another result of the tax deferral provisions is that host countries are able to obtain tax revenue from the reinvested profits of the U.S. multinationals; until the profits are repatriated, the United States does not. The reinvested earnings of American multinationals increased from $3 billion in 1970 to $22.4 billion in 1989.[49] Also of concern is the tax credit provision that allows American firms to deduct directly from their U.S. tax bill monies paid in taxes to host countries. It should be pointed out that most of the major capital-exporting countries have tax provisions similar to the deferral and tax credit arrangements.

American multinationals have also been attacked for what is alleged to be the "ruthless" way in which their money managers brought about a series of monetary crises during the period 1971–1973 by shifting large amounts of currency from a weak dollar to stronger currencies. There was in this action little consideration of what was good for the United States. National loyalty was subordinated to what was best for the corporation. American critics of multinational firms charge that their preoccupation with more efficient and profitable operations generally makes them prone to disregard national concerns about employment, balance of payments, monetary crises, and other matters. Their internationalism allows these firms to operate above and beyond the boundaries of specific states, including their parent country. Indeed, such firms are flexible enough even to dissolve themselves legally in countries such as the United States, Canada,

---

[48]U.S. Department of Labor, Bureau of Labor Statistics, "Hourly Compensation Costs for Production Workers," telephone conversation, November 1990.

[49]U.S. Department of Commerce, *Survey of Current Business*, August 1990, p. 60.

and the United Kingdom and to establish legal residence in tax havens such as the Netherlands Antilles.

The effect of American multinational corporations on U.S. foreign policy and foreign relations is another matter of great concern. It has been charged that, because of the vast amount and wide scope of American investment abroad, the United States is obliged to protect its multinationals around the globe. The American economy has become so dependent upon foreign investment in the aggregate and upon the critical raw materials obtained by its extractive firms in the developing countries, it is alleged, that U.S. foreign policy is designed to ensure that host countries continue to be receptive to American investment. This relationship between U.S. foreign policy and U.S. foreign investment is enhanced by the links between executives of big business and the important political appointees in Washington. Both issues are discussed in subsequent chapters.[50]

Although New Left critics typically focus upon these concerns, another aspect of the relationship between corporations and foreign policy needs to be understood. The independent, insensitive, or perhaps even stupid actions of multinational corporations and their subsidiaries can seriously damage relations between the United States and host states. In such cases, the actions of the corporation are taken out of the private context in which they are often undertaken and are transferred into the public domain by elements of the host state that fail to perceive, understand, or accept the distinction between official policies and those of private international firms. When official relations are harmed by private actions, it falls to U.S. foreign policy to try to improve the relationship. Moreover, in some cases American multinational corporations appeal directly to the U.S. government for help in their conflicts with host countries. For example, they may call for the application of U.S political power through diplomacy, aid reductions, or other mechanisms by which the American government can attempt to influence other states. In these situations, the American government may be pulled into a situation not of its own doing but as a result of a multinational firm's actions. Again, the multinational corporation acts as an entity unto itself; it imposes few restraints upon itself in the form of feelings of national loyalty to any state. Yet, it sometimes demands protection by the U.S. government when it confronts trouble abroad.

There is also the danger that the parent government may attempt to use its multinational corporations as instruments of its foreign policy, thus causing conflict with the host country. For example, the U.S. government may enforce provisions of the Trading with the Enemy Act, and parent states generally may pursue other less formal actions through the multinational firm. This has already been discussed as a negative aspect of foreign investment for host states. The mere existence of American, French, or Japanese multinationals may tempt parent state government

---

[50]The question of American dependence on foreign sources of raw materials is discussed in depth in Chapter 7. The relationship between American business executives and U.S. foreign policy is examined in Chapter 8.

officials to meddle in the international affairs of host countries by means of these firms, an issue discussed in Chapter 6.

For the most part, parent country concerns about multinational corporations are caused by the fear that these firms operate largely beyond the control of the parent state. Public officials in parent states fear that, contrary to the broader interests of their nation, their government will be pushed or pulled into difficult situations by their own multinationals. Furthermore, to the extent that international businesses link the economies of the parent state and host states, these firms increase the interdependency of the parent state with other states, thereby reducing parent state autonomy. This is particularly true of natural resource companies, such as oil multinationals, where the firm may become the "captive" of the host country, with the parent state also being a prisoner of the need for a stable source of supply. Consequently, a parent state may be less able to manage either its domestic economy or its international trade and monetary policy. As a result of these concerns, particularly the feelings of helplessness, various groups in parent states are urging their governments to adopt more stringent regulations concerning the operations of their own multinationals. In many respects, these concerns of parent states are similar to those of host states; both feel that the internationalism of multinational corporations gives these firms an alien character and a flexibility that threaten national sovereignty.

Parent States' Benefits

Since the beneficial consequences of foreign investment for parent countries have been questioned seriously by the American labor movement and by other critics, supporters of these enterprises have had to develop a convincing rationale, with accompanying evidence, to counteract the charges. Several of the major arguments offered in support of multinational corporations, specifically those headquartered in the United States, will be examined here. These enterprises are said to contribute generally to a U.S. balance-of-payments surplus; their international involvement keeps U.S. enterprises competitive in both domestic and foreign markets; and their international nature fosters rather than retards employment in the United States.

A cautious and comprehensive Tariff Commission report based on 1966 and 1970 data found that American multinational corporations do, indeed, contribute to an American balance-of-payments surplus.[51] Their performance far surpasses that of the nonmultinational sectors of the economy. The outflow of funds involved in American direct foreign investment was outweighed by the returns from export activity and the income from repatriated profits, royalties, interest payments, and other fees.

Evidence gathered by the Department of Commerce suggests that multinational enterprises are particularly active exporters, especially to their own affiliates in other countries. In 1977, for example, 36 percent of

---

[51]U.S. Congress, Senate Committee on Finance, *Implications of Multinational Firms*, p. 173.

all non-agricultural U.S. exports involved the flow of goods from the American facilities of U.S.-based multinationals to their foreign subsidiaries.[52]

A corollary argument proposes that, if American firms were not multinational in scope, the overseas markets that are now filled by foreign subsidiaries with significant exports from the United States would be captured by foreign companies. Thus, it is not a question of serving a particular foreign market by either a foreign subsidiary or by increased exports from the United States. In most cases the latter alternative is not available. This is, non–U.S.-based multinationals would move into the market and take away the export option, since local facilities are often less costly in terms of production, transportation, and service costs and are more responsive to local conditions and sales opportunities. A report by Arthur Andersen & Company indicates that in 1965, 69 percent of the 100 largest industrial companies in the world were American, whereas by 1984 only 46 percent of them were.[53] Thus, supporters of the multinational corporation claim that an either/or proposition does not exist in this case. Rather, the multinational enterprise must use foreign installations to service foreign markets; otherwise the foreign market would be lost entirely to U.S. companies and their workers.

Employment is a third factor of great importance in this dialogue. U.S. multinational corporations and their supporters point to the export figures and conclude that American employment would decrease if American firms were not international in scope. Furthermore, not only do multinational enterprises export more than their strictly domestic counterparts, but their domestic investment and employment increase at a more rapid rate than do those of the purely domestic firms. The keystone of the argument is that international operations stimulate the domestic component of a business. International facilities are not a substitute for domestic production for domestic markets nor for domestic production for foreign markets. In many industries, off-shore production is essential to being competitive at home, for non-American firms have gained U.S. market share by exporting into the United States.

Quite naturally, supporters of the multinational corporation reject the charge that the activities of these firms tend to draw the United States into conflicts with host countries. Although advocates admit to a few instances of such conflict, they believe it is more often the case that the efforts of a firm to increase the benefits to parent and host states are hindered by the policies and behavior of the U.S. government. Such policies—for example, the Vietnam war, the favoritism shown the Israelis over the Arabs, the reaction to the Soviet invasion of Afghanistan, governmental concentration on human rights violations in certain South American countries under the Carter administration, and the often assertive and unilateral

---

[52]U.S. Department of Commerce, *U.S. Direct Foreign Investment Abroad*, 1977, p. 340.

[53]Arthur Andersen & Company, "U.S. Companies in International Markets—The Competition Factor in Tax Policy," before the Committee on Finance of the U.S. Senate, April 20, 1976. Also derived from *Fortune* magazine 1985 are lists of the 500 largest U.S. firms and the 500 largest foreign firms. *Fortune*, April 29, 1985, pp. 266, 268; and August 19, 1985, pp. 183, 185.

actions regarding monetary and trade matters—have all tended to make life more difficult for the multinational corporations, not the reverse.

Moreover, U.S.-based multinationals, along with their counterparts in France, Germany, the United Kingdom, and Japan, emphasize that their internationalism helps to find, mine, and then process raw materials critical to the health and welfare of the parent state economy and society. American multinational oil companies were criticized strongly in 1974 and afterward for their inability to control the source of supply of foreign crude oil and thus prices, largely as a result of the nationalizations of such sources by some OPEC countries. Similarly, manufacturing industries develop important foreign markets for the products of American or other parent state factories. Thus, the conclusion of this argument is that parent states should aid and foster their multinational enterprises because of the many positive effects of their activity. It is interesting to note regarding this issue that one of the conscious strategies adopted by advanced industrial states and many developing countries to meet the challenges of foreign investment is the development of their own multinationals. Thus, multinationals must have some benefit to parent states.

MULTINATIONAL CORPORATIONS AND CONFLICT IN INTERNATIONAL POLITICS

Thus far, we have focused on the impact of multinational corporations on host states.[54] Also important, but the subject of far less attention by both academicians and policymakers, are the effects that multinational firms may have on relations among these types of states. It is important to examine the ways in which multinational corporations, by conscious policies or by unintended effects of their actions, may contribute to the worsening of relations among these other international actors.

Relationships between parent state and host state are particularly susceptible to strain as a result of the actions of multinational enterprises. Since both states seek to utilize the international firm for their own objectives, basic questions of sovereignty and jurisdiction arise, and the corporation may be caught in the middle: Antitrust provisions, the Trading with the Enemy Act, and technology embargoes have already been mentioned

---

[54]In earlier chapters we have discussed how countries have responded to the growth of trade and the increasing importance of the international monetary system by developing the GATT and the IMF as vehicles to "manage" the international nature of these transactions. Regarding the multinational corporations, there is no comparable overarching organization to deal with the internationalization of production and marketing. Instead, a number of largely uncoordinated efforts have been made by many different organizations to control and regulate the international firm. The control efforts of some of these regional and international organizations are discussed in a subsequent section of this chapter. However, the perspective of these organizations has for the most part been to protect their members (states) in dealings with multinational corporations. Thus, the international organizations have acted largely as an extension of their member states and not so much as international political-economic actors in their own right. Even with the IMF and the GATT, little analysis has been made by academics or policymakers of the impact of multinationals on the workings of the international monetary and trade systems and their respective international organizations.

as sore points in the relationship between the United States as a parent government and other countries as host states. Questions of jurisdiction have on several occasions been raised in Canada and in other states regarding legal demands on American multinationals by the U.S. government or its courts. For example, in 1950 the provinces of Ontario and Quebec tried to prevent American subsidiaries from providing documents in compliance with U.S. court rulings by passing laws prohibiting such actions. The Canadian government also prohibited Canadian subsidiaries of U.S. firms from providing data to the U.S. government for use in possible judicial action involving the isssue of a uranium cartel. At times, diplomatic negotiations are necessary to unravel the complications resulting from jurisdictional disputes. In all such cases, the existence of the transnational corporation brought into question the fundamental issue of which political entity had jurisdiction. Such problems are inevitable for the corporations are multinational and the countries are only local. These problems will continue to plague relations between parent and host states.

The potential for conflict between host states and parent states is exacerbated by the fact that host states and parent states may have very different objectives for the same multinational enterprise and thus may clash in their attempts to achieve these objectives. Balance-of-payments policies constitute an excellent case in point. A parent state trying to correct a deficit might enact regulations designed to hasten and enlarge the repatriation of profits and management fees from the subsidiary; to hinder and restrict the outflow of new capital for investment, thereby provoking the use of local sources of funds within host states; and to expand exports from the parent company and to inhibit imports from the subsidiary. Of course, a host state troubled by a balance-of-payments deficit may institute regulations designed to produce results that are exactly the opposite of those desired by the parent state.

Similarly, parent and host states may also have different objectives about trade, domestic employment problems, currency stability and valuation, location of research and development efforts, and foreign policy matters. It is possible to develop a conflict matrix, such as that in Table 4-4, to specify these and other differing objectives of host and parent states regarding the actions and effects of multinational corporations. A conflict matrix could also be constructed to illustrate the various policy actions that might be undertaken by parent or host states in pursuit of their essentially conflicting objectives. The purpose of such an exercise and of this discussion is to emphasize that the behavior and existence of multinational corporations may be the source of and vehicle for worsening relations between parent and host states, as each attempts to harness such corporations to advance its own interests.

Parent states and host states may also clash as a result of specific actions taken by either host or parent states in the attempt to influence the behavior of multinational corporations. Over the years the efforts of Cuba, Peru, Bolivia, and Chile to nationalize American business enterprises within their jurisdiction has produced important conflicts in official governmental relations between these countries and the United States. Canadian govern-

TABLE 4-4   Parent State—Host State Conflicts In Objectives: Multinational Corporations' Effect on Balance of Payments

ISSUE	HOST STATE DESIRES	PARENT STATE DESIRES
Investment capital	Obtained from parent state	Obtained from host state and other foreign sources
Profits	Reinvest	Repatriate
Licenses, royalties, management fees	No payment for services rendered	Full payment for services rendered
Exports	From subsidiary to other subsidiaries and to parent country headquarters	From parent country plants to subsidiaries in host states

ment efforts to "Canadianize" the oil industry in the early 1980s caused problems with the U.S. government in support of U.S. foreign investment in that country. Similar problems have occurred involving French firms operating in Africa and Japanese enterprises in Asia.

In addition to the fact that multinational corporations may be the object or the source of conflict between parent and host states, they also may be the vehicle by which host and parent countries try to influence each other. There is a widespread fear, with some justifying examples, that multinational corporations may serve as a conduit for foreign policy actions by parent states. The U.S. government sought to hinder the development of a French nuclear force by prohibiting IBM from selling needed equipment. The IT&T-CIA case regarding the Allende government in Chile is a widely remembered example that heightens fear and suspicion that multinationals are vehicles for U.S. foreign policy efforts.

The reverse is true also. Host states have attempted to influence parent states through multinational firms. In response to President Nixon's 10 percent import surcharge in August 1971, many U.S. firms with subsidiaries in Latin America decried the measure and sought its rapid repeal since Latin America was already running a trade deficit with the United States. Whether out of enlightened self-interest or as a result of direct requests from host state officials, these firms were seeking to influence U.S. policy on behalf of the Latin American host states. The Arab oil embargo of 1973–1974 was accompanied by Arab efforts to have multinational petroleum companies influence U.S. and Western policy toward the Middle East. Even prior to the embargo and the Arab-Israeli war, stockholders of Standard Oil of California were sent a letter urging "understanding on our (America's) part of the aspirations of the Arab people, and more positive support of their efforts toward peace in the Middle East." This statement is a good example of a multinational's efforts to influence parent state policy on the behalf of host states. The petroleum shortages and rapidly rising price of oil in the 1970s encouraged some Middle Eastern host countries to try to influence policies of parent nations through the vehicle of the multinational corporation. The "special" relationship between Saudi Arabia and the United States is based in part on the long-term active involvement of U.S. corporations in that nation.

The potential impact of multinational corporations on relations between a parent state and a host state is widely appreciated. Less obvious is the possibility of competition among parent states on behalf of their own multinational firms. The expansion and success of American-based multinational corporations in the 1960s and the threat of Japanese companies led a number of European states to rationalize and consolidate their own companies with the objective of forming sizable multinationals of their own to compete with the foreign firms. Since these combined firms are often created as a result of government initiative and sometimes with government funds, it is reasonable to expect that the parent governments will sometimes seek to ensure that their firms are successful in their efforts by actively supporting them, to the detriment of international enterprises of a different nationality. Some of the giant European multinationals, such as British Petroleum and ENI, are owned partially by their respective governments. The concept of Japan Inc., if often exaggerated, suggests the very close relationship between the Japanese government and its multinational enterprises.

A further stimulus of conflict among parent states stemming from competition among multinational corporations will emerge when there are concerns about raw material shortages. For example, the lack of sufficient domestic supplies of petroleum, in conjunction with the successful efforts of oil-producing states to control petroleum prices and supplies, prompted the Japanese government in the 1970s to help its firms explore for oil in other areas. At the same time an oil-hungry and dependent Europe attempted to establish new sources of supply for itself and its own firms, to the disadvantage of Japanese and American firms. Consequently, competition among multinational firms of different nationalities, in concert with the policies of their home governments, for access to and control over scarce natural resources can produce great tensions among states. Off the record, some major political figures in Europe, like Jacques Chirac, viewed the U.S.-led military intervention of 1990–1991 to liberate Kuwait and to punish Iraq as a long-term American strategy to secure control over global oil supplies for the purpose of equalizing rising EEC and Japanese economic power.[55]

Conflict among host states is likely to occur as they compete to attract the benefits of foreign investment. Many host states already compete with one another by offering various kinds of inducements to foreign investors. During a 1971 visit to the United Kingdom, Henry Ford made it clear to Prime Minister Heath and the British people that unsatisfactory labor relations in Great Britain might cause Ford of England to restrict new investment or even transfer some existing investment from Britain to other countries. The next day, a group of Dutch business managers and gov-

---

[55]Flora Lewis, "A Shabby French Sulk," *The New York Times*, February 20, 1991, p. A15.

ernment officials invited Ford to consider further investment in the Netherlands. Although this situation might not happen often in such a blatant fashion, competition for foreign investment does exist among advanced industrial states and among the developing nations.

There are several possible effects of this competitive courtship of multinational corporations. If the competition is severe enough, one result may be an increase in the various states' incentive packages and/or a reduction in the investment risks and costs for the corporations. If states actively pursue foreign investment, they may undercut one another in offering inducements, thereby generally increasing the level of the returns or benefits accruing to multinational corporations and reducing the gains of the host states.

Moreover, the uneven pattern of foreign investment within a region may help to sour relations among potential host states. For example, within a particular region the combination of natural and human endowments, geographical advantages, governmental policies, and other factors may mean that one or two states receive much of the foreign investment and other states very little at all. To the extent that multinational corporations are thought to bring more advantages than disadvantages, the less fortunate states in a region may seek to gain a greater share of the foreign investment through political efforts directed against the more successful host countries.

As a result of competition for investment and concern about the unequal distribution of such investment, some states in a particular region have formed regional groups to distribute foreign investment more equitably and purposefully, to harmonize the laws and incentives regarding these enterprises, and generally to reduce the possibility of intraregional conflict over these firms. Among other reasons, the desire to present a united front to foreign investors was a major stimulus for the formation of the Andean Common Market, which is comprised of Venezuela, Colombia, Ecuador, Peru, Bolivia, and at one time but no longer Chile. The ASEAN countries of Singapore, Malaysia, Brunei, Thailand, Indonesia, and the Philippines have also joined together to present a combined and more rational approach to regional economic development and the role of multinational firms in the planned development. Thus, in an almost dialectical fashion, competition among host states to obtain the benefits of multinational enterprises may lead to the development of regional strategies designed to prevent this conflict. This may be thought by some to be a positive result of the activities of multinational corporations.

On the other hand, regional or international efforts to contain interstate conflict may be perceived by some host states as interfering with their ability to try to attract foreign investment or at least to determine their own policies on these issues. Colombia and Venezuela were reluctant initially to join the Andean pact because both countries had relatively satisfactory experiences with a sizable foreign investment sector. Chile withdrew from the pact, and in 1980 the military government of Bolivia intimated a similar possibility. In another example, Belgium was disturbed when the European Common Market commission disallowed investment incentives for a certain region of Belgium, an action that the government felt was necessary for the promotion of industry and creation of employment. In essence, the commission felt that the incentives provided an unfair advantage to the Belgians relative to other states in the Common Market. Host state conflict with international or regional organizations emerges when a state feels that it will be able to obtain greater benefits from foreign investment by not subscribing to an international or regional agreement that establishes a common policy toward multinational corporations.

Conflict at the international or regional level may emerge when international organizations, in the form of producer cartels, align host states against a coalition of multinational firms and their parent states. Conflict of this sort threatened to develop between the major petroleum-consuming countries and OPEC. In the winter of 1974, the United States attempted to organize major petroleum-consuming countries as a counterweight to OPEC; leadership would have supposedly been assumed by those states that had a number of multinational petroleum companies. The lack of success in this endeavor does not undermine the basic point that conflicts between organized groups of host states and an alignment of parent states are likely to be particularly severe when the dispute involves scarce natural resources or food products.

According to the views advanced by Stephen Hymer, from a more global perspective, it has been suggested that multinational corporations widen the gap between developing countries, as the recipients for foreign investment, and those few advanced industrial states in which the headquarters of the multinational enterprises are located.[56] Thus, a stratified international political and economic system is created, with significant power accruing to the few headquarters states. There also exists a second tier of regionally important states, similar to middle-management levels of the corporation, that have influence only to the extent to which they serve the interests of the center states. Finally, a large number of passive and very dependent states exist that are the hewers of wood and haulers of water for the rich states and their multinational enterprises. Hymer and other regional critics predict that this international stratification of states, caused partially and furthered by multinational corporations, will provoke the seeds of its own destruction, for the peripheral states will attempt to overturn the system that dominates them. This will not be achieved readily or without substantial conflict.

POSITIVE IMPACT OF MULTINATIONAL CORPORATIONS ON INTERNATIONAL POLITICS

Advocates of multinational corporations claim that these enterprises have had and will continue to have a beneficial impact on relations among states. In several different ways, multinational enterprises are thought to contribute to regional or functional integration and to other cooperative efforts. First, the threat posed by the existence of multinational corporations

---

[56]Stephen Hymer, "The Multinational Corporation and the Law of Uneven Development," in *Economics and World Order: From the 1970s to the 1990s*, ed. Jagdish N. Bhagwati (New York: Macmillan, 1972), pp. 113–40.

may prompt states to adopt common policies to counteract, adapt to, or get the most benefit from them. Concerns about the ability of multinational enterprises to exploit their common market led the Andean group to adopt a set of stringent barriers and regulations to control closely multinational business activities. Similarly, OPEC in its heyday was able to present a more united front to the giant multinational oil companies and the oil-consuming states. In these cases and others, the multinational enterprise has had a catalytic effect on the formation of coordinated efforts among states that were previously too much in conflict to cooperate.

Second, multinational corporations, as a result of their own integrated nature and their impact on other social units, may help to provide an environment conducive to the promotion of integration among states, which is thought by some world leaders to be a desired goal. The ability of these enterprises to surmount national boundaries in the production and marketing of a product contributes to the establishment of a common regional culture and life style. Integrated production means that workers in a number of different states are linked closely to one another in terms of their work and, of course, their employer. In Europe particularly, regional unions are springing up to represent regionwide interest. Management personnel in Europe are beginning to develop a European perspective and to perceive themselves as having interests and opportunities that range beyond those of their own country.[57] In some multinational automobile companies, there have been exchanges of workers among headquarters and subsidiaries to break down national barriers and to provide training experiences leading to greater productivity. The Japanese style of management and labor relations has been introduced by Japanese firms in their U.S. subsidiaries, often with great success. In sum, the multinational corporation may help both to overcome the barriers of separateness and to crystallize some of the common interests and culture that foster regional interest groups and regional orientations. Evidence seems to suggest that multinational corporations within the EEC have been useful in promoting integration rather than retarding it. Indeed, European-based multinationals were actively behind the movement to create a single internal market within the EEC by 1992.

Some supporters of the multinational corporation claim that it is a force for peace among states since it represents an extremely successful form of internationalism, one that links states and people more closely. In spite of the political impediments of different national systems and national characteristics, the multinational corporation has succeeded in overcoming some of these barriers and in making states more interdependent and thus less likely to engage in violent conflict. The former president of the Bank of America and the World Bank expressed this thesis clearly:

> the idea that this kind of business enterprise can be a strong force toward world peace is not so far fetched. Beyond the human values involved, the

---

[57]See Bernard Mennis and Karl P. Sauvant, "Multinational Corporations, Managers, and the Development of Regional Identification in Western Europe," *The Annals*, 403 (September 1972), 22–33.

multinational firm has a direct, measurable, and potent interest in helping prevent wars and other serious upheavals that cut off its resources, interrupt its communications, and kill its employees and customers.[58]

Donald Kendall, the former chairman of Pepsico who maneuvered that company into an early commercial relationship with the Soviet Union in 1969, was a strong advocate of détente even when that position was not popular.

The previous section indicated many ways in which multinational corporations may adversely affect the patterns of relations between states and international or regional organizations, either as a matter of policy or merely because of competition for their benefits. In this section, we have offered arguments to show the beneficial impact of the multinational corporation on interstate relations. Although serious conceptual and methodological problems as well as fundamental value positions make it difficult to determine precisely the net impact of these enterprises on international politics, it is important to be aware of the positive as well as the negative implications of their existence for relations among states.

MULTINATIONAL CORPORATIONS AND CHANGES IN THE INTERNATIONAL POLITICAL SYSTEM

Up to this point we have examined multinational corporations largely in terms of their relations with states. However, a different perspective is imperative, for these firms not only have important consequences for states but also have stimulated the development of international cooperation among other nongovernmental actors. Within this relatively neglected area, some far-ranging and basic changes may be occurring. To oversimplify a bit, it appears that an international economic and political system may be emerging in which multinational corporations are the major institutions as well as the prime stimuli for the development of other structures. However, all this is occurring without a central international political authority.

Because of the importance of the international economic system, various international groups organized around common interests are beginning to participate in the international system, as their domestic counterparts do in individual states. The reason for this activity is simply that international economic transactions have direct consequences for the interests of these groups, and as a result the groups seek to exert control over these transactions. Nations have not been particularly responsive to or effective in protecting these organized interests from the impact of the international economic system. Domestic groups are relatively powerless to protect their interests in the context of a highly interdependent world. Finally, the various intergovernmental institutions have not yet developed the ability or the will to represent effectively the concerns of these domestic

---

[58]Reprinted from "The Internationalized Corporation: An Executive's View," by A. W. Clausen in vol. 403 of *The Annals* of the American Academy of Political and Social Science, p. 21, 1972, © by The Academy of Political and Social Science.

groups. Thus, there is a need to develop new forms of direct international action among like interests within the global economy.

The lack of a systematic investigation of this phenomenon requires us to illustrate these developments by means of specific examples. The Council of the Americas is a business-oriented group somewhat analogous to a lobbying organization in that, among other things, it seeks to promote actions by Latin American governments that favor multinational corporations. The Council also seeks to aid and educate American corporations regarding the problems and prospects of doing business in Latin America. In addition to the Council and a number of other similar organizations, various international trade associations of some importance exist. More broadly, the International Chamber of Commerce made a significant effort to develop a set of guidelines for multinational corporations, parent governments, and host governments on a variety of issues. At one point the international chamber had been especially eager to assume a leadership and watchdog role on the issue of eliminating improper payments by corporations. It too seeks to represent business interests in the councils of various international organizations.

As a response to the many business-oriented organizations in this emerging international system, other groups are seeking to develop a countervailing force to the multinational corporation. The efforts of international labor union organizations in this regard are most revealing, for the patterns of response that these union organizations are developing may prove to be a model for the actions of other groups. The various national labor movements often feel helpless in the face of the international mobility, flexibility, and strength of the multinational corporations. For a variety of reasons, the strategies and tactics used by unions on domestic employers are frequently ineffective when used on multinational employers.[59]

To overcome this disadvantageous position, unions have designed a number of activities to exert some control over the corporations. At the national level, unions from two or more states have cooperated to aid one another in their conflicts with the same multinational employer. At times, this has entailed meetings to exchange information and plan a common strategy for eventual confrontations with management. In other instances, coordinated action has actually been taken against the employer in several different countries. At the regional level, groups of unions have formalized their efforts to coordinate actions taken toward corporations. Through the leadership of the European Metalworkers' Federation, representatives of unions from several states have met with the management of such multinational employers as Philips, AKZO, and others to discuss various issues. Moreover, when a union in one country has struck a multinational employer, counterpart unions in other countries have sometimes refused to work overtime to take up the slack caused by the disruption in production, or they have applied similar types of pressure to the common employer.

---

[59]For a discussion of trade union weaknesses and their responses, see David H. Blake, "Trade Unions and the Challenge of the Multinational Corporation," *The Annals*, 403 (September 1972) 34–35; and David H. Blake, "The Internationalization of Industrial Relations," *Journal of International Business Studies*, 3 (Fall 1972), 17–32.

Similar activities have occurred at the international level. A number of the international trade secretariats (international union organizations organized according to type of industry), such as the International Metalworkers' Federation and the International Chemical and General Workers' Federation, have formed company councils composed of many of the national unions associated with the same multinational employer. Such company councils were formed for General Motors, Ford, Volkswagen, Philips, General Electric, Shell, Nestlé, and many others. Information exchange, consultation and planning, and joint solidarity actions have been planned and coordinated by these international trade secretariats.

Although these activities do not represent the prevailing pattern of union responses to multinational corporations and the international economic system, they do represent both formal and informal efforts to confront multinational corporations on a regional and international level. To a limited but increasing extent, industrial relations are being internationalized.

This type of development, which is stimulated by multinational corporations, is leading to the emergence of a more truly international economic and political system. Processes and procedures limited formerly to nations are being introduced at the regional and international level because of the international nature of these firms. Although this trend is just developing, evidence suggests that it may well be one of the most important long-run effects of the multinational corporations. These enterprises have provoked an operational internationalism that has not yet been achieved by formal political mechanisms. However, in the following section we will discuss the ways in which international organizations have been attempting to increase their monitoring and control of the activities of multinational enterprises.

POLICIES FOR CONTROL

It is natural that some attempts (particularly by host states) would be made to control the extensive impacts of multinational corporations on domestic interest groups, parent and host states, and regional and international organizations and systems. These efforts vary greatly in nature and in degree of success. Some states have not bothered to institute any controls at all, other than those already existing for domestic enterprises. At the other extreme is outright nationalization, whereby the host state obtains total ownership and control of the corporation and the foreign investment is eliminated completely. Between these two extremes is a wide variety of control mechanisms designed to preserve foreign investment while increasing the benefits received by the host state and reducing the associated disruptions and costs.

Overall, the substance of these control policies is quite varied and incorporates most of the concerns expressed by host states. Regarding balance-of-payments questions, some host states insist upon a specific degree of export activity by the multinational enterprise. In addition, they may impose barriers on the import of goods and limits on the repatriation of profits, royalties, licenses, and management fees to the foreign headquarters. Local content regulations require the products of the foreign enterprise to have increasing amounts of domestically produced components or raw materials as opposed to imported parts, and naturally this will reduce a state's balance-of-payments deficit. Brazil, during the space of little more than fifteen years, for example, brought about change in the sourcing procedure of its large car industry to the point where about 99 percent of the component parts are produced in Brazil.

In terms of exerting local control over foreign enterprises, host states often establish requirements regarding the number and position of both foreign and local employees and managers. Some states require a majority of host country citizens on the enterprise's board of directors. Other states go much farther, insisting that the foreign enterprise share ownership—in varying proportions—with national enterprises, local citizens, or government agencies. These demands have been widespread and have affected the global operations of many multinational corporations. Even IBM, which historically had been able to maintain its 100 percent ownership policy because of its high-technology character, encountered problems of mandated local ownership requirements in India, Indonesia, Nigeria, Malaysia, and Brazil and is now more open to joint venture arrangements.[60]

Some of these measures, and others as well, enhance the domestic benefits of the foreign investment. Increasing tax rates or the pretax governmental share of profits is a common way by which host countries seek to enlarge their benefits. Mexico and several other states have sought actively to have foreign investors conduct research and development in the host state, thereby increasing the opportunities for local scientists and enhancing the indigenous research and development capability of the host country.

Of course, host states have adopted many other measures to exert some kind of control over the multinational corporation. Some of these efforts to increase the benefits and reduce the costs for the host state take the form of barriers to or requirements for entry. Multinational corporations seeking to invest must meet the specific demands of the host state, often through long, complex negotiations. Some of these provisions may apply to all foreign concerns; others may be ad hoc and specific to the particular investment.

Host state control is also increased through the establishment of new requirements, which must be met by existing foreign enterprises. The firms must then decide whether compliance or withdrawal is the best course to follow. Singapore, for example, instituted an unorthodox policy in the summer of 1979, designed to get multinational corporations to enhance particular state objectives regarding creation of capital-intensive investment. The Singapore government pushed up wage levels countrywide, ranging from 14 percent to 20 percent, to induce multinational corporations to employ fewer people and set up more capital-intensive operations because of the rising cost of labor.[61] Having made the initial investment

[60]"Erosion Extends Around the World," *Datamation*, April 1978, p. 182.
[61]*The Economist*, December 30, 1978, p. 51.

and incurred the costs associated with starting a new venture, it is difficult for a corporation not to respond in a fashion that allows it to continue making a profit and at the same time comply with the demands of the state. However, if the operation is marginal at best, or if the process can be easily closed down and opened up in another country, the bargaining power of the state is reduced. As with requirements for entry, these new measures may be applied generally or may be designed for a specific firm.

Just as it is impossible to examine all the types of incentives offered by host states, so it is impossible to discuss the many types of controls placed on foreign investment by host states. As we suggested earlier, the complexity and severity of these restrictions vary widely. States such as Belgium, the Netherlands, Great Britain, and a fairly large number of developing countries are quite receptive to foreign investment and impose few regulations. However, this attitude can change easily, as illustrated by the Spanish government's efforts to increase its control and benefits from foreign investment and then more recently to be more receptive to foreign investment. Brazil, too, is a country that has moved from a posture of enthusiastic openness to foreign investment to a more restrictive policy and back again somewhat to a more open environment.

Even in the United States, greater attention is being directed at controlling inward foreign investment in recent years. The Exxon-Florio provision, included in the Omnibus Trade and Competitiveness Act of 1988, authorizes the President to block foreign acquisitions of American companies if they are considered a threat to national security. Such legislation is aimed, especially, at foreign takeovers of high-tech companies in the United States with process and product technologies deemed important in defense industries and in maintaining the international competitiveness of U.S. firms.[62] With a view toward possible future controls on direct foreign investment, increasing pressure is also being exerted in Congress to improve the quality and precision of data-collection in relation to the activities and impacts of multinationals at the national, state, and local levels.[63]

Other states have a much more stringent set of controls. For a long time, Japan made it exceptionally difficult for many multinational corporations to establish investment in that country, particularly in those industrial sectors deemed to be most important for Japan's economic plans and success. This policy has been liberalized considerably since 1971, as a consequence of the pressure of the U.S. government and its multinationals. Mexico, too, has traditionally controlled foreign investment in pursuit of its own national objectives. In the 1970s and 1980s Mexican laws regarding foreign investment specified not only a majority share of Mexican ownership but also a high degree of Mexican, as opposed to foreign, management. Coupled with these requirements were regulations overseeing the

---

[62]See, for example, "Capitol Hill Considers National Security, Foreign Investment Links," *JEI Report*, August 10, 1990, pp. 6–9.

[63]"Bill Aims to Improve the Quality of Foreign Investment Data," *Congressional Quarterly*, October 27, 1990, pp. 3583–584. For more elaboration on the need for such data collection, see Norman Glickman and Douglas Woodward, *The New Competitors: How Foreign Investors Are Changing the U.S. Economy* (New York: Basic Books, 1989), pp. 276–85.

nature of technology transfers between Mexican enterprises and the subsidiaries of foreign firms and foreign business concerns. The registration of all technological contracts allowed the Mexican government to determine whether the arrangement was in Mexico's best interests. Although these laws were applied rather flexibly, the new economic policy of President Salinas has aggressively courted foreign investment.

Other states have taken an even more restrictive posture on foreign investment, exhibiting a basic reluctance to welcome multinational corporations, but this stand is tempered sometimes with an awareness of the necessity of having some foreign investment in certain specified industries. The terms for admission and operation are much stricter than existed in Mexico, for instance. Salvador Allende's Chile exhibited this tendency, as did Indonesia in 1965 and Ceylon in 1962 and 1963. The Soviet Union and the Central European countries are currently seeking to attract foreign investors as part of their development drive. Multinational corporations often are willing to operate under these more difficult conditions, but such restrictions, particularly if coupled with governmental instability, tend to scare off many potential investors. Thus, there is the interesting anomaly of President Allende's nationalizing most investments from the United States and other countries and at the same time attempting to attract foreign investment in Europe, without much success. On the other hand, multinational corporations of many nationalities find the huge Soviet market and the stable Soviet investment climate in pre-Gorbachev times to be potentially interesting in spite of the extensive restrictions on business activities. The adaptability of multinational corporations to restrictive foreign investment climates in the face of great market potential is borne out by the rush of firms to develop relations with the People's Republic of China. Even in the face of unfamiliarity, recent antagonism, abridgement of human rights, and confusing governmental policies, business corporations remain hopeful about the business possibilities with China, as, for example, the Procter & Gamble executive's comment on the market potential of selling one billion toothbrushes to the Chinese.

The success of host state efforts to control the activities and impact of multinational corporations while still obtaining desired benefits varies with such factors as the nature of the controls, the stability of the investment climate, the size of the market, the dependence on the raw material, and of course the specific nature of the foreign investment. To put it in different terms, the multinational enterprise weighs the costs of doing business under restrictions with the possible benefits to be received. Nations perform the same type of calculus but from a different perspective. Speaking generally, a restricted Chinese environment is potentially attractive because of the very large market, in terms of population and stage of industrial development, and the existence of important raw materials. A much smaller and poorer market, even with less onerous and cumbersome restrictions, may be far less attractive to many manufacturing firms. However, if this smaller and poorer country has scarce and critical raw materials, the extractive multinational may put up with governmental controls to gain access to the raw material. In sum, a set of restrictions that controls, without driving out, foreign investment in one country or in a specific industry may be ineffective and disastrous in another country or in a different industry in the same country.

In a general way, it is possible to identify the sources of strength that multinational corporations and host states bring to their negotiations. These are listed in Table 4-5. In the abstract it is not possible to determine whether a specific host country or multinational corporation has the greater power in their conflicts, but some general points can be made.

Both sides have an ultimate source of power. The host country is well within the bounds of international law to nationalize properties owned by foreign corporations. Conversely, companies can decide to shut down their investment and leave the country.[64] This type of situation occurred in 1978 between the government of India and IBM. The former said that IBM could continue to operate only if it was willing to share ownership. The company was unwilling to comply and thus withdrew partially from the Indian market.

TABLE 4-5   Sources of Strength in Host Country Negotiations with Multinational Corporations

HOST COUNTRY	MULTINATIONAL CORPORATION
Controls factors that multinationals want (natural resources, labor, market)	Controls benefits desired by host state (capital, employment, technology, management skill, industrialization, and all the other benefits)
Legislative power	International advantages not duplicated easily (integrated production, established international distribution networks)
Power of the bureaucracy to delay and withhold	Potential parent state pressure
Police and military power	Negative host country actions will scare away other investment and international credit
Competition among multinationals for access to factors	Competition among host states for multinationals' investment
Ability to obtain advantages of multinationals from several different sources ("unbundling")	Refusal to expand investment
Nationalize foreign investment	Ultimate power to close down investment

[64]In some countries, particularly in Europe, a company's ability to close its operations is becoming severely restricted. Numerous firms have found it extraordinarily expensive to go out of business in Europe because of the high price extracted by labor unions and host governments.

However, in most conflicts between multinational corporations and host states, reliance upon the ultimate weapons are rare and frequently counterproductive. In the India-IBM case, both parties lost the benefits of the investment. Consequently, most bargaining between host states and multinational corporations involves strategies designed to increase or maintain the benefits and reduce the costs without causing the situation to deteriorate to where both parties lose.

Parent states have also attempted to control the impact of multinational corporations. Since World War II, most capital-exporting countries have at one time or another imposed controls on outward-bound capital investment. These measures were designed to preserve scarce currency. Other types of controls have been established in response to concerns about antitrust, national security, protection of domestic industry and employment, and punishment leveled at specific countries, such as Rhodesia prior to the formation of Zimbabwe or the Soviet Union after its armed intervention in Afghanistan.

Sometimes the control efforts of the parent state have been designed to ensure that its multinationals behave in an appropriate fashion in host countries. Japan has become quite concerned about the poor Japanese image and hostile relations stimulated by the expanding and insensitive presence of Japanese firms in Asia. Japan has established a set of guidelines in response. Both Sweden and the United States have provisions in their investment-guarantee programs that try to foster good behavior. But, although Sweden has an extensive list of "social conditions," the impact of such efforts is quite limited.

On certain specific items, the U.S. government has attempted to control the behavior of its own multinational firms. Stringent regulations have been imposed on participation by U.S. firms in the Arab boycott of Israel. Companies that comply in any fashion with the boycott, including providing information about trade with Israel to the boycott office, are in violation of the antiboycott legislation. Similarly, in 1977 Congress passed the Foreign Corrupt Practices Act, which leveled severe penalties on firms that engaged in bribery of foreign government officials to obtain business. Both laws are exceedingly complex, ambiguous, and changing, but nonetheless, managers of multinational corporations must be aware of the potentially serious penalties that they and their firms face if they violate these laws.

Of a different sort has been the wide promulgation and acceptance of the Sullivan principles for multinational corporations operating in South Africa. Leon Sullivan, an activist on behalf of black economic development in the United States and a member of the board of General Motors, proposed a voluntary nongovernmental code that established principles of behavior for U.S. firms with investments in South Africa. These principles seek desegregation at the work place and demand fair employment practices, equal pay, training programs for nonwhites, increased nonwhite representation in management, and efforts to improve the employees' lives outside work. In addition, on-site inspections and reporting of compliance with the principles are basic to the agreements. Many of the major multinationals have abided by the provisions of the principles. The Sullivan principles came under fire as being too protective of U.S. investment in

South Africa and indeed were denounced by Reverend Sullivan himself. Thus, in 1985 and 1986, demonstrations on many college campuses, joined by many notables, decried U.S. investment in South Africa under any conditions as long as apartheid was the prevailing rule in that country. In spite of the freeing of Nelson Mandela and the legalization of the African National Congress by the South African government, there has not been a flood of new U.S. investment in that country.

Thus, far, we have discussed control efforts undertaken by nations acting alone. An alternate control strategy is concerted action by a group of states regarding the conditions under which multinationals are allowed to operate. Because of the commonly agreed-upon rules and regulations for foreign investment adopted by a specific group of states, their coordinated efforts tend to overcome to some degree the advantages of mobility and flexibility enjoyed by the corporations. These groupings may be organized along geographic and regional lines, as is the case with the Andean Common Market and the European Economic Community, or they may involve cooperation because of a common natural resource, as in the case of OPEC.[65]

The Andean Common Market is an interesting example of a regional attempt to control the actions and effects of multinational corporations and still obtain the desired benefits. With respect to control, the five member states agreed upon a relatively stringent set of rules regarding foreign investment. With respect to benefits, they joined together as a common market, so that investors abiding by their rules can produce and sell in a market of five states with a combined population of more than 90 million people. Therefore, from the perspective of the investor, the costs of operating in a more controlled environment need to be measured against the benefits of doing business in a much larger market with a significant reduction of intraregion tariffs.

The Andean experiment is comprehensive in its approach, and, thus, a brief look at some of its early but since modified provisions regarding foreign investment may be instructive. First, foreign investment was prohibited in a number of industries, including banking, insurance, broadcasting, publishing, and internal transportation. Second, new investment and most existing investment had to divest itself of majority ownership (the fade-out formula) within fifteen years in Columbia, Peru, and Venezuela and within twenty years in Bolivia and Ecuador, so that national investor participation would be at least 51 percent. Third, annual earnings repatriated by the foreign firm cannot exceed 20 percent (previously 14 percent) of the investment. Fourth, a foreign subsidiary may not pay its parent company or other affiliate for the use of intangible technological know-how; in addition, clauses or practices that tend to restrict competition or production or otherwise increase the cost of the technology to the host state were prohibited. The Andean code contained other provisions, but these four suggest the extent to which the Andean countries attempted to control the actions and impact of the multinationals. These five states de-

[65]OPEC is discussed in detail in Chapter 7.

sired foreign investment on their own terms, although they have had to soften those restrictions.

At the international level, a growing number of attempts have been made to deal with the international and national challenges presented by multinational corporations. The United Nations and its family of organizations have been especially active. Upon the recommendation of an international panel of experts, the United Nations established a Centre on Transnational Corporations that collects information about multinational corporations and prepares studies on various aspects of their operations. In addition, technical assistance programs are organized to improve the negotiating and regulatory capabilities of host countries. A list of consultants is maintained to aid host countries in these negotiations.

The United Nations has developed a series of codes of conduct on various issues associated with foreign investment, including a code on restrictive business practices. The International Labor Organization has produced a code on labor-related matters. In addition, UNCTAD has been working on developing a code on technology transfer, and after more than ten years the debate continues about a wide-ranging code for foreign investment.

While other international and regional organizations are developing codes, the most celebrated effort was undertaken by the Organization for Economic Cooperation and Development (OECD). Its Guidelines on International Investment and Multinational Enterprise sought to "improve the foreign investment climate, encourage the positive contribution which multinational enterprises can make to economic and social progress, and minimize and resolve difficulties which may arise from their various operations."[66] After substantial input from labor and business advisory committees, the "guidelines" were agreed to by OECD member countries in 1976 and slightly revised in 1979. This rather comprehensive code is voluntary, but subsequently it has been referred to in court cases. The OECD itself has attempted to monitor the extent of compliance with the code. In other words, these voluntary guidelines have now become an important part of the environment within which multinational enterprises must operate, in some cases actually incorporated into state law. The OECD has also drafted a code on the protection of privacy and the transborder flow of information that seeks to restrict the unfettered and insensitive collection and use of information by multinational corporations and other agencies. Other efforts have been and will be mounted, for the international nature of the activities and impact of the multinational corporation have provoked efforts by governmental organizations and also nongovernmental ones to develop a comparable international presence.

In assessing the effectiveness of attempts to control the behavior and impact of multinational enterprises, a few general patterns can be observed. The efforts to control multinational corporations focus primarily on their relationship with host states and domestic interests within the host states. Parent states have imposed controls to advance their own economic interests

[66]*The OECD Observer*, July 1976, p. 9.

and in a few cases to regulate the foreign behavior of these firms. The issue of the impact of foreign investment on the relations among states has received scarcely any systematic attention, and there has been little action to remedy any of the resulting problems.

With respect to the efforts to control multinationals and their actions in host states, much evidence indicates that these firms are willing to operate under regulated conditions as long as it is profitable for them to do so. In other words, those states that have much to offer multinational corporations can effectively harness the activities of these enterprises toward national objectives with the corporation readily adapting to the new environment. However, not all states are in this fortunate position, and the adaptability of industries and specific firms varies quite widely. Again, the decision to adapt or not depends largely upon management's assessment of the benefits to be gained from continuing operations versus the costs to be incurred.

Developing states and small countries without the benefit of deposits of scarce natural resources or thriving markets are not in a position to exert significantly greater control over foreign investment without threatening to drive away the investments. Basically, the larger and richer state has the best chance to impose controls since this type of state has the most to offer the multinational corporation: expanding markets, labor supply, natural resources. As with trade and monetary matters, it appears that many developing countries are less able than are the more advanced states to obtain the greatest amount of benefit from foreign investment. This peripheral relationship may be improved by joint action such as the Andean Common Market, but the obstacles to such efforts are great.[67]

Of course, if one rejects the objective of industrialization and growth, there is no need for a state to accept investment by multinational corporations. Furthermore, if one views the relationship between host states and these firms in strict zero-sum terms (meaning that corporate benefits are offset by host state costs), then the implied policy is to nationalize all existing investment and prohibit the entrance of new operations. However, if the relationship is viewed in positive-sum terms, then the challenge for host states is how best to maximize the benefits and reduce the costs associated with foreign investment.

THE MULTINATIONAL CORPORATION AND THE FUTURE

In the late 1960s and the 1970s, the issue of the multinational corporation was a critical one for host states and for the United States as the largest parent country. Trade unionists, academicians, journalists, politicians, bureaucrats, and ideologues focused their attention on the multinational corporation as a highly visible and tangible manifestation of global interdependency. Many kinds of social, political, and economic dislocations were blamed on the international firm. However, since those years, the debates about the multinational corporation have become less strident as the problems of interdependency and the need for economic development became more immediate and complex. Worldwide economic recession and infla-

---

[67]Chapter 7 examines in-depth various strategies available to developing countries.

tion, energy dependency, balance-of-payments disequilibrium, huge national debt burdens, domestic unemployment, and threats to survival of major companies and industries as a result of foreign competition have reduced somewhat the fixation on the multinational firm. In addition, the collapse of communism has led to the multinational corporation being seen as a desirable force for economic development. Thus, the multinational corporation is a less controversial issue in global economic and political relations.

Nations seem to have more confidence in their ability to structure and shape corporate impacts to achieve national goals. This is not to say that there are not major problems and issues to be resolved; rather, there seems to be the recognition by many that multinationals and states will continue to exist together, and efforts are underway to develop the patterns of relationships that will foster this accommodation.

Some feel that slowly but steadily multinationals will change in a way that is more acceptable to the concerns of host states in reestablishing control. Peter Drucker foresees the development of a transnational confederation that takes advantage of its technological, marketing, and managerial skills to link together production-manufacturing centers in various countries.[68] These production-manufacturing centers would be located in developing countries, would be owned by local interests or agencies, and would be woven into a transnational system of production, management, technology, and marketing. The locally owned "subsidiary" would provide labor and perhaps raw materials to manufacture the component parts of the product. The "headquarters" or center firm, erstwhile the multinational headquarters, would contribute technology, management skill, and well-developed marketing skills and international networks. In the transnational confederation, each component part provides the element of the process in which it has a comparative advantage. However, none of the component parts is competitively self-sufficient; instead, each depends upon the complete network for its success.

The confederation arrangement would remove the issue of equity ownership by foreigners, but the complexity of the system does reduce the ability of the host state to influence the whole process, although it can affect the activity taking place within its borders. Central direction is still important in the transnational conferation, but the permanent character of foreign ownership is eliminated.

Whether the multinational corporation evolves into a transnational confederation or not, the international firm as we know it today will likely continue to adapt to the pressures and concerns of state efforts to reduce the costs of foreign investment and general international interdependency. The multinational is still the most tangible and visible element of global interdependency. While states and managers have become more adept at working within this environment, the fundamental issues raised earlier will continue to challenge policy makers and corporate executives even in an environment that is much more supportive of the concept of foreign investment as an essential force for economic growth.

[68] Peter F. Drucker, *Managing in Turbulent Times* (New York: Harper & Row, 1980), pp. 103–110. Note how similar this is to the Japanese trading company discussed on pp.113–114.

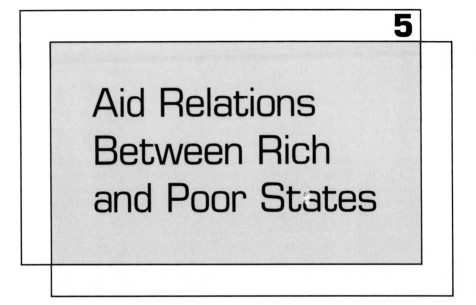

Aid Relations Between Rich and Poor States

5

During the 1950s and 1960s, foreign aid[1] was perceived as perhaps the most critical aspect of economic relations between rich and poor states. While it still constitutes an important and unique dimension of relations between advanced industrial states and less developed countries, other economic channels (such as trade, direct foreign investment, and commercial bank lending) have assumed greater importance over the course of the 1970s and 1980s. In 1984, for example, economic aid accounted for less than 30 percent of the $71.5 billion in net financial flows to less developed countries.[2] Nevertheless, foreign aid remains a critical factor in the development prospects of numerous states in the Third World, especially the poorest among them.[3] This is so not only because of the concessional character of aid but also because aid can be targeted to specific development priorities by a government in ways not possible with export earnings, direct foreign investment, or private bank loans from abroad.

The value of economic aid flowing to less developed countries and to multilateral aid agencies in 1988–1989 is presented in Table 5-1. Western states account for approximately 87 percent of total aid disbursements. The United States has been surpassed as the largest aid donor by Japan. Its

---

[1]This discussion, consistent with the focus of this volume, will be confined to economic assistance and will exclude military aid. By economic assistance, we mean flows to less developed countries and multilateral institutions provided by governments for the ostensible purpose of development; such flows are concessional in character (lower interest rates, longer repayment periods, grace periods, and so forth) relative to commercial terms.

[2]International Bank for Reconstruction and Development, *World Development Report, 1985* (Washington, D.C.: IBRD, 1985), p. 145.

[3]Ibid., p. 94. During 1981–1982, official development assistance represented 82 percent of the net capital receipts of low-income countries.

TABLE 5-1   Foreign Economic Assistance, 1988—1989 ($ billions)

DONOR STATE	VALUE	% OF WORLD TOTAL	% OF DONOR's GNP
Western States[1]	$47.7	86.8%	0.35%
France	5.1	9.2	0.52
Germany	4.9	9.0	0.40
Japan	9.3	16.9	0.32
United Kingdom	2.6	4.8	0.32
United States	8.7	15.9	0.18
Arab OPEC States	1.5	3.5	0.54
Saudi Arabia	1.2	2.9	1.46
Kuwait	0.2	0.3	0.54
USSR and East Europe	4.5	8.2	—
China	0.1	0.2	0.03
WORLD TOTAL	$55.0	—	—

[1]States represented in the Development Assistance Commitee of the Organization for Economic Cooperation and Development. In addition to the states specified in the table these include Australia, Austria, Belgium, Canada, Denmark, Italy, the Netherlands, Norway, Portugal, Sweden, and Switzerland.

Source: Organization for Economic Cooperation and Development, *Development Cooperation, 1990 Report* (Paris: OECD, 1990), pp. 186—187.

major economic partners have increased their aid to less developed countries at a much faster rate than the United States has over the past twenty-five years.[4] Between 1961 and 1988 the American share of total Western aid fell from 59 percent to 18 percent. By the customary measure of aid as a percentage of the donors GNP, the United States presently ranks last among all the Western aid donors.

Total aid to less developed countries almost doubled from 1979 to 1989 (see Figure 5-1). However, during these years less developed countries' increasing financial requirements outran aid growth by a wide margin in the face of a fifteen-fold increase in oil prices, two recessions in the global economy that severely depressed LDCs' export earnings, declining terms of commodity trade, austerity programs required to manage foreign debt service payments, and other developments in monetary relations discussed in Chapter 3.

As critical as economic assistance may be to less developed countries, it is clear that most of them cannot depend on it to meet their development needs. This is especially true in view of the politically motivated concentration of bilateral aid disbursements from most major sources. Aid from the Arab oil exporters has declined markedly since 1980 (see Figure 5-1). It has been distributed primarily to Islamic states in the Middle East, Africa,

[4]Overseas Development Council, *The United States in World Development, Agenda 1980* (New York: Praeger, 1980), p. 230.

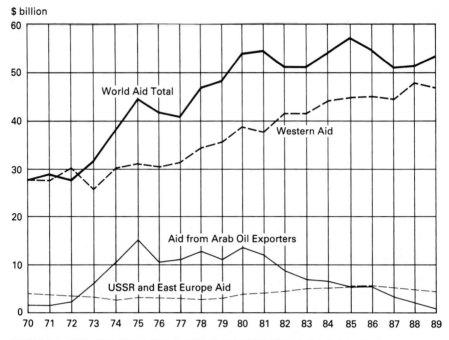

FIGURE 5-1 Aid by Major Donor Groups, 1970–1989 (at 1988 prices and exchange rates)

Source: Organization for Economic Cooperation and Development, *Development Cooperation, 1990 Report* (Paris: OECD, 1990), p. 15.

and South Asia—led by Syria and Jordan. Cuba, Mongolia, and Vietnam received about three fourths of Soviet and East European aid during the 1980s. Recent political and economic reforms (discussed in Chapter 9) in these donor states will likely lead to aid reductions for their traditional recipients. Israel and Egypt were, by far, the leading recipients of U.S. aid disbursements in the 1980s. French aid has long been concentrated in its overseas departments, territories, and former colonies. Japanese aid has flowed predominantly to Asian states, especially Indonesia and the People's Republic of China in recent years.[5] Only two dozen of the world's 140 less developed countries are the primary beneficiaries of the major bilateral aid programs.

THE FRAGILE POLITICAL BASE FOR AID IN THE DONOR STATES

It is very difficult to generalize about Western aid efforts in the aggregate— so many diverse tendencies are present simultaneously. Scandinavian states with few historical ties to the Third World have emerged as strong supporters of development assistance since the 1960s. These countries, along

[5]For a detailed summary of the direction of aid disbursements, see Organization for Economic Cooperation and Development, *Development Cooperation, 1990 Report* (Paris: OECD, 1990), pp. 233–42.

with some of the smaller European states such as the Netherlands, have assumed heavy aid burdens for their size. They are also among the most responsive advanced industrial states to less developed country demands for a wide variety of international economic reforms. Japan and Germany were in a defensive international position economically and politically after World War II. They moved into the economic assistance field boldly only in the late 1970s. Japan was increasing its aid substantially at the end of the 1980s and implemented a program to recycle $30 billion of its current account surplus to less developed countries through private channels. It emerged alongside the United States as the largest aid donor among the advanced industrial states (both countries extended aid of over $9 billion in 1988)[6], but its economic assistance carries less concessionary terms than most Western aid and is linked more explicitly to its commercial interests. The United States, as we have seen, has been unwilling to sustain its earlier postwar posture as the initiator, advocate, and purveyor of massive amounts of bilateral and multilateral aid to less developed countries. Its aid commitment has immense implications for the global aid picture because of America's economic importance and the leadership it has traditionally exercised on international economic assistance issues.

Several factors help to account for the fragile political base upon which U.S. aid rests currently. Over the years congressional liberals have been the major political constituency for American development assistance. During the 1960s much support from this quarter was lost as a result of a close association between the aid program and America's role in the Vietnamese war. Out of the Vietnam experience many came to view economic aid as a program that deeply involved the United States in the internal affairs of recipients—even to the point of helping draw the United States into military commitments of questionable value to core American interests. Congressional liberals began to argue for a lower foreign profile that recognized limits to the desirability and capacity of America to shape the political fabric of states throughout the Third World through aid or other means.

Support for U.S. economic assistance eroded further as doubts emerged in the 1970s concerning the impact of development aid on the lower income elements of society in less developed countries. Even if aid helped promote economic growth in Third World states, there was little evidence that the benefits of growth were serving the basic human needs (education, health, and nutrition) of the majority of the population. Questions about the aid program's effectiveness in this regard led to attacks upon it from the ranks of its traditional political supporters.[7]

A series of domestic social, economic, and political challenges since the 1960s have also gradually undercut domestic political support for U.S. development assistance. During the 1960s, Americans became sensitized to tremendous social challenges confronting them at home—such as civil rights,

---

[6]Joseph Wheeler, "The Critical Role for Official Development Assistance in the 1990s," *Finance and Development*, 26, no. 3 (September 1989), 40.

[7]John Sewell and Christine Contee, "U.S. Foreign Aid in the 1980s: Reordering Priorities," in *U.S. Foreign Policy and the Third World*, eds. J. Sewell, R. Feinberg, and U. Kolleb, (New Brunswick Transactive Books, 1985). Overseas Development Council: Wash. D.C. p. 104.

medical care, urban decay, and deterioration in public transportation. Programs were initiated to confront these challenges that involved major new commitments of public capital. Even in a period of great affluence, foreign economic assistance fared poorly as it faced greater political competition from "domestic aid" programs for shares of the national budget.

During the 1970s and 1980s, confidence in continued domestic prosperity gave way to reduced rates of economic growth, higher levels of unemployment, and rapidly escalating prices. As the opportunity costs for foreign economic assistance increased in this economic atmosphere, so, too, did political opposition to the program. For example, food exports to less developed countries are one thing when the United States enjoys large, unmarketable grain surpluses; they constitute quite another matter when grain reserves are low and rapidly rising food prices in the United States are helping to drive the country's rate of inflation to record peacetime levels. Thus, proposals for increased food aid to less developed countries in 1973 confronted tough opposition in the United States on the grounds that such aid would aggravate inflation in the American economy.

Additional domestic political opposition to foreign economic assistance comes from American industries and labor fearing loss of domestic production and jobs to less developed countries industrializing with the help of aid. Steelworkers and basic steel manufacturers in advanced industrial states, for example, have lived since the late 1970s with plant closings and massive layoffs because of global overcapacity in steelmaking. They vigorously oppose economic assistance to less developed countries for expanding steel industries—even if poor states view this as a vital step toward their overall industrialization goals. Increased economic assistance efforts by the United States and other donors are likely to become casualties of both neomercantilist and anti-inflationary foreign economic policies of such states in periods of stagflation.

During the 1980s, the Reagan administration imposed severe cuts in virtually all nondefense components of the U.S. federal budget, and Americans witnessed the prospect of annual $200-billion-a-year budget deficits. These developments helped produce such a poor domestic political climate for development assistance that funding for United States aid programs between 1981 and 1985 had to be obtained through a series of ad hoc continuing resolutions rather than the customary practice of passing annual foreign aid legislation. At the same time the administration shifted the emphasis of American foreign aid from development assistance to military assistance as part of a renewed effort to bolster defense. The cold war once again was providing the primary rationale for U.S. foreign assistance. In 1985 development assistance comprised only one third of American aid expenditures while security assistance accounted for two thirds. Between 1981 and 1985, increases in U.S. security assistance were almost five times those of development aid.[8]

To account for the erosion of support for economic assistance, we must also note the emergence of "donor fatigue," particularly on the part of the United States. Most major aid donors deny that they expect gratitude or allegiance from less developed countries as a condition for economic

---

[8] Ibid., p. 99.

assistance. Nevertheless, they resent the fact that long-time aid recipients so seldom evidence either in sufficient measure. Relative to the early years of economic assistance efforts, there is considerably less conviction in Western states that aid programs bring with them clearly identifiable influence over a recipient country's foreign policy orientation and its domestic political-economic processes. Over the years, all major aid donors have witnessed votes against their position on crucial issues before the United Nations, as well as public displays of hostility (such as attacks on embassies or other facilities) within the less developed countries to which much of their economic aid has flowed. This holds true for Communist aid donors as well as Western states. The Soviet Union has seen anti-Soviet rallies held in stadia constructed with Soviet aid. During the Cuban missile crisis in 1962, Guinea refused to permit Soviet aircraft bound for Cuba to land for refueling at the Conakry airport, which had been constructed with Soviet aid. After years of experience with aid programs, the accumulation of incidents such as these inevitably gives rise to skepticism about the political returns from economic assistance. This is true even if donors insist that no political obligations are connected with development assistance.

In addition to frustration with the foreign policy results of economic aid, the United States and other Western countries have lost confidence in their capacity to determine the development path of poor states through aid programs. Relative to the early postwar years, for example, aid donors are much less confident of their ability to produce predictable political, social, and economic results in poor states through transfers of technology[9], population control programs, duplication of Western public education and health systems, and capital flows designed to increase the GNP of aid recipients. There is, in addition, much more reluctance on the part of aid donors than there was decades ago to argue that economic assistance is linked in any clearly direct manner to the forging of Western democratic political systems in recipient states. In short, those officials in donor states who see economic assistance as a means of guiding the development efforts of poor states toward preconceived social, economic, and political ends are more sensitive to their limitations than in the past. They are also less prone to exaggerate claims about results to be expected from aid programs. These uncertainities about economic assistance make it more difficult in rich states to secure additional resources for economic aid programs.

A similar erosion of confidence in the development results of aid is evidenced in appraisals of aid by Soviet analysts. They have expressed doubts about the results of Soviet aid to the state sector in non-Communist less developed countries, as well as about the consequences of Soviet aid recipients' precipitously nationalizing the private sectors of their economies.[10] Soviet leaders have also expressed more general doubts about the nature of socialism espoused by many leaders of Third World states and about the profound differences between these forms of socialism and the "scientific socialism" of Moscow.

---

[9]For a discussion of the politics of transfer of technology, see Chapter 6.

[10]See Robert S. Walters, *Soviet and American Aid* (Pittsburgh, Pa.: University of Pittsburgh Press, 1970), pp. 65–67.

REASONS FOR MAINTAINING AND REINVIGORATING AID PROGRAMS

The decline in American support of economic assistance efforts is explained largely by these changes in the international political environment, by the erosion of domestic political support for aid appropriations, and by the emergence of "donor fatigue." In spite of these developments, the United States and other Western states continue to have sufficient interests in less developed countries to maintain economic assistance programs—albeit at reduced levels in relation to their economic capabilities. Economic aid will continue to be a valuable instrument in the diplomacy of advanced industrial states. For example, large requests for aid were an integral part of the American military withdrawal from Indochina and its efforts to settle the Middle East conflict. Two weeks after Secretary of State Kissinger's marathon negotiation of an Israeli-Syrian troop disengagement, and one week before President Nixon's visit to the Middle East in 1974, the administration requested $100 million in economic aid to rebuild Syrian towns along the disengagement line, $350 million in economic aid to Israel, $207 million for Jordan, and $250 million for Egypt. Following the U.S.-inspired Camp David Agreement on the Middle East in 1977, Israel and Egypt became by far the largest recipients of American economic assistance. Similarly, France has over the years sustained a large economic aid program designed to maintain political and extensive cultural (education) ties between itself and its former colonies. Economic aid will be maintained as a permanent instrument employed by rich states in pursuit of their disparate political goals in less developed countries, whatever the alterations in the philosophical underpinning of their aid efforts or the trend in overall aid flows.

Rich states will also continue economic assistance programs in an effort to promote their national and private economic interests in the Third World. The scarcity in global supplies of certain mineral resources emerged as a clear constraint to the prosperity of all advanced industrial states following oil shortages in 1973. More than ever before, rich states can be expected to use economic aid, along with other incentives, to secure access to vital raw materials in less developed countries. Japan, for example, made massive aid commitments to oil-producing states in the Persian Gulf and to Indonesia in the aftermath of the Arab embargo on oil shipments during 1973 and 1974.

Rich states also use aid to finance their exports to less developed countries. The provision of financing by Western states for high levels of imports by less developed nations in the 1970s helped to soften the severity of economic stagnation in the West. Western prosperity will continue to be linked importantly with provision of adequate financial assistance (through private and public channels) for less developed states to continue their purchases in Europe, the United States, and Japan. As long as neomercantilism continues to be an important part of advanced industrial states' overall trade policies, rich states are likely to continue economic assistance to poor states as a means of preserving export-related jobs at home and improving their balance of trade. The United States sends 38 percent of its exports to less developed countries. Aid as a supplement to private lending will remain a vital element in stimulating American commerce.

The connection between economic assistance and the creation of a hospitable climate for direct private foreign investment is still another reason for the continuation of aid programs by Western states. The United States and other Western aid donors have spoken frequently of economic assistance in the forms of resource surveys, feasibility studies, and infrastructure projects in less developed countries (ports, communication facilities, roads, rail transportation, electric power networks, and so forth) as crucial in creating the necessary preconditions for poor states to finance their future development through private resource flows. In these and other ways (such as investment guarantees for firms operating in poor states, and the threat of denying future foreign aid to less developed countries that nationalize private foreign investment without adequate compensation), economic aid programs are an integral part of securing investment opportunities for firms in donor states. In an age of burgeoning private foreign investment, most Western states will continue to have a vested interest in supporting aid programs on this ground alone.

The Third World debt crisis has since the mid-1980s refocused international attention on the importance of economic assistance. The success of both the Baker and the Brady plans for managing the debt crisis depend upon bolstering aid to heavily indebted less developed countries.[11] Increased infusions of public loans carrying concessionary terms (such as longer repayment periods and lower interest rates) are imperative for many less developed countries to sustain growth rates sufficient to service their existing private, commercial debts. Since the major Western aid donors are also the home of the world's leading commercial banks, potent domestic as well as international reasons exist to link economic assistance more closely with strategies for debt management. It seems inevitable that internal political-economic turmoil and threats of international economic instability unleashed by the burdens of servicing less developed states' foreign debt will be important reasons for elevating aid levels in the 1990s.

Finally, advanced industrial states will continue to engage in economic aid efforts because they contribute a unique type of resource transfer to less developed countries. Export earnings and private foreign investment combined may dwarf aid flows to less developed countries, but export earnings and private investment flow, in the first instance, to firms and individuals in poor states. Economic assistance, on the other hand, supplies new investment capital directly to governments in poor states for their use in priority development activities. Thus, systematic improvements in agriculture, education, health, and a variety of other activities to promote economic infrastructure and to meet human needs crucial for development are much more likely to be produced through aid than through revenues generated by trade or private investment in many instances.

The importance of aid in a poor state's overall development is greater than one would expect from looking at the volume of aid flows, shown

---

[11]The Baker and Brady plans are discussed in Chapter 3. pp. 97–99.

either as a proportion of total foreign exchange receipts or as a proportion of total investment by less developed countries. It is politically unfeasible for advanced industrial states today to deny their interest in the development of the Third World. Because of aid's unique characteristics, rich states that claim to have an interest in poor state's development must continue aid disbursements, notwithstanding their doubts about the political and economic results.

MULTILATERAL AID

Multilateral aid comprises one fourth of the total Western economic assistance. The International Bank for Reconstruction and Development (IBRD) and its affiliates, the major source of multilateral aid, disburses half as much economic assistance each year as the United States does. There are contradictory explanations as to the reasons for and larger significance of multilateral aid. One view is that multilateral aid is a means by which both donors and recipients can eliminate some of the more nettlesome problems they each associate with bilateral economic assistance. Another view (the radical perspective) is that multilateral aid is a more subtle and effective means than bilateral aid for exercising Western influence over less developed countries.

According to the first view, multilateral aid substantially removes politics from economic assistance; consequently, it is preferred by both donors and recipients to bilateral aid. Multilateral aid is a way in which to continue economic assistance with less direct involvement on the part of a donor state in the internal affairs of recipients. Thus, liberal U.S. Congress members can support multilateral aid as a means of maintaining an internationalist orientation and simultaneously reduce a specifically American presence in less developed countries; a former colonial power such as the Netherlands can give multilateral aid and thereby avoid charges that its aid efforts are merely an attempt to reimpose its dominance over former colonies. From the donors' perspective, multilateral aid permits a rich state to demonstrate its commitment to the development of poor states in a way that minimizes political attacks from aid critics at home and abroad.

Improved management of certain aid-related problems also provides incentives for increased multilateral cooperation by donors. Bilateral aid flows, for example, have typically been tied to purchases from the donor state. This places constraints on the aid recipient's choice of trade partners and usually results in higher prices for imports flowing to "captive" aid purchasers. Economic assistance must be untied to maximize its effectiveness for promoting development, but few states are willing to do this on a large scale unless all other donors do so. Multilateral aid encourages joint action toward this end.

Recipients, too, can see some major advantages to multilateral aid. Development assistance can be separated more clearly from the narrow political and security interests of various donors if aid is disbursed through an international organization. Even if multilateral aid disbursements are conditioned upon specified policy changes by a recipient, it is easier for a less developed state to accept these conditions from an international institution of which it is a member than to accept them from another state. Membership in the international agencies that disburse aid also gives less developed countries a voice in establishing the criteria for aid allocations. However small their voices, compared with those of rich states in these institutions, it is greater than the voice they have in shaping the bilateral aid policies of donor states. Hence, multilateral aid is attractive to both donors and recipients because it places an international organization between the parties to buffer what is usually a bittersweet relationship.

From the radical perspective, however, Western aid—multilateral as well as bilateral—has never been designed to facilitate the development of poor states. Indeed, in this view aid is merely another instrument that ensures the subordination of states in the periphery to Western states that control the capitalist global economy. This exploitation is crucial for the indefinite continuation of the rich states' prosperity. International economic institutions are purportedly essential to the efforts of rich states to subordinate and exploit less developed countries. The radical perspective with regard to aid is entirely consistent with their view of the function international organizations perform in trade and monetary relations, which we discussed in Chapters 2 and 3. Rich states remain fully in control of the aid policies of international institutions by virtue of their budgetary contributions and voting power, whereas the participation of poor states merely creates the illusion of a genuinely multilateral aid enterprise.

The International Monetary Fund and the International Bank for Reconstruction and Development are the focus of radical critiques of multilateral aid. The IBRD was established as a sister institution to the IMF. They share the same buildings in Washington, D.C., and, like the IMF, voting in the IBRD is weighted in rough proportion to the amount of capital each country pledges to the institution. In contrast to medium- and short-term IMF loans for financing balance-of-payments deficits, however, loans from the IBRD are repayable over much longer periods of time and are linked to internationally approved development programs of recipients. Over the years the IBRD has established the world's most extensive capabilities for monitoring and evaluating development plans and economic assistance. In 1988, over $15 billion in aid was disbursed under its auspices.

As the major source of multilateral short-term credit for less developed countries, the IMF and IBRD impose stringent conditions on their borrowers; conditions, stress the radical analysts, that open the door for their penetration by the trade and investment of rich states. They would view as consistent with this analysis the U.S. call for less developed countries' adoption of market-oriented domestic and foreign economic policies as a precondition for further access to international finance. Less developed countries not willing to conform to IMF and IBRD suggestions find themselves denied not only loans from these institutions but also credit through private channels or bilateral aid programs. These and other multilateral aid agencies, thus, are merely a subtler and more effective means of attaching poor states to the international imperialist system than is the cruder device of explicit political control.

We are likely to see renewed emphasis on multilateral assistance in coming years as the financial needs of Third World states continue to present a chronic challenge to the stability of the international economy. The IBRD, and especially its soft window (the International Development Agency), has firmly established itself as the centerpiece of multilateral aid efforts.

THE AID DIALOGUE AT THE INTERNATIONAL LEVEL

Global inflation, increased prices for oil dictated by OPEC, and economic stagnation of the advanced industrial states raise the aid needs of most less developed countries and inhibit the willingness of rich states to expand their aid programs. Less developed countries, cognizant of these facts, have attempted to rivet international attention on minimal aid levels "appropriate" for rich states and to push for comprehensive forms of debt relief for the least developed states among them.

Since the U.N.-declared First Development Decade in the 1960s, less developed countries have sought commitments from all developed states to extend economic assistance in amounts equal to at least seven tenths of 1 percent of their GNP. They were pressing in the 1980s for an increase in this aid target to 1 percent of donors' GNP. The United States has never accepted these or any aid targets as legitimate, in the sense that donor states have any obligation to meet them. Indeed, American aid would have to more than triple to comply with the 0.7 percent target. Among the Western states only Norway, the Netherlands, Denmark, Sweden, and France meet or exceed the aid target.[12] The less developed countries persist in attempting to hold rich states accountable to these international "standards" of aid giving. Even if compliance is rare, a political burden has been placed on every donor country to explain why its aid levels are below the target in virtually all international forums. Without exaggerating their importance, the presence of these targets has placed many rich states on the defensive over the years and has certainly encouraged most advanced industrial states of the West to expand their aid commitments, notwithstanding U.S. intransigence on the issue.

Debt relief has emerged as a major theme of the international aid dialogue since the late 1970s. Two very different types of LDC debtors have figured prominently in the evolution of aid policies. The heavily indebted countries concentrated in Latin America have been the focus of the Baker and Brady plans. As we saw in Chapter 3, their debt is largely owed to commercial banks. Multilateral aid efforts, as they relate to these countries, can be thought of as a means to help "socalize" the risks of their private foreign debt. Increased multilateral aid is necessary, in combination with other policies, to help such countries service their debt through growth rather than austerity, which threatens to undermine their domestic social-political-economic systems.

---

[12]Table 5-1 shows where various major donors stand in relation to these targets. Aid from the USSR and East Europe would have to increase two and one-half times. The Western states as a group would have to double their aid.

As development assistance becomes more closely linked to debt management, the traditional roles of the IBRD and the IMF have become less distinct. The IMF has supplemented its focus on short-term balance-of-payments concerns with longer-term adjustment and development concerns. The IBRD has supplemented its focus on long-term development assistance with greater attention to short-term balance of payments relief for heavily indebted LDCs. Some tensions have arisen between the two institutions over conflicting advice about economic policy to less developed states.[13] The IBRD enjoys much greater acceptance by most LDCs for its sustained support of development goals than the IMF, with its traditional emphasis on austerity for managing payments crises. As the World Bank assumes a higher profile in debt strategies, it seeks to maintain its posture as a champion of LDCs' development and to avoid becoming perceived in the Third World as a debt manager for commercial banks, like the IMF.

A group of heavily indebted states in sub-Saharan Africa present a very different challenge to the international system than the largest LDC debtors receiving the most attention. As very poor, underdeveloped states they were never able to borrow extensively from international banks in the 1970s. They carry a large foreign debt accumulated through bilateral and multilateral aid. Unlike the leading LDC borrowers, 65 percent of their debt is owed to governments and international institutions.[14] Since the mid-1980s Western governments have coordinated debt relief and forgiveness efforts through the Paris Club,[15] and special facilities were created in both the World Bank and the IMF to ease their debt service burdens.[16] These bilateral and multilateral aid developments are distinct from the international debt strategies discussed in Chapter 3.

The myriad challenges of Third World debt will certainly remain a central focus of international aid deliberations in coming years. Multilateral aid, and the IBRD in particular, will likely assume greater salience in international political-economic relations as a component of international debt management strategies.

---

[13]"World Bank and IMF in a Conflict Over Roles," *The New York Times*, February 28, 1989, pp. 25, 30.

[14]The World Bank. *Annual Report, 1988* (Washington, D.C.: IBRD, 1988), p. 27.

[15]The Paris Club is an ad hoc mechanism used by Western states over the decades to jointly negotiate repayment relief for aid recipients on a case-by-case basis. The main purpose is to maintain equitable burden sharing among creditors, so one donor state's largess to an aid recipient (e.g., forgiving some part of an aid debt) does not simply wind up financing the LDC's obligations to other donors. Joint action in negotiating concessions to aid recipients allows movement that might never be possible through unilateral policies. As of 1990, the United States had pledged to cancel debts of $735 million owed by twelve sub-Saharan countries. "U.S. Forgives Loans to 12 African Countries," *The New York Times*, October 10, 1990, p. 30.

[16]The World Bank, *Annual Report, 1988*, pp. 35–37; Organization for Economic Cooperation and Development, *Development Cooperation, 1987 Report*, pp. 14, 75.

TABLE 5-2   The Development Gap between Rich and Poor States, 1987

	77 Low and Middle Income States	OECD States
GNP per capita, 1987 dollars	700	14,670
Population, millions	3,861	747
Infant mortality per 1,000 live births	71	9
Life expectancy at birth, years	62	76
Calorie supply per capita	2,509	3,390
Population per physician	8,300	870
Percentage of age group enrolled in Secondary Education	40	93

Source: Table generated from data found in International Bank for Reconstruction and Development, *World Development Report, 1989* (Washington, D.C.: IBRD, 1989), statistical appendices.

CONCLUSION

The development gap between rich and poor states is a glaring reminder of tremendous inequalities present in the world (see Table 5-2). As long as it persists, demands for new forms and increased levels of economic assistance will confront the advanced industrial countries, no matter how generous they may feel they have been in the past. The development gap will be a source of increasing international political tensions in the future, just as inequalities among elements of domestic society have been in national politics throughout the world. The focus of the aid dialogue will change from time to time as the various needs of poor states take on greater or less urgency—such as debt service burdens or food supplies. But economic assistance in various forms will remain a critical need for all but one or two dozen of the 120 less developed countries for years to come.

At the same time, it is now more widely recognized than in the past than economic assistance programs can bear only a small share of the burden in producing development for most states. That requires extensive political, economic, and social alterations in the domestic systems of poor states as well as greater progress in improving the gamut of international trade, investment, monetary, and technology transfer relations between rich and poor countries. Economic assistance is likely to take a back seat, except intermittently, to these other pressing challenges to development and international economic peace keeping in future years.

6

Technology and International Relations

Developments in science and technology are increasingly important elements in world politics, with widespread international ramifications. Technology has become an objective of national policy, a means to achieve military, political, and economic goals, and an instrument to carry out foreign policy. Technological advances have become almost synonymous with economic growth and constitute major factors in assessing shifts in the balance of economic and political power. This is why the issues of technology and technology transfer have generated so much heated debate among researchers and policymakers alike. Technology transfer has become a prism for a constellation of related issues, among which are the role of science and technology in industrialization, the gap between rich and poor nations and its implications for both, the transnational corporations as both the culprit and savior, and the "new international economic order."[1]

Several different dimensions of the technology issue will be examined in this chapter. One focus is the technological gap between rich and poor nations, as viewed from the perspective of both types of countries. This issue has important international implications made more complex by the concerns of domestic interest groups. Similarly, among advanced industrial states, technological capability has substantial bearing on the perception and reality of a state's domestic and international strength and power. Thus, technology as a point of contention among advanced industrial states will also be considered. Finally, the use of technology as a weapon of foreign

[1]Taghi Saghafi-nejad and Robert Belfield, "Transnational Corporations, Technology Transfer and Development: A Bibliography," Worldwide Institutions Research Group, The Wharton School, University of Pennsylvania, Philadelphia, 1976, Introduction, p. 1.

policy will also be discussed. But first, it is useful to discuss what is meant by science, technology, and the transfer of technology.

Science and technology are closely related, but different, phenomena. *Science* "refers to a body of verifiable knowledge and an associated conceptual framework that attempts to structure the observable features of the natural world and to predict the outcome of observations and experiments yet to be conducted. . . . The driving forces of science are largely intellectual: curiosity, skepticism, and the search for order. But science also responds to social forces—the pursuit of prestige, the availability of public funds, the insatiable appetite for the new and different."[2] "*Technology*, by contrast, is action-directed, concerned with doing things, solving practical problems, the creation of goods and services that are marketable, in the commercial sense or in the sense that they fill the perceived needs of nations as a whole. The values of technology, then, are both internal, in that good technology usually derives from good science, and external, in that they are derived from the worth society places on the applications of technology."[3]

National scientific and technological capacities, as well as national capacities for innovation so important for developing and maintaining wealth and power, of course, vary widely. Factors important in influencing national innovation capacity include the entire spectrum of science and technology activities (research, development, production, and distribution) and a wide range of national policies and cultural traits (science and technology policy, macroeconomic policy, management skills/strategies and socio-technical factors such as research infrastructure, labor attitudes, bureaucracy, risk-taking inclinations, and risk-sharing mechanisms in the public and private sectors).[4]

As with international trade, investment, and monetary relations, technological innovation and leadership have been highly concentrated in the advanced industrial states of North America, Western Europe, and Japan. In 1963 and 1964, these states accounted for 98 percent of the world's expenditures on research and development (a total of $29 billion). The United States alone accounted for 70 percent of the total expenditures.[5] Ten years later, total global expenditures on research and development (R&D) increased to $63.5 billion, with advanced industrial states accounting for 97.2 percent of that amount. While the share of the developing countries hardly increased in that period, the U.S. share fell drastically from 70 percent to 50.7 percent, with Western Europe and Japan increasing proportionally. In 1985 of the 72,651 patents granted in the United States, 42 percent were awarded to residents of other nations, 38 percent of these

[2]John V. Granger, *Technology and International Relations* (San Francisco: W. H. Freeman, 1979), p. 9.

[3]Ibid., p. 10.

[4]See, for example, Frank Press, "Technological Competition and the Western Alliance," in *A High Technology Gap? Europe, America, and Japan*, ed. Andrew Pierre (New York: Council on Foreign Relations, 1987), pp. 14–27.

[5]Jan Annerstedt, "On the Global Distribution of R&D Resources," Occasional Paper 79: 1, Vienna Institute for Development, 1979, Figure 1, p. 4.

to Japanese. Between 1971 and 1975, about 30 percent of the patents were granted to foreigners and between 1961 and 1965 non-Americans were awarded only 17.5 percent of U.S. patents.

Since developing countries generate little indigenous technology, their source of supply for new technology has historically been from the advanced industrial states through the mechanism of technology transfer. Consequently, the developing countries, individually and through vehicles like the United Nations, have included technology in the North-South dialogue and discussions of the new international economic order. Technology has become linked inextricably with trade, monetary issues, and direct foreign investment, and at the same time it has become a critical issue in its own right.

The term *technology transfer* itself does not necessarily have a transnational connotation. For example, a distinction has been made between *vertical transfer*, as in the stages of the product cycle (e.g., from applied research to product development), and *horizontal transfer*, that is, transfer between places or institutions at a given stage of the product cycle.[6] For our purposes, international technology transfer "occurs whenever production in one country benefits from technical knowledge previously available only abroad."[7] The concept of the international transfer of technology as used in this book is the flow of purposeful knowledge across national boundaries "in whatever context for whatever reason to whatever country.[8]

International transfers of technology take place through numerous mechanisms. They include, for example, exported goods and services embodying product and process technologies, turnkey factories, direct foreign investment, license agreements, patent transfers, technical assistance through bilateral and multilateral aid programs, trade exhibits, educational exchanges, published trade and scientific literature, international colloquia and seminars, consulting, and theft.[9] Different mechanisms of transfer will clearly affect the amount, composition, and control of technology exchanged.[10] In one form or another, technology has been transferred across national boundaries throughout history. The issue has assumed greater salience in recent decades as the pace of technological change has accelerated in information-based industries and as the commercial life cycle of many high-technology products, such as integrated circuits and computers, is measured in just a few years.

---

[6]E. Mansfield, "International Technology Transfer: Forms, Resource Requirements and Policies," *American Economic Review* (May 1975), as reported in Philip Hanson, "Technology Transfer to the Soviet Union," *Survey: A Journal of East-West Studies*, 23, no. 2 (Spring 1977), 73.

[7]Philip Hanson, "Technology Transfer to the Soviet Union," p. 73.

[8]Henry R. Nau, *Technology Transfer and U.S. Foreign Policy* (New York: Praeger, 1976), p. 3.

[9]John McIntyre, "Introduction: Critical Perspectives on International Technology Transfer," in *The Political Economy of International Technology Transfer*, eds. Japan McIntyre and Daniel Papp (New York: Quorum Books, 1986), p. 11.

[10]Ibid., pp. 11–12.

TECHNOLOGY GAPS AND NORTH-SOUTH ISSUES

It is difficult to measure the exact magnitude of the technology gap between rich and poor states, for there are so many approximate or surrogate measures. Nonetheless, the gap is dramatic. A U.N. study that used 1975 per capita gross domestic product of the economically active population as a surrogate measure of technology estimated that "it would take 80 years (for the developing countries) to reach the 1975 levels (of the developed countries) with an annual GDP growth of 3 percent, 60 years with an annual growth of 4 percent, and 50 years with one of 5 percent."[11] In the meantime, of course, the advanced industrial states would not be standing still in technological developments and improvements. The gap can be illustrated further by the fact that 87.4 percent of the world's R&D scientists in 1973 lived in the advanced industrial states compared with only 12.5 percent in the developing countries.[12] Moreover, R&D expenditures per capita of the economically active population were $3.00 for developing countries and $182.10 in the developed countries, according to 1973 figures.[13] The data show clearly that most poor countries presently lack the capital and human resources necessary for industrialization and economic growth in the future.

The international political controversies surrounding the technology gap are centered in the almost universal desire of states to exercise control over science and technology—as opposed to acquiring it from external sources, no matter how accessible the technology or generous the terms. Nations want to harness technology to economic, social, and national security policies as defined by the state itself and not as determined by a foreign government or corporation. Many developing countries seek greater self-reliance in technology in all sectors of their economies, although many do not possess the capital or human resources to develop a strong technological base. Furthermore, effective control and use of technology is perceived to enable a country to compete more effectively in the international economy.

The developing countries seek new technology at low cost, and the advanced industrial states demand a significant return for transferred technology that was developed in their countries. Between these parties, and tied inextricably to the points of contention, are the multinational corporations as a major vehicle for technology transfer. The concerns and aspirations of each of these parties are important to an understanding of the technology issue.

---

[11]UNCTAD Secretariat, report of the Secretariat, *Towards the Technological Transformation of Developing Countries* (New York: United Nations, 1979), p. 34.

[12]Annerstedt, "On the Global Distribution of R&D Resources," p. 4.

[13]Ibid., p. 6.

CONCERNS OF DEVELOPING COUNTRIES

Probably the overriding concern of the developing countries has been what they consider to be their excessive dependence on the advanced industrialized states for their development (particularly in such areas as industrial technology) and what appears to be an inevitable perpetuation of that dependence. The developing countries feel entangled with the advanced industrial states by a variety of asymmetrical relationships largely the result of the dominant role that the industrialized states exercised during the colonial era. Trade patterns that developed between the advanced industrial states (i.e., the North) and the developing countries (i.e., the South) during colonial times form a key historic element of this asymmetric dependence.

For instance, the commodities produced in the South and sold in the international market largely reflected the demands and tastes of the markets in the North. Similarly, the consumer goods of interest to developing countries reflected the production patterns and tastes of the North. Because the Northern states possessed more elaborate technical know-how, patents, finance, and management techniques, the underdeveloped Southern states looked to the North for their supplies of capital-intensive consumer items, which were too complex to manufacture in the South. To industrialize, the developing countries had to import expensive technology, often in the form of products, from the already industrialized states, and that required them to expand their export base, selling more commodities primarily to the commodity-hungry North. Efforts by the developing countries to establish their own manufacturing industries threatened some of the exports from the industrialized states. The North's advocacy of freer international trade to facilitate the most efficient and profitable distribution of factors of production served to undermine the efforts of the developing countries to build a manufacturing base with its attendant technological advantages. The Southern states thereby felt relegated to becoming "hewers of wood" and had to be dependent on the North for whatever transfer of technology would be forthcoming, at the latter's own inclination and pace.

The asymmetry of technical knowledge in favor of the advanced industrial states is seen most vividly in the negligible ownership of patents by developing countries compared with the developed countries. Studies by UNCTAD have revealed that only 6 percent (200,000) of the world's 3.5 million patents in existence in 1972 were held by the developing countries and that less than one sixth of that total (30,000) were held by nationals of those countries.[14] The remaining 170,000 patents were held by foreigners, mostly multinational corporations.[15] Apparently, Western dominance

---

[14]UNCTAD Secretariat, "Transfer of Technology—Technological Dependence: Its Nature, Consequences and Policy Implications," TD/190 (New York: United Nations, 1975), p. 11.

[15]Issam El-Ziam, "Problems of Technology Transfer—A Point of View from the Third World," Occasional Paper No. 78/6, Vienna Institute for Development, 1978, p. 2.

of Third World patents has, if anything, been increasing. In Chile, for example, nationals held 34 percent of all patents in 1937, but only 5 percent thirty years later.[16]

Another concern of the developing countries relates to the "appropriateness" of the technology transferred by the advanced industrial states.[17] The developing countries maintain that much of the technology transferred is typically capital intensive and labor saving whereas the chief problem in most developing countries is unemployment. The different circumstances under which such technology is developed and the unwillingness of the developed countries and the multinational corporations to adapt it to the local setting make it inappropriate for the developing countries given their need to provide employment. Conversely, machinery and equipment transferred to the developing countries have been labeled "inappropriate" because they were machines of older vintage. Not only was the technology out of date but also the developing countries or consumers in these countries were being charged high prices for the old technology. The contradiction between these two arguments is a function of the differing values that exist within a country.

Even where the technology transferred from the developed countries is welcomed by the developing countries, there is generally a dissatisfaction with its price. The developing countries maintain that the cost of transferred technology is unnecessarily inflated. For example, it is charged that members of the pharmaceutical industry are among the highest-cost sellers of technology and dramatically overprice their products. An OECD report stated (on the evidence of U.S. Senate reports) that some ingredients were overpriced by 1,000 percent or even 5,000 percent.[18] The developing countries consider technology already developed to be part of human heritage and that all countries have a right of access to such technology to improve their standards of living. Moreover, they are of the view that they have paid enough to the developed countries through the exploitation of their natural resources that facilitated the development of the advanced industrial states at their expense. The developing countries are therefore incensed by the fact that payments for technology, in their attempt to industrialize, strain their balance-of-payments position. An UNCTAD study estimated that the Third World would pay over $10 billion for the right to use patents, licenses, process know-how, technical services, and trademarks by the end of the 1970s.[19] In 1988 receipts by U.S. firms from the export of royalties and license fees totaled nearly $10.7 billion.[20]

---

[16]Ibid.

[17]See, for example, Luis de Sebastián, "Appropriate Technology in Developing Countries," in *Mobilizing Technology for World Development*, eds. Jairam Ramesh and Charles Weiss, Jr. (New York: Praeger, 1979), pp. 66–73.

[18]A. C. Cilinigiroglu, "Transfer of Technology for Pharmaceutical Chemicals," October 1974, as reported in *Transfer of Multinational Corporations*, Vol. II, ed. Dimitri Germidis (Paris: Development Center of OECD, 1977), p. 26.

[19]UNCTAD Secretariat, report of Secretariat, *Major Issues Arising from the Transfer of Technology to Developing Countries* (New York: United Nations, 1973), p. 2.

[20]U.S. Department of Commerce, *United States Trade Performance, 1988* (Washington, D.C.: GPO, September 1989), p. 89.

One contributor to the unnecessarily inflated price of technology, as seen by the developing countries, is the fact that technology is often sold in packages. For example, tie-in clauses in certain contracts compel a licensee to purchase unpatented goods from the licensor; in other cases, technology may be supplied only through turnkey operations where the supplier undertakes full responsibility for construction of a plant and managing it until local personnel are ready to do so. Particularly where the recipient of the technology is a subsidiary of the supplier, as often is the case, the recipient country acquires little, if any, "new" technical know-how. What the developing countries find repugnant is that some elements of the package may be overpriced, unnecessary, or available locally. One study revealed that 83 percent of Bolivia's contracts and 86 percent of Ethiopia's involved such clauses.[21] There has consequently been a drive for disaggregation or "unbundling" of package contracts by the developing countries. In the Andean pact countries, for instance, royalty payments from subsidiaries to parent companies are prohibited. Moreover, a requirement is imposed for disaggregation: The import of every item of technology must be cost justified separately on the basis of comparison with other available technology.[22]

As part of their strategy to facilitate technological development and minimize the cost of imported technology, the developing countries have been trying to get the multinational corporations operating in their jurisdiction to establish research and development centers in the local setting. One OECD-sponsored study of sixty-five subsidiaries of more than twenty multinational corporations in twelve countries of varying levels of development, economic structure, size, and geographical locations revealed that R&D activities in centers attached to subsidiaries were practically nonexistent[23] but were concentrated mostly in the parent company's home country. There are good reasons for this, including the economies of scale involved in centralizing R&D, the availability of highly trained scientific and engineering personnel, close interactions between members of the scientific community, and more effective management of the R&D function.[24] But the technology gap is widened, not narrowed, as a result of such policies. However, some countries have been able to trade off access to markets for local R&D facilities. In July 1985 Mexico allowed IBM to build microcomputers in that country, but among other things IBM promised

[21]El-Ziam, "Problems of Technology Transfer," p. 31.

[22]Chamber of Commerce of the United States, report of the Task Force on Technology Transfer, "Technology Transfer and the Developing Countries: Guidelines and Principles for Consideration in Development of National Policies Governing Transfer of Technology Between Industrial and Developing Countries" (Washington: Chamber of Commerce, April 1977), p. 7.

[23]Dimitri Germidis, *Transfer of Technology by Multinational Corporations: A Synthesis and Country Case Study*, Vol. I (Paris: Development Center of the OECD, 1977), p. 52.

[24]William A. Dymza, "Regional Strategies of U.S. Multinational Firms That Affect Transfers of Technology to Developing Countries," in *Transfer of Technology by Multinational Corporations*, Vol. II, ed. Dimitri Germidis, p. 99.

to establish a semiconductor technology center to assist Mexico's electronics industry.[25]

One of the results of this phenomenon, which is of great concern to the developing countries, is what is known as "reverse transfer of technology" or "brain drain." Not only are the developed countries and their multinational corporations reluctant to establish R&D and other facilities that could employ and train local skilled labor, but, paradoxically, the developing countries in need of foreign assistance are an important source of highly qualified personnel for the developed countries. UNCTAD studies estimate that, for the fifteen-year period from 1960 to 1975–1976, skilled migration from the developing countries (consisting of engineers, scientists, physicians and surgeons, and technical and kindred workers) to the three major developed countries of immigration—the United States, Canada, and the United Kingdom—amounted to over 300,000 persons.[26] That estimate does not take into account skilled migration to other developed countries. At the same time there has been a gradual shift in the skill-level composition of persons emigrating from the developing to the developed countries. Officials in the latter have attempted to make their immigration policies responsive to their domestic labor markets by applying more selective criteria for immigration applicants.[27] For example, in the United States, high on the list of priorities are those people with education and skills needed in the U.S. labor market; very low on the list are unskilled workers. Consequently, scientists, engineers, doctors, and the more highly skilled are more likely to gain permission to immigrate to the United States than are other less skilled categories; this contributes to the brain drain from those countries desperately in need of building their indigenous technological capabilities. In terms of absolute flows, nearly 61,000 physicians and surgeons, over 100,000 engineers and scientists, and another 123,000 technical and kindred workers migrated from the developing regions to the United States, Canada, and the United Kingdom between 1961 and 1975–1976.[28] In the latter part of the 1970s, the migration of people from the developing countries represented 70 percent to 80 percent of the total migration of skilled persons to the United States. From 1961 to 1965, the developing countries provided only 37 percent of the total migrants.[29] Approximately half of the graduates of medical schools in the Philippines go abroad, and 80 percent of the Taiwan Chinese who are studying in the

[25]On the subject of bargaining between LDCs and multinational firms over technology, see Constantine Vaitsos, "Government for Bargaining with Transnational Enterprises in the Acquisition of Technology," in *Mobilizing Technology for World Development*, eds. Jairam Ramesh and Charles Weiss, Jr., pp. 98–107.

[26]UNCTAD Secretariat, report of Secretariat, *Technology: Development Aspects of the Reverse Transfer Technology* (New York: United Nations, 1979), para. 6.

[27]Ibid., para. 9.

[28]Ibid., para. 12.

[29]Ibid., para. 10, based on unpublished data supplied by the U.S. National Science Foundation.

United States do not return home. The brain drain is working to the disadvantage of the developing countries.

These considerations provide substantial justification for developing countries' skepticism regarding reliance upon the "trickling down" of technology from the advanced states. Some developing countries have sought to develop indigenous R&D capacities that would simultaneously facilitate growth, preserve their self-reliance, and enhance national security. Brazil has attempted to build its own software capability by deliberately restricting foreign involvement in this industry. One outcome of the present system is an uneven distribution of the fruits of technology transfer and a substantial widening of domestic income gaps. The consequences of this situation have been stated succinctly by Frances Stewart, an Oxford economist:

> 5–15 percent of the labor force is equipped with modern technology. The rest suffers from complete neglect. The minority, equipped with advanced-country methods, have high productivity and high incomes; the majority, lacking all modern equipment and deprived of most investment resources, suffer from very low productivity. The wide disparities in incomes between the sector using advanced technology transferred from the advanced countries and the rest of the population is largely responsible for the unsatisfactory income distribution in many developing countries, and for the employment problem.[30]

Because of a dependency upon technology transfer via multinational corporations, many developing countries feel unable to control either the direction or the pace of technological and industrial development. While some remedies of control are possible, the economic realities of their position mean that in many cases countries are largely passive recipients of the technological efforts of others. Autonomy and self-direction are difficult to achieve.

In addition, the tendency for some multinational corporations, in pursuit of more favorable costs, to allocate low-skill-level operations to subsidiaries in developing countries may have long- and short-term effects on the international division of labor. The developing countries may be frozen into production activity characterized by low wage costs and low technology levels, whereas the more high-paying functions requiring the development and application of new technology will remain the province of the advanced industrial states. Thus, the developing countries retain their status of economic and technological colonies with few opportunities to develop their own technological strength.

---

[30]Frances Stewart, "Technological Dependence in the Third World," paper prepared for OECD Seminar on Science and Technology and Development in a Changing World, DSTI/SPR/75.33, Paris, April 21–25, 1975, as quoted in Ward Morehouse, "Science and Technology and the Global Equity Crisis: New Directions for United States Policy," Occasional Policy No. 16, The Stanley Foundation, Muscatine, Iowa, 1978, p. 18.

ADVANCED INDUSTRIAL STATES' VIEWS AND THE TECHNOLOGY GAP

The concerns of the developed nations with respect to technology transfer differ significantly from those of the developing countries; hence, the debate. One primary issue upon which there is disagreement is the view that existing technology is part of human heritage and should therefore be free. The advanced industrial states maintain that technology is proprietary knowledge, a human product based on ingenuity and capability that merits commercialization and that should be sold only at the owner's (and developer's) discretion. Its transfer, however achieved, should neither be interfered with nor should it be compelled.

The arguments by the developed countries on this issue may be summarized as follows: First, the developing countries fail to realize that the majority of transferable technology is privately owned by corporations and that the governments of the advanced industrial states cannot mandate transfer of technology even if they wanted to. A report by the Chamber of Commerce of the United States stated that

> The ownership of technology constitutes a property interest entitled to recognition as such. There is no doubt that this statement represents the position of the United States government of both political parties, of economists and lawyers of nearly every persuasion and of both American business and American labor.[31]

Second, as with any other commercial item, technology will be transferred only if the conditions for it are suitable. Moreover, the owners of the technology usually seek profits from its use. A report that contributed to the development of U.S. policy for the General Conference on Science and Technology for Development in Vienna in August 1979 stated that

> it seems clear that the extent of private technology flows to developing countries will depend on whether conditions in each country (markets, regulations, institutional and business capabilities, and so forth) attract such flows.[32]

Third, it is only appropriate that the developed countries demand a "fair" return for the technology transferred to the developing countries because technology is expensive. It is estimated that American government agencies, firms, and universities spent $132 billion on research and development in 1989.[33] Also, funds earned from existing technology are needed for the development of new technology. The advanced industrial states, especially the multinational corporations, maintain that survival and growth of their enterprises are dependent on profits often generated by the de-

---

[31]Chamber of Commerce of the United States, "Technology Transfer," p. 20.

[32]National Research Council, report of the Council, *U.S. Science and Technology for Development: A Contribution to the 1970 U.N. Conference*, Background on Suggested U.S. Initiatives for the U.N. Conference on Science and Technology for Development, Vienna, 1979 (Washington, D.C.: GPO, 1978), p. 5.

[33]United States, National Science Board, *Science and Engineering Indicators, 1989* (Washington, D.C.: GPO, 1989), p. 264.

velopment and application of new technology. Consequently, bowing to the demands of the developing countries for free or undervalued technology is considered suicidal and furthermore would greatly reduce technological breakthroughs of benefit to the world.

Instead of allowing economic forces to regulate technology flows, the aggressive political activism of the developing countries in their quest for technology is objectionable to many of the advanced industrial states and the multinational corporations. This posture of the developing countries is thought to be counterproductive to the long-term growth interests of the developing countries. The chairman of OECD's Development Assistance Committee has stated that the developing countries "do themselves a disservice by not recognizing more clearly that a further unleashing of the international market mechanism at this juncture is the most promising means for moving toward their goal of a new international economic order.[34] In effect, many in the advanced industrial states feel that developing countries should seek expansion of technology and its application rather than pursue policies that will restrict technology and its transfer to countries needing its benefits.

The interests and concerns of the advanced industrial states coincide largely with those of the multinational corporations that serve as the major conduit for the transfer of technology. They are particularly disturbed by the restrictive practices of the developing countries, ranging from national legislation to the call for international codes of conduct, many of which are considered to inhibit economic activity and efficiency. A growing number of developing countries have adopted laws and created regulatory agencies to control the flow of technology and the payments for such technology. For example, the Andean pact members made technology transfer payments an important part of their overall regulation of foreign capital.[35] In Brazil, payments for technology are screened by a National Institute on Industrial Property before foreign exchange is released by the central bank.[36] Argentina has a similar law. Mexico, among other countries, has denied or severely restricted patent protection for pharmaceuticals, fertilizers, pesticides, and the like as well as for a variety of chemical and metallurgical processes, antipollution apparatus, and nuclear technology.[37] At the international level, the code of conduct proposed by the developing countries in UNCTAD is seen as a list of "do's and don'ts" for multinational companies. In response, the Chamber of Commerce of the United States has stated in its guiding principles that

> the United States should react to impairment or threats of impairment of industrial property rights of American citizens as it does to the impairment of rights in tangible property.[38]

[34]Report of the OECD Development Assistance Committee, John P. Lewis, chairman. "A Possible Scenario for the Development Strategy," *OECD Observer*, 101 (November 1979), 6. This view was also propounded by President Reagan at the Cancun Conference in 1981.

[35]Chamber of Commerce of the United States, "Technology Transfer," p. 12.

[36]Ibid., p. 12.

[37]Ibid., p. 15.

[38]Ibid., p. 20.

The developed countries and the multinational corporations sometimes find confusing the apparent contradiction between the often-expressed demands for easier transfer of technology to developing countries and their demands for the strengthening of local capability to innovate and produce or adapt technologies more appropriate to the local environment and markets. The developing countries are seen to be undecided and unclear about their needs and capabilities and consequently frustrate the potential development of adequate technology flows.

In addition to the disagreement over how the developing countries should react to technology, some groups in the advanced industrial states have serious misgivings about the export of technology from such states. Some in the United States have even agitated for a curb on the export of technology to both developing and developed countries.

The most vocal and persistently critical group in developed countries on the issue of technology transfer is the labor movement. It has spearheaded the verbal assaults on the multinational corporation for excessive transfer of technology. The gist of their protectionist position in the United States is that the export of technology, be it in the form of know-how, machinery, or plants, has a long-term damaging effect on the U.S. economy as a whole and on U.S. employment in particular. Earlier chapters discussed American labor's concerns about the effect of American subsidiaries overseas and the "unfair" trade practices of other countries that threatened employment levels in the United States.[39]

The current protectionist stance of U.S. labor is a major shift from labor's position in the 1950s and 1960s when it advocated freer trade. Then, labor felt that removing impediments to trade facilitated potential growth in U.S. exports, thereby creating more jobs for U.S. workers who enjoyed a substantial technological advantage over workers elsewhere. With the increasing interventions in markets by the developing countries, such as export performance requirements, local content regulations, and technology review boards, U.S. labor has become frustrated and has been pressing both industry and the government to take actions to prevent a loss of U.S. industrial employment.

One reason why labor is disturbed by the export of technology to the developing countries is the latter's tendency to erect high tariff barriers to restrict the inflow of American products based on that technology, once the domestic expertise is developed. A case in point involves light aircraft trade between the United States and Brazil. Until the early 1970s, Brazil was a leading purchaser of light aircraft manufactured in the United States; in 1974, 408 Cessna aircraft were purchased by Brazil. The Brazilian government wanted to create a domestic light aircraft industry and entered into co-production with the Piper Aircraft Corporation to manufacture in Brazil. The Brazilian government later put a 50 percent tax on all imported planes even from Piper. In 1976, Piper Aviacao do Brasil supplied about

---

[39]See the discussions on this point in Chapters 2 and 4.

75 percent of the domestic Brazilian market, while the United States export market share fell from about 100 percent in 1970 to less than 1 percent in 1976. Moreover, in 1976, the Brazilian Piper subsidiary had begun to export aircraft to Uruguay, Chile, Peru, Colombia, Venezuela, and some African nations. It even sought to sell Brazilian-made planes in the United States.[40] By labor's estimate, the creation of a light aircraft industry in Brazil has damaged employment in the U.S. aircraft industry. Similar developments have occurred in other industries, especially as developing countries established local content regulations for subsidiaries of foreign multinationals.

The liberal arguments of the developed countries and multinational corporations about technology appear so contrary to the neo-Marxist arguments of the developing countries that the two sides seem to be on a no-win path. However, the desire to resolve the conflict and work out an accommodation has led to a variety of formal and ad hoc agreements that seek to make the system better as opposed to dismantling it. As in so many cases described in this book, the North and the South each have legitimate concerns about the other party's point of view. As a result, the conflicts are not easily resolved. Particular problems between a multinational corporation and a developing country are often settled through negotiations, although in some cases no agreement can be reached. However, there are also major efforts to address, if not resolve, the North-South technology issue in a variety of international settings. UNCTAD has been a pivotal forum for attempts to reach an understanding.

In 1974 the developing nations proposed an International Code of Conduct on Transfer of Technology that sought initially to curtail drastically the concept of ownership of technology. The issue is so sensitive and so linked with other international economic issues that drafts are still being debated. The developing countries feel that mandating technology transfer will provide increased and cheaper access to technology. The advanced industrial states are convinced that practices that undermine the ownership and control of technology by its developers will reduce the transfer of technology, for there will be little incentive to engage in such transfers.

The Andean Common Market and ASEAN countries have also established their own rules and regulations regarding technology. The Organization of American States has sought to develop an understanding about the different perspectives of advanced and developing countries. The OECD has addressed the issue of technology transfer directly in several ways, including having a section on that issue in its Guidelines for Multinational Enterprises, which was discussed in Chapter 4.

In spite of these and other efforts, the issue of technology transfer

---

[40]See the National Research Council, *Technology, Trade and the U.S. Economy* (Washington, D.C.: National Academy of Sciences, 1978), pp. 74–75; and Harold W. Berkman and Ivan R. Vernon, *Contemporary Perspective in International Business* (Chicago: Rand McNally, 1979), p. 138.

from developed countries to the developing countries is unlikely to be resolved soon. Technology transfer is linked inextricably with the other international political economy issues addressed in this book. In addition, technology is an important part of the demand of the developing countries for a dramatic transfer of resources and wealth from the North to the South. The issues are clear; the different viewpoints are well-founded, but the controversy is so linked to different sets of values that its resolution is extraordinarily difficult.

TECHNOLOGY, POWER, AND COMPETITIVENESS AMONG DEVELOPED STATES

Technology gaps are not exclusive concerns of less developed countries confined to the North-South conflict. Advanced industrial states place great emphasis on their relative technological strength as it affects their growth potential, national security, and political-economic independence. In the mid-1960s, fears of America's seemingly unassailable scientific and technological predominance relative to Europe prompted the French, especially, to politicize this issue. In the decade 1957–1966, the United States devoted over three times the resources to research and development ($158 billion) as did all the industrialized states of Western Europe combined ($50 billion).[41] From 1951 to 1969, scientists in the United States received twenty-one of thirty-eight Nobel prizes in chemistry and twenty-three of forty Nobel prizes in medicine and physiology.[42] Giant American-based multinational firms such as IBM and Kodak were capable of devoting resources to research and development equal in magnitude to the gross sales of their competitors in Europe.[43] Indeed, from 1965 to 1970,[44] IBM spent as much on the development of its model 360 computer ($5 billion) as the French government planned to spend on the Force de Frappe, its nuclear deterrent.

Taking note of these and similar developments, Robert Gilpin summarized the French position on the centrality of science and technological capability to leadership in international relations:

> Today Great Power status accrues only to those nations which are leaders in all phases of basic research and which possess the financial and managerial means to convert new knowledge into advanced technologies. In the case of the two superpowers, eminence in science and technology go hand-in-hand,

[41]Organization for Economic Cooperation and Development, *Gaps in Technology*, analytical report (Paris: OECD, 1970), p. 115. During the mid-1960s American expenditures on research and development were fifteen times those of West Germany and ten times those of Britain. Raymond Vernon, *Sovereignty at Bay* (New York: Basic Books, 1971), p. 90.

[42]Vernon, *Sovereignty at Bay*, p. 90.

[43]Kenneth Waltz, "The Myth of National Interdependence," in *The International Corporation*, ed. C. Kindleberger (Cambridge, Mass.: M.I.T. Press, 1970), p. 217; and John Dunning, "Technology, United States Investment and European Economic Growth," in *The International Corporation*, p. 165.

[44]Waltz, "The Myth of National Interdependence," p. 217.

and it appears unlikely that any nation or group of nations can ever again aspire to a dominant role in international politics without possessing a strong, indigenous scientific and technological capability. International politics has passed from the era of traditional industrial nation states to one dominated by the scientific nation states.[45]

The vulnerability of even an advanced industrial state that is dependent upon an ally for foreign sources of technology was revealed when the U.S. government initially prohibited the French purchase of certain IBM computers required for its Force de Frappe on the grounds that the nuclear test ban treaty forbade America's assisting a nonnuclear power to obtain nuclear weapons.[46] In the eyes of the French and numerous other states on the wrong side of the technology gap, the achievement of a greater degree of self-sufficiency in science and technology is a prerequisite for the capacity to forge an independent stance in global political and economic relations.

During the 1980s and 1990s, fears of technological decline in the United States relative to Japan, Europe, and the newly industrializing countries of East Asia emerged as a major concern among analysts of American national security and international competitiveness—even though the picture remains very complex. The United States in 1986 still spent more on research and development than the next four largest countries combined (Japan, West Germany, France, and Britain).[47] Yet, the U.S. share of the combined R&D budgets of these five leading states declined from 68 percent in 1966 to 54 percent in 1986.[48] Both West Germany and Japan spend a larger share of their GNP on research and development than the United States, and a larger portion of both German and Japanese R&D has been focused on commercial applications than American R&D, which is more defense-oriented.[49] The share of U.S. patents granted to foreigners rose from 30 percent in 1970 to 48 percent in 1986—the highest share of U.S. patents that foreign inventors have ever achieved.[50] Japanese inventors accounted for 21 percent of U.S. patents in 1986.[51]

Most alarming of all has been a dramatic decline in America's trade balance in high-technology manufactures during the 1980s, traditionally a strong point in U.S. trade performance. The United States actually imported more high-technology manufactured goods than it exported in 1986. Japan and the newly industrializing Asian countries have been the

[45]Robert Gilpin, *France in the Age of the Scientific State* (Princeton, N.J.: Center of International Studies, Princeton University Press, 1968), p. 25.

[46]Ibid., p. 54. These IBM computers were to be purchased from the French affiliate of IBM. This case is a good example of the political implications of multinational corporations for host state–parent state relations. These implications are discussed in Chapter 4 of the present volume.

[47]United States, National Science Board, *Science and Technology Indicators, 1989*, p. 3.

[48]Ibid.

[49]Ibid.

[50]Ibid., pp. 133, 134.

[51]Ibid., p. 135.

major threat in this regard. For a summary of U.S. high-technology trade developments during the 1980s, see Figure 6-1.

These trends have immense impacts on American national security, competitiveness, and international leadership, as noted by Charles Ferguson: "U.S. technological decline in an era of globalized economic activity implies that foreign and national security policy now depends upon economic and technology policy to a degree not seen since the advent of nuclear weapons. The future economic and geopolitical security of the United States will be determined ever more heavily by the fundamental health of its technology-intensive industries."[52] Yet, as the trade data in Figure 6-1 indicate, these industries are not faring as well as they used to in the United States.

Ferguson and others attribute this decline to a combination of domestic and international developments. Domestic factors involve shortcomings in U.S. government policies, industrial structures and corporate strategies—including such things as tax and economic policies biased toward consumption; fragmented political and economic structures impeding long-term technological and strategic coordination; research, higher education, trade, and military policies that afford other countries asymmetric access to American science and technology; and entrenchment of outdated manufacturing processes within American industry.[53] International factors include developments in financial markets, the pace of international technology transfers, rises in foreign competition, lower capital costs in other countries, industry structures and corporate strategies abroad that more

FIGURE 6-1 U.S. Trade Balance, High-Tech Manufactured Goods ($ billion).

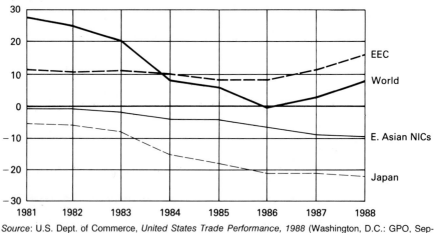

Source: U.S. Dept. of Commerce, *United States Trade Performance, 1988* (Washington, D.C.: GPO, September 1989), p. 87.

[52]Charles Ferguson, "America's High-Tech Decline," *Foreign Policy*, No. 74 (Spring 1989), 124.

[53]Ibid., p. 125.

effectively commercialize new product and process technologies, and the diminishing importance of the U.S. market to total global demand—Japan is clearly perceived to pose the greatest external threat to American technological leadership.[54]

Concerns such as these have led to numerous conflicts involving technology competition and transfers between the United States and its closest military and economic partners. The Reagan and Bush administrations opposed a Japanese effort to develop and construct a new fighter airplane (FSX) on its own, based on the F-16, and insisted upon a joint U.S.–Japanese project involving American contractors. The Japanese accommodated these demands only to face bitter outcries from Congress that the United States was giving Japan access to American technology that the Japanese would certainly use to develop into a strong future international competitor in civil and defense aviation. The arrangements for joint U.S.–Japanese development and production of the FSX were maintained in 1989 with limits on Japanese access to particularly sensitive U.S. technologies. The conflict created over technology transfers by the United States in connection with the project will accelerate pressures for indigenous Japanese defense production including an aviation industry to compete with American and European firms.[55] Moreover, we can certainly expect more difficulty in future military cooperation between these allies as issues of technology and competitiveness intrude more directly on defense production in both states.

At the outset of the 1990s all of the advanced industrial states were competing vigorously through public policy and private initiatives for leadership to develop and commercialize important technologies associated with potential high-growth industries in the international economy. Within months after the discovery of new materials with superconducting properties at liquid nitrogen and higher temperatures in 1986, for example, both Japan and the United States launched highly publicized national policies to accelerate the commercialization of new superconductivity technologies with myriad commercial and military applications in areas such as energy (production, storage, and transmission), transportation (magnetic levitation trains, ship propulsion), and medicine (magnetic resonance imaging).[56] Europe, Japan, and the United States were competing at the outset of the 1990s to establish national and international standards for high definition television (HDTV) that will largely determine which countries' industries will assume the lead in the next generation of products for television transmission and reception, computer terminals, and defense-related electronic displays.

Leadership in important dual-use (military and commercial) technologies has assumed such importance for national military and economic

---

[54]Ibid., p. 126.

[55]See "Tokyo, Unsure of U.S., Talks of Developing Its Own Arms," *The New York Times*, June 28, 1989, pp. 1, 7.

[56]Robert S. Walters and Ellis Krauss, "Science, Technology, and Economic Competitiveness: U.S. and Japanese Efforts To Commercialize High Temperature Superconductivity," Mimeo, Paper delivered at the annual meeting of the International Studies Association, London, April 1, 1989.

security that the United States, as most states, has experimented with new forms of state-industry relations to position its important national industries more favorably in the international division of labor. During the 1980s Japanese firms seized the lead in semiconductor manufacturing from the United States "merchant" firms (producers of semiconductors for end-users other than themselves) that pioneered the industry. By the middle of the decade several U.S. government studies "concluded that the nation was falling behind Japan in most of the key process and manufacturing technologies necessary for the production of future generations of semiconductor technology. Indeed, for over five years Japanese producers have been first to market with new memory chips that represent the next advance in miniaturization."[57] In an electronic age, surrender of technological leadership in semiconductor products and manufacturing processes has important connotations for international economic preeminence and defense. Accordingly, with the support of the Defense Department a consortium of leading U.S. semiconductor firms, chip tooling and materials suppliers pooled resources to advance and disseminate semiconductor manufacturing techniques in an effort to overtake the Japanese—Sematech, the Semiconductor Manufacturing Technology Initiative located in Austin, Texas.[58] The results of this effort are not yet clear. However, an active role by the federal government to promote generic, process technologies to strengthen the domestic semiconductor industry's competitive position in international commercial markets marks a bold departure from its traditional non-interventionist role in the civilian economy. In this regard the federal government of the United States is engaged in the same game that Americans criticize Japan's Ministry of Trade and Industry (MITI) for playing. Indeed, it is attempting to emulate the Japanese model of close government-business cooperation through state funding for the creation of industrial consortia in critical, high-technology sectors.[59]

The United States, the European Economic Community, and Japan bring different strengths and weaknesses to their competition for technological leadership in the world. Technological innovation is reflected in nations' research, development, production, and distribution capabilities. In very general terms, U.S. strengths lie in research and development as manifested in high funding levels for R&D, the unparalleled research capacity of its universities and national laboratories in basic science, the numerous ties between universities and industry, commercial spillovers from large federal defense and space programs in the postwar period (computers, semiconductors, civil aviation, for example), and the world's largest domestic market.[60]

American industries' weaknesses in technological innovation tend to lie more in production and distribution—in commercializing new scientific discoveries and technologies. Several factors are important in this regard.

---

[57]Michael Borrus, *Competing for Control: America's Stake in Microelectronics* (Cambridge, Mass.: Ballinger, 1988), p. 3.

[58]See Ibid., pp. 216–22.

[59]This is a celebrated instance of industrial policy discussed previously in Chapter 2.

[60]Press, "Technological Competition and the Western Alliance," p. 29.

Research in universities and national laboratories contribute importantly to basic science in the United States, but their research agendas are not driven by considerations of commercialization. The national laboratories, especially, have a poor track record for transferring technology to civilian industry.[61] While the U.S. federal government spends far more on R&D than any other state, over 70 percent of that was directed toward defense in the late 1980s. It is often argued that dual-use technology is spun off to the private sector from defense R&D, but there is a widespread sense that the increasingly specialized nature of defense applications is diminishing the commercial impact of dual-use technologies in the United States.[62] In more commercially relevant, nondefense R&D expenditures as a percent of GNP, the United States ranks fourth behind Japan, West Germany, and France.[63]

In both Japan and Germany a higher percentage of national R&D expenditures are derived from business sources than in the United States, and the late 1980s witnessed declines in the rate of growth of U.S. corporate funding for research.[64] Xerox and Eastman Kodak, long noted for their vigorous research programs, have sharply curtailed and reorganized their research, especially in basic sciences.[65] Factors inhibiting corporate research spending in the United States relative to Japan and West Germany include greater fragmentation within industries and heavier reliance on equity-based investment requiring more attention to short-term returns on capital. The surge of leveraged buyouts in the United States also inhibits R&D as management looks for ways to cut back on long-term investments to focus on higher immediate returns to stockholders and on generating higher cash flows to service heavy financial debts. The purchase of RCA by General Electric, for example, resulted in less research for both.[66]

Japan's innovative strength has been more in its rapid commercialization of innovative technologies, production, and distribution than in basic science, research, and development. Its "remarkable success, at first with traditional manufacturing and later in the advanced technology sectors, emphasized the application of good engineering to both manufacturing processes and production technology, and the release of high-quality, competitively priced products on world markets."[67] Its capacities in overtaking American firms in automobiles, electronic consumer goods, and semiconductors clearly reflect these strengths. The Japanese have been somewhat

---

[61]U.S. Congress, Office of Technology Assessment, *Commercializing High Temperature Superconductivity* (Washington, D.C.: GPO, June 1988), p. 83.

[62]Harvey Brooks, "Technology as a Factor in U.S. Competitiveness," in *U.S. Competitivenes in the World Economy* eds. Bruce Scott and George Lodge (Boston: Harvard Business School Press, 1985), p. 332.

[63]United States, National Science Board, *Science and Engineering Indicators, 1989*, p. 4.

[64]"A Corporate Lag in Research Funds Is Causing Worry," *The New York Times*, January 23, 1990, p. 1.

[65]Ibid., p. C6.

[66]Robert Reich, "Leveraged Buyouts: America Pays the Price," *The New York Time Magazine*, January 29, 1989, p. 36.

[67]Press, "Technological Competition and the Western Alliance," p. 30.

less impressive than might be expected from such a technological giant in basic science and the creation of innovative technologies.[68] However, much greater emphasis in Japan is now being placed on these activities, especially as American firms and public officials demonstrate increased reluctance to share technology as they did in the earlier postwar period (witness the FSX episode). This trend is evident in recent increases in R&D budgets in both the private and public sectors; in attempts to strengthen Japan's weak university research structure and to connect it more effectively to high-tech industries and government laboratories through regional "Techno-polis" plans modeled after Silicon Valley in the United States; in attempts to develop venture capital markets as Japan's financial strength continues to grow; and in MITI's attachment of priority status to the advancement of science and basic technology in its vision of the "Third Technological Revolution" at the turn of the century.[69]

The science and technology challenge of West Europe, despite the EEC and its high-technology projects such as ESPRIT and RACE, lies in the fact that "the whole of European technology is less than the sum of its (national) parts, many of which are individually impressive."[70] N tional R&D efforts among the member states of the Common Market are five to six times those at the level of the EEC, but there is relatively little transfer of technology from one country to another. Simply put, unlike both the United States and Japan as technological rivals, Europe is not "techno-logically unified."[71] The EEC's creation of a single "domestic" market in 1992 will become a pivotal factor in overcoming Europe's competitive disadvantage in the technology race among the advanced industrial states.

Competition for scientific and technological leadership, generally reflecting the neomercantilist orientation to political economy, conditions all aspects of relations among the developed states. Trade balances, competitiveness of important domestic industries, employment levels, international investment patterns, and national economic and military security all are functions of the changing distribution of technological capabilities among the leading states. Technology issues among even the closest economic partners will certainly assume ever larger importance in the international political economy.

TECHNOLOGY AND FOREIGN POLICY: EAST-WEST RELATIONS

The most highly politicized, contentious issues of technology transfer in the postwar period involve relations between the leading Western states and Communist countries. Here technology is linked directly to consid-

[68] Ibid., p. 31.

[69] See Walters and Krauss, "Science, Technology and Economic Competitiveness," pp. 16–19.

[70] Press, "Technological Competition and the Western Alliance," p. 32.

[71] Ibid.

erations of national security and goals of foreign policy, in addition to competitiveness in world markets.

Through legislation to control exports over more than four decades, the United States has sought to make it as difficult as possible for the USSR to acquire Western product and process technologies useful for defense. It has led an effort since 1950 to administer uniform controls over Western technology exports to the USSR and other Communist states through the Coordinating Committee for Multilateral Export Controls (COCOM)— composed of the United States and fourteen of its allies. The conduct of these policies has raised deep conflicts not only between East and West but also among the Western allies, with their diverse political-economic and foreign policy interests.

There is no question that the USSR and other Communist states have devoted great effort to acquiring Western technology through legal and illegal means. Examples of industrial espionage and other illegal technology transfers to the USSR abound. A Soviet acoustic buoy designed to keep track of U.S. submarines was found to have been so closely copied (reverse engineered) from American equipment that it included a "signature" screw having no purpose other than to identify the original designer. In 1984, the United States interdicted two Digital Equipment Corporation VAX minicomputers about to be shipped to the USSR via trans-shipments through Norway, South Africa, and Sweden—in violation of American export laws. Legally obtained technology transfers have also had important military implications for the West. Trucks used in the Soviet invasion of Afghanistan were designed and manufactured in the Karma River factory using technology and production processes imported some years earlier from Italy.

American defense leaders have argued that both defense and dual-use technologies from the West are critical to Soviet military capability as well as for economic growth upon which its domestic political stability has become increasingly dependent. The views of Secretary of Defense Casper Weinberger are illustrative of this orientation: "Without constant infusions of advanced technology from the West, the Soviet industrial base would experience a cumulative obsolescence, which would eventually also constrain the military industries. . . . By allowing access to a wide range of advanced technologies, we enable the Soviet leadership to evade this dilemma."[72] Logic such as this has led the United States to argue typically over the years for expansive lists of controls on exports to the USSR that include commercial goods (for example, Apple II personal computers in 1984) as well as products and manufacturing processes that are directly related to defense.[73]

American emphasis on expansive export controls to the USSR has created tension between the United States and its allies. The latter press

[72]Bruce Jentleson, "The Political Basis for Trade in U.S.–Soviet Relations," Mimeo, Paper delivered at the 1984 annual meeting of the American Political Science Association, Washington, D.C., August 30–September 2, 1984, p. 27.

[73]"An Opening to the East for Tiny Computers," *Business Week*, May 28, 1984, pp. 31–32.

for limiting controls on exports of equipment and technology to the USSR only on items with direct military relevance. Sustaining commercial relations with the USSR, East Europe, and China has been of much greater political and economic importance to West European states and to Japan than has been the case for the United States, historically. Consequently, the allies argue for less inclusive lists of export controls within COCOM than does the United States.

American firms and the Department of Commerce have frequently argued that America's more restrictive policies on technology transfers to Communist states (reflecting the views of the Defense Department) places U.S. firms, like computer manufacturers, at a substantial competitive disadvantage relative to other Western firms operating in Eastern markets.[74] The result is that the USSR procures the technology or product, competitors in Europe and Asia get the business, and American firms lose commercial opportunities and market shares to the economic detriment of the United States. For these reasons, American officials press their allies hard for uniform technology export policies in East-West relations. However, the further one moves from equipment and technology with direct military relevance, the less success the United States has enjoyed in these efforts.

A corollary issue that has caused great distress among allied countries and U.S. business executives is the use of technology export controls as a foreign policy weapon to "punish" the Soviet Union, Poland, or others. As a case in point, the United States imposed sanctions against the Soviet Union in 1982 in response to the declaration of martial law in Poland, a stance that was warmly supported by Polish dissidents. One sanction was restriction on the technology needed to complete the Yamal pipeline to carry gas from the Soviet Union to Europe. Not only did the restrictions apply to U.S. firms but also to the foreign subsidiaries of U.S. multinational corporations. In the celebrated case of Dresser Industries, the U.S. policy outraged the parent company in Texas, its French subsidiary that could no longer use the parent's technology, and the French government relying on the pipeline to expand and diversify its access to energy supplies. The issue of extraterritoriality of U.S. law raised in Chapter 4 was critical, for the French felt that it was wrong for a company located in France to be subject to U.S. laws—applied retroactively in this instance, by the way. The French position was supported by the governments of West Germany and Great Britain.[75] The results were that U.S. allies distrusted the judgment of the U.S. government; U.S. companies and their subsidiaries felt they were being used as pawns in a Cold War struggle; foreign governments doubted the wisdom of reliance upon U.S. foreign investment for technology transfer and economic growth; and foreign customers questioned the reliability and stability of U.S. or U.S.-related suppliers. The resultant uncertainty and discord hindered U.S. business and harmed relations among allies. Furthermore,

---

[74]Ibid.

[75]For a summary of the pipeline crisis, see U.S. Congress, Office of Technology Assessment, *Technology and East-West Trade: An Update* (Washington, D.C.: GPO, 1983), pp. 30–32.

the policy itself had little real impact in changing the Polish government's internal policy toward Solidarity and other dissidents.

Controlling technology exports as an instrument of foreign policy in East-West relations has proven to be highly problematic for the advanced industrial states of the West. East-West trade is of much less economic importance to the United States than to its allies. Widespread skepticism exists in Europe and Japan regarding the utility of trade sanctions in achieving political objectives vis-á-vis the USSR. For both reasons, West European states and Japan are much less prone than the United States to use foreign controls on technology exports as an instrument of foreign policy to punish the USSR for policies with which they disagree—such as the invasion of Afghanistan in 1979. Nor do they have national legislation providing legal mechanisms to control technology exports to the East comparable to the United States[76]—as evidenced by the Toshiba Corporation's export of technology for manufacturing highly sophisticated ship propellers to the USSR in the mid-1980s (propellers allowing Soviet submarines to operate with much less risk of detection). These differences have often made technology transfer to Communist states a politically charged issue among the leading Western countries.

Soviet surrender of control over East Europe, the unification of Germany and internal Soviet political and economic reforms have begun to transcend some of these conflicts over technology transfers. In 1990, the COCOM countries agreed to drastically reduce controls on exports to the USSR and East Europe that will give them greater access, for example, to much more sophisticated computers, telecommunications equipment, and machine tools. A new, more limited list of items subject to review by COCOM will be developed focusing only on very sensitive military items. This should remove much of the tension underlying past disputes among the allies over technology controls. With the demise of the Warsaw Pact, the reunification of East and West Germany, the democratization of much of East Europe, and the transformation of NATO, COCOM itself could become an anachronism.[77] Notwithstanding this fact, the United States and Britain in 1990 vetoed proposals by domestic firms to build a fiber-optic cable across the USSR, arguing that it would involve technology with potential military applications.[78] However, should Gorbachev's economic and political reform efforts fail,[79] and Soviet relations with the West sour, technology policy would resurface as a contentious issue among the Western states.

For all the reasons discussed above, technology has become a vital factor in the economic, political, and military strength of a country. As a result, technology now plays an unaccustomed role in the economic and

---

[76]Ibid., pp. 63–64.

[77]"The Dismantling of a Cold-War Icon," *Business Week*, June 25, 1990, pp. 41–42.

[78]"U.S. to Relax Standards on High-Tech Exports," *The New York Times*, June 8, 1990, p. A4.

[79]For a discussion of political-economic reforms in the USSR and East European states, see Chapter 9.

political councils of national and international governments. Its critical nature has led to restrictions, sanctions, thievery, and espionage, all of which prohibit the free flow and testing of ideas so essential to the betterment of man's condition. In the area of technology, the prevalent notion among advanced states seems to be more mercantilist than a liberal economic philosophy. The stakes are deemed to be widespread, have long-term implications, and are very costly.

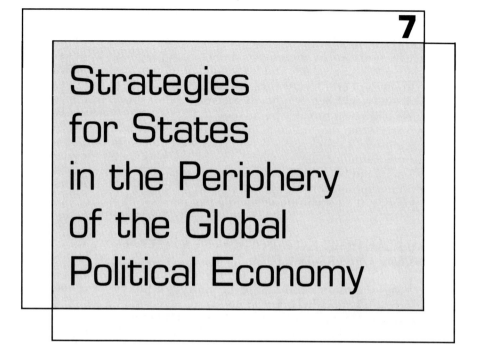

7

Strategies for States in the Periphery of the Global Political Economy

In the view of most observers, less developed countries have failed to maximize their position in global economic and political relations. Why this is true, however, is a matter of dispute. It may be the result of their own social-political-economic choices, of a purposeful or *de facto* policy on the part of advanced industrial states to exploit them over several centuries, or of the rich states' preoccupation with economic relations among themselves and their relative neglect of the impact of these relations on poor states. Whatever the explanation, it is important to examine alternative strategies that less developed countries, acting individually and in concert, can employ to augment their share of the benefits from international economic transactions.[1] Success, of course, implies that Third World countries will simultaneously strengthen their political position in the international arena.

The oil cartel administered through the Organization of Petroleum Exporting Countries (OPEC) has been far and away the most successful exercise of leverage among a variety of strategies pursued by states in the periphery of the global political economy. The emergency and impact of OPEC deserves and will receive primary attention in our discussion of alternative strategies being pursued by Third World states to enhance their international and domestic positions. Yet, it is important to recognize that,

---

[1]Less developed countries' policies toward foreign investment will constitute the focus of this chapter, although other forms of economic transactions, such as trade and aid, will be discussed in passing. Strategies for poor states to secure greater gains from trade were discussed in Chapter 2.

for all OPEC's success, it is a technique of applying economic and political leverage that very few less developed states can employ. Also, after a decade of rapidly increasing wealth and international influence, the political economic strength of OPEC states dissipated over the course of the 1980s. For these reasons a number of other strategies—less dramatic in impact, but applicable to a much broader population of less developed countries—will be outlined. While the strategies are outlined separately, they are related with each other. Less developed countries will sometimes pursue several approaches simultaneously. At other times, states will adopt a particular development and bargaining strategy as a remedy to deficiencies revealed in previous experience with a different approach. We will come back to these points at the conclusion of the discussion.

NEOMERCANTILIST EXPLOITATION OF A LIBERAL ECONOMIC ORDER—THE NICs

If the leadership of a less developed country accepts the basic tenets of liberal economic thought, one way to enhance that state's benefits from global economic transactions is simply to attract more of those transactions to it. The strategy here is to forge national policies in a manner designed to exploit the highly sensitive international economic interdependence characterizing the contemporary world.[2] Taking advantage of the sensitivity of multinational corporations to business opportunities all over the globe, a less developed country can occasionally attract foreign capital, increase its exports, and otherwise channel foreign capital and technology in accordance with its national economic priorities by the use of selective economic incentives and implementation of well-conceived industrial policies.[3] This strategy has been adopted most successfully by a number of newly industrializing countries (NICs)—most notably South Korea, Taiwan, Singapore, and Hong Kong in Asia, and Brazil, Chile, and Mexico in Latin America. The NICs have relied upon different combinations of export-oriented growth and import-substitution policies as means of promoting rapid industrialization. Generally speaking, the Asian NICs have stressed the former while the Latin American NICs have stressed import substitution.[4] Their policies typically include special tax incentives to local and foreign investors (especially for production of exportable goods); duty-free entry of imports (raw materials, intermediate goods, machinery) necessary for producing goods to be exported; currency devaluations to maintain a competitive position for national production in world markets; income policies designed to keep wages low; and maintenance of a hospitable en-

---

[2]See Richard Cooper, "Economic Interdependence and Foreign Policy in the Seventies," *World Politics*, 24, no. 2 (January 1972), 159–81.

[3]For a more complete presentation of an "exploitative response" to international economic interdependence, see ibid., p. 168.

[4]S. Haggard, "The Newly Industrializing Countries in the International System," *International Organization*, 38, no. 2, 343–70. See also Haggard, *Pathways from the Periphery* (Ithaca: Cornell University Press, 1990).

vironment for direct foreign investment,[5] at least in sectors not targeted by the state for national control. In addition, these countries possess a disciplined, skilled labor force; an active, indigenous entrepreneurial class; and a stable (often authoritarian) government controlled many years by a single political party or the military. The state typically has an active, interventionist developmental strategy which it implements by its control over finance and other policy tools to favor certain industries and firms over others—although Hong Kong is an exception in this respect among the countries mentioned here.[6]

The less developed countries mentioned here have, through these sorts of policies, enjoyed spectacular economic success over the past two decades. They have achieved higher rates of domestic economic growth and trade growth than advanced industrial states and other less developed countries. They have become vigorous exporters of a variety of increasingly sophisticated industrial goods across many stages of the product cycle. Eight newly industrializing countries accounted for 74 percent of all manufactured goods exported from less developed states in 1980.[7] South Korea, for example, has successfully challenged Japanese steelmakers in Japan's domestic market during the 1980s, which steel firms in Europe and the United States have been unable to do. Samsung, a manufacturing giant in South Korea, entered world markets producing one-megabit semiconductor chips in 1988—a high-technology product few American semiconductor firms could produce profitably at the time.[8]

These newly industrializing countries succeeded through outward-looking growth policies exploiting opportunities afforded by a liberal economic order. Most of them began their rapid development in the 1960s during a period of vigorous global economic growth, a great advantage unavailable to the next wave of less developed countries (such as Indonesia, Malaysia, Thailand, the Philippines, and China) trying to emulate their industrialization strategies. The success of newly industrializing states will depend upon continued access to international finance despite a large accumulated private foreign debt. It also depends upon the willingness of advanced industrial states to accommodate rather than to resist structural shifts in international production that transfers much manufacturing to the Third World. The efficacy of these policies as a strategy for growth and industrialization by less developed countries will be undermined if the advanced industrial states resort to protectionism in the face of the LDCs increased international competitiveness—a process many see as already

[5]Organization for Economic Cooperation and Development, *The Impact of the Newly Industrializing Countries* (Paris: OECD, 1979), p. 48.

[6]For an insightful contrast and comparison of the NICs' development patterns and strategies, see Frederic C. Deyo, ed., *The Political Economy of the New Asian Industrialism* (Ithaca: Cornell University Press, 1987); and Organization for Economic Cooperation and Development, *The Newly Industrializing Countries: Challenge and Opportunity for OECD Industries* (Paris: OECD, 1988), pp. 34–66.

[7]Organization for Economic Cooperation and Development, *The Newly Industrializing Countries*, 1979, p. 48.

[8]"South Korea's High-Tech Miracle," *The New York Times*, December 9, 1988, p. 33.

underway. Among the advanced industrial states, the United States has far and away been the most open to exports of manufactured goods from the NICs, yet, they were clearly targets of the Super 301 process established under the new U.S. trade law. In 1988, the four Asian NICs ran a combined trade surplus of $32 billion with the United States.

The growth and development strategy of these rapidly industrializing states entails certain costs that make it unpopular, or even politically impossible, to sustain in many less developed societies. To maximize a nation's international competitiveness and its attractiveness to foreign investors, a premium is often placed upon ruthlessly imposed political stability and suppression of wages at the expense of domestic economic and social justice. Successful efforts to attract direct foreign investment may result in extensive foreign control over, and denationalization of, the host state's economy. Financing growth and trade deficits through commercial borrowing can lead to staggering debt-service burdens and exposure to intrusion upon domestic political and economic decisions by one's international creditors.

All these criticisms have been leveled against Brazil's economic miracle, for example. For years, a military regime maintained a tight grip on political life in Brazil until the mid-1980s. Inequalities in the distribution of income between the richest 5 percent of the population and the rest of the country increased during the period of rapid economic growth[9]—due largely to a repressive wage structure for laborers. Foreign firms accounted for over 40 percent of Brazil's exports of manufactured goods and a similar proportion of the country's total sales in manufacturing.[10] Brazil has accumulated the largest foreign debt of any Third World nation ($115 billion in 1988) through its extensive commercial and public borrowing. Its debt service exceeded one third of its exports of goods and services in 1987. Brazil went through several highly contentious debt negotiations during the 1980s. It has now come under close scrutiny by the international banking community and the IMF. The government finds itself in periodic confrontations with the IMF over Brazil's compliance with conditions attached to the release of further credit from the IMF and international banks.

Brazil, therefore, exemplifies the best and the worst of the outward-oriented growth strategy followed by a number of rapidly industrializing less developed countries. Its growth in production, industrialization, and exports as well as its access to foreign capital and technology through foreign investment and bank lending make Brazil the envy of the Third World, in some respects. On the other hand, its remarkable economic success has been accompanied by an authoritarian political regime, an erosion of national autonomy, an exacerbation of income inequalities within society, and dependent development.[11]

The newly industrializing countries are frequently cited as models of development by liberal analysts while at the same time radical analysts

---

[9]Werner Baer, "The Brazilian Growth and Development Experience," in *Brazil in the Seventies*, ed. Riordan Roett (Washington, D.C.: American Enterprise Institute, 1976), p. 48.

[10]Peter Evans, *Dependent Development* (Princeton, N.J.: Princeton University Press, 1979), p. 80.

[11]See ibid., for a thorough discussion of these points.

condemn them. In fact, these countries' experience defies assessment in simple liberal or radical terms. Some NICs, such as Taiwan and South Korea, exhibit far less income inequality, less dependence on foreign investment controlled by Western-based multinational firms, and greater success in exporting high-value-added manufactured goods than radical thought leads us to expect. By the same token, liberal analysts claiming that NICs illustrate the success of market-driven, political-economic systems, tend to ignore the extraordinary significance of active state leadership and interventions in the development experience of these countries.[12]

REGIONAL EFFORTS TO ATTRACT AND REGULATE INVESTMENT

The common investment code of the Andean Common Market was an example of an attempt by six less developed countries[13] to avoid the economic denationalization associated with the Brazilian-type experience while seeking the capital, technology, and services of foreign investors. Through regional integration, these countries hoped to create a unified market that would strengthen their economic and political position in relation to the large states in Latin America (Brazil, Argentina, Mexico) and to advanced industrial states outside the continent.

Multinational firms are uniquely equipped to take advantage of the opportunities presented by regional integration efforts—as previous events in Western Europe had indicated. The Andean pact states sought to spur direct foreign investment in manufacturing industries through offering the attractions of a common market. On the other hand, they wanted to prevent loss of control over the course of their national and joint industrialization plans as a consequence of multilateral corporations' policies. A common investment code (Decision 24) of the Andean Common Market was designed to strengthen the bargaining leverage of host states and local firms vis-à-vis multinational corporations operating in the region.[14]

The members of the Andean pact varied greatly in their inclinations and capacities to administer their common investment code. Since the code relies upon national implementation, its effectiveness in controlling multinational corporations fell considerably short of the objectives formulated in 1970.[15] Nevertheless, for most less developed countries, concerted action vis-à-vis foreign investors is likely to offer greater potential than individual action if the aim is both increased investment and more stringent host state regulation. If a single state imposes strict investment controls, multinational

[12]For a more developed argument on this point, see Cal Clark, "The Taiwan Exception: Implications for Contending Political Economy Paradigms," *International Studies Quarterly*, 31, no. 3 (September 1987), 327–56.

[13]Peru, Colombia, Ecuador, Bolivia, Venezuela, and Chile (which withdrew in 1975).

[14]The types of controls exercised by the Andean pact states through their common investment code are described in Chapter 4, p. 148.

[15]For an assessment of the investment code's implementation, see Lynn K. Mytelka, *Regional Development in a Global Economy* (New Haven, Conn.: Yale University Press, 1979), pp. 62–113.

corporations sensitive to differences in national regulation of their activities will avoid that state and locate elsewhere in the region.[16] If, on the other hand, a number of states in a region adopt and implement an identical investment code, multinationals that wish to operate in the region will find it much more difficult, perhaps impossible, to avoid the constraints. The connection of such investment controls with movement toward a regional common market is a particularly interesting strategy because the prospect of an integrated regional market, rather than a number of small national markets, may offer the incentive necessary to attract foreign investment even under strict controls. The Andean Pact generates far less attention today than it did during the 1970s; however, it will be intriguing to see if "Europe 1992" helps renew interest in developing regional economic policies, including foreign investment strategies, among certain less developed countries.

NATIONALIZATION

The approach of the Andean pact may appear as a halfway measure to economic nationalists in less developed countries. The Andean states are, after all, still interested in attracting foreign investment, albeit under stringent conditions. Nationalization of major foreign operations within the state is sometimes prescribed as a more appropriate strategy for an individual less developed country in its attempts to increase its share of benefits from global economic relations. The strategy of nationalization, usually on a highly selective basis, is likely to appear most attractive to those less developed countries in which government revenues are generated largely from exports of primary products whose extraction and international sales are controlled by foreign capital.

This is true for several reasons. Foreign-owned extractive enterprises engaged in the exploitation and shipment abroad of finite natural resources give the appearance of removing national wealth rather than creating it, as a manufacturing enterprise does. Thus, foreign investment in extractive industry is particularly resented in less developed countries, and it is more prone to nationalization than is foreign investment in the manufacturing sector, for example.[17] In addition, the return on foreign direct investment in extractive industries is typically much higher than is the return on investment in manufacturing industries.[18] Even though the host state's share

[16]This is more the case for small states than for larger, more highly developed countries. For example, Mexico has attracted foreign capital quite successfully with investment controls similar in some respects to the Andean investment code. See Chapter 4 for a more detailed discussion of controls imposed on foreign investors by host states.

[17]Stephen Kobrin found that, in states expropriating only the most sensitive foreign investments, extractive industries accounted for 59 percent of all takeovers. Manufacturing investments accounted for only 11 percent of all expropriations by these states. See his "Foreign Enterprise and Forced Divestment in the Less Developed Countries," *International Organization*, 34, no. 1 (Winter 1980), 77.

[18]See U.S. Congress, Senate Committee on Finance, *Implications of Multinational Firms for World Trade and Investment and for U.S. Trade and Labor*, 93rd Cong., 1st sess., 1973, p. 445.

of earnings from extractive enterprises controlled by foreign capital has increased substantially over the years, host states have a compelling urge to nationalize these enterprises and to acquire *all* the earnings from these particularly lucrative investments.

The nationalization of foreign investments in extractive enterprise is an extraordinarily appealing strategy for those less developed countries fortunate enough to possess major supplies of primary products.[19] Nationalization holds the promise of increased government revenues and foreign exchange earnings in a way that appears to reduce the dependence of a poor state upon rich states and the multinational corporations operating from them. This policy has immense domestic political appeal in those less developed countries in which the general population is highly sensitive to dependence upon, and perceived exploitation by, rich states and foreign firms.

Seductive as this policy may be for less developed countries, it does not necessarily result either in increased revenues or in reduced dependence upon multinational firms. Unless a number of special circumstances are present, nationalizing local production of primary products for sale abroad is likely to place a less developed country in the unenviable position of being a supplier of last resort. As a result, it faces great uncertainty in the amount of its export earnings and government revenues from year to year. Moreover, it is also likely to remain as dependent upon multinational corporations for marketing the product internationally as it had been dependent upon them previously for production of the primary product.[20]

The production and sales of most mineral resources, such as petroleum, copper, tin, nickel, and aluminum, are typically controlled by an oligopoly of vertically integrated multinational corporations that are at once the major producers *and* the major consumers of the mineral resource. Vertical integration is a compelling goal of large enterprises that seek to avoid risk either as suppliers or as consumers of mineral resources. A firm that begins as a producer of, say, copper creates affiliates that process and/ or fabricate products from the mineral in an effort to assure its sales of copper in a buyer's market. A firm that begins as a producer of finished goods requiring massive amounts of copper inputs creates affiliates to produce copper itself in an effort to assure its supply of the mineral in a seller's market.[21] This behavior results ultimately in the oligopolistic control of

---

[19]We will focus our discussions of nationalization on extractive industry since this is such a salient export sector to many Third World states. It is very difficult to analyze the pros and cons of nationalization with any precision unless one focuses on particular economic sectors or products.

[20]In addition to these problems, one must also take into account the effect that nationalization of extractive industry might have on efforts to attract foreign investment in other economic sectors or efforts to secure international loans. The discussion that follows relies heavily upon the work of Theodore Moran. In particular, see "New Deal or Raw Deal in Raw Materials," *Foreign Policy*, No. 5 (Winter 1971–1972), 119–36; "Transnational Strategies of Protection and Defense by Multinational Corporations: Spreading the Risk and Raising the Cost for Nationalization in Natural Resources," *International Organization*, 27, no. 2 (Spring 1973), 273–88; and *Multinational Corporations and the Politics of Dependence: Copper in Chile* (Princeton, N.J.: Princeton University Press, 1974).

[21]Moran, "New Deal or Raw Deal in Raw Materials," pp. 122–23.

international markets in mineral resources, a condition faced by almost any less developed country contemplating nationalization of foreign-owned extractive industry. This situation often reduces the efficacy of nationalization as a strategy to enhance the economic returns and national autonomy of a less developed country possessing valuable mineral resources.

Nationalization is likely to bring a steady increase of economic returns to a less developed country to the extent that (1) the stage of production represented by a foreign firm's operations in the country is the greatest barrier of entry into the vertically integrated production and sales process,[22] (2) the state that nationalizes the foreign firm either continues to cooperate with, and participate within, the oligopoly controlling international distribution of the mineral resource[23] or to develop an international distribution capability of its own—one that is seen by refiners, fabricators, and consumers of the mineral as a dependable source of supply at stable prices.[24] Unless these circumstances prevail, the state that nationalizes foreign-controlled extractive operations will find itself a supplier of last resort, because multinational firms will seek "safer" sources of supply, even at higher cost.

If the stage of production represented by the foreign firms' operations within a particular less developed country is not the greatest barrier of entry into the vertically integrated production and sales process, nationalization of the foreign operations will not result in increased revenues or in control over marketable production of the mineral for international consumers. If alternate sources of supply of the mineral can be developed, the multinational firm whose mining operations are nationalized will develop them. Even if these alternate deposits are more expensive to develop, they will be attractive to multinational firms seeking to avoid risk in securing supplies of the mineral. Thus, in response to the threat of nationalization of their mining operations in Chile and other areas, large corporations in the copper industry focused their efforts on extracting copper from lower-grade ore deposits in more "secure" areas of the world, such as Australia, Canada, and the United States.[25] Copper is a mineral resource for which access to unprocessed reserves is the greatest barrier of entry to a vertically integrated production and sales process. Even so, after nationalizing foreign-based copper industries in 1971, Chile faced the loss of its major consumers and thus, reduced economic returns from its international sales of copper. Attempts at nationalization by less developed countries to maximize revenues from international sales of other mineral resources, such as aluminum and tin, are even less likely to succeed over the long run because the greatest barrier of entry to the vertically integrated production and sales of these minerals is possession of highly sophisticated processing technology and immense amounts of capital, not access to ore deposits.[26]

[22]Ibid., pp. 124–27.

[23]Ibid., pp. 129–31.

[24]Moran, *Multinational Corporations*, p. 242.

[25]Ibid., pp. 32–33. For an interesting discussion of the corporate strategy employed by Kennecott in anticipation of and defense against nationalization of its operations in Chile, see Moran, "Transnational Strategies of Protection and Defense by Multinational Corporations."

[26]Moran, "New Deal or Raw Deal in Raw Materials," p. 126.

The other major requirement a less developed country must meet to sustain increases in economic returns from the nationalization of extractive industry is to maintain its reputation as a dependable supplier of the mineral to consumers abroad. This means continued participation within the international oligopoly of multinational firms which often control the bulk of international sales of mineral resources. In this way, the production of the nationalized operation continues to enjoy a sustained volume of sales at controlled price levels in international markets. Unless this is accomplished, or unless the less developed country develops an international sales network of its own that is just as dependable in supplying the mineral at steady price levels, the income generated from nationalizing production is likely to be reduced or very uneven from year to year.[27] The development of its own sales and distribution network is often beyond a less developed country's economic capacity or administrative skills; it is, in addition, always a long-term enterprise. The threat of interrupting supplies for political purposes is, in any case, not compatible with maximizing earnings from nationalized production over the long run. Thus, the country that nationalizes foreign-controlled production of its mineral resources finds that it must continue to cooperate with the same firms, or with firms similar to those it nationalizes at home, for the sales of its products abroad.

Finally, nationalization of extractive industry exposes the government of a less developed country to economic and political pressures that the foreign firms used to absorb. Zambia's nationalization of copper, for example, forced the government to guarantee foreign loans to finance copper investments, previously provided by the foreign firms. This added to Zambia's foreign debt burden, inhibiting development. Domestically, the government found itself, rather than the foreign mining firms, to be the target of union demands for higher wages and benefits. A government that previously found domestic political strength by allying itself with unions against the mining companies, alienated its labor support by taking the side of management in the newly nationalized copper industry. In short, nationalization can result in a government's losing insulation from international economic developments and domestic political pressures important for its stability, or even its political survival.[28]

These facts pose a major dilemma for less developed countries attempting both to maximize revenues from sales abroad and to reduce dependence upon multinational corporations (and their parent states) by nationalization of local operations of extractive industry. The government that chooses this policy will usually have to decide which of these goals to pursue, since they tend to be mutually exclusive. Policies designed to obtain steadily increasing, or even stable, economic returns from international sales of nationalized mineral exploitation require cooperation with, and continued dependence upon, multinational corporations. But this is politically difficult and often unacceptable for a regime whose domestic support rests upon its confrontation with foreign firms over the production and

[27] Ibid., pp. 129–33; and Moran, *Multinational Corporations*, pp. 240–41.

[28] Michael Shafer, "Capturing the Mineral Multinationals: Advantage or Disadvantage?" in *Multinational Corporations: The Political Economy of Foreign Direct Investment*, ed. Theodore Moran (Lexington: Lexington Books, 1985), pp. 25–54.

sale of these economic resources. Refusal to cooperate with multinational firms may minimize dependence upon them (and their parent states), but a less developed country will thereby most likely suffer great fluctuations in its receipts from international sales. The regime may feel that a redistribution of income within the country and a sense of national identity and pride accompanying nationalization are more than adequate compensation for the loss of stable or increased export earnings. Our point, however, is simply that nationalization of foreign capital in local extractive industry seldom results in *both* increased revenues and reduced dependence upon foreign firms.

This analysis of nationalization as a strategy for less developed countries suggests in most cases that it is not likely to produce all the results that at first glance make it attractive to economic nationalists. We have focused upon nationalization of extractive industry, but the basic argument can, with minor adjustments, be applied to the nationalization of numerous types of production marketed internationally. Of course, a very different situation and calculus exist with regard to the efficacy of nationalization of foreign firms that produce only for consumption within the domestic market of a less developed country.

In the end, there is no clear conclusion as to how successful less developed countries can be in harnessing foreign firms to their national interests. Leading analysts of multinational firms have moved to bargaining models which stress situationally specific features of the host state and foreign firms at specific points in time, rather than models which draw sweeping conclusions about the relative strength of states and foreign investors (see Chapter 4). Important factors in bargaining include such things as the structure of the international industry; whether the enterprise depends upon repeated infusions of rapidly changing technologies; the amount of capital needed for upcoming investments; the entrepreneurial and technological skills of host state nationals; and the capacity of the host state's public and private officials to raise capital in domestic and international financial markets.[29] Much attention has been focused on theories of the "obsolescing bargain" in which foreign firms are seen as having greatest bargaining leverage during periods when they are initiating large investments in less developed countries involving new process and product technologies, as well as the development of new markets. After the investment is "sunk," the new products and production processes have become familiar to host state nationals, and markets have been secured, the original bargain struck between the firm and the host state (typically favoring the firm) progressively becomes obsolete. Under these new conditions host states are often able to renegotiate the original distribution of benefits to enhance its revenues and exercise greater control over the firm's operations.[30]

---

[29]An excellent summary and analysis of these and other bargaining factors applied to Peru, can be found in Alfred Stepan, *The State and Society: Peru in Comparative Perspective* (Princeton: Princeton University Press, 1978), pp. 230–89.

[30]For a concise presentation of the "obsolescing bargain" as well as possible strategies for firms to protect themselves against it, see T. Moran, "International Political Risk Assessment, Corporate Planning, and Strategies to Offset Political Risk," in *Multinational Corporations: The Political Economy of Foreign Direct Investment*, ed. Theodore Moran, pp. 107–18.

COMMODITY PRODUCER CARTELS:
THE EXTRAORDINARY CASE OF OIL

If, in general, nationalization of foreign-controlled extractive industry by individual less developed countries has little chance of yielding all the benefits claimed, unified action by a group of less developed countries that together possess the major deposits of the same mineral resource should offer greater hope of success. In this case, the strategy involves concerted action by major producer states confronting an industry or oligopoly as a whole, rather than a single producer state confronting only the firm (or firms) located within its borders. If less developed countries possessing the major sources of a particular mineral resource can maintain a common front vis-à-vis all the major multinationals in that industry, presumably none of these states can be relegated to the position of a supplier of last resort. Collectively, they would still be able to exert considerable weight in international distribution and sales. This is, of course, the strategy that was employed so successfully by oil-producing states between 1973 and 1979.

The oil-producing states were in a very weak bargaining position relative to the international oil industry prior to 1970. The seven giant oil majors (Exxon, Texaco, Mobil, Standard of California, Gulf, Shell, and British Petroleum) dominated international oil markets. These firms determined both the level of production and the price for oil in virtually all oil-producing states. Throughout the postwar period until about 1970, there was a substantial surplus of oil relative to global demand. As a result, the posted price of oil, upon which the producing states' royalties and tax revenues were based, remained very low. Indeed, in 1959, oil firms imposed a *reduction* in the posted price of oil from all oil-producing states. This act prompted the creation of OPEC in 1960.[31] Less developed oil-producing states heavily dependent upon oil export receipts vowed to oppose, through OPEC, any future attempts by the international oil firms to reduce their oil revenues. Joint action was imperative because any oil-producing state confronting the international oil industry alone risked reduction of its oil output and revenues. The international firms could freeze "troublemakers" out of world markets since they controlled production and marketing networks throughout the non-Communist world and had access to alternative sources of crude oil supplies in numerous countries. OPEC's activities had little economic or political impact for the first decade of its existence, however, in the face of abundant global oil supplies.

The convergence of several developments enabled the oil-producing states to wrest control of pricing and production of their oil from the international oil firms in the early 1970s.[32] During this period, all the advanced industrial states in the West were enjoying economic prosperity

[31]OPEC is composed of Iran, Iraq, Kuwait, Saudi Arabia, Venezuela (the original members), Indonesia, Algeria, Libya, Nigeria, Ecuador, Qatar, Abu Dhabi, Dubai, Sharjah, and Gabon.

[32]The discussion that follows is treated in greater detail in numerous publications. Two brief recitals of these events are Edith Penrose, "The Development of a Crisis," in *The Oil Crisis*, ed. Raymond Vernon (New York: W. W. Norton, 1976), pp. 39–57; and John M. Blair, *The Control of Oil* (New York: Pantheon, 1976), pp. 211–34.

and were operating simultaneously near the peak of their business cycles. This extraordinary level of aggregate economic activity placed immense pressure on existing global oil production. The international oil market that was characterized previously by great surpluses became very tight.

At about the same time, America's voracious consumption of oil began to exceed its capacity to supply its needs from domestic production. The United States lost its virtual self-sufficiency in petroleum production in the late 1960s and was forced to enter world markets for oil purchases in increasing amounts yearly.

The oil-producing states in the Middle East occupied the pivotal position in the world oil market of the early 1970s. Middle Eastern production costs could not be matched anywhere. The region accounted for approximately 40 percent of the world's oil production, and it provided the logical location for future expansion of oil production as 60 percent of proven global oil reserves were located there.

These dramatic developments in the global energy picture at the end of the 1960s had been preceded by a gradual, and exceedingly important, alteration in the structure of the international oil industry. During the 1950s and 1960s, the oil majors that had long dominated international petroleum markets found themselves in vigorous competition with oil independents (such as Occidental, Marathon, Hunt, and Getty) seeking to develop access to their own supplies of crude oil.[33] The independent oil companies were able to secure concessions alongside the oil majors as new oil fields were developed and expanded rapidly over the course of the 1950s and 1960s in states such as Algeria and Libya. In short, the number of important firms in the international oil industry was expanding. The oil majors were less firmly in control of the oligopolistic international oil market that they had dominated successfully for decades.

Against this backdrop of developments Qaddafi, the aggressive new leader of Libya, made a bold move in 1970 to renegotiate the terms governing the oil industry's development of Libya's oil concessions. His success set in motion a chain of events that culminated in OPEC's dramatic assertion of control over oil pricing and production in just three years (after a decade of frustration and impotence).

Qaddafi took advantage of Libya's unique attractiveness as an oil exporter in the tight oil market of 1970. He argued that the price of Libyan oil should be increased and maintained above the price of Persian Gulf oil (including production from Iraq, Iran, Kuwait, Saudi Arabia, and others) because (1) Libyan crude has a very low sulfur content, making it especially attractive to refiners and consumers of heating oil in Western economies facing strict environmental standards, and (2) Libyan oil was far more economical to deliver to markets in Europe and the United States than was Persian Gulf oil, which, after 1967 and the closure of the Suez Canal, had to be shipped all the way around the continent of Africa. Accordingly,

---

[33]The oil independents were following the traditional pattern of vertical integration seen so frequently in the emergence of multinational corporations (see section on Nationalism). Price competition between the oil majors and the independents led directly to the reduction in oil prices of 1959 that spurred the creation of OPEC.

Qaddafi demanded an increase in Libyan oil prices and threatened to shut down Libyan oil production to sustain the price increase, if necessary (i.e., he sought greater revenues through a lower volume of output at higher prices, thus conserving Libya's oil reserves). In early 1970, oil companies in Libya were told to raise the posted price of oil they produced there or face confiscation of their Libyan oil operations. The oil firms were extremely vulnerable to pressure from Qaddafi, not only because of Libya's market position but also because of the deep divisions within the international oil industry between the independents and the majors.

Both the independents and the majors operated concessions in Libya. The independents such as Hunt, Occidental, Continental, and Marathon had little alternative but to accede to Qaddafi's demands. They controlled few or no alternative sources of crude oil outside of Libya and, hence, could not afford to risk the loss of their Libyan concessions. The oil majors (such as Exxon, Mobil, and British Petroleum), on the other hand, had numerous alternatives to their Libyan crude supplies. Giving in to Qaddafi's demands would invite all other oil-producing states in which the majors operated to raise similar demands for revenue increases and for a voice in determining production levels. The oil majors' access to alternative supplies of crude oil and the prospect of having to renegotiate their numerous concessions elsewhere gave them the capability and the incentive to orchestrate oil industry resistance to Qaddafi's demands.

A common front by the oil companies against Libyan demands proved impossible to sustain, however, because of the differing vulnerabilities and interests of the oil majors and independents. Exploiting this division, Qaddafi successfully negotiated a price increase with Occidental Petroleum— a particularly vulnerable independent international oil firm that relied almost totally upon its Libyan concession for crude oil. With this break in the ranks, other oil independents and majors in Libya quickly followed Occidental's precedent in renegotiating the terms of their oil concessions.

As the oil majors feared, Libya's success prompted other oil-producing states in the Middle East to demand price increases for their oil production as well. The oil majors were caught in a cycle of leap-frogging demands between Libya and other oil-producing states on the Persian Gulf. If the Middle Eastern oil-producing states secured price increases, the price premium Libya demanded for the lower transportation costs and lower sulfur content of its oil would be negated. Middle Eastern producer states' success, therefore, would generate a new round of Libyan efforts to renegotiate its oil prices. This, in turn, would prompt Middle Eastern producers to renegotiate, and so on.

To avoid this terrifying prospect, the oil industry as a whole took the unprecedented move of engaging all the oil-producing states in the Persian Gulf and North Africa in comprehensive, multilateral negotiations to establish a mutually acceptable, stable price structure for oil. These efforts culminated in the Teheran and Tripoli Agreements of 1971, which called for an increase in the posted price of oil from $1.80 to $2.50 per barrel with orderly annual price increases of 2.5 percent through 1975.

Unfortunately for the international oil industry, events during 1972 and 1973 outran the Teheran and Tripoli Agreements. Global demand for oil pushed actual market prices higher than the posted prices negotiated in 1971. Devaluations of the dollar in 1971 and 1973 meant a loss of real earnings for the oil-producing states, which received payment for oil exports in dollars. The OPEC countries scheduled a meeting with the oil industry for October 1973 to revise price levels to take account of these unanticipated developments in the oil market following the Teheran and Tripoli Agreements. Of course, in October 1973 the world also witnessed the outbreak of war in the Middle East. Arab oil-producing states shortly thereafter imposed a selective embargo of oil shipments to the United States, the Netherlands, and Portugal in retaliation for their support of Israel in the war. The embargo and concomitant production cutbacks tightened global petroleum markets even further and introduced great uncertainty throughout the world about assured access to uninterrupted supplies of oil. Oil-importing states responded by competing frantically for oil deliveries at even higher prices. At the end of 1973, all OPEC states (Arab and non-Arab) took advantage of this volatile market situation to impose a fourfold increase in the posted price of oil to $11.67 per barrel.

This extraordinary series of events in the early 1970s constituted a revolution in world oil markets. The oil firms that had traditionally maintained unilateral control over oil prices and production levels found themselves unable to do so any longer. Changes in the structure of the international oil industry brought about by the rise of independents, and a very tight oil market altered fundamentally the bargaining strength between the industry and oil-producing states. The Teheran and Tripoli Agreements initiated by the oil industry to assure market stability revealed, instead, a new-found strength for oil-producing states after decades of impotence. Within the next two years, through OPEC the oil-producing states were able to determine unilaterally prices and production levels for their crude oil entering world markets.

In addition to securing control over pricing and production levels, the oil-producing states systematically assumed majority or complete national ownership of the companies' crude oil concessions within their jurisdiction. While they pushed the oil multinationals into a minority equity position, they did so without forcing the firms to disengage from the oil-producing states. The companies surrendered their exclusive equity position but remained for the time being as operators of their previous concessions and continued to distribute and market much of the OPEC states' oil internationally. In this way, the producing states gained national control over their natural resources while still securing the benefits of the oil corporations' technological expertise, managerial skills, capital, and distribution and sales networks. Sheik Yamani, the Saudi Arabian minister of oil and minerals, referred to the post-1970 arrangements between OPEC states and the oil industry as a "catholic marriage between the producer countries on the one hand and the consumers and the major or independent oil companies on the other hand by linking them to a state where it is almost impossible for any of them to divorce."[34] It was clearly a marriage, however,

---

[34]*The New York Times*, October 8, 1972, Sec. 3, p. 7.

that the producing states forced upon reluctant partners and in which they held the upper hand. Oil industry officials referred to it as a "shotgun wedding."[35]

These arrangements differ significantly from the nationalization efforts outlined previously. The traditional form of nationalization seeks to expel selectively foreign firms from the host state whereas OPEC states seek to exploit them. Nationalization leads to open conflict with foreign firms upon which the less developed countries often depend for new technology, capital mobilization, and international sales. OPEC states were able to forge continued cooperation between themselves and the multinational investors at all stages of the production and sales process. In a seller's market host states remained firmly in control of the terms of the relationship since the oil firms were hostage in the short and medium terms to the OPEC states' crude oil supplies.

Political-Economic Impacts of OPEC during the 1970s: A Seller's Market

OPEC's assumption of control over production and pricing in international petroleum markets introduced massive alterations in the global political economy and, of course, immensely enhanced the political-economic salience of OPEC states. During the 1970s two thirds of the world's oil reserves and just over half of the world's oil production were accounted for by OPEC. The Middle Eastern and North African OPEC states occupied a particularly pivotal role; they possessed about 90 percent of OPEC's reserves and generated over three fourths of OPEC's total production. Late in the decade Western Europe and Japan relied upon oil imports from OPEC states in the Middle East and North Africa for over 75 percent of their oil consumption.[36] The United States met over 25 percent of its oil needs from these OPEC states at the time.[37]

The OPEC states exploited their dominance over global oil supplies by raising the price of oil fifteenfold in the seven years following 1973. Oil price developments are presented in Figure 7-1 for Saudi Arabian market crude. These price increases produced the largest "peacetime" international transfer of wealth in history. OPEC revenues from oil exports, which amounted to $15 billion in 1972, reached a peak of over $300 billion in 1980. Indeed, between 1974 and 1982 OPEC states accumulated $339 billion in current account surpluses—oil export earnings in excess of their purchases of goods and services abroad.[38] Of course, these OPEC payments surpluses must be reflected in huge payments deficits for oil-importing

---

[35] Ibid., Sec. 4, p. 3.

[36] American Petroleum Institute, *Petroleum Industry Statistics* (Washington, D.C.: API, July 1978), Section X, Table 5.

[37] Ibid., Section XIV, Table 3.

[38] Richard Mattione, *OPEC's Investments and the International Financial System* (Washington, D.C.: The Brookings Institution, 1985), p. 8. These revenue surpluses are concentrated in a few OPEC countries—Kuwait, Libya, Qatar, Saudi Arabia, and the United Arab Emirates. Saudi Arabia alone accumulated $160 billion in surpluses, or 47 percent of the OPEC total. Ibid., p. 11.

$ per Barrel

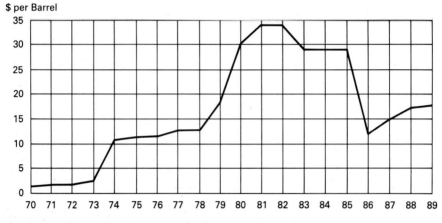

FIGURE 7-1   Saudi Arabian Oil Prices, 1970–1989 ($ per barrel)
Source: *BP Statistical Review of World Energy, 1984 and 1989.* Prices in 1986, 1987, and 1989 are estimated.

states. America's oil import bills, for example, increased from $4.8 billion in 1972 to $80 billion in 1980. This was a key factor in America's persistent balance-of-trade deficits throughout the 1970s.

Domestically, these jumps in oil prices increased inflation dramatically, produced wrenching imbalances among various sectors of the economy, and retarded economic growth. OPEC's financial gains from international oil sales were, therefore, obtained at high domestic and international costs to America and the rest of the world.

The dramatic, intermittent price increases for OPEC oil confronting all oil-importing states followed a well-established pattern between 1973 and 1980. Oil consumers competed with each other in frenzied pursuit of oil at virtually any price during periods when an unanticipated reduction in oil production occurred in a major oil-exporting country for any length of time. A tight international oil market, maintained by OPEC production shut-ins, amplified the effect of short-term price escalations accompanying uncertainties in oil deliveries. When OPEC states saw frenetic competition among consumers generating short-term price escalation, they captured and perpetuated the "temporary" panic market by formally raising the posted price of oil governing their longer-term oil contracts. For example, the posted price of Saudi Arabian oil increased relatively slightly from $11.65 per barrel in 1974 to $14.34 per barrel on January 1, 1979. During 1979, however, domestic turmoil in Iran, which resulted in the Shah's departure and continued long after Khomeini's assumption of power, reduced Iranian oil production and exports abruptly. In the face of this unanticipated shortage of global oil supplies, prices for oil in the "spot" market (auctions of discrete lots of oil to the highest bidder, unlike longer-term contractual oil sales at posted prices) in 1979 shot up to $40 per barrel. The OPEC states, arguing that spot market prices indicated clearly that the posted price of oil was too low, responded by more than doubling their posted prices of oil. By January 1, 1980, Saudi Arabian oil under long-term contract sold at $30 a barrel (versus $14.34 two years earlier). The same dynamic occurred in 1973 during the Arab oil embargo, when oil prices were increased fourfold.

The dramatic success of OPEC between 1973 and the early 1980s is one of those seismic events in world affairs that directly affects virtually all dimensions of international political activity. Among other things, OPEC intensified the sharpness of the Third World's demands for a new international economic order (NIEO), it introduced severe strains among the Western allies over energy policy and diplomacy in the Middle East, and it thrust the Persian Gulf region into the forefront of America's security concerns.

Most Third World countries took great pleasure in seeing the non-Western oil-producing states of OPEC wrest control over the international oil market from Western states and their oil multinationals. It marked an end to the West's previous domination of virtually every important dimension of international economic exchange. The OPEC states moved quickly and adroitly to cement ties with the Third World states by using their oil power to press the long-standing demands for international economic reform of importance to all less developed countries. (We have already examined the less developed countries' concerns in the areas of trade, aid, investment, and monetary relations.)

Just months after the oil price hikes and the Arab oil embargo of 1973, OPEC states led the call for convening a special session of the United Nations General Assembly to address the problems of raw materials and development. At this session was passed the U.N.'s "Declaration on Establishment of a New International Economic Order" of interest to all Third World states. OPEC states declined Western initiatives during 1974 to negotiate an orderly oil production and pricing scheme for the sake of reducing turmoil in the international economy. Instead, the OPEC states succeeded in creating a negotiating forum including other Third World states as well as the Western states and OPEC. These negotiations were based on an expanded agenda that addressed the gamut of less developed countries' commodity trade, industrialization, and international financing interests in addition to oil production and pricing. The OPEC states linked the threat of further oil price increases in late 1975 to the Western states' willingness to negotiate seriously with the Third World within this larger framework. These negotiations took place in Paris in the form of a specially created Council on International Economic Cooperation (CIEC) that functioned from late 1975 through early 1977. While the substantive accomplishments were modest, it was within the CIEC framework that the Western states agreed to create and contribute to the Common Fund as part of UNCTAD's Integrated Program for Commodities (see Chapter 2).

OPEC states also initiated economic assistance programs for less developed countries amounting to over $5 billion per year by the late 1970s. At these levels, OPEC aid, as a percentage of the donors' GNP, was several orders of magnitude higher than Western aid during the same period. OPEC aid has been concentrated primarily in a half dozen states with large Moslem populations and amounts to only a small fraction of the increased import bills that less developed countries must now pay for oil. But, the initiation of these aid efforts helped OPEC to retain good relations with Third World countries.

Through all these activities OPEC managed to forge a loose economic coalition with Third World states and to provide the cutting edge in their dialogue with Western states over international economic reforms. Yet the concrete financial burden placed upon oil-importing less developed countries by OPEC's price increases certainly introduced severe strains on this relationship. For example, Brazil's oil imports increased from $4.2 billion in 1979 to $10.5 billion in 1980 due to oil price increases imposed by OPEC. These financial burdens aggravated an already imposing foreign debt challenge facing Brazil. Taken as a whole, less developed countries' oil import bills doubled between 1978 and 1980 when they rose to $50 billion. The current account deficits and debt accumulation during the 1970s by these states, due largely to higher oil prices, were examined in Chapter 3. However, Third World states did not challenge OPEC openly in spite of these burdens, because Western nations gave little indication that less developed countries could expect additional economic assistance to meet their increasing energy and development needs by joining Western efforts to oppose OPEC.

The pivotal position of the Middle East in international oil markets since 1973 altered Western states' diplomacy dramatically vis-à-vis the region and opened up deep cleavages among the advanced industrial states. Through implementation of their embargo in 1973 against the United States, the Netherlands, and Portugal along with production cutbacks, the Arab oil-producing states demonstrated their capacity to employ the oil weapon with political success. European and Japanese dependence on oil supplies from the region since that time led them to virtually embrace the Arab position in the conflict with Israel to assure uninterrupted access to oil. The United States, whose imports from the Middle East and Arab states in North Africa increased substantially over the course of the 1970s moved from a clearly pro-Israeli position in the 1960s to that of a mediator between Israel and Arab states between 1973 and 1976. Under the Carter administration, the United States became an active participant in forging an Israeli-Egyptian bilateral peace treaty and a framework for a more comprehensive Arab-Israeli agreement. OPEC's success in 1973 and since has permanently altered politics in the area.

Asymmetries in the degree of dependence upon Middle Eastern oil have rendered deep cleavages between the United States and its Western allies. The United States is a major producer of oil. Immense reserves of coal and oil shale provide the United States with viable, if costly, alternatives to OPEC oil in the long term. In contrast, Europe and Japan rely upon imports from this region for over three fourths of their oil needs and do not possess fossil fuel alternatives in abundance, as is the case for the United States. These differences are an important factor leading European states and Japan to shy away from bold challenges to OPEC or to important oil-producing states in the Middle East, which the United States has sought on occasion. Such was the case in the unwillingness of Japan and the European states to apply stringent economic sanctions in support of the United States during its confrontation with Iran over the seizure of American diplomatic personnel as hostages between 1979 and 1981. Similarly, they opposed U.S. bombing of Libya in 1986; U.S. aircraft based in Britain were denied permission to fly over French airspace on the mission.

More generally, it is important to note that, in the Middle Eastern war of 1973 and in the Iranian revolution in 1979, the United States, not Europe or Japan, was the primary target of OPEC states' threatening to use supply interruptions as a political weapon. It is not surprising that America's allies would attempt to put some distance between themselves and the United States in its Middle Eastern confrontations, given their greater dependence on Middle Eastern oil and the fact that the United States has typically been the target of the oil states' wrath, not they. Differences in energy vulnerability and in preferred political-economic-military strategies in the Middle East will continue to create major strains among the Western allies. That has been an important legacy of oil politics since 1973.

OPEC's Decline in the 1980s: A Buyer's Market

The second of the great price hikes by OPEC in 1979–1980 marked the high-water mark of OPEC's political-economic power. OPEC oil production dropped from over 31 million barrels a day in 1979 to fewer than 17 million in 1985. Its oil revenues in 1984 were less than half those in 1980.[39] After a decade of current account surpluses, well in excess of $100 billion in 1980, OPEC states as a group fell into a deficit position on current account in 1982. Over the course of the decade, OPEC accounted for approximately one third of global oil production, compared to about one half in the 1970s (see Figure 7-2).

A combination of factors led to this precipitous decline of OPEC's position in global oil markets during the 1980s. The worst global recession in the postwar era reduced overall demand for energy at the outset of the decade. Conservation efforts in the advanced industrial states, spurred by the fifteenfold increase in oil prices in the 1970s, began to manifest themselves. Even with economic recovery in the United States, for example, oil consumption per unit of economic growth in the 1980s had declined approximately 28 percent from levels a decade earlier. Higher prices for OPEC oil accelerated shifts to alternative sources of energy (such as coal and nuclear power) and reliance upon oil supplies from sources outside of OPEC (see Figure 7-2). Production of oil in the North Sea, Mexico, and Alaska brought an additional 6 million barrels a day of non-OPEC oil to the world market between 1973 and 1982.[40]

A buyer's market for petroleum reemerged in the 1980s. OPEC had become a supplier of last resort to firms and countries whipsawed by threats of supply interruptions and price increases after 1973. When conditions allowed, oil purchasers diversified their sources of supply. The OPEC states were forced to absorb most of the slack in demand and production existing

---

[39]"Cheaper Oil," *The Economist*, July 6, 1985, p. 18.

[40]Bijan Mossavar-Rahmani, "The OPEC Multiplier," *Foreign Policy*, No. 52 (Fall 1983), 143.

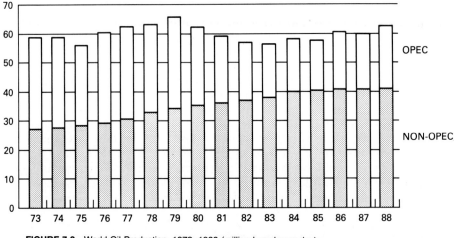

FIGURE 7-2   World Oil Production, 1973–1988 (million barrels per day)
Source: *BP Statistical Review of World Energy, 1985 and 1989*, p. 5.

in world oil markets during the 1980s. This not only had devastating economic impacts on the OPEC states but also introduced much greater strains in relations among the members of OPEC, threatening the cohesion upon which the viability of the cartel depends.

During OPEC's heyday, Saudi Arabia could operate as a swing producer for the cartel, shutting down production or expanding it to keep world oil markets in balance. Saudi Arabia was ideally suited for this role with substantial international reserves, annual current account surpluses, excess production capacity, and oil export revenues well beyond annual government expenditure needs. Its unilateral role in controlling oil markets over the course of the 1970s permitted OPEC states to avoid the difficult political problem of jointly allocating production quotas among themselves to defend cartel prices. This system collapsed in the 1980s.

As petroleum supplies exceeded demand in the 1980s, OPEC production shrank to a low of 17 million barrels a day in 1984—approximately 15 million barrels per day less than OPEC's production capacity. Even Saudi Arabia found it impossible to bring OPEC production and global oil demand into equilibrium. The OPEC states were required for the first time to forge formal agreements on production ceilings for all members of the cartel. In 1984 production quotas were set at 17.5 million barrels per day to defend official OPEC oil price levels. Production at such levels proved insufficient to meet the financial needs of any but several low population OPEC states. By the mid-1980s there was extensive price discounting and widespread cheating on national production quotas by most members of the cartel.

The extent of the challenge facing OPEC producers in the mid-1980s is well illustrated by the case of Saudi Arabia. In 1985 Saudi Arabia's balance-of-payments deficit of $20 billion was exceeded only by that of the United States. With a production capacity in excess of 10 million barrels,

Saudi Arabia was pumping only 2.5 million barrels per day. Its oil revenues had declined from $102 billion in 1981 to just $17.5 billion in 1985,[41] requiring it to draw upon its international reserves at the rate of $15 billion a year to cover government expenditures.[42] Such circumstances compelled the Saudis in 1985 to discount their oil sales below the official price of $28 per barrel and to expand production beyond the 2.5 million barrels a day to which they had confined themselves to defend OPEC prices. World oil markets were in such turmoil that the Saudis and OPEC could no longer control production and prices. In 1986 oil prices plummeted (see Figure 7-1).

Have we witnessed the demise of OPEC? Such a conclusion is certainly premature. Lower oil prices are eroding energy conservation efforts in advanced industrial states; witness the return of American fascination with large, less fuel-efficient automobiles, for example. Lower prices also have led to much diminished efforts to develop new wells and to employ energy substitutes for oil. North Sea, U.S., and Soviet oil production outside of OPEC is expected to decline in the 1990s. OPEC states still possess two-thirds of the world's proven reserves of oil. Should global economic growth rebound and rekindle demand increases for oil, OPEC will have to supply it.[43] The Middle East remains a most unstable area, as Iraq's invasion of Kuwait during 1990 and the Gulf war of 1991 prove. International war, civil war, revolution, and acts of terrorism all are realistic threats to interrupt oil supplies from major producers to world markets in future years without warning. These developments taken together suggest that the world is not free from a possible replay of events that gave OPEC great political-economic leverage during the 1970s. It is a mistake to assume that the oil crisis is today no more than an artifact of history.

The American Response to OPEC

The United States has attempted through both multilateral and unilateral efforts to deal with the security and economic challenges posed by OPEC's seizure of control over international oil markets. In 1974 Western states, with the exception of France, created the International Energy Agency (IEA) to coordinate their response to OPEC. Its major accomplishment to date has been the erection of a multilateral mechanism to deal with any significant supply interruptions from OPEC, whether directed consciously at Western states (as the Arab oil embargo of 1973) or not (such as the elimination of production through domestic turmoil or war). IEA agreements call for each member state to accumulate an emergency petroleum reserve equivalent to at least 90 days' supply of its national oil consumption. In addition to being able to draw upon these reserve stocks in a future oil emergency, states in the IEA have commitments to share equally any reduction in oil consumption in excess of 7 percent due to an interruption of imports. In a word, a selective embargo of oil of the sort

[41]"Texaco Deal: A New Saudi Strategy," *The New York Times*, June 27, 1988, p. 29.

[42]Mattione, *OPEC's Investments and the International Financial System*, p. 186.

[43]For an interesting discourse on the multiplier effects of supply and demand changes for OPEC oil, see Mossavar-Rahmani, "The OPEC Multiplier," pp. 136–49.

imposed by the Arab states in 1973 would be met by a common IEA strategy for Western states to share equally their available supplies of energy oil reserves, oil imports, and domestic oil production. It is hoped that knowledge of these commitments among Western states will deter or render ineffective any OPEC states' efforts to bring pressure on Western countries through interrupting oil supplies in the future.

While these multilateral arrangements would, presumably, provide some security for Western states in the face of supply interruptions, they do not confront the threat to their economic security posed by massive OPEC oil price increases during supply shortages. To do that, Walter Levy, a prominent oil consultant, suggests that through the IEA the Western states must forge an agreement to refrain jointly from competing for oil in world markets at spot market prices above OPEC price levels. They would also need to agree to share equally the burdens of adjusting to oil shortages that might well arise by their refusal to purchase oil at high spot market prices.[44] An agreement of this sort would directly confront the dynamic underlying the pattern of OPEC price increases prevailing in periods of a seller's market such as that in the 1970s.

American vulnerability to OPEC has varied considerably since the oil crisis of 1973. From Figure 7-3 we can see that domestic U.S. oil production has declined slightly since the early 1970s, even with Alaskan oil coming on stream. Increases in U.S. oil consumption must be met by greater reliance upon imports. During the 1970s America's unabated thirst for oil led to increased dependence on oil imports. Late in the decade the United States was importing more than twice as much oil as it did in the years prior to the 1973 crisis. Particularly alarming was the increased reliance upon imports from the Middle East and North Africa—the most volatile and politicized sources of petroleum. It is no wonder that the oil supply interruptions and price increases of 1979 had such a devastating impact on the American economy.

This situation of acute oil vulnerability gave way to a much improved position during the 1980s. Energy conservation efforts initiated in the 1970s began to yield dividends (reliance upon fuel-efficient automobiles decreased gasoline consumption, and greater energy efficiency in commercial and residential buildings was achieved, for example). Problems on the supply-side were attacked by extracting residual oil from previously worked reserves, expanding exploration and production in Alaska and in offshore waters, initiating greater exploitation of petroleum reserves on federally owned land, and making additions to the nation's strategic oil reserves as called for under the IEA arrangements. Imports were shifted to take advantage of non-OPEC oil production in the North Sea and Mexico, for example, which was much less subject to unforeseen supply interruptions. These developments were spurred both by public policies and market forces. The latter became especially salient with the abandonment of U.S.

[44]See Walter Levy, "Oil and the Decline of the West," *Foreign Affairs*, 58, no. 5 (Summer, 1980), 999–1015. Note that in the absence of such arrangements oil prices doubled in 1990 after Iraq's invasion of Kuwait, even though only 7 percent of global oil production was affected and other suppliers quickly expanded output to replace the shortfall.

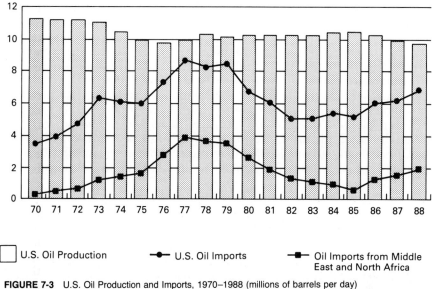

U.S. Oil Production   —●— U.S. Oil Imports   —■— Oil Imports from Middle
                                                                East and North Africa

FIGURE 7-3   U.S. Oil Production and Imports, 1970–1988 (millions of barrels per day)
Source: *BP Statistical Review of World Energy*, various years 1970–1989.

energy price controls during 1980–81. Moreover, economic recession in the early 1980s led to a decline in U.S. oil consumption and imports.

In 1985 the United States enjoyed much greater immunity to OPEC pressure than it had any time during the previous decade. The bulk of U.S. oil imports were coming from relatively secure sources in Latin America, Western Europe, and Canada—all outside of OPEC. Oil imports from Iran and Arab states in the Middle East and North Africa were less than 25 percent of their peak during 1977–1979, accounting for fewer than 1 million of the 15 million barrels of oil consumed daily in the United States. The United States' strategic petroleum reserves contained 450 million barrels—enough to replace imports for more than three months. The world petroleum market was so soft that OPEC found itself incapable of successfully defending its official price levels. It appeared that U.S. oil problems were a thing of the past.

Even in the presence of the favorable energy environment of the mid-1980s, however, concerns were expressed that changes in the structure of international oil markets could limit Western capacity to cushion the impacts of future oil crises. The IEA strategy for responding to possible future oil shortages relies primarily upon movements of oil by the major international oil firms. Yet these companies occupy a much diminished position in international markets. In the early 1970s the seven sisters controlled two thirds of the oil reserves outside the Communist world, two thirds of oil production, and 60 percent of the market for refined petroleum products. In the 1980s their shares had declined to less than 20 percent of reserves and production and 40 percent for refined products.[45] This suggests that

[45]"Oil and the Gulf," *The Economist*, July 28, 1984, p. 14.

Western oil firms are in nowhere near as commanding a position to help manage global oil shortages possibly emerging in future crises as they were in the crises of 1973 and 1979. Moreover, since 1981 all price controls and rationing schemes for dealing with oil emergencies have been dismantled in the United States in favor of market forces. A future crisis could wreak far greater havoc on the American economy than earlier experience suggests. In a 1983 simulation of the International Energy Agency program for coping with a world oil crisis, assuming reliance upon market forces as preferred by the United States, oil prices skyrocked to $98 per barrel.[46] Although the oil picture looked bright for consumers in the mid-1980s, the United States found itself dangerously exposed to untoward developments in global energy markets as the decade came to a close.

The Third Oil Crisis: Iraq Invades Kuwait, 1990

Depressed oil prices of the mid-1980s (see Figure 7-1), rising oil consumption, and declining domestic oil production—all in a decade of slack interest in an energy policy—combined to make the United States more dependent on foreign oil in 1990 than at any time in its history. United States oil production in 1989 was at its lowest level in twenty-five years.[47] Domestic drilling and exploration levels were the lowest since record keeping began in 1940.[48] Oil imports, which amounted to 31 percent of domestic U.S. oil consumption in 1984, had risen to 50 percent during the first half of 1990—well above the highest level of U.S. oil import dependence during the two oil crises of the 1970s.[49] Oil imports during 1989 accounted for 44 percent of the U.S. trade deficit, approaching the level of its trade deficit with Japan. The United States, moreover, was importing a larger proportion of its oil from the Middle East in 1989 than it had in 1973.

From the narrow perspective of U.S. energy posture, upheaval in the Middle East could scarcely have come at a worse time. Saddam Hussein threw the region into turmoil in August 1990 when he invaded Kuwait, declaring it an integral part of Iraq on the basis of historical claims. By March 1991 the venture had collapsed in shambles. Iraq suffered a humiliating military defeat at the hands of an international coalition, but only after Hussein shook political, economic, and military relations in the area to their foundation.

Iraq's military action against Kuwait involved much more than oil. Hussein had built the world's fourth largest army in Iraq. Iraq was asserting itself as the dominant regional power in the Persian Gulf after its costly war with Iran during the 1980s. Hussein advanced himself as a leader of

[46]"Next Time the Persian Gulf Shuts Down, the U.S. May be Ready to Act," *National Journal*, February 25, 1984, p. 367.

[47]"Greater Reliance on Foreign Oil Feared as U.S. Output Tumbles," *The New York Times*, January 18, 1990.

[48]"Drilling for Oil Falling in U.S., Price Rises Seen," *The New York Times*, February 2, 1989, p. 31; "Prices Encourage Search for Oil, but Labor Is Short," *The New York Times*, September 11, 1990, p. 1.

[49]"U.S. Imports Record 49.9% of Oil," *The New York Times*, July 19, 1990, p. C1. See Figure 7-3 for trends in U.S. oil production and imports during the late 1980s.

the Arab world in its conflicts with non-Arab adversaries, such as Israel, Iran, and the West. He verbalized impoverished Arabs' resentment of the richest, traditional Arab regimes' (especially Kuwait and Saudi Arabia) refusal to share their immense oil wealth and financial reserves more generously with the wider Arab community.

In 1990, Iraq and Kuwait were locked in a bitter political-economic conflict. Kuwait was insisting that Iraq maintain its burdensome repayment schedule for loans connected with the Iraq-Iran war. Iraq criticized Kuwait for depressing oil prices and Iraq's oil export revenues by vastly exceeding its production quota under OPEC agreements. Moreover, Hussein accused Kuwait of stealing Iraq's wealth by extracting far more than its share of petroleum from the rich Rumaila oil field straddling the Iraq-Kuwaiti border. Iraq's position was that the economic costs of these actions by Kuwait exceeded the value of the loans in dispute.[50] Hussein "settled" the dispute by invading Kuwait in August 1990, driving the ruling family into exile, and declaring Kuwait an integral part of Iraq under historical claims preceding Britain's colonial rule of the area following World War I.

Iraq's conquest of Kuwait gave it much easier access to the Persian Gulf and, of course, much greater potential wealth through control over Kuwait's oil resources. Its military supremacy in the region and the demonstration of its use against Arab rivals directly threatened Saudi Arabia and the smaller, oil-rich regimes in the Persian Gulf. Iraqi troops immediately took up provocative positions along the Saudi border.

By invading Kuwait, Iraq controlled 20 percent of the world's oil reserves. Were Iraq to invade Saudi Arabia, with the world's largest oil deposits, Hussein would have obtained direct control over 45 percent of global oil reserves. If unopposed, Iraq would not only have established itself as the hegemonic state in the region but also would have been able to determine oil production levels and prices in OPEC through intimidation of other oil producers in the Gulf region—with all that implies for the energy needs of the world and the international economy. No one doubted that Saddam Hussein would exploit this position to the fullest in pursuit of his unbounded political ambitions, were he able to achieve it. The potential implications for rival Arab regimes, Arab-Israeli relations, regional and international power balances, and Western political, economic, and military interests were incalculable.

The United States quickly committed forces to defend Saudi Arabia from the Iraqi threat and forged a broad international coalition to oppose Iraq's aggression. Under authority of the United Nations Security Council, virtually all countries of the world imposed a trade and financial boycott on relations with Iraq and occupied Kuwait.[51] A coalition of twenty-nine states assembled under American leadership, including several Arab countries (most notably Egypt, Saudi Arabia, Syria, and exiled Kuwaitis), warned Hussein in November 1990 that they would force his withdrawal from

[50]"The Oilfield Lying Below the Iraq-Kuwait Dispute," *The New York Times*, September 3, 1990, p. 7.

[51]"Text of Resolution for Sanctions on Iraq," *The New York Times*, August 7, 1990, p. A5.

Kuwait by military means if he did not leave by January 15, 1991. The military forces of the coalition deployed in the region numbered more than 500,000 by early 1991. They faced an Iraqi army of at least comparable size but with much less technological sophistication. Coalition forces engaged Iraq militarily on January 16, 1991. Six weeks of war restored Kuwait's independence, destroyed most of Hussein's armed forces, and left the economic infrastructure of Iraq in ruins. The crisis marked the beginning of a period during which the political, economic, and security relations of the Middle East must be redefined in the most fundamental terms. The consequences will not be fully understood for years.

This complex crisis and destructive war was about much more than oil. But it cannot be understood apart from oil. Neither Iraq's territorial claims on Kuwait nor Hussein's political enmity toward the ruling family in Kuwait were new; but Hussein's pressing them in 1990 was occasioned by a desperate need for additional oil revenues to finance his political, economic, and military ambitions. President George Bush's commitment of military force to defend Saudi Arabia and to restore the deposed Kuwaiti leadership was certainly related to the Western states' dependence on foreign oil and the desire to maintain friendly regimes astride the world's largest oil reserves. (It is hard to imagine the same response were the Gulf states major producers of tropical fruit, for example.) Beyond pressures exerted by the United States, the international community's refusal to accept Iraq's absorption of Kuwait was related directly to fears of periodic turmoil in energy markets and international economic stability in future years were Hussein to successfully harness OPEC policies to his political agenda through military conquest and intimidation of oil-producing states in the Gulf.

During the crisis international oil prices soared to over $36 a barrel, despite the fact that additional output by other OPEC states quickly made up for supplies lost because of the embargo on oil from Iraq and Kuwait. (See Figure 7-4 for a summary of oil prices over the course of 1990, as related to major crisis developments.) President Bush was reluctant to release large amounts of oil from America's Strategic Petroleum Reserve to mitigate price increases, preserving stocks in the event that the need to go to war in the area would threaten Saudi production (it did not as things turned out). When the war commenced in 1991, oil prices fell quickly as the dominance of the coalition forces arrayed against Iraq became evident.

The postwar period will severely challenge OPEC. Iraq, if permitted by the coalition that defeated it, and Kuwait will seek to resume oil exports at high levels to finance their reconstruction. Of course, the destruction of Kuwait's oil producing intrastructure will slow the process. Yet, other states that expanded production (most notably, Saudi Arabia) to make up for Iraqi and Kuwaiti output lost during the crisis will find it difficult to cut back to their previous quota agreements in OPEC. This could well lead to period of downward pressure on oil prices in world markets and income difficulties for all petroleum exporters.[52]

---

[52]For a discussion of OPEC's challenges in the aftermath of the war, see "Assessing the Damage to OPEC," *The New York Times*, February 11, 1991, pp. C1, C5.

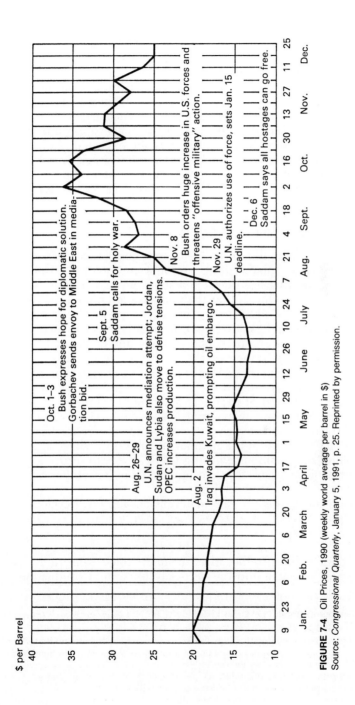

$ per Barrel

FIGURE 7-4 Oil Prices, 1990 (weekly world average per barrel in $)
Source: *Congressional Quarterly*, January 5, 1991, p. 25. Reprinted by permission.

Oct. 1–3
Bush expresses hope for diplomatic solution.
Gorbachev sends envoy to Middle East in media-
tion bid.

Sept. 5
Saddam calls for holy war.

Aug. 26–29
U.N. announces mediation attempt; Jordan,
Sudan and Lybia also move to defuse tensions.
OPEC increases production.

Aug. 2
Iraq invades Kuwait, prompting oil embargo.

Nov. 8
Bush orders huge increase in U.S. forces and
threatens "offensive military" action.

Nov. 29
U.N. authorizes use of force, sets Jan. 15
deadline.

Dec. 6
Saddam says all hostages can go free.

The Gulf crisis and war of 1990 and 1991 underline the dangers of substantial energy dependence on oil from this politically volatile region. This is true despite the buildup of petroleum stockpiles and energy efficiency improvements in the United States and other advanced industrial societies since the oil crises of the 1970s.[53] Whatever its benefits, letting market forces drive American energy policy means perpetuating dependence on oil from the Middle East at higher levels than those found unacceptable during the 1970s. Accordingly, United States economic and security interests will continue to make it particularly vulnerable to developments in the region. Periodic crises threatening supply interruptions and dramatic price swings in oil simply must be expected. At a minimum, it would make sense to expand stocks held in the Strategic Petroleum Reserves to permit quick release in large amounts to counter oil price escalations of the magnitude experienced in each of the three Middle East crises since 1973.[54]

The Generalizability of OPEC

OPEC's success and durability despite conflicts and even wars among its members has so enhanced the economic and political position of the oil-producing states that less developed states possessing large shares of raw materials or commodities other than oil have attempted since the 1970s to develop variants of OPEC's producer cartel strategy. Associations now exist among producers in less developed countries of such diverse commodities as bauxite, copper, iron ore, rubber, timber, and bananas. These producer associations have tested their market strength over the years. Some of them have enjoyed intermittent success in increasing government revenues from existing and future concessions, securing the location of processing facilities within the jurisdiction of producer states, and assuming minority or majority ownership over raw materials' production. However, they have not had much success in exercising decisive control over world market prices and production levels in the manner of the OPEC states after 1973. The combination of conditions enabling OPEC states to secure a stranglehold over world oil markets does not appear to be present for Third World producers of other commodities.

Producer cartels for raw materials among less developed countries are likely to succeed as a strategy for seizing market control under the following circumstances:

1. Access to the product in its primary stage constitutes the greatest barrier of entry into the vertically integrated production and sales process.

[53]See, for example, "Oil Crisis Like 1973's? It's Not Necessarily So," *The New York Times*, August 13, 1990, p. A7.

[54]This not only would afford greater economic security but also might reduce incentives for American interventions in the politics of an area we do not comprehend and are unable to control. Even as modest an energy policy change as this would be resisted in the United States, in the face of large fiscal deficits. Yet, the costs of this or any energy policy ought to be measured against the lives lost and the tens of billions of dollars associated with war and a permanent U.S. military presence in the Middle East required by continued energy dependence on oil from the region.

2. The dominant portion of the world's supply of the mineral is concentrated in a very limited number of less developed countries whose political outlook and economic situation are sufficiently congruent to make concerted economic action possible.

3. Global demand for the product is rising steadily over the years.

4. Natural and synthetic substitutes are not available or are extremely costly to employ.

5. Production cutbacks to hold or increase prices do not significantly increase unemployment in the producing states.

6. Financial reserves are large enough to allow limits in output without seriously curtailing imports necessary for development.

Oil would appear to be the exception, not the rule, for commodity producers in the Third World.

It should also be noted that, even if all these conditions for successful cartel activity should emerge for another commodity, there is no raw material that approaches crude oil's economic and political potency as a lever on advanced industrial states. Crude oil exports from less developed countries exceed the value of less developed countries' exports of all other commodities and manufactured goods combined.[55]

A NEW INTERNATIONAL ECONOMIC ORDER

OPEC exemplifies a strategy whereby less developed states cooperate and bargain along industry lines to enhance their economic and political position in international relations. There are also numerous multilateral efforts structured along regional and universal lines by less developed countries that extend well beyond confrontation with a particular industry. These efforts have seldom provided the drama of OPEC confrontations with advanced industrial states and the oil multinationals, but they constitute an important dimension of less developed countries' attempts to extract more benefits from their economic relationships with rich states and multinational firms.

Universalist multilateral strategies for systemic economic reform took shape with the creation of the United Nations Conference on Trade and Development (UNCTAD) in 1964. The cleavage between periphery and center states in the global economy was formalized in UNCTAD by a group system[56] in which 120 poor states (originally 77) adhered to united positions in making concrete proposals for reform in the gamut of international economic relations between rich and poor states. During the 1970s common less developed countries' proposals for international economic reforms (first made explicit and given coherence by UNCTAD) evolved to comprise a set of formal demands for a new international economic order. Since

---

[55] United Nations, *Handbook of International Trade and Development Statistics, 1984* (New York: United Nations, 1984), p. 154.

[56] For a discussion of the group system, see Branislav Gosovic, "UNCTAD: North-South Encounter," *International Conciliation*, No. 568 (May 1969), 14–30.

1974 the NIEO has provided the agenda for North-South diplomacy in a wide variety of institutional settings.

In substance, the NIEO consisted of the aggregated demands for economic reforms of interest to less developed countries in the various issue areas discussed throughout this volume. The demands would assure increased resource transfers from rich to poor states on improved terms and with little accountability on the part of the less developed countries. Among other things the list included:[57]

1. Implementation of UNCTAD's Integrated Program for commodities along with the establishment of the Common Fund as its centerpiece.
2. Liberalization and extension of the Generalized System of Preferences for less developed countries' exports of manufactured and semimanufactured goods to advanced industrial states.
3. An increase in the less developed countries' share of the world's industrial output to 25 percent by the year 2000. (In 1979 less developed countries accounted for only 9 percent.)
4. Establishment of a link between the creation of new special drawing rights in the IMF and development assistance.
5. Increased stabilization of the value of international reserves and exchange rates by movement away from the dollar as the linchpin of the international monetary system.
6. Increased access to IMF and commercial loans with lower interest rates, longer repayment periods, and less conditionality.
7. A comprehensive international approach to the management of debt rescheduling or cancellation confronting less developed countries.
8. Conformity of all advanced industrial states with the target of 0.7 percent of GNP in official development assistance to less developed countries.
9. Development of an enhanced research and development capacity within less developed countries.
10. Enhancement of science and technology transfers most appropriate to the particular needs of less developed countries, at reduced cost.
11. International regulation of multinational firms to prevent their most pernicious impacts on the social, cultural, economic, and political development of poor states.

As we have seen before, the less developed countries made these and additional demands with the conviction that the liberal international economic system dominated by Western states has produced a maldistribution of income and influence at the expense of Third World states. The resource transfers demanded in the NIEO would, in their view, eliminate the international sources of their economic and political weakness.

In addition to resource transfers, NIEO demands also focused on the

[57]For an excellent, concise summary of less developed countries' demands for a new international economic order, see Donald J. Puchala, ed., *Issues Before the Thirty-Fifth General Assembly of the United Nations, 1980–1981* (New York: United Nations Association of the United States, 1980), pp. 73–104.

need for universal recognition of new principles that less developed countries would like to see guiding international economic relations. In this sense, the NIEO was as much a demand for alteration in standards of conduct and norms governing economic relations as a demand for resource transfers. Less developed countries pressed hard to legitimize these new principles through passage of numerous U.N. resolutions.[58] The principles advanced in the NIEO assert the rights that less developed countries claim for themselves and the duties they would impose upon advanced industrial states. Consider the following points taken from the Charter of Economic Rights and Duties of States passed by the General Assembly of the United Nations in December 1974:

1. "Every state has and shall freely exercise full permanent sovereignty, including possession, use and disposal, over its wealth, natural resources and economic activities."

2. "Each state has the right to nationalize, expropriate or transfer ownership of foreign property in which case appropriate compensation should be paid by the state adopting such measures taking into account its relevant laws and regulations and all circumstances that the *state* considers pertinent. In any case where the question of compensation gives rise to controversy, it shall be settled under the *domestic law of the nationalizing state and by its tribunals . . .*" (italics added).

3. "It is the duty of states to contribute to the development of international trade of goods particularly by means of arrangements and by the conclusion of long term multilateral commodity agreements, where appropriate, and taking into account the interests of producers and consumers."

4. "All states have the right to associate in organizations of primary commodity producers [such as OPEC] in order to develop their national economies to achieve stable financing for their development, and in pursuance of their aims assisting in the promotion of sustained growth of the world economy, in particular accelerating the development of developing countries. Correspondingly, all states have the *duty to respect the right by refraining from applying economic and political measures that would limit it*" (italics added).

These and similar norms for international economic relations advanced by less developed countries would result in enhancing the sovereignty of Third World states, altering long-standing principles of international law regarding rights of foreign investors, and replacing the market mechanisms with commodity agreements and/or commodity cartels in international commerce for raw materials. The advanced industrial states

---

[58]See, for example, "The Charter of Economic Rights and Duties of States," *UN Monthly Chronicle*, 12, no. 1 (January 1975), 108–18; "The Declaration on Establishment of a New International Economic Order," *UN Monthly Chronicle*, 11, no. 5 (May 1974), 66–69 and "Program of Action on the Establishment of a New International Economic Order," pp. 69–84. For an excellent study of the NIEO as an effort to replace market mechanisms with administered or authoritative forms of resource allocation, see Stephen Krasner, *Structural Conflict* (Berkeley: University of California Press, 1985).

rejected these principles being advanced by less developed countries in the NIEO. The U.N. resolutions asserting them carry no legal or politically binding authority. Through the resolutions the less developed states are attempting to draw public attention to their aspirations and to establish a foundation for altering international economic practices in the future.

A third dimension of less developed countries' demands for a new international economic order involved institutional reforms that enhanced their power in international economic decision making. Most Third World states had not obtained independence at the time the major international economic institutions were established after World War II. They were able to exercise little influence over the formulation of international law or the operation of international organizations affecting most directly their conduct of international economic relations. To enhance their position and voting power in multilateral economic decision making, less developed countries have pressed for (1) expanding the membership of existing organs of the U.N. family of institutions (such as tripling the size of the U.N. Economic and Social Council with increased participation by less developed countries, (2) bringing negotiations of economic importance from forums excluding less developed countries into institutions where they are represented (such as moving key deliberations on international monetary relations from the Organization for Economic Cooperation and Development to the International Monetary Fund's Group of Twenty), and (3) creating entirely new international economic institutions to champion particular less developed countries' interests (such as UNCTAD, the United Nations Industrial Development Organization [UNIDO], and the U.N. Commission on Transnational Corporations). Overall, the developing states have attempted to subordinate multilateral decision making on economic matters in the IMF, IBRD, GATT, and elsewhere to the authority and supervision of organs in the United Nations, where less developed countries have enjoyed an overwhelming voting majority. This was at the core of their dispute with the United States and other advanced industrial states in the North-South negotiations at Cancún, Mexico, in 1981.

A new international economic order along the lines advocated by less developed countries would constitute wholesale redistribution of resources and political-economic power in the international system from the advanced industrial states of the West to countries in the Third World. For this reason Western states refused to move voluntarily toward a comprehensive implementation of the NIEO. In addition to considerations of wealth and power losses, however, the leading Western states profoundly disagree with the basic premises of the NIEO demands. As opposed to the NIEO assumption that underdevelopment is primarily a result of past and present inequities in the international economic system, the United States and others are inclined to view domestic policies of less developed countries as the greatest obstacle to their development. Western states are opposed to a massive restructuring of international economic institutions and the norms of behavior that, in their view, have served most states well. They are very reluctant to replace market mechanisms, despite their imperfections, with an elaborate array of formally negotiated agreements governing resource flows as called for in the NIEO.

The advanced industrial states responded to the NIEO demands by agreeing to highly specified, selective reforms in international trade, financial, or investment relations that take into greater account the particular economic needs of less developed countries and with which most Western states are in agreement (such as the Generalized System of Preferences). They essentially isolated and "domesticated" a few of the most palatable demands for a new international economic order on which they were willing to negotiate. The Western states remain opposed to sweeping alterations of the basic principles and institutions that have provided the framework for international economic relations since World War II.

While the aggregated demands of 120 less developed countries for reform of the international economic system are unlikely to be met in any comprehensive fashion, the continued emphases in the NIEO performed an important agenda-setting function for less developed countries. It provided the means by which Third World states placed their political-economic priorities alongside Cold War issues and intra-Western economic concerns in international diplomacy. This is a considerable accomplishment for a group of states that only forty years ago were objects of world politics rather than actors in it.

The NIEO demands also provide legitimacy and a more coherent rationalization for bolder regional and national policies of less developed countries in their foreign economic relations. In short, the greatest impact of the NIEO is likely to be seen in increased multilateral economic cooperation among Third World states and emboldened unilateral bargaining by less developed countries with foreign firms, public and private financial institutions, and advanced industrial states. We should not look only at formal universal agreements consummated between advanced industrial states and less developed countries in evaluating the success or failure of the NIEO as it evolves.

RADICAL STRATEGIES

With the exception of nationalization, this discussion of alternative strategies for states in the periphery seeking to improve their position in the global political economy has focused on a positive-sum view of international economic relations. That is, both poor and rich states are believed to secure benefits from their various economic transactions; the struggle is over attempts to increase the relative share of these benefits going to the poor states. Radical thinkers see the global economy in zero-sum terms, however. Benefits secured by rich states in their economic transactions with states in the periphery are seen as a direct measure of the economic loss suffered by the poor states. In short, the contemporary poverty of states in the periphery is seen by radicals as the product of their continued economic relations on present terms with advanced industrial societies. When prescribing strategies by which less developed countries might reduce losses or increase benefits from international economic relations, radicals emphasize the need to interrupt economic transactions with rich Western states—indeed, to rebel against the existing global system.

Consistent with this logic, a less developed country might choose to withdraw from international economic relations to the maximum extent possible. Such a strategy is an insulatory response to a situation in which a poor state associates economic exploitation and political and cultural penetration with active participation in the contemporary global economy. Burma under Ne Win, for example, adopted a variant of this basic posture in its insistence upon isolation and self-sufficiency. It minimized international economic contacts and subordinated the values of rapid economic growth and development to the values of national autonomy. Burma pursued its own application of Buddhism and socialism to preserve indigenous socio-cultural-political interests—under a very repressive regime, it should be noted.

When taken to its logical conclusion, the radical position implies an aggressive strategy of confrontation between states in the periphery and the center states.[59] The United States and other Western powers are seen as owing their commanding economic and political position in the world to their capacity for continued access to and exploitation of states in the periphery. The only way for less developed countries to improve their lot significantly is to act in concert to destroy existing exploitative economic relations and the present American role in the world economy. Radicals have implied that this could be done by denying the United States and other Western countries the export markets, investment opportunities, and raw materials of the Third World upon which the center states' prosperity depends. Unlike the other strategies for which one can find some empirical referent, this strategy is exclusively theoretical at the present time. Because of this, we will address only briefly the question of the extent of the center states' dependence upon Third World states and the economic capacity and political efficacy of this proposed action. Since most of the relevant literature pictures the United States as the linchpin of contemporary international economic relations, this examination will be confined to the United States as the target of the Third World.

There is no question that the United States would be hurt economically if all less developed countries joined together to terminate their imports of U.S. goods and denied their markets to direct foreign investment by U.S. firms. What position do the less developed countries occupy in American trade and investment? In 1989, U.S. trade turnover (exports plus imports) with less developed countries amounted to 6 percent of its Gross National Product.[60] During 1987, the cumulative book value of U.S. direct foreign investment in less developed countries amounted to 1 percent of its GNP.[61] Income from U.S. direct foreign investments in less developed countries amounted to $9 billion in 1987, out of a total of $52 billion in

[59]See, for example, André Gunder-Frank, "Sociology of Development and Underdevelopment of Sociology," in *Dependence and Underdevelopment*, eds. J. Cockroft, A. G. Frank, and D. Johnson (Garden City, N.Y.: Doubleday, 1972), pp. 321–98.

[60]Calculated from International Monetary Fund, *Direction of Trade Yearbook, 1990* (Washington, D.C.: IMF, 1990), p. 404.

[61]Calculated from U.S., Department of Commerce, *Survey of Current Business*, August 1988, p. 42.

income from direct foreign investments the world over.[62] U.S. direct foreign investment in less developed countries during 1987 generated a 13.7 percent rate of return.[63]

These data suggest that U.S. trade and investment in less developed countries are certainly important to American economic prosperity. In the aggregate, however, there is little to suggest that the United States could not cope with an attempt by less developed countries to sever trade and investment relations with it. The American economy remains more self-sufficient than all but a handful of countries in the world—as measured by the ratio of foreign economic activity to domestic activity. The less developed countries as a group occupy a relatively small proportion of America's international economic transactions. Sixty percent of U.S. trade and 77 percent of its direct foreign investment are directed to other advanced industrial states. Rates of return on direct foreign investment were higher in advanced industrial states than in less developed countries in 1987.[64] More to the point, it is hard to conceive of realistic situations in which a large group of less developed countries would unite effectively to confront the United States with a cutoff of trade and investment ties, even assuming the emergence of highly radicalized leadership. The more likely pressure would be toward maintaining or increasing trade and investment relations with alterations in their terms of exchange and composition, not an abrupt interruption of economic relations that less developed countries need more than the United States.

The capacity of less developed states to secure global economic reform by threatening to withhold mineral resources appears more impressive than their capacity to do so through the denial of their markets to American exports and capital. For example, Harry Magdoff listed six critical materials necessary for the production of jet engines and points out that imports account for 75 to 100 percent of American consumption of four of these materials (columbium, nickel, chromium, and cobalt).[65] By means of this illustration Magdoff very dramatically made the point raised by many radicals that the overall American economy is highly dependent on raw material imports that in many cases are supplied by less developed countries. It is a small step to conclude that concerted action by the Third World to deny these resources to the United States would indeed accomplish the goal of forcing the United States to agree to major alterations in the terms upon which it conducts foreign economic relations.

The major problem in implementing a collective denial of mineral resources vital to the American economy is the extremely remote possibility that major suppliers would agree to such a policy. Table 7-1 explains why. It is unlikely that states such as Brazil, Canada, Mexico, and Malaysia would elect to cooperate in this endeavor. To implement a concerted strategy of denying mineral resources to the United States would require the emer-

[62]*Ibid.*, p. 44.

[63]*Ibid.*, p. 45.

[64]*Ibid.*

[65]Harry Magdoff, *The Age of Imperialism* (New York: Monthly Review Press, 1969), pp. 51–52.

gence and cooperation of radical regimes in most of the states listed in Table 7-1. But even radical regimes might not wish to take such action. Those states that have individually nationalized foreign-owned extractive enterprises have usually done so to increase their returns from sales of the mineral resources to advanced industrial states rather than to halt deliveries to major consumers and purposefully disrupt the global economy. This is true notwithstanding the Arab oil embargo of the United States in 1973 and 1974. It must also be realized that the United States retains considerable capabilities of its own to which it could resort should a direct confrontation along these lines be attempted by producers of mineral resources. Most notably, credits and capital flows from the U.S. government as well as from American banks and firms critical for many LDCs' economic development could be cut off. No one would "win" in an economic war waged between the Third World and the United States. More pointedly, a conflict along these lines is too improbable to take seriously.

Short of actually denying raw materials to the United States, there are possibilities for securing changes of American policy for long-standing issues of economic importance to less developed countries through the leverage afforded by OPEC states. Radicals would presumably like to see the oil-producing states demand in concert the construction of a new economic order that would be more beneficial to all poor states as the quid pro quo for assurances of adequate supplies of oil at stable prices to the United States and other rich states. In addition, should less developed countries be successful in instituting producer cartels in commodities other than oil, the opportunity would be present for a confrontation between *coalitions* of commodity producer cartels and advanced industrial states. This would add even more leverage to demands for radical reforms in the conduct of global economic and political relations.

Radical thinkers are prone to assert that aggregate data on the Third World's portion of American export trade, foreign investment, and raw material supplies both understate American economic dependence on the poor states and miss the point. They hold that the economies of advanced industrial nations, particularly the United States, "are so intricate that the removal of even a small part, as in a watch, can stop the mechanism."[66] Most evidence suggests, however, that the leverage the less developed countries have is basically that of raising costs and producing some major, but probably manageable, adjustment throughout the American and global economies. Pursuit of concerted action of this sort might result in increasing a few less developed countries' share of the benefits in various types of international economic transactions, but it is likely overall to produce further stratification among rich and poor states. Moreover, except in the broadest terms, radical thinkers fail to identify the mechanisms through which, and the terms upon which, international trade, capital, technology, and services will be conducted should this strategy succeed in revolutionizing the existing global economy.

---

[66]Gabriel Kolko, *The Roots of American Foreign Policy* (Boston: Beacon Press, 1969), p. 50.

TABLE 7–1   Major Suppliers of Mineral Resources of Which 50 Percent or More of American Consumption is Imported

MINERAL OR METAL	% CONSUMPTION IMPORTED, 1983	MAJOR FOREIGN SUPPLIERS, 1983	U.S. ABSORPTION[1]
Aluminium	97	Australia, Jamaica, Brazil, Guinea	34
Antimony	97	Bolivia, Rep. South Africa, China	56
Arsenic	93	Phillipines, Sweden, Canada, Mexico	55
Asbestos	68	Canada, Rep. South Africa	5
Barite	73	China, Mexico, Peru	45
Cadmium	72	Canada, Australia, Mexico, Peru	22
Cesium	100	FR Germany, Canada	100
Chromium	100	Rep. South Africa, Zimbabwe, Yugoslavia	9
Cobalt	100	Zaire, Zambia, Belgium	31
Colombium	100	Canada, Brazil, Nigeria, Australia	27
Diamond— Industrial	100	Rep. South Africa, Ireland, United Kingdom	15
Flourspar	68	Mexico, Rep. South Africa	12
Gallium	100	Switzerland, FR Germany, France	40
Indium	86	France, Italy, Belgium-Luxembourg	28
Iodine	67	Japan, Chile	27
Lead	59	Canada, Mexico, Australia, Peru	34
Manganese	99	Rep. South Africa, Gabon, France, Brazil	8
Mica (sheet)	100	India, Brazil	16
Platinum Metals	100	Rep. South Africa, United Kingdom, USSR, Canada	31
Potash	75	Canada, Israel, GDR, FR Germany	21
Selenium	65	Canada, Japan, United Kingdom, FR Germany	31
Silver	63	Canada, Peru, Mexico	30
Strontium	100	Mexico, Spain	39
Tantalium	100	Canada, Malaysia, Thailand	63
Thallium	64	Canada, Europe	10
Tin	99	Bolivia, Thailand, Brazil, Indonesia	18
Titanium	81	Australia, Canada, Rep. South Africa	30
Tungsten	85	Canada, Bolivia, Brazil, Peru	17
Zinc	73	Canada, Mexico, Peru	16

[1]U.S. Absorption: U.S. demand/Total World Production in %.

Source: U.S., Department of Interior, Bureau of Mines, *Mineral Facts and Problems* (Washington, D.C.: GPO, 1985).

CONCLUSION

Less developed countries never rely exclusively on a single strategy to improve their position in the global political economy. Often, the simultaneous pursuit of different strategies can lead to mutually reinforcing results. For example, the regional investment code of the Andean states may help to stimulate universal oversight of multinational corporate behavior through UNCTAD, which in turn would strengthen the hand of many less developed countries struggling with unilateral foreign investment policy. However, a special difficulty arises for a less developed country when it approaches one economic sector (such as extractive industry) in radical terms, and at the same time wishes to cooperate within other economic sectors (manufacturing or service industries) on the basis of liberal economic assumptions. Thus, Chile's nationalization of copper was inconsistent with its efforts through its membership in the Andean pact to attract foreign capital in other economic sectors.

It would be gratifying if on the basis of this discussion a general policy prescription could be suggested that would dramatically enhance these states' position in the global political economy,[67] but it would be a mistake to do so. Some of today's less developed countries such as Brazil, the Asian NICs, and certain oil-exporting state with small populations and immense petroleum reserves may in the future move into the center of the international system by virtue of their wealth and political importance. Other poor states may someday be catapulted into a position of economic and political potence should they sit astride mineral resources that are subject to intense global demand of the sort we saw for petroleum during the 1970s. Dankwart Rustow's observations about political modernization seem compelling as a general assessment of the problem:

> When one starts searching for causes, a country's rapid progress will always turn out to be closely related to very special and very favorable circumstances in its location or heritage [or in international market conditions]. The most admirable achievement seems least susceptible of imitation. . . . What is encouraging is the length and diversity of the list. . . . There is no reason to search for a single universal recipe, and even less to despair if any of its alleged ingredients are missing. Instead, each country must start with a frank assessment of its particular liabilities and assets; and each will be able to learn most from those countries whose problems most closely resemble its own.[68]

---

[67]This is not to say that less developed states employing these and other strategies are unlikely as a whole to increase their economic or political position in the global economy. Advanced industrial states and multinational firms can expect to find states in the periphery extracting a greater share of the benefits from international economic transactions than they were able to do prior to the 1970s. The era of virtually complete control of international commodity markets by Western firms has passed. However, notwithstanding some alteration of the less developed states' general position in the global political economy, these states are unlikely overall to secure economic and political gains, *relative to advanced industrial states*, that will even approach the magnitude that will be necessary to alter their perception that they must function in a global economy in which they are relegated unjustly to a peripheral position.

[68]*A World of Nations: Problems of Political Modernization* (Washington, D.C.: The Brookings Institution, 1967), pp. 275–76.

In efforts to prescribe policies by which less developed countries might obtain greater benefits from global economic relations, it is important to make explicit the values that are to be maximized (for example, aggregate economic growth or national autonomy), the costs (social and economic) involved in the pursuit of these values, the political and economic conditions at home and abroad that must obtain for the successful pursuit of a specific policy, and the probability that such conditions are likely to be present or produced. These considerations will generate different assessments of the prospects for different countries, and even for the same country as it operates in different economic sectors. Proponents of both liberal economic thought and radical thought would do well to focus on these basic considerations instead of indulging their penchant to propose policies that are deduced from prior assumptions and that are seen as generally applicable to all states in the periphery and to all varieties of their economic transactions.

8

Foreign Economic Policymaking in the United States

The United States is still the leading economic and political power among the center states and within the global economic system. However, its hegemony is challenged at home and abroad; frequently it is unable to get its own way; and in some regions of the world, other states exercise more economic influence than does the United States. Yet, in terms of the breadth and intensity of its economic and political links throughout most of the world, it remains the preeminent state in the global economic system. Developments within the United States as well as specific American policies are likely to have widespread implications for countries throughout the world. Consequently, an analysis of the politics of the global political economy requires an examination of the policymaking process in the United States. This will be done by juxtaposing radical, liberal, and mercantilist perspectives of the American foreign policy process, recognizing that important differences exist among analysts within all of these orientations toward political economy.

THE RADICAL PERSPECTIVE

The Substance of Foreign Policy

Our purpose is to examine the foreign economic policymaking process within the United States. From the perspective of various radical analysts, however, the assumption must first be made about the substance of U.S. foreign policy. Basically, although with some variation, radical critics feel that the foreign economic and political interests of the United States are synonymous. Therefore, the process by which foreign policy is made is essentially the same, regardless of whether the issue is an economic or a political one. Indeed, for most radicals a distinction between the two is not appropriate.

On this question and on others as well, there is some disagreement among radical analysts.[1] One group, of a Marxist-Leninist orientation, tends to feel that the capitalist system of the United States largely determines its political concerns and that capitalism demands international economic and political involvement to overcome its many domestic shortcomings. According to this view, perhaps represented best by Harry Magdoff, capitalism is a system that inequitably withholds from its workers their fair share of income and wealth. Consequently, the limited purchasing power of the proletariat, coupled with an insatiable appetite for growth by corporations, results in a surplus of manufactured goods and investment capital. The domestic U.S. market cannot absorb enough new production to sustain corporate growth since the proletariat is not earning enough to purchase more goods. Less new investment capital is needed and less is able to be employed profitably in the United States. Therefore, the capitalist American system needs foreign outlets for its excess goods and investment capital. The foreign political and military policy of the United States is designed to secure and maintain these foreign markets for the benefit of the American economy. As Magdoff states, "the underlying purpose [of imperialism] is nothing less than keeping as much as possible of the world open for trade and investment by the giant multinational corporations."[2] In the neo-Marxist world view, foreign economic expansion by American enterprises and financial institutions, supported through an imperalist foreign policy by the state, is a necessity—not a policy choice. Capitalism and American imperialism are inseparable.

Magdoff and others go beyond this relationship to point out how dependent the United States is upon a host of critical raw materials found elsewhere in the world. Because these natural resources are necessary for the continued functioning of the highly developed American economy, American foreign policy seeks to safeguard the sources of these materials. This leads quite naturally to an expansionist and adventuresome foreign policy that knows few geographical or political limits.[3] Because of natural resource dependency and the need to have foreign markets absorb goods and capital, the foreign political policy of the United States is designed primarily to serve and advance its economic interests. The U.S. response to Iraq's invasion of Kuwait in 1990 and the bold deployment of American troops in Saudi Arabia to prevent Saddam Hussein from being able to

[1]Pat McGowan and Stephen Walker identify five radical approaches to the formulation of foreign economic policy. The general discussion that follows does not explore the diversity of these views or the richness of each. For a more comprehensive treatment, see Pat McGowan and Stephen G. Walker, "Radical and Conventional Models of U.S. Foreign Economic Policy Making," *World Politics*, 33 (Winter 1981), 347–82. See also, Stephen Krasner, *Defending the National Interest* (Princeton: Princeton University Press, 1978), pp. 20–26.

[2]Harry Magdoff, *The Age of Imperialism* (New York: Monthly Review Press, 1969), p. 14. See Vladimir I. Lenin, *Imperialism* (New York: International Publishers, 1939) for the classical Marxist-Leninist view of imperialism.

[3]This issue has been examined in greater depth in Chapter 7, pp. 221–25.

dictate production and price levels in world oil markets offer a perfect illustration of radical views on how economic imperatives drive an expansionist U.S. foreign policy as the leading capitalist state.

Another group of radical critics, especially Michael Hudson, feels that American economic interests and policy are really servants of an expansionary political policy.[4] He observes a self-assertive U.S. government that seeks to dominate other countries or at least to ensure their compatibility with the American system. The expansion of American investments and trade is a conscious policy fostered by a government that is anxious to enhance the overall power of the United States. This outward thrust of state capitalism is based on a different cause-and-effect relationship than that advanced by Magdoff, but in both cases foreign economic policy and foreign political policy are thought to be so highly correlated as to be synonymous.

Richard Barnet combines the two previous radical positions when he ascribes American expansionism to its society and institutions. Like Hudson, he emphasizes the importance of the national security managers (officials in the State Department, Defense Department, National Security Council, CIA, and so forth) who have decision-making authority in foreign policy matters. However, Barnet, like many other radicals, stresses the business background of these officials and the dominance of business interests and attitudes in the government and in the society more generally. The crux of the relationship as he views it is that "the corporations continue to exercise the dominant *influence* in the society, but the *power* keeps passing to the state."[5] The congruence of foreign economic and political interests in American international relations is once more clearly indicated.

Regardless of differences among them, radical critics rarely make a distinction between the American foreign policymaking process regarding political and security matters and the process for economic issues. Since the interests and objectives of business and government regarding both economic and security matters are basically similar, separate policymaking processes do not exist. In other words, decisions on Cuba, arms limitation agreements with the Soviet Union, trade reform, and revision of the international monetary order spring from the same fountainhead of policymaking. The imperative of U.S. foreign policy is to reproduce capitalism around the globe for the sake of avoiding a domestic political-economic crisis in the United States leading to a socialist revolution.

The Formulation of Foreign Policy

Admitting the differences among radical analysts but recognizing their shared conviction that American foreign economic and political interests are similar, several views of how foreign policy is made in the United States can now be examined. It is important to note that discussions of the foreign policymaking process by radical analysts focus frequently on the

---

[4]Michael Hudson, *Super Imperialism: The Economic Strategy of American Empire* (New York: Holt, Rinehart & Winston, 1968).

[5]Richard J. Barnet, *The Roots of War* (Baltimore: Penguin Books, 1972), p. 185.

procedures by which policy is made on political, security, and military issues. Some radical critics like Magdoff discuss the *substance* of American economic policy, but they fail to explore specifically the process by which foreign economic policy is made. Others have addressed this issue more directly. Consequently, an examination of radical analysts' views of the formulation of foreign economic policy in the United States rests upon a combination of direct statements about the policy process and interpretations of their writings on other subjects like political and security issues.[6]

One group of radical thinkers, the instrumentalist school, perceives a U.S. foreign policymaking process that is primarily a reflection of and a response to the interests of the capitalist class and its big corporations.[7] It is a system in which economic and political interests, as defined and advanced by large business enterprises, dominate the substance of political and economic policy as well as the process by which foreign and domestic policies are made.

These radical analysts argue that business dominance is achieved as the result of congruence between what is good for the United States and what is good for its large business concerns. Radical critics often rely upon statements by policymakers and corporate executives to prove their point. One of the most often-quoted remarks is that of Assistant Secretary of State Dean Acheson in 1944 before a congressional committee concerned about postwar economic planning. Drawing upon the frightening possibility of a new depression after the war, Acheson said, "We have got to see that what the country produces is used and sold under financial arrangements which make its production possible. . . . You must look to foreign markets."[8] The prospect of limiting production only to what could be consumed in the United States "would completely change our Constitution, our relations to property, human liberty, our very conceptions of law. . . . Therefore, you find you must look to other markets and those markets are abroad."[9] Thus, he continued, "We cannot have full employment and prosperity in the United States without the foreign markets."[10] Businessman Bernard Baruch was more succinct when he emphasized the "essential one-ness of United States economic, political, and strategic interests."[11]

---

[6]One further caveat is that we are attempting to describe briefly views of a number of analysts as if there were no differences among them. Of course, there are; thus, what follows is a short synthesis of the thoughts of many.

[7]For a summary of instrumental Marxism, see McGowan and Walker, "Radical and Conventional Models of U.S. Foreign Economic Policy Making," and Stephan Krasner, *Defending the National Interest*. A leading statement of this position can be found in Ralph Miliband, *The State in Capitalist Society* (New York: Basic Books, 1969).

[8]Quoted in William Appleman Williams, "The Large Corporation and American Foreign Policy," in *Corporations and the Cold War*, ed. David Horowitz (New York: Monthly Review Press, 1969), p. 95. Parts of this passage have also been quoted in David Horowitz, *Empire and Revolution* (New York: Random House, 1969), pp. 233–34; and Lloyd C. Gardner, *Architects of Illusion* (Chicago: Quadrangle Books, 1970), p. 203.

[9]Williams, "The Large Corporations and American Foreign Policy," p. 96.

[10]Ibid.

[11]Quoted in Benjamin J. Cohen, *The Question of Imperialism: The Political Economy of Dominance and Dependence* (New York: Basic Books, 1973), p. 125.

Business influence over the foreign policymaking process is ensured by the recruitment of foreign policy officials from the highest ranks of the corporate and financial elite. Consequently, many of the national security managers not only represent business interests but in essence are corporate officials serving the government for a few years in the foreign policy apparatus. In the process, of course, they also further the interests of their corporations and of business in general. G. William Domhoff and Richard J. Barnet present analyses of foreign policy managers in the White House and the departments of State, Defense, and Treasury that reveal that a significant proportion of these officials held top-level positions in corporations, financial institutions, and related corporate law firms prior to their recruitment into government service. Barnet points out, for example, that between 1940 and July 1967, seventy of the ninety-one secretaries and undersecretaries of Defense and State, secretaries of the three branches of the armed forces, chairmen of the Atomic Energy Commission, and directors of the Central Intelligence Agency came from large corporations and leading investment houses.[12] Among President Reagan's inner circle of top foreign policy cabinet officials, Secretary of Defense Weinberger and Secretary of State Schultz were recruited from the Bechtel Corporation (one of the largest construction firms in the world with extensive international operations), and Secretary of the Treasury Regan was recruited from his position as president of the financial giant, Merrill Lynch. Weinberger and Shultz had served previously in important positions of government during the Nixon and Ford administrations, as had President Reagan's first secretary of state, Alexander Haig, who returned to Washington in 1981 from his post as president of United Technologies. Thus, the link between business and foreign policy in the United States is continually maintained through a direct sharing of executives by government and big business.

More indirectly, but just as critical, is the unrepresentative social and educational background of many of the most important foreign policy officials and their counterparts in business. The similarity in their background would tend to provide them with basically the same outlook on many economic and political issues. They are likely to move in similar social and intellectual circles. Many of them share the characteristics of significant family wealth, membership in exclusive clubs, listing in *The Social Register*, attendance at select private preparatory schools, and graduation from Ivy League–type colleges. For example, a study by the Brookings Institution revealed that 32 percent of the political appointees to the departments of State, Treasury, Defense, Army, Navy, and Air Force (all of which are important in the making of foreign policy) attended a select list of eighteen private preparatory schools.[13] Political appointees to Cabinet departments, regulatory agencies, and other commissions that are less involved in foreign

---

[12]Richard J. Barnet, "The National Security Managers and the National Interest," *Politics and Society*, February 1971, p. 260.

[13]These figures were derived from Table D.9 in David T. Stanley, Dean E. Mann, and James W. Doig, *Men Who Govern* (Washington, D.C.: The Brookings Institution, 1967), pp. 124–25.

policy matters were much less likely to have attended these prep schools (only 11 percent of them did so).

All this means that this corporate-based power elite will find it quite easy to move between business and government positions, thereby ensuring a foreign policy posture that is compatible with and supportive of big business interests. In the words of a leader in this type of analysis of the elite, "American foreign policy during the postwar era was initiated, planned, and carried out by the richest, most powerful, and most international-minded owners and managers of major corporations and financial institutions."[14] Thus, the unrepresentativeness of foreign policy managers in terms of socioeconomic background and previous positions in and allegiances to corporate America suggest strongly that big business interests help determine the foreign policymaking process.

According to the instrumentalist view, the influence of big corporations on the foreign policymaking process is enhanced further by the activities of a number of important groups that serve to transmit the business point of view to government officials. These transmission belts include a few of the large foundations based on corporate wealth, special blue-ribbon presidential advisory committees, and a small number of research and discussion committees. The Ford Foundation, the Carnegie Corporation, and to a lesser extent the Rockefeller Foundation have been active supporters of programs at universities and of foreign-policy related groups that represent business concerns in the foreign policymaking process. The special presidential committees are blue-ribbon citizens groups selected largely from corporate elites to analyze and to make recommendations regarding specific foreign policy issues. These committees have reported on such things as the nature of American military preparedness and the direction of its foreign aid programs. Seven of the eight most important committees concerned with foreign policy matters were chaired by corporate executives; the eighth chairman was the president of the Massachusetts Institute of Technology.[15] The research and discussion groups referred to are organizations such as the Council on Foreign Relations, the Committee for Economic Development, the Foreign Policy Association, the Trilateral Commission, and RAND, many of whose members and boards of directors come from a big business background.

All these groups act as links between corporations and government officials, and they ostensibly provide expert but nonbiased advice from nongovernmental sectors. In fact, though, the interests, perspectives, and alternatives advantageous to business are conveyed to governmental decision makers through the activities of these groups. These transmission belts sponsor formal face-to-face meetings that allow their largely business membership to exchange ideas and information with American and non-American foreign policy officials. These information and access advantages, combined with good organization and competent staffs, mean that these groups are able to develop thoughtful and comprehensive recommenda-

[14]G. William Domhoff, "Who Made American Foreign Policy 1945–1963?" in *Corporations and the Cold War*, ed. David Horowitz, p. 25.

[15]Ibid., p. 46.

tions about foreign affairs. Indeed, there are almost no other sources out-side of the government that can consistently provide such well-informed and coherent analyses of foreign policy issues of direct relevance to foreign policy officials. In other words, these transmission belts enjoy a virtual monopoly of effective interest representation regarding foreign economic and political policy. Moreover, the similar background characteristics of business and government elites ensure the receptivity of the latter to the concerns of the former.

This influence relationship is fostered as a result of the social, intel-lectual, and value similarities between foreign policy officials and the active membership of these transmission belts. This both follows from and leads to these groups serving as a major source of recruitment for high-level foreign policy officials. As an example of the two-way flow of personnel, prior to becoming secretary of state for President Kennedy, Dean Rusk was president of the Rockfeller Foundation. In the opposite direction, McGeorge Bundy left his position as national security adviser to the White House to become president of the Ford Foundation. There are many more such examples.

Domhoff suggests that the Council on Foreign Relations is probably the most important transmission belt for foreign policy matters. The large foundations and a number of major corporations provide the prime fi-nancial support for the council. In addition, top corporate executives are members of boards of directors of the major foundations and are also members of the Council on Foreign Relations. Thus, according to Domhoff, it should not be surprising that the council consciously attempts to increase the interaction between Washington officialdom and its largely corporate membership. These efforts have obviously paid off. For example, John J. McCloy, who had been among many things chairman of the board of Chase Manhattan Bank, high commissioner for Germany, and coordinator of American disarmament activities, once remarked, "Whenever we needed a man [to help direct foreign policy activity during World War II] we thumbed through the roll of Council members and put through a call to New York."[16]

To stimulate this interaction, the council arranges off-the-record speeches and question-and-answer sessions by important foreign policy officials of the United States and other countries. The information learned, the insights gained, and the views exchanged draw together more closely corporate interests and Washington officials. In addition, the council pub-lishes a number of important books and reference works as well as the prestigious journal, *Foreign Affairs*, which frequently contains articles by foreign policy officials.

However, Domhoff feels that the most important activity of the council is the discussion and study groups that examine a specific issue in great detail. Twenty-five business executives, government officials, a few military officials, and a small number of nonradical scholars conduct extensive discussions, often off the record, which eventually result in a book that presents a thorough statement of the problem. Some of the topics consid-

---

[16]Quoted by Joseph Kraft, "School for Statesmen," *Harper's Magazine*, July 1958, p. 67.

ered by these study groups have been instrumental in shaping U.S. policy regarding the nature of the United Nations charter and the development of the Marshall Plan for European recovery and in the early 1970s a full-scale reassessment of American relations with China. In sum, the council, along with the other groups mentioned, serves to encourage business participation in the formulation of foreign policy and to transmit business influence to foreign policy officials in multiple ways. At the very least, such institutions provide an important means of access to and maintenance of contacts with foreign policy makers. "Among 90 advisers, consultants, and members of the Reagan administration in 1981, 31 were members of the Council on Foreign Relations"—including Alexander Haig, George Shultz, Donald Regan, the director of the CIA, the secretary of commerce, the special trade adviser, the deputy secretary of defense, and eight top-level appointments at the State Department.[17]

A more recently founded vehicle for implanting corporate views in the councils of governments is the Trilateral Commission. One radical critic referred to it as "the executive committee of transnational finance capital."[18] Indeed, the following members of the Carter administration were all listed on the 1974 roster of the Trilateral Commission: the President, Vice President, the secretaries of state and defense, the national security adviser, and a number of undersecretaries in the Treasury and State departments. In 1981, twelve of President Reagan's policy advisers were participants in the Trilateral Commission.[19] It is important to note that this organization is comprised of government officials and private persons from the United States, Japan, and countries in the European Common Market. This internationalism is an attempt, some would say, to ensure cohesion within the capitalist class across national boundaries and to maintain the dominance of the international capitalist system.

The basic argument of the instrumentalist view is that American foreign policy reflects and represents the interests of big corporations in foreign affairs. Whether governmental political objectives conveyed through state capitalism lead to foreign economic involvement, or vice versa, is not a crucial distinction for our purposes. Either way, the result is a foreign policy that is linked closely and substantively to the interests of corporate America through a foreign policy formulation process that is subject to immense and almost exclusive influence from big business on the executive branch of the government. Congress, the radical analysts feel, is a largely impotent body in foreign policy matters since it often meekly upholds the policies and actions of the executive without acting as an alternate decision-making center. Consequently, corporate efforts to influence foreign policy are logically directed primarily to the executive branch. As William Domhoff characterizes it, "The policy-planning process begins in corporate

[17]G. William Domhoff, *Who Rules America Now? A View for the '80s* (New York: Simon & Schuster, 1983), p. 140.

[18]Jeff Frieden, "The Trilateral Commission: Economics and Politics in the 1970's," *Monthly Review*, 29, no. 7 (1977), 11.

[19]Domhoff, *Who Rules America Now?*, p. 140. For a treatment of the Trilateral Commission as an extension of U.S. hegemony, see Stephen Gill, *American Hegemony and the Trilateral Commission* (New York: Cambridge University Press, 1990).

board rooms, where problems are informally identified as 'issues' to be solved by new policies. It ends in government, where policies are enacted and implemented. In between, however, there is a complex network of people and institutions that plays an important role in sharpening the issues and weighing the alternatives . . . policy groups, foundations, think tanks, and university research institutes."[20] The entire network is led and funded by a "social upper class in the United States that is a ruling class by virtue of its dominant role in the economy and government"[21] as outlined in the manner of instrumental Marxists.

Not all neo-Marxian analyses agree with instrumental Marxists about the nature of politics and of state-society relations in capitalist countries. Structural Marxists[22] do not view capitalist states as directly responsive to the explicit interests of corporate and financial elites in the manner outlined by instrumental Marxists. They see capitalist states as exhibiting more autonomy from direct social-political-economic pressures of the bourgeoisie. Structural Marxists "see the state playing an independent role within the overall structure of the capitalist system."[23] The role of the state is determined by the very structure of the capitalist political-economic foundation upon which it rests. There is no need to find a one-to-one correspondence between corporate and government leaders through social-economic class as Miliband, Domhoff, and others attempt to document. The state is not simply the executive committee of the ruling class in the United States.

To structural Marxists, the United States government functions to reproduce and maintain capitalist society at home and abroad. It contains/ manages the contradictions inherent in capitalist economic structures and class conflict in order to sustain an inherently unstable capitalist system. Indeed, the interests of the dominant class in the United States may on many occasions be served more effectively by government officials and political leaders who are not always responsive to the pressures and petitions of leading corporate and financial interests. During the Depression, Franklin Roosevelt may well have saved American capitalism by introducing welfare state policies which the corporate and financial elite in the United States found abhorrent and vigorously opposed. Yet his policies, from the perspective of structural Marxists, enhanced the legitimacy of the capitalist state to the majority of the population, not part of the dominant class, and they enabled the United States to avoid a socialist revolution or a Fascist reaction in the face of great social turmoil. "To appear to follow the explicit preferences of powerful capitalists too slavishly would weaken the stability of the whole [capitalist] system. Compromises, such as the recognition of unions and higher social welfare payments, are essential, even if they are opposed by the capitalist class. Such policies protect the existing structure

---

[20]Ibid., p. 84.

[21]Ibid., p. 1.

[22]For a further elaboration of structural Marxism, see Krasner, *Defending the National Interest;* McGowan and Walker, "Radical and Conventional Models of U.S. Foreign Economic Policy Making"; and Nicos Poulantzas, *Political Power and Social Classes* (London: New Left Books, 1975).

[23]Krasner, *Defending the National Interest,* p. 22.

of economic relationships by disarming and disuniting potential opposition from the opposed."[24]

Structural Marxists, like instrumental Marxists, understand United States foreign policy to be driven by the economic imperatives of capitalism. Yet the former would expect the U.S. government to pursue international relations in a manner that does not always back particular U.S. corporate or financial interests in their activities abroad. The policymaking process permits the government to operate in a somewhat more activist and autonomous position relative to the economic interests of the dominant social-economic class in the United States. The function of the state in American foreign policy is advancing the interests of capitalism in the United States by reproducing capitalism abroad and prohibiting the implementation of policies contrary to its structural needs.

Myriad radical explanations of the foreign policymaking process have been advanced, but substantial agreement exists among them that the United States, as the premier world power since World War II, has been relatively less constrained by the interests and concerns of other countries and thus enjoys a correspondingly wide decisional latitude. American political and military policies, in conjunction with foreign economic policies that change economic partners into economic dependents, have enabled the United States to ensure the compliance of most states to its wishes. The radical literature is replete with examples of how the United States has imposed its will on recalcitrant friends and enemies to enrich itself and its corporations and to extend it global dominance at the expense of other countries. Thus, the United States has consciously attempted to structure and use the global economic system in a way that promotes its economic and political hegemony and the subjugation of other states. This gives American businesses free rein to develop and implement the kinds of domestic and foreign policies that will advance their interests the most.

A CRITIQUE OF THE RADICAL VIEW

Admittedly, this brief sketch of several radical conceptions of the American foreign policymaking process fails to do full justice to both the richness of the arguments and the many significant differences that do exist among radical analysts. Nevertheless, it is appropriate to raise questions about the substance of the instrumentalist view, the methodology used to develop these positions, and the way in which each contributes to an understanding of the foreign economic policymaking process.

Historically, much of the instrumentalist argument has been based on an analysis of American foreign political, security, and military policy. The role of domestic U.S. interests in these policies has been examined extensively, but far fewer attempts have been made to focus on how foreign economic policy has been made. One of the results of concentrating on political and military policy as the outcome of the policymaking process is that frequently there has been much greater unanimity within the United

[24]Krasner, *Defending the National Interest*, p. 25.

States on these issues because of the perception of serious external threats. Given the Cold War environment as the historical (though not the only) focus of the instrumentalists,[25] the coincidence of national policy and economic interests is not surprising. With large segments of the American population perceiving the existence of the Soviet Union and other Communist states as having broad and largely singular implications for all of American society, the concept of bipartisanship or the submerging of different and parochial interests was undertaken for the sake of national unity against a common threat. Business, labor, and government all joined together to protect the American system from what was perceived to be both a political and economic threat. Thus, the view of business dominance is based largely upon an analysis of political and security issues on which there was and still is, wide agreement as to the nature of the situation and American objectives. This is likely to change dramatically as we enter the post–Cold War era of U.S. foreign policy in the 1990s. On the other hand, to the extent that economic interests displace concerns about defense against the USSR in defining American foreign policy, others are coming to think in terms of what neo-Marxists have been saying all along—U.S. economic interests and its foreign policy *are* synonymous.[26]

A Multiplicity of Business Interests

By focusing on such political, security, and military issues, instrumentalist critics have largely neglected a rich panoply of bureaucratic and political maneuvering that is found in the making of foreign economic policy. Here, the common perception of threat and the unified external posture (with many internal differences and disputes about tactics) dissolves into wrangling associated with the promotion of specific and contradictory objectives by many competing economic and business interests. Thus, the concept of a business interest dominating the foreign economic policymaking process seems inappropriate for those economic groups that are often at odds with one another. In short, because the instrumentalist view is founded primarily on analyses of overarching political, military, and security issues, some serious problems are created in the transferring of their conclusions to discussions of the formulation of foreign economic policy.

As a result, the analysis fails to define, much less operationalize, the notion of *the business interest.* Instead, it is simply assumed that an overarching business interest is self-evident—one that is specific enough to serve as a guide to U.S. foreign policy. An examination of the policy formulation process on trade or investment issues reveals something quite different. In

---

[25]Most radicals say that the Cold War was contrived by the United States. See Joyce Kolko and Gabriel Kolko, *The Limits of Power* (New York: Harper & Row, 1972).

[26]This is not to say, however, that this has always been the fact in years past, that the substance and processes of formulating U.S. foreign policy have been unaltered by the disintegration of the Soviet bloc in 1989, or that Marxian analyses of U.S. policy are completely accurate even if they do attach primacy to economic relations. The implications of developments in the Communist countries for understanding international political economy will be addressed in Chapter 9.

the first place, different types of industries disagree greatly about the consequences of various foreign economic policy alternatives. For example, imposing tariffs or import quotas to protect the steel, textile, and shoe industries in the United States has been resisted by those industries who can successfully meet foreign competition and who themselves export to other countries. They fear that protectionist moves by the United States will be countered with similar actions by other countries and that their export activities will thereby by harmed. Also, if, for example, the U.S. steel industry seeks import restrictions to protect its domestic market share and increase prices, it will face opposition from other important industries in the United States using large quantities of steel in their manufacturing processes (such as appliances, machine tools, and automobiles), because they would be placed at a competitive disadvantage by such policy. To further illustrate these differences, consider this partial list of industries and products that were the subject of congressional testimony by interested unions, trade associations, and companies on the Trade Reform Act of 1973–74:

Agriculture
Automobiles
Bicycles
Chemicals
Clay
Dinnerware
Eggs
Flowers
Glue
Leather goods
Marbles
Musical instruments
Petroleum
Potash
Poultry
Shears
Shoes
Steel
Textiles
Tools
Vegetables
Wine

These specific groups differed greatly on their positions regarding the desirability of raising or lowering tariffs. Moreover, some of them have changed their views since that time, such as the auto industry. A precise and unanimous business interest cannot be observed among these industries, as a brief review of some of the conflicting testimony will indicate. Radical analysts may be right in emphasizing the influence of business interests on American foreign economic policy, but that does not provide nearly as clear a guide to policy as their analyses imply.

On certain issues, different firms within the same industry perceive different patterns of gains and losses to result from foreign economic policy. In the coffee industry, giant multinational corporations such as General Foods, Procter & Gamble, and Coca-Cola disagree over the nature of American policy toward the International Coffee Agreement. General Foods was quite concerned about the import of soluable coffee products from abroad, but P&G and Coca-Cola, joined by other smaller firms, did not wish to stem the flow. Quite naturally, each side used political influence in an effort to ensure that its position was advanced or protected by the policy that emerged.

An issue such as tariff reform may also highlight the very real areas of disagreement among different divisions of a multiproduct firm. In their careful study of the politics of tariff policy, Bauer, Pool, and Dexter point out that within the DuPont corporation the division manufacturing paint supported liberalization of trade whereas the rayon yarn division tended to be protectionist. Other parts of the corporation were little interested in the issue.[27] Similar differences can be observed within other corporations that manufacture a variety of products.

In the area of foreign economic policy, at least, American business interests rarely support a single policy position solidly except on the broadest levels, such as enthusiasm for the concept of private enterprise. Instead, the various alternatives available have different implications for different industries, firms, and divisions within specific corporations. As a result, the process by which foreign economic policy is made seems to be subject to the same type of political struggles thought to be characteristic of the domestic policymaking process.

Foreign economic policy has important and varying implications for businesses. Thus, businesses and other economic interests—including unions and a potpourri of various social groups each with their own conceptions of desirable goals—become actively involved in the domestic political process to influence the outcome of policy deliberations. As a result, the formulation of foreign economic policy provokes extensive and at times heated domestic political activity. For example, the hearings before the House Ways and Means Committee on the 1973 Trade Reform Act produced testimony by 96 industry associations and trade groups, 36 companies, 18 union organizations, 17 agricultural groups, 15 public interest groups, and 15 individuals. In addition, the committee received written statements from 111 other such groups and individuals. An examination of the hearings emphasizes the lack of consensus among these groups or within each type of group. The positions advanced reflected very specific conceptions of self-interest—not some overall consensus position by business.

Business executives tend to become preoccupied with and most active in specific issues that have definite implications for their business. They are not usually trying to establish and promote a grand design regarding the foreign political and economic posture of the United States. For in-

---

[27]Raymond A. Bauer, Ithiel de Sola Pool, and Lewis Anthony Dexter, *American Business and Public Policy* (New York: Atherton, 1963), p. 270.

stance, there is some suggestion that business involvement in organizations such as the Council on Foreign Relations amounts to little more than political dilettantism. Even a leading radical analyst, Domhoff, quotes a study by Bernard C. Cohen that concludes that members of the Foreign Policy Association "seldom seriously discuss political policies at all, let alone alternative policies. They tend to keep discussions apolitical, emphasizing the social, economic, cultural, and historical aspects of foreign affairs."[28] Barnet claims that corporate executives "do not seem to know how to manipulate this great wealth to influence the great decisions of war and peace. Nor do they seem to be particularly interested in doing so."[29]

Differences Within Government

The political, military, and security perspective of the radical analysts has led them to understand the governmental process in a way that may not be applicable to the formulation of American foreign economic policy.[30] Just as they assert *a* business interest, so also do they perceive *a* government view of U.S. foreign policy. Such an approach ignores the significance of the different perspectives and interests of various government agencies. Moreover, it neglects the specialized clientele and constituents of each department. Thus, the departments of Labor, Commerce, and Agriculture have different interests and objectives regarding American foreign economic policy as a result of the different sets of pressures they are subjected to by labor, business, and farmers and as a result of different conceptions of the nature of their tasks. Furthermore, within these broad economic sectors and within each of these departments there are disagreements on the consequences of policy alternatives. Thus, it is an oversimplification even to view various departments as passive instruments of their constituencies (labor, business, farmers, and so on) in society, for these groups themselves are not united on all issues.

Another critical assumption at the base of the instrumentalists' view of the American foreign policymaking process involves the nature of the relationship between business and government. As we discussed earlier, they feel that business interests dominate the government. However, there are numerous examples of U.S. policy that contradict this view. The Trading with the Enemy Act prohibits U.S. firms and their subsidiaries from trading with specified enemy countries in a number of defense-related products. In the mid-1970s and early 1980s, this act inhibited some business interaction with the Soviet Union and Cuba, in spite of the requests of American firms to rescind its restrictive provisions. Antitrust concerns of the Department of Justice have also served to retard the growth and success of the foreign subsidiaries of American firms. Moreover, the years of Cold War between the Soviet Union and the United States as well as the many years of American nonrecognition of China meant many missed oppor-

---

[28]Domhoff, "Who Made American Foreign Policy 1945–1963?" p. 61.

[29]Barnet, *The Roots of War*, p. 186.

[30]This topic is discussed at greater length later in this chapter when we examine the pluralist view of the foreign economic policymaking process.

tunities for doing business with these countries. The inability of American business to change government policy on these matters long after allies and their corporate competitors had opened lucrative business and political contacts is another important instance in which the interests of many corporations were not served by government policy. Despite official U.S. government hostility toward the Marxist regime in Angola, Gulf Oil successfully pursued its oil-drilling operations in that country with excellent relations with the government. Thus, one has to question the degree to which business in fact controls government policy.

Bauer, Pool, and Dexter suggest that in many ways Congress tends to use business lobbyists, rather than vice versa.[31] This study, which examines business and government interactions on the question of tariff reform, indicates that lobbyists are most effective when they aid an already favorably disposed legislator in the attempt to sway colleagues in the House or Senate. Moreover, members of Congress frequently utilize lobbyists to obtain information about an issue so that they can make up their minds on the issue. Although practices obviously vary widely, the basic conclusion of the authors is that Congress is not captive of business lobbyists or of any lobbyists for that matter.

However, instrumentalist radical critics feel that the legislative branch is relatively impotent in the foreign policymaking process. Thus, much of their argument is based on the extent of business control over the administrative branch. Basically, some radical thinkers *infer* business control from the socioeconomic backgrounds of top-level officials recruited into executive agencies, without offering substantial evidence as to the precise nature of the linkage between background and decision making.

Such critics insist that former corporate employees carry their predispositions and parochial interest directly into their positions in government. Although there is substance to this argument, it is possible that the new experiences and role expectations accompanying their office expand the horizons of former corporate executives beyond their previous views. For example, in assessing the influence of foreign travel on business executives' conceptions of self-interest, Bauer, Pool, and Dexter found that it "made a man see the trade issue in national terms, rather than in the parochial terms of his own industry."[32] One cannot help but wonder whether journeys into government service do not have a similar effect.

The radicals insist that the legislative branch has little to do with the making of foreign policy on political and security issues. (This is the view of many nonradicals as well.) This is probably not the case in regard to international economic issues having important domestic implications. In these instances, different business interests and other economic interests actively urge members of Congress to represent their concerns in the legislative process. In the mid-1980s, some members of Congress, in response to constituency concerns, were forceful advocates for retaliatory measures against Japan and the latter's huge trade surplus with the United States. Congress does fulfill an active and important role in many issues involving

---

[31]Bauer, Pool, and Dexter, *American Business and Public Policy*, p. 488.
[32]Ibid., p. 168.

foreign economic policy. Yet this role is disregarded by most radical analysts because their frame of reference tends to be focused on military and security issues. It is useful to note, though, that national security policy and executive branch leadership in such matters often overwhelm strong domestic economic interests. The Carter administration's imposition of a grain embargo on the Soviet Union in response to the invasion of Afghanistan is a case in point, for the interests of the American farm community were severely hurt by this action.

The instrumentalist conception of American foreign policymaking implies or asserts that only high-level political appointees determine the content of foreign policy. Barnet suggests that these national security managers revel in their jobs because of "the sense of playing for high stakes."[33] These foreign policy officials are exhilarated and "intrigued by power, more than money and more than fame."[34] Even if we accept Barnet's characterization, it is hard to imagine these national security managers experiencing much thrill and excitement over attempts to get Japan to reduce automobile exports to the United States or attempts to change the discriminatory trade policies of the European Common Market. Participation in many of these economic issues does not often yield fascinating memoirs testifying to one's diplomatic astuteness and importance.

Instead, many of these economic issues involve exceptionally technical details that are managed more competently by the technical experts in the civil service who inhabit the departments of Treasury, Commerce, and Agriculture. Thus, the important role of the technostructure, on economic issues at least, should not be, but often has been, ignored by some critics, who perceive American foreign policy to be the preserve of a small number of political appointees in the State and Defense departments. It is important to note that there is much more diversity in social backgrounds, educational experience, and career patterns among career civil servants than there is among the top political elites, upon whom some radical critics focus. Moreover, the relationship between the bureaucracy and business interests, especially where regulation is concerned, is often adversarial, reflecting in part the lack of common objectives and career backgrounds.

The point is that business control of government, as proclaimed by followers of the instrumentalist approach, is probably overstated. Radical thinkers fail to specify either what they define as control of foreign policy or the precise nature of the foreign policy decision-making process. They presume that broad conclusions about overall policy outcomes and the backgrounds of certain types of government officials are sufficient evidence to infer the control of business interests over the American foreign policy process. But radical analysts do not tell us what control is and how it can be observed. Their concept of the foreign policy decision-making process is developed from the presumption that a highly unified business interest dictates government policy. No inputs into the foreign policy process other than business interest are examined seriously. The role of Congress and the intense struggles among and within executive agencies, if they receive

[33]Barnet, *The Roots of War*, p. 98.
[34]Ibid., p. 97.

any attention at all, are considered inconsequential for American foreign economic policy.[35]

Structural Marxists, in contrast with instrumental Marxists, understand U.S. government officials to have considerable autonomy from direct influence by business pressures in the formulation and implementation of foreign economic policy. They are not preoccupied with specifying the circulation of elites between business and key foreign policy decision-making positions or the linkage of business interests to specific acts of U.S. foreign policy. They see no need to operationalize *the business interest* or *the government view* in the conduct of American foreign policy. In-depth studies of foreign policy decision-making processes and the relative influence of various government and business interests in the conduct of foreign policy (often in conflict with one another) are trivial exercises, largely besides the point. The role of the state in the leading capitalist country is to maintain and to reproduce capitalist structures and processes at home and around the world. American foreign policy is structurally determined by the needs of capitalism and the position of the United States as the leading state in the international capitalist system, regardless of who makes foreign policy decisions or whether identifiable U.S. business interests are promoted or overriden in the process. But this identity of foreign policy and the promotion of capitalism tells us little about either the specific content or the formulation of American foreign policy. *Every* act of American foreign policy is understood as promoting capitalism—protecting beleaguered U.S. industries, free trade, war, peace, insistence on foreign debt repayment, forgiveness of foreign debt, intervention in crises around the world, non-intervention, supporting the claims of U.S. multinational firms, leaving U.S. multinationals to their own devices, arms races, arms control, and so on. If this is so, the promotion of capitalism can hardly serve as a *guide* to American foreign policy or to U.S. foreign policymakers in any specific, meaningful sense. It becomes a truism that is categorically asserted—irrefutable but of little use in concrete terms.

Nonetheless, the analyses of the instrumentalist and structuralist critics do provide important insights into the nature of foreign economic policymaking. Whether through the prevalence of common backgrounds or interests among officials or through the structure of the state allowing participation in the process only to those societal institutions that foster the prevailing view, there are wide areas of consensus. In spite of conflicting and vigorous expressions of self-interest about the nature of U.S. foreign economic policy, the fundamental concepts of capitalism and the internationalism of capitalism are widely accepted and rarely debated, much less challenged seriously, in the United States.

---

[35]This point is made by Gabriel Kolko, *The Roots of American Foreign Policy* (Boston: Beacon Press, 1969), pp. 4–5.

THE PLURALIST PERSPECTIVE

There are a number of different liberal views of American foreign economic policy and the process by which it is formulated. While some analysts feel that there are basic differences between the making of foreign economic policy and that of foreign political and national security policy, others do not observe such differences. Still others classify the foreign policy-making process (economic or not) by types of issues involved.[36] However, for purposes of highlighting differences with the radical views discussed, in this section we will examine perspectives based on concepts of pluralism, bureaucratic politics, and politics between the executive and legislative branches of the U.S. government.[37]

Rather than a dominant business interest, the pluralist approach perceives the existence and importance of a wide variety of internal interests and constraints that greatly complicate foreign economic policymaking. Second, this view contends that American foreign policy in the economic arena is constrained severely by the economic objectives and actions of other states, whose own domestic groups have a vested interest in their government's actions.[38] In short, the process by which U.S. foreign economic policy is formulated is subject domestically to widespread political bargaining and maneuvering and internationally to the actions and concerns of other states.

Domestic Constraints on Foreign Economic Policy

The extensive domestic political activity associated with American foreign economic policy occurs because some domestic interest groups stand to gain or lose as a result of the particular policy adopted. To achieve an outcome favorable to their particular set of interests, each of the affected groups mobilizes to protect and advance its concerns. For example, trade issues have both international and domestic implications; thus, labor, business, consumer, and other groups who feel that they may be affected by

---

[36]McGowan and Walker, "Radical and Conventional Models of U.S. Foreign Economic Policy Making," pp. 365–77, provides a useful interpretation of the issue-area analysis approach as it relates to the formulation of foreign economic policy. See also William Zimmerman, "Issue Area and Foreign Policy Process," *American Political Science Review*, 67 (December 1973), 1204–12.

[37]Books representing these views include Bauer, Pool, and Dexter, *American Business and Public Policy*; Morton H. Halperin, *Bureaucratic Politics and Foreign Politics* (Washington, D.C.: The Brookings Institution, 1974); Robert Pastor, *Congress and the Politics of U.S. Foreign Economic Policy* (Berkeley: University of California Press, 1980); Stephen D. Cohen, *The Making of United States International Economic Policy*, 3rd ed. (New York: Praeger, 1988); I. M. Destler, *Making Foreign Economic Policy* (Washington, D.C.: The Brookings Institution, 1980) and *American Trade Politics: System Under Stress* (Washington, D.C.: Institute for International Economics, 1986).

[38]The international constraints on foreign economic policy making are examined in Robert O. Keohane and Joseph S. Nye, *Power and Interdependence: World in Transition* (Boston: Little, Brown, 1977).

the U.S. policy will seek to influence it. A proposal to reduce tariffs in the 1973 Trade Reform Bill received the support of such diverse groups as the Aerospace Industries Association of America, the American Importers Association, the National Grain and Feed Association, the National Farmers Union, the League of Women Voters, and the U.S. Council of the International Chamber of Commerce. Those seeking to maintain the current tariff structure or to increase the duties included the Manufacturers of Small Tools and Metal Fasteners; the National Association of Marble Producers; the American Iron and Steel Institute; the United Rubber, Cork, Linoleum and Plastic Workers of America; the Nationwide Committee on Import-Export Policy; the AFL-CIO; and the Liberty Lobby.

Investment issues provoke the same type of widespread and deeply committed interest-group activity and conflict. As we discussed in Chapter 4, the AFL-CIO and some of its affiliates were active promoters of the Burke-Hartke Bill to restrict the ability of American corporations to invest abroad. This pressure was countered by the activities of numerous multinational corporations that were designed to protect their interests. Other American firms had little interest one way or the other in the proposed restrictions. Again, the determining factor of interest-group involvement is the perception that self-interest may be advanced or injured by the various policy options available. However, the critical point is that foreign economic issues directly affect various domestic interests in different ways, and these interests in turn seek to influence the substance of U.S. foreign economic policy by actively engaging in the policymaking process.

Regarding foreign economic matters, especially those involving trade issues, Congress is an important target of interest-group pressures and conflicts. The various interests affected by specific legislation and policy decisions present their concerns to individual legislators, who represent a region according to how that region stands to gain or lose as a result of the policy adopted. For example, on trade issues, labor and/or business interests are able to demonstrate precisely how an increase or decrease in tariffs will lead to more or less business and consequently to more or less employment in a specific geographical area. Since the policy has a direct impact on constituents, the congressperson at least takes notice. When determining the overall impact on the district in light of his or her own interests in future elections, the representative may well actively seek to champion the interests of those groups with electoral power who will be significantly affected by governmental policy.

The nature of most foreign economic issues is such that different regions of the country are affected differently by a policy. Thus, the textile interests in the South have obtained widespread support for their attempts to reduce foreign competition by enacting protectionist legislation. Similarly, Senator Edward Kennedy and other members of Congress from New England have advocated measures to protect the domestic shoe industry. And in steel-producing areas, such as Pittsburgh, local members of Congress are leaders in protecting companies and unions who are disadvantaged by the imports of foreign steel. However, regional coalitions such as these face opposition from American farmers, who wish to reduce trade barriers, not increase them. Representatives from the Midwest advocate a free trade position, especially with respect to EEC barriers, because it will aid their farming constituents. They are joined by other representatives whose constituents would benefit from a reduction of trade obstacles. The politically conservative farmers of the Grain Belt objected strongly to "punishing" the Soviet Union for invading Afghanistan by withholding grain shipments.

It is important to note, however, that with respect to trade reform these coalitions of interests and representatives from many parts of the country join together for the purpose of advancing common interests only at the most general level. These are coalitions of convenience and self-interest, not coalitions reflecting deep-seated consensus on the nature of American foreign economic policy. Large multinational firms may be concerned about how a policy under consideration affects their global operations. Executive branch career civil servants and technocrats may have their eye on how certain policy proposals affect the fortunes of their department or office within the U.S. government apparatus. Members of Congress, state and local officials, and most business and labor groups evaluate policy proposals in terms of the potential effect on production and employment in their particular geographic area or economic sector. The policy process in the United States must accommodate *all* these important economic and political forces. As a result, foreign economic policy involves much more, and usually produces much less, than a coherent strategy that maximizes American power and advances American private interests around the world.

Many interest groups supplement their efforts to influence congressional deliberations with a strategy to gain access to decision makers in the executive branch. There are two basic objectives associated with such efforts: to influence the specific policy alternatives proposed and choices made as they emerge from the bureaucracy and to influence the technocrats within the bureaucracy as they implement the policies established in the legislative or administrative sectors of government. In either case, interest-group involvement in the executive branch is frequent and widespread. Moreover, the congressional allies of interest groups also attempt to influence the appropriate parts of the bureaucracy through well-established patterns of communication and what amounts to congressional lobbying of the executive agencies. Thus, the pluralistic struggles of interest-group activity are carried directly into the bureaucracy.

Some analysts view political bargaining between the executive and legislative branches in the United States, not interest group activity, as the most important process to understand in explaining American foreign economic policy, with its many internal contradictions.[39] I. M. Destler, for example, explains American trade policy since the Reciprocal Trade Agreements Act in 1934 as an effort by Congress to insulate itself from domestic political pressures for protectionism, bringing on the depression of the 1930s, by delegating trade policy to the executive branch.[40] In this vein, he explains the resurgence of protectionism in the United States during

---

[39]Pastor, *Congress and the Politics of U.S. Foreign Economic Policy.*
[40]Destler, *American Trade Politics.*

the 1980s as an effort by Congress to force President Reagan to pay greater attention to trade problems and to implement long-standing provisions under U.S. trade law that would reduce the political pressures being raised from constituents in the face of declining U.S. competitiveness. Indeed, Destler suggests that the politics of trade in the United States are primarily designed to protect Congress, not American industry.[41] Trade policy is guided by domestic politics, defined in terms of inter-branch relations, not by a coherent strategy of foreign economic policy to advance American interests around the world.

Yet another group of analysts explain foreign policy in the United States and elsewhere as the outcome of conflicts and competition between various agencies and departments constituting government bureaucracies.[42] This bureaucratic paradigm stresses important differences among the perceptions, attitudes, goals, and operating procedures prevalent in different administrative units. Moreover, these units have different constituencies, whose views they are likely to adopt to at least some degree. Thus, in general, the Department of Agriculture represents the interests of farmers, the Department of Labor promotes the labor view, the Treasury Department looks after the concerns of banks and financial organizations, and the Department of Commerce tends to represent business. However, as we discussed earlier, it is inappropriate to speak of a single labor view or a single business view on specific issues, such as tariff reform. Various units or bureaus *within* the agencies have their own, more specialized constituencies, whose interests they often seek to represent and from whom they often receive support during budgetary allocations and other intradepartmental conflicts. It is also misleading to assume that the agencies are total captives of their natural constituency in society. A former official in the international division of the Bureau of the Budget has noted, "Perhaps more than in any other area of policy international trade pits agency against agency, advisor against advisor."[43]

These conflicts produce intra- and interagency struggles in which the many parties to these disputes utilize a host of political techniques to represent their concerns. In their relations with one another, they resort to the use of raw power, appeals to higher authority (the President), persuasion, manipulation, negotiation, and bargaining. The result is often a policy that is a mixture of the contending positions. Rarely does one set of interests succeed in obtaining all its objectives, for this essentially legislative process involves bargaining and compromise over different goals and strategies, and the eventual acceptance and incorporation of contradictory positions in the policy adopted. Thus, political conflict and political maneuvering are characteristic of the bureaucratic policymaking process regarding for-

[41]Ibid.

[42]For a classic presentation of bureaucratic politics and foreign policy, see Graham Allison, *Essence of Decision* (Boston: Little, Brown, 1971).

[43]Donald S. Green, "Government Organization for Policymaking and Execution in International Trade and Investment," in Commission on International Trade and Investment, *United States International Economic Policy in an Interdependent World*, Vol. II (Washington, D.C.: GPO, 1971), p. 420.

eign economic issues. The differences within society are mirrored in and affect the nature of the decision-making process in the bureaucracy. The substance of foreign economic policy reflects the results of these intense battles in the policymaking process.

Harald Malmgren, a former deputy special representative for trade negotiations, observed that for the most part the State Department has "consistently avoided taking the necessary steps to deal directly with domestic political and economic interests."[44] Instead of incorporating and organizing for these matters, the Department of State has been willing to allow other agencies to handle functionally or politically related matters. One result is that at one time in the 1970s over sixty agencies, departments, or other institutions had "direct interests and decision-making powers in international economic issues."[45] Consequently, there is extensive interagency bargaining and compromise on such matters but very little central planning and direction regarding U.S. foreign economic policy. The proliferation of multiagency coordinating committees in which some of this negotiation occurs is evidence of the fragmented nature of the process by which American policy and actions are developed. Indeed, Malmgren wishes that American foreign economic policy exhibited the degree of coherence and consistency imputed to it by radical analysts.

This tendency for a fragmented and political decision-making process to occur in regard to foreign economic policy is heightened by the fact that during most of the Cold War era few high political officials took much interest in the specific issues raised. The President and his major advisers were not much concerned with the rather mundane and often exceedingly complex and technical matters of international economics. This is illustrated by President Nixon's response to being told that the chairman of the Federal Reserve, Arthur Burns, was concerned about the speculation against the Italian lira. His response, as captured on the White House tapes of June 23, 1972, was, "Well, I don't give a (expletive deleted) about the lira (unintelligible)." Similar disinterest was expressed about the problems of the British currency.

Moreover, these issues, because of their domestic content and their repercussions in the many countries concerned, often involve long, drawn-out negotiations and trade-offs among technical specialists who are subject to severe domestic pressures and constraints. It is difficult to emerge from such a grueling process with an international reputation that will have much historical impact. In the absence of the direct and continuing interest and participation of top political officials, these difficult and technical matters have tended to be the concern of bureaucratic technocrats. These specialists do not operate according to some grand design but rather in a professional but limited way to advance their bureaucratic and constituent interest. Thus, the political disputes are frequently carved out in a bureaucratic arena that is not at the top level of political officials. This lack of ongoing involvement by high-level political actors emphasizes the importance of

[44]Harald B. Malmgren, "Managing Foreign Economic Policy," *Foreign Policy*, No. 6 (Spring 1972), 46.

[45]Ibid., p. 43.

interest groups promoting their objectives at the level of bureaucratic implementation, for sometimes the decisions of consequence are made during this implementation process.

Direct White House involvement in foreign economic policy typically occurs when it is linked clearly to the international power and leadership position of the United States or when foreign economic policy has demonstrable domestic political (electoral) implications for an administration. The oil crises of 1973, 1979, and 1990, prompted by wars and revolutions in the Middle East, would be salient instances when U.S. foreign economic policy was intertwined with the national security and international power position of the United States. On such occasions top foreign policy officials (including the President himself) exhibit great interest in international economic matters, and they certainly exercise control over the formulation and implementation of foreign economic policy. Indeed, they seek attention in exercising this role in such circumstances. Examples of White House involvement in foreign economic policy because of their implications for domestic political considerations also abound. Despite a principled commitment to free trade, the Reagan White House in 1984 orchestrated a highly restrictive, five-year voluntary restraint agreement restricting steel imports to the United States. Top political advisers to the President were preoccupied with the need to retain a Republican majority in key states as the 1984 election approached. Steel-producing states in the industrial Midwest accounted for one third of the 270 electoral college votes required to win the presidency. A policy to deal with the impact of imports on a declining steel industry was an imperative in the campaign. Trade restrictions were implemented by the White House against the advice of the leading economic administration officials. In this instance, as in many others, White House direction of foreign economic policy was motivated by domestic political considerations, not by a larger sense of international economic strategy.

A rich literature produced by practitioners and analysts of international economic policy views the policy process in the United States as the outgrowth of an open political system in which organized interest groups of all sorts, government bureaucracies promoting their parochial agency interests, Congress, the White House and a fractionated executive branch vie for control with each other. The result is a foreign economic policy lacking in coherence or internal consistency over time. Representative of this view is the following observation by a leading scholar on U.S. international economic policy:

> The society of the United States is hopelessly pluralistic. Government in general and international economic policymaking in particular reflect this situation. As a consequence, the strengths and weaknesses of American society and government can be found here. In a democracy with a population whose interests are so diverse, there is a degree of virtue and logic in providing each of several constituencies a designated pipeline to the decision-making process. The resulting pluralism is manifested in a large, decentralized, shifting, and overlapping organization. Despite this untidiness, the process at times can work efficiently, blending contrasting views into a consensus that serves the

national interest and attracts broad support. But when the system is working poorly, policy usually is delayed, deficient, or both.[46]

The same analyst goes on to identify seven models of decision making as evidence of the complexity in the formulation and conduct of U.S. foreign economic policy.[47] This conventional picture of an open, pluralistic political system producing a highly indeterminate American foreign economic policy could hardly be more at odds with the views of neo-Marxist analysts examined previously.

External Constraints on Foreign Economic Policy

As we have seen throughout this study, the United States and other advanced industrial countries are linked together by a dense network of international economic ties. Over two thirds of world trade and direct foreign investment flows among these countries, and their currencies are used around the world to settle international payments. This economic interdependence limits the ability of all these states, including the United States as the leader among them, to formulate and implement foreign economic policy in disregard of accommodating the interests of others.

Paradoxically, the United States is frequently constrained by the fact that it is the most important economic and political power. There have been numerous instances where the necessity of being a reliable leader of the international political economy has often required it to forgo policies of narrow self-interest and to adopt policies that serve the broader interests of its partners in the international system. Examples would include the underwriting of European economic recovery, maintaining the position of the dollar as the key international currency facilitating international transactions, accepting Japanese and European protectionist policies to help their political economic revival in the early postwar years, acting as a lender of last resort in the international financial system, and providing military security for the Western states at considerable economic expense to itself. The United States certainly reaped benefits from these actions, but international obligations have also constrained its latitude and muted American opposition to some of its allies' policies. The United States, like others, finds itself losing autonomy in an interdependent global economy, despite its preeminence in the international system.

Domestic politics in countries abroad also constrain American foreign economic policy and its ability to prevail upon others to follow its leadership in international economic relations. Despite huge, if diminishing, disparities in the economic and political power of the United States, Europe, and Japan, the strong domestic political position of farmers in the latter two states has repeatedly frustrated American insistence on international agreements to reduce or eliminate subsidies for agricultural production and trade. Moreover, as we saw in the discussion of international finance in Chapter 3, America's capacity to manage its trade and payments balances

---

[46]Cohen, *The Making of United States International Economic Policy*, p. 223.
[47]Ibid., pp. 143–77.

as well as the value of the dollar is increasingly a function of the coordination it can achieve between U.S. economic policy and the domestic economic policies of the other leading market economies.

The pluralist perspective places great emphasis on the manner in which states abroad and various domestic sub-national interests, in addition to big business and finance, shape the formulation and substance of American foreign economic policy. Taking explicit account of these forces leads them to the conclusion that U.S. foreign economic policy is not nearly as consistent, as successful, or as guided by a larger strategic purpose as neo-Marxian analysts assume.

A CRITIQUE OF THE PLURALIST VIEW

The pluralist image of U.S. policymaking stressing extensive conflict among interested economic groups, among various agencies in the fractionated executive bureaucracy, and between Congress and the White House conveys an exaggerated sense of disorder and purposelessness in American foreign economic policy. On specific issues various interests in society and the government do clash over objectives and strategy, but these clashes take place within identifiable boundaries of "acceptable" policy options widely held among the important, interested, and active segments of society and government typically participating in the policymaking process. For example, among the options for increasing the international competitiveness of American business and structural adjustment of its industries in decline, no serious consideration is given in the United States to state-led strategies for restructuring firms in an industry or to the development of public enterprises. Such approaches to these challenges are not uncommon in other market-oriented economies around the world. Moreover, although various government agencies certainly seek to advance their narrow bureaucratic and clientelistic interests, numerous interagency coordinating groups at all levels of government force compromises among them, producing a greater degree of consistency and coherence in policy than most pluralist analyses convey.

The conflicts and compromises among myriad societal and governmental interests that are the focus of pluralist assessments of U.S. foreign economic policy take place, of course, within a capitalist political economic system which by its structure and its history favors private enterprise and market solutions to social problems. The liberal world view of political economy, outlined in the first chapter, pervades thinking in the policymaking process. One does not have to embrace neo-Marxist constructs to recognize that among the interests competing to shape policy in the United States, business interests are especially potent. For example, noted non-Marxist political economist Charles Lindblom speaks of the "privileged position of business" relative to all other interests in American society.[48] Beyond the unparalleled economic resources, expertise, organizational ap-

---

[48]Charles Lindblom, *Politics and Markets* (New York: Basic Books, 1977). The summary of his argument presented here is taken from pp. 170–88.

paratus, and access to government decision makers that businesses can mobilize to influence public policy, its privileged position derives from the extraordinary array of functions critical to society that America's market system delegates to business enterprises—employment levels, prices, levels and location of production, economic growth, income levels and distribution, payments balances, and so on. These functions are so central to society, to the economy, and to the success of public policy that government's success depends upon the success of business. Thus, government officials seek to insure their own performance by getting businesses to perform well the social and economic tasks delegated to them. This is done through regulations constraining businesses, but, more importantly, by continually offering inducements to the private sector (for example, tax breaks and interest rates that the businesses argue will be required to sustain investment, growth, price stability, and so forth). Business access to public authorities and its unmatched role in legislative and electoral processes occurs by virtue of this unique, indispensable role in American society relative to all other interests. The American political system is open, as pluralists assert, and business interests do not always prevail; but if neo-Marxists overstate the capacity of business to control U.S. foreign economic policy, pluralists understate it.

The privileged position of business in the United States is so internalized that we often fail to recognize it. A State Department report drafted in 1972 to consider alternative postures toward American direct foreign investment outlined three possible approaches. The negative alternative examined ways in which the government could actively seek to inhibit the activities of American-based multinational corporations. The positive position suggested ways of promoting American investment in other countries. The third view—in the paper's terms, a "neutral" approach—was to maintain the existing policy of neither promoting nor hindering multinational enterprises. This "neutral" view failed to recognize the supportive character of the important set of incentives that is offered by the U.S. government for foreign investment. Tax credits, tax deferrals, a host of preinvestment services, and many other policies cannot be termed a neutral approach to American investment abroad. Neutrality, like beauty, is in the eyes of the beholder, and the neutral view of the State Department and American society is based on an acceptance and approval of American business and private enterprise.

Pluralist analyses view the substance of U.S. foreign economic policy as reflecting the success of different coalitions of interests in capturing the policy process. Interest coalitions differ from issue to issue, producing different winners and losers over time. Consequently, pluralists view American foreign economic policy as unpredictable and lacking in continuity. Despite many contradictions and inconsistencies, however, we have seen that in its trade, investment, monetary, and aid relations, the United States has sought to promote a liberal international economic order since World War II. This policy pattern stems from diverse sources such as its domestic political economic system, its history, it political economic philosophy, and its position of economic and political power in the international system. It is easy to point out deviations from it, but the general pattern has remained fairly consistent even in the face of significant alterations in its power position relative to other states and of new policy challenges. The preoccupation of pluralists with the clashes of numerous interests in the policymaking process and changes in the process from issue to issue, tends to obscure this larger continuity in the substance of American foreign economic policy—even if it falls short of a singleness of purpose guiding foreign policy to which neo-Marxists allude.

Finally, while recognizing the external constraints on American foreign economic policy stressed by pluralists, it is important not to overlook the political, economic, and military strength that the United States can bring to any controversy. If events of the last thirty years have shown that Europe, Japan, the oil-producing states, and newly industrializing countries in the Pacific can themselves wield significant amounts of influence in international affairs, events have also shown that none of them has the combination of size, unity, industrial capacity, technological innovation, natural resources, agricultural reserves, and military strength that the United States possesses. The United States cannot often dictate international economic policy in its relations with other advanced industrial states, but it retains a capacity to act unilaterally in ways even its strongest rivals simply cannot, notwithstanding increased international economic interdependence. Witness the leadership of the United States in contrast to the marginal roles of the other advanced industrial states (especially the strongest economies, Japan and West Germany) in their response to Iraq's conquest of Kuwait in 1990 which posed a direct threat to them all through Saddam Hussein's bid for control over OPEC oil production and pricing.

THE STATIST PERSPECTIVE

During the 1980s a statist analytical perspective emerged in the United States that is highly critical of both Marxists and pluralists for their view that the state merely registers and implements foreign economic policies determined by societal forces.[49] Marxists see American foreign economic policy as serving the narrow interests of the owners of capital, either in direct response to business leaders well connected to government decision makers (instrumentalists), or in a less direct manner as an inevitable reflection of the domestic structure of capitalism in the United States and the needs of the international capitalist system (structuralists). Pluralists understand American foreign economic policy as a reflection of the preferences of organized interest groups in shifting coalitions with segments of the government bureaucracy that succeed in "capturing" policy on particular issues. While very different from each other, both view the state as more or less passive in relation to these societal forces; a vehicle used by

---

[49]Classic statements of the statist perspective can be found in Krasner, *Defending the National Interest*; and Peter Evans, Dietrich Rueschemeyer, and Theda Skocpol, eds., *Bringing the State Back In* (Cambridge: Cambridge University Press, 1985). Our discussion is taken primarily from Stephen Krasner's work since it focuses explicitly on U.S. foreign economic policy.

particular classes or other organized interests to advance their parochial needs/preferences at the expense of others in society. Neither views U.S. foreign economic policy as consistently serving a larger "national interest" in a manner that transcends the different, disaggregated elements of society. Both look to society not the state to understand foreign policy.[50]

Statists argue that these emphases of Marxists and pluralists are misplaced. Indeed, they convey an erroneous understanding of the conduct of U.S. foreign economic policy. In a study of American foreign policy relating to raw materials investments, Stephen Krasner concludes that state officials have developed goals and pursued strategies largely independent of the interests of investors. While U.S. foreign policy on raw materials has sometimes supported American business interests, it has often been at odds with pressures exerted by raw materials firms and with the larger interests of industrial and financial elites in U.S. society. He concludes from his series of case studies that interest-group pluralism and instrumental Marxism are clearly inadequate for explaining the foreign economic policy behavior he observes.

While somewhat harder to dismiss, he also argues that U.S. foreign policy is inconsistent with the views of structural Marxism. There were not demonstrable domestic economic interests pressing for the American intervention in Vietnam, for example. American involvement in the war is not explained by the government's response to domestic societal pressures in favor of such a policy, as both interest-group pluralism and instrumental Marxism would lead us to expect. Structural Marxists view U.S. government leaders as capable of action independent of direct pressures from the dominant capitalist class. But the imperatives of international capitalism and the domestic capitalist structure of the United States would lead structural Marxists to expect only U.S. foreign policy conduct which would strengthen its domestic political, economic, and social order and would enhance the stability of the international capitalist order. Krasner argues America's Vietnam policy did just the opposite. Accordingly, he also finds structural Marxism deficient for explaining American foreign policy.[51]

Krasner advances a statist view that American foreign policy officials have demonstrated a capacity for defining U.S. goals in international relations autonomous of interest groups and economic class. He sees these goals as deriving primarily from an ideological commitment held by state policymakers to project the principles of Lockean liberalism and democracy as understood in the United States throughout the world, once we assumed the position of a leading economic and military power in the international system—and especially a hegemonic position after World War II. In his view, U.S. foreign policy goals encompass economic and security interests as well as ideological interests. The latter are consistent with virtually all acts of policy he examines, whereas the others are not. For example, he argues that Vietnam was neither central to U.S. economic interests nor to its military security; but American involvement there, and its behavior in

---

[50]For a further elaboration of these points, see Krasner, *Defending the National Interest*, pp. 20–34 and Evans et al., *Bringing the State Back In*, pp. 3–37.

[51]Krasner, *Defending the National Interest*, pp. 320–26.

all the cases of foreign policy relating to raw materials investment he examines, is most consistent with an ideologically driven foreign policy.[52]

In summary, Krasner argues that there has been great continuity in American foreign policy. American foreign policy is defined by state officials who operate with considerable autonomy from societal pressures exercised by special interests. The state is viewed as much more activist in relation to societal interests in its conduct of foreign policy than either pluralist or Marxist analyses suggest. Pursuit of a national interest, defined in ideological terms by state officials (transcending special interests in domestic society), offers a more persuasive explanation of American behavior in international relations than explanations emphasizing economic or national security interests.

Krasner's advocacy of the statist view is a useful supplement to pluralist and Marxist conceptualizations of U.S. foreign policy formulation and conduct, but it is open to criticism as well. The empirical evidence upon which he makes conclusions about U.S. policy is drawn from cases involving American investments in raw materials. As he notes, himself, the patterns of state-society relations in a country are likely to differ in different issue areas.[53] In choosing to focus on raw materials investment policy, Krasner may have found state officials more insulated from societal pressures of the sort pluralists and Marxists define than had he chosen trade policy, for example. Before accepting his conclusions we need to obtain a better sense of how representative raw materials policy is of U.S. foreign economic policy more generally. Moreover, while dismissing pluralist and instrumental Marxists on meticulous development of case studies of raw materials policy, he switched to the case of Vietnam (not raw materials policy) to challenge structural Marxists and to assert the superiority of statism. Yet, he does not develop the Vietnam case as he did the others. Krasner makes reference to the interests of the United States in Vietnam as if they were self-evident; he nowhere documents the policy formulation and implementation process or the positions of societal interests and state actors on Vietnam as he does in the raw materials cases. One might well agree with his views, but they are not based on evidence presented in the body of his case studies.

Finally, his conclusions regarding U.S. foreign policy might be altered by major events occurring since the book appeared. Among the forces driving the massive American military intervention in Saudi Arabia and the blockade of Iraq in 1990 in response to Iraq's conquest of Kuwait, economic interests and the implications of Iraq's control over global oil markets for American power and international leadership would, indeed, seem to offer far more persuasive explanations of U.S. behavior than an interest in projecting Lockean liberalism and democracy—an important element in the foundation of his argument for the statist orientation. Notwithstanding these criticisms, Krasner's work is representative of a rapidly growing interest in more systematically specifying state-society relations in

---

[52]Ibid., pp. 329–52.
[53]Ibid., p. 58.

the foreign economic policy of the United States[54] and other countries—a subject to which we will return in the concluding chapter.

CONCLUSION

Our purpose is not to designate one view or another as being the most accurate or most useful perspective for explaining American foreign economic policy. These three analytical traditions do not nearly exhaust explanations of foreign policy important for political scientists and public officials. Political realism and analyses of hegemonic stability, for example, view U.S. foreign policy as determined primarily by changes in power distributions among states in the international system. Political realists see power distributions in an anarchic international system as compelling the United States to preserve its national security through prudent participation in the ever changing requirements of the balance of power as the guide to its foreign policy.[55] Analysts of hegemonic cycles see certain periods of international relations characterized by the political, economic, and military dominance of one state, such as the United States after World War II. They advance an explanation of U.S. policy during this period in terms of the requirements of occupying this hegemonic position in the international arena—such as assuming a disproportionate share of the defense burdens among its allies and underwriting, at increasing costs, the functioning of an open international economy.[56] Both of these approaches deduce the conduct of U.S. foreign policy from properties of the *international* political system and America's position in it, rather than addressing the actual *formulation* of policy. For this reason they are not examined in the depth afforded to Marxist, pluralist, and statist explanations of American foreign economic policy.

All of these explanations of U.S. foreign economic policy are flawed when pushed to their logical extremes. However, each alerts us to particular forces, structures, and processes that are present in American policymaking and implementation. To ignore or reject any of them out of hand is a mistake. We would do well to learn from the subtleties that each has to offer, even if one chooses not to accept all of the intellectual baggage accompanying them. The complexities of making and conducting foreign economic policy in the United States and elsewhere have defied any universally acceptable effort at specification.

[54]See, for example, John Ikenberry, David Lake, and Michael Mastanduno, eds., *The State and American Foreign Policy* (Ithaca: Cornell University Press, 1988).

[55]See Hans Morgenthau, *Politics Among Nations, The Struggle for Power and Peace*, 4th ed. (New York: Knopf, 1967).

[56]Robert Gilpin, *War and Change in World Politics* (Cambridge: Cambridge University Press, 1981).

9

The International Political Economy: Contemporary Trends

Writing a conclusion to a volume such as this is a difficult task. The intent is to introduce international political economy in a way that takes account of very different conceptions/understandings of the nature and consequences of international economic relations for national societies and for world order. We have shown how different analytical orientations help us to understand various sources of conflict and cooperation in relation to specific issue areas—such as trade, investment, monetary relations, aid—and to the formulation of American foreign economic policy. Our purpose throughout the study has been to focus upon issues and forces of enduring consequence in international economic relations, rather than to present a comprehensive, institutional or historical narrative capturing all developments in detail. It is evident that international political economy lies at the intersections of politics and economics, of domestic and international affairs, of relations between states and elements of their domestic societies, and of public policy and private action. It is no wonder that in a subject matter of such complexity a high degree of uncertainty pervades both its analysis and its practice.

Yet, as we enter the 1990s, a discernable pattern of great importance is clearly emerging in the international political economic order. An international economy with increased internationalization of production and finance, as well as growing trade and policy interdependence, offers tremendous opportunities for expanding wealth and international economic exchange. Yet, it also poses staggering challenges to domestic social, economic, and political order. Increased international economic interdependence and changes in the dynamics of world markets are important forces reordering conventional arrangements in state-society relations throughout the globe. In the advanced industrial states of the West, this is posing severe challenges in policy orientations and stimulating significant new institutional developments. Among the debtor countries in the Third World it is forcing sharply reduced standards of living, social disorder, and major political realignments. Throughout the Communist world it is along with other factors, undermining the legitimacy of political regimes.

SOCIALIST STATES AND THE CONTEMPORARY INTERNATIONAL ECONOMY

The most important long-term development for international politics and economic relations over the past decade has been the transcendence of the Cold War and steps toward the reintegration of previously insulated Communist societies with the global economic system dominated by the advanced industrial states of West. The political and economic character of this process has taken distinctly different forms in the various socialist states of Central Europe, the USSR, and China. Yet, together, developments in these states over the course of the 1980s reveal a "crisis of socialism"[1] that has profoundly transformed domestic societies in all of these countries as well as the international political-economic order itself.

So striking are these developments that they took analysts and political leaders throughout the world almost completely by surprise. Who would have anticipated in early 1989 that by 1990 the USSR would relinquish its control over East Europe? That Germany would be reunified? That the Soviet Union itself would face economic chaos, ethnic conflicts, and a constitutional crisis between central and regional authorities threatening the viability of its political system? Or that a democracy movement would grow to such proportions in China that the Communist party leadership would feel compelled to crush it militarily in the presence of the world's media— at the risk of aborting its extraordinary opening to the world economy of twelve years standing?

Virtually every regime in what had been the "Communist world," entered the 1990s with a crisis of political legitimacy. Each in its own manner was engaged in a desperate search for ways to restructure its domestic economy, society, and political system as well as for ways to forge more effective ties with a global economy that had left them all behind. Of course, this crisis of socialism did not emerge full bloom in 1989. It grew out of a conjuncture of forces that had been evolving many years. We will examine some of the major developments in this regard as they were manifested in the Chinese, Soviet, and East European experiences.

China

Between 1978 and 1989, China was the socialist state that had moved furthest to introduce domestic economic reforms and to construct closer

---

[1]Ellen Comisso, "Crisis in Socialism or Crisis of Socialism?" *World Politics*, XLII, no. 4 (July 1990), 563–606.

ties with the international economy. This was especially remarkable in light of Mao's political-economic legacy.[2]

After the emergence of the Sino-Soviet split in 1957, China pursued economic ties with socialist and other countries that stressed China's economic self-sufficiency and cultural separateness. The country was closed to foreign investment, it eschewed foreign borrowing, and it permitted minimal scientific and cultural exchange. These autarkic policies were reinforced during the 1960s by Soviet and American economic embargoes on significant economic and technological exchange with China. Domestically, Mao emphasized egalitarianism by relying upon political-ideological commitment and compliance rather than material rewards to stimulate production and efficiency. Central planning rather than markets and prices were used to guide economic decisions and resource allocation. Intellectuals and scientific and technological experts were distrusted for their lack of conformity to revolutionary and cultural norms as defined by Mao. They, along with entrenched political, economic, and bureaucratic elites felt to be lacking in revolutionary fervor, were ruthlessly purged during the Cultural Revolution (1966–1969) by political activists unleashed by Mao. China was turned upside down as an act of social and political reconstruction during this period—a development from which the country has not yet fully recovered.

Nevertheless, at the time of Mao's death in 1976, China had developed an impressive industrial base, achieved higher growth rates than other large Asian states like Indonesia and India, joined the nuclear club, and developed a primitive rocket and space capability.[3] Despite its political-economic isolation, during the 1960s, China's trade as a share of national output had expanded from 8 percent in the late 1950s to 11 percent in the mid-1970s.[4] In the aftermath of a border clash with the USSR in 1969, China during Mao's last years, normalized diplomatic relations with the United States, assumed its seat in the United Nations, and enhanced its political and economic ties throughout the non-Communist world.

At the same time, however, China in the mid-1970s faced grave economic challenges. Central economic planning, stifling controls over enterprises, underdeveloped domestic markets, and the absence of prices reflecting scarcities resulted in chronic economic inefficiencies.[5] The country lacked adquate investment capital. Chinese technology, overall, was decades behind world levels.[6] Distrust of intellectuals and neglect of education for decades under Mao had resulted in an undereducated administrative bureaucracy directing the economy.[7] China's economic development required bold reforms.

[2]This discussion of Mao's economic legacy is taken largely from Harry Harding, *China's Second Revolution: Reform After Mao* (Washington, D.C.: The Brookings Institution, 1987), pp. 11–39.

[3]Ibid., p. 30.

[4]Ibid., p. 23.

[5]Ibid., p. 31.

[6]Ibid., p. 33.

[7]Ibid., pp. 34–35.

Upon his consolidation of political power in 1978, Deng Xiaoping launched a series of domestic economic reforms to address these problems, to accelerate China's rate of development, and to reintegrate China with the global economy and the key international economic institutions. Higher prices for agricultural output and experimentation with family-enterprise alternatives to collective forms of agricultural production led to great increases in farm output and rural income in the early 1980s.[8] Industrial production was redirected toward consumer goods from its traditional emphasis on heavy industry and military production.[9] Market mechanisms and price reforms were introduced to supplement centralized planning in the economy. State controls over large and medium enterprises were loosened to give them more autonomy over production. Enterprises were allowed to retain profits, make their own investment decisions, determine their own wage structures, and establish their own prices on production beyond that committed to the state at prices still determined by central planners. State ownership was supplemented with various forms of collective and private economic activity. Retail commerce in consumer goods and services was opened to private enterprise, stimulating a surge of entrepreneurship and, often, the accumulation of great personal wealth. Egalitarianism and political-ideological persuasion gave way to material incentives for stimulating production and greater economic efficiency during the 1980s.[10]

These domestic reforms were accompanied by a series of moves to link China with the international economy after 1978. It sought to attract foreign investment, expand trade and acquire technology from abroad through decentralizing economic power and focusing foreign access to the Chinese economy in specially designated coastal areas. Four "Special Economic Zones" (SEZ) were first established along China's southeast coast in 1979, offering incentives to attract foreign investment, trade, and technology. These were more than export processing zones such as those used by other developing countries in Asia:

> They are bridges linking China to Hong Kong and Macao, and through them to the rest of the world; laboratories in which new management techniques and economic policies can be tested before being adopted in the rest of China; filters than can screen out those aspects of foreign technology and culture that are not considered appropriate for Chinese needs; and lubricants that can facilitate the reunification of Hong Kong, Macao, and Peking hopes, Taiwan, with the rest of the Chinese mainland.[11]

By 1985, fourteen coastal cities, three river deltas on the eastern coast, and an additional SEZ were opened to expand a coastal development strategy reintegrating China with the international economy.[12]

---

[8]Barry J. Naughton, "China's Economy," *Problems of Communism*, 39, no. 2 (March–April 1990), 115.

[9]Ibid.

[10]For a concise summary of China's economic reforms, see Immanuel Hsu, *China Without Mao*, 2nd ed. (New York: Oxford University Press, 1990), pp. 168–205.

[11]Harding, *China's Second Revolution*, p. 164.

[12]Hsü, *China Without Mao*, p. 235.

Within these designated areas, Beijing gave regional and local officials considerable authority to collect taxes, retain and allocate foreign exchange, borrow in foreign capital markets, offer trade and investment incentives, and purchase foreign technology. In this manner, trade, foreign investment, technology imports, and foreign borrowing in the most developed areas of the Chinese economy were stimulated through decentralizing political and economic decision making during the 1980s.[13]

At the same time, Beijing made a concerted effort to join the international economic institutions at the center of the global economy. In 1980 China joined the International Monetary Fund and the International Bank for Reconstruction and Development, giving it greater access to financial and development assistance from the international community. Over the course of the decade the World Bank Group, for example, authorized over $7 billion in development loans to China.[14] As a major textile producer, China joined the international Multifiber Arrangement in 1984. It obtained observer status in the GATT in 1983 and initiated a formal application for full GATT membership in 1986. Negotiations for full participation in the GATT focused on China's price system, forms of regional and administered protectionism, and the seriousness of its commitment to implement market-conforming economic reforms. Until China's political crisis in 1989, these negotiations seemed destined to result in its eventual membership in the GATT. Since then, the eventual outcome has become much less clear.[15] These and other arrangements negotiated with leading multilateral institutions in the international economy (China also joined the Asian Development Bank in 1986) not only helped China gain greater access to foreign markets and to resources on a nondiscriminatory basis but also buttressed Deng Xiaoping and the Chinese political leadership in the face of conservatives' opposition to the process of domestic economic reforms.[16]

The economic reform efforts launched in 1978 and expanded through the 1980s, notwithstanding some periods of consolidation and retrenchment, yielded impressive results. China's economy grew at an average rate of 10.5 percent between 1980 and 1986—a higher growth rate than that of the Asian newly industrializing countries in the same period.[17] The ratio of exports to China's national output more than doubled, to 14 percent, between 1978 and 1986.[18] Less than 8 percent of its trade was directed toward the USSR and East European states in 1985.[19] China be-

---

[13]See Harding, *China's Second Revolution*, pp. 131–171; and Mario Blejer and Gyorgy Szapary, "The Changing Role of Macroeconomic Policies in China," *Finance and Development*, June 1990, pp. 32–35.

[14]Harold K. Jacobson and Michel Oksenberg, *China's Participation in the IMF, the World Bank, and GATT* (Ann Arbor: University of Michigan Press, 1990), p. 119.

[15]Ibid., pp. 83–105. See also, William Feeney, "Chinese Policy Toward Multilateral Economic Institutions," in *China and the World*, ed. Samuel Kim (Boulder: Westview Press, 1989), pp. 254–57.

[16]Feeney, "Chinese Policy," p. 256.

[17]Jacobson and Oksenberg, *China's Participation in the IMF*, p. 133.

[18]Harding, *China's Second Revolution*, p. 138.

[19]Jacobson and Oksenberg, *China's Participation in the IMF*, p. 166.

came one of the leading host states among the less developed countries to foreign private investment. By 1988, China had entered into 16,000 direct foreign investment contracts worth $28 billion.[20] During this period China rapidly expanded its reliance on foreign capital. Its foreign debt more than doubled to $28 billion between 1984 and 1986.[21] China's reintegration with the international economy and the prospects of greater access to its huge domestic market were viewed with great enthusiasm in the West. Its course during the 1980s seemed destined to make it a central actor in the burgeoning political-economic development of the Pacific Basin.

Countertrends to these developments, however, called China's political-economic trajectory into question at the end of the decade. Domestic economic reforms led to severe economic and social distortions in the late 1980s. Price reforms and the introduction of market mechanisms had resulted in inflation rates estimated, unofficially, at 30 to 40 percent in 1988.[22] Administrative reforms opened serious tensions between central and regional authorities regarding the degree of autonomy the latter could exercise on tax and other economic policies. A society that had stressed equalitarianism was exhibiting profound income inequalities. The coastal development strategy exacerbated economic differences between the coastal areas linked to the global economy and the more remote, backward interior regions of the country. Socially contentious income disparities emerged between successful entrepreneurs operating in the private sector and employees in the state sector on fixed wages and salaries.[23] Owner-drivers of taxis, for example, could earn ten to thirty times the salaries of professors and surgeons.[24] "By official admission, corruption [was] rampant at all levels of party and state administration."[25] Economic reforms, resulting in several prices for the same goods distributed through different channels, invited corruption. People in positions of authority could procure items at low, state determined prices and resell them at higher, free market prices.[26]

Inflation, income inequalities, corruption, growing incompatibilities of a highly centralized political regime and economic reforms relying on markets and greater autonomy for enterprises and entrepreneurial activity, and an aging political leadership increasingly distant from the Chinese population were all important factors contributing to the emergence of a democratization movement between 1986 and 1989. This extraordinary

---

[20]Shen Xiaofang, "A Decade of Direct Foreign Investment in China," *Problems of Communism*, 39, no. 2 (March–April 1990), 63.

[21]Harding, *China's Second Revolution*, pp. 152–53.

[22]Jan Prybyla, "China's Economic Experiment: Back from the Market?" *Problems of Communism*, 38, no. 1 (January–February 1989), 4.

[23]Ibid., p. 5.

[24]Hsü, *China Without Mao*, p. 242.

[25]Prybyla, "China's Economic Experiment," p. 6.

[26]James Mittelman, "The Dilemmas of Reform in Post-Revolutionary Societies," *International Studies Notes*, 15, no. 2 (Spring 1990), 68.

political development captured the world's imagination in the spring of 1989, with demands for sweeping political reform led by students demonstrating in Beijing and other large cities. As their numbers grew and their influence spread to other elements of the population in Beijing, Deng Xiaoping and the top political leadership purged moderates within their ranks (most notably Zhao Ziang, general secretary of the Communist party) and moved to repress the movement through brutal military means on June 3–4, 1989. The events leading up to this terrible climax were played out before the world's media in a manner never before permitted in China.[27] To make matters worse, accounts of events offered by Chinese officials in the aftermath of the violence simply did not square with what millions around the world had seen for themselves on their television screens.

The consequences of the violence on Tiananmen Square in 1989 are still unfolding in China's domestic and foreign policy. Political order was restored under Deng's (unofficial) leadership. This was accomplished by harsh treatment of political dissidents and indoctrinization of the Chinese population that muted observable political activity. These actions in 1989 and 1990 cost the regime dearly in terms of the confidence and legitimacy it commanded in the eyes of China's politically alert population. The regime insisted that these political events would not affect the course of China's domestic economic reforms or its reintegration with the global economy. Yet, they certainly did.

The Western states initially responded to the political repression with condemnation, diplomatic isolation, and the interruption of financial flows to China through bilateral and multilateral channels for a year following Tiananmen. While economic relations continued between China and the West, they were conducted under a cloud of uncertainty. The U.S. Congress threatened to terminate most-favored-nation treatment for China in light of its human rights abuses—even though it renewed China's MFN status in 1990 at President Bush's insistence. America and other Western nations opposed new World Bank loans to China. Negotiations were suspended on China's application for full membership in the GATT. Foreign investors' interest in China cooled.

By the second half of 1990, however, the advanced industrial states showed diminishing interest in continuing their isolation of China in the post–Cold War era. At the July economic summit in Houston, Japan announced its intention to resume loans to China under a five-year program of financial assistance negotiated prior to Tiananmen. The EEC lifted economic sanctions, international lending agencies and banks began freeing up funds for China, and foreign investors showed renewed interest in the country.[28] China's international position in 1990 was especially improved

---

[27]For a brief summary of these political events, see Hsü, *China Without Mao*, pp. 276–94. For an account of the democracy movement, Chinese politics, and the Tiananmen crackdown from the perspective of an important figure in the movement, see Liu Binyan, *Tell the World* (New York: Pantheon Books, 1989).

[28]"A Quiet Comeback: How China Broke Out of Isolation," *Business Week*, December 24, 1990, pp. 34–35.

by its cooperation with the United Nations Security Council in imposing sanctions against Iraq and in authorizing the use of military force to reverse Iraq's conquest of Kuwait. China's veto power in the Security Council could have prevented effective international action through this preferred U.N. channel.

Eighteen months after the events of Tiananmen the international community seemed disposed to gradually resume more normalized relations with China, albeit with an altered, and more realistic, sense of the character of China's political-economic system. Experimentation with price reforms, greater reliance on market mechanisms, and decentralization of economic decision making do not necessarily place China on a path toward a market economy or political liberalization with which the advanced industrial states of the West would feel comfortable. Expectations along these lines were clearly exaggerated by many Western observers before June 1989, despite the conclusions of more astute analysts of China's political-economic development.[29] Domestic economic reforms and closer integration with the international economy may well characterize China's future development. But, if it is moving away from a model of orthodox socialism, it is not evolving into a capitalist system. China is groping toward a "mixed economy that combines state planning, a government regulation, and market forces, and that melds private, collective, and state ownership."[30] Its unique manner of doing this is consistent with its special domestic and international circumstances. Despite frequent references to its trade and investment strategies in the 1980s as an "open door policy," the Chinese economy depends primarily on the growth of its internal market.[31] While seeking expansion of its access to foreign trade, investment, and technology, China does not embrace the concept of free trade and open access of foreign enterprises to its domestic economy. It retains formidable controls over imports of goods, capital, and technology. China seems more interested in a trade strategy of import substitution than export-led growth.[32] "China, much like the rest of East Asia, has adopted a neo-mercantalist strategy aimed at promoting foreign economic relationships that will, in the end, help produce a relatively self-reliant nation"[33]—consistent with its historical sense of cultural superiority and separateness.

Even within this more constrained sense of how markets and greater use of international economic ties are being managed by the Chinese, the introduction of these reforms have unleashed pressures for social, economic, and political changes that are inevitably redefining state-society relations in the country. In 1989, the leadership attempted to repress these forces in Tiananmen Square. No doubt, from their perspective, the turmoil associated with political and economic reforms in East Europe and the USSR since 1989 convinces Deng Xiaoping and his colleagues that their

[29]See, for example, Harding, *China's Second Revolution*, from which this assessment is derived.

[30]Ibid., p. 130.

[31]Ibid., p. 170–71.

[32]Ibid.

[33]Ibid.

actions saved the Communist party and socialism in China. But neither will ever be the same.

The Soviet Union and East Europe

Political and economic reforms in the Soviet Union and the countries of East Europe took a very different course than those in China during the 1980s, but they have been no less profound. They altered a long-standing postwar pattern of economic and political isolation from the international economic community[34] toward one in which renewed political-economic vitality depends upon developing close ties with the leading Western states.

East European countries emulated the Soviet Union's political and economic system as it consolidated its power in the region after World War II.[35] Communist parties modeled after that of the Soviet Union exercised a monopoly on political authority and organization within these states. Leadership of the Communist parties in most East European states derived from ties to Moscow rather than from ties to the domestic population. The Soviet Union controlled policies in the region through a combination of an extensive network of highly intrusive bilateral political, economic, and military ties and its leadership of the Council of Mutual Economic Assistance (CMEA) and the Warsaw Pact.[36] CMEA was initiated in 1949 as a formal Eastern counterpart to the cooperation between the United States and Western Europe under the Marshall Plan. It later evolved into a kind of Eastern reflection of the European Economic Community, stressing regional development cooperation and economic exchanges between the USSR and East European states—under Moscow's direction. The Warsaw Pact was the Soviet answer to NATO after West Germany was rearmed and integrated into NATO following the Korean War. It provided the framework legitimating the stationing of Soviet troops throughout Eastern Europe—important not only for meeting the international security concerns of the Soviet Union during the Cold War but also for establishing domestic political order under Communist rule in East Europe, on occasion.[37] Indeed, after the Czechoslovakia crisis in 1968, the Warsaw Pact, through the Brezhnev Doctrine, formally became an instrument for external intervention in the domestic affairs of any socialist state deemed by

---

[34]For a brief overview of this traditional pattern, see Joan Spero, *The Political Economy of International Economic Relations*, 4th ed. (New York: St. Martin's Press, 1990), pp. 305–19.

[35]This discussion of East Europe necessarily focuses on central tendencies. For example, after its ouster from the Soviet camp by Stalin in 1948, Yugoslavia followed a different political-economic path from that outlined here. Later developments in Albania and Rumania removed them from this pattern also. Of course, Yugoslavia, Albania, and Rumania faced grave challenges to their domestic political order during the nineties like other East European states. East Europe as generally described here refers primarily to Bulgaria, Czechoslovakia, East Germany, Hungary, and Poland.

[36]For an excellent survey of the structure of Soviet control over East Europe, see Zbigniew Brzezinski, *The Soviet Bloc* (New York: Praeger, 1961).

[37]Such occasions arose, for example, in Poland and Hungary in 1956 and in Czechoslovakia in 1968.

the USSR and other East European leaders to be in danger of abandoning its Marxist-Leninist character.[38]

Before the political-economic transformations in the region during the late 1980s, this general structure of Soviet control had been threatened by periodic economic and political crises challenging Communist political authorities in some East European states—most notably Poland and Hungary in 1956, Czechoslovakia in 1968, and Poland in 1980–1981. Notwithstanding their many differences, these past disorders shared some important features. They were triggered by domestic economic collapses in East European states requiring political and economic reforms responsive to indigenous social developments. These reforms, excepting Hungary in 1956 where the Communist party was hopelessly divided, were undertaken within limits of experimentation understood *by national Communist leaders* as likely to be tolerated by the Communist Party of the Soviet Union (CPSU) on the basis of economic and political developments within the USSR. Acceptable political-economic experimentation was generally perceived to involve (1) maintenance of a monopoly on political authority and leadership by the national Communist party in the process of reform, (2) reaffirmation of the commitment by national authorities to the Warsaw Pact under Soviet leadership, and (3) confidence across the rest of Eastern Europe that reforms introduced, even with the acquiescence of a national Communist party, would not threaten to unleash turmoil and similar demands for reform that Communist leaders elsewhere in the region could not control. Where these circumstances existed during periods of crisis, external military intervention was avoided (Poland in 1956 and 1980–1981). Where one or more of these limits were exceeded *in the view of the CPSU*, demands for reform were brutally repressed, and a change in Communist party leadership of the Eastern European state was imposed by external military intervention (Hungary in 1956 and Czechoslovakia in 1968).

Within this political context, the centrally planned economies of Eastern Europe modeled after the USSR and the Soviet economy itself exhibited a mixed pattern of economic performance. During the early postwar period these countries experienced rates of economic growth comparable to those in the leading market economies of the West[39] by means of "extensive" development strategies. That is, growth was produced by large increases in labor and capital inputs as well as in easily accessible natural resources through central planning and political control under Communist parties.

Significant declines in economic performance, however, plagued these countries during the 1970s and 1980s. Mobilization of massive increases in labor, capital, and natural resources proved unsustainable. "Intensive" development strategies, relying on increased efficiency and greater productivity, proved illusive to all of the centrally planned economies. They fell further behind the Western economies, especially during the 1980s.[40]

[38]Joseph Nogee and Robert Donaldson, *Soviet Foreign Policy Since World War II*, 3rd ed. (New York: Pergamon Press, 1988), p. 247.

[39]International Monetary Fund, *World Economic Outlook, May 1990* (Washington, D.C.: IMF, 1990), pp. 65, 68.

[40]Ibid.

The most dramatic indication of this was an unprecedented *decline* in life expectancy in East Europe and the USSR.[41] Also, during the period 1983–1987, Soviet trade performance deteriorated (exports, imports, and trade balances), its gross foreign debt increased from $23 billion to $36 billion, and its debt service payments in relation to exports rose from 11 percent to 24 percent.[42] Growth of the East European economies stagnated in the 1980s as well. Bulgaria and Poland actually recorded negative growth in 1987.[43] Indeed, Poland's per capital GNP was lower in 1987 than in 1975.[44] The foreign debt of the East European states grew by over 50 percent between 1984 and 1988, to almost $100 billion.[45] Poland accounted for about 40 percent of this amount; Hungary about 20 percent—they were carrying debt service burdens similar to those of the most heavily indebted less developed states.[46] The USSR and Eastern Europe, whose trade was directed primarily toward one another,[47] were being left behind by the global economy in the late 1980s.

Against the backdrop of these political relations with East Europe and of stark economic conditions in all CMEA states, Mikhail Gorbachev assumed leadership of the USSR in 1985. The political and economic reforms he initiated produced stunning consequences during the remainder of the decade for the USSR, for political and economic systems throughout East Europe, and for the international order.

Gorbachev sought to revitalize and restructure the stagnant Soviet economy (*Perestroika*) by offering greater autonomy and economic incentives to enterprises and workers, essentially passive and unproductive in the command economy of centralized planning. To energize the population and to harness it in support of his proposed reforms, Gorbachev invited the public to openly express long-standing frustrations with entrenched state and party bureaucracies (*Glasnost*) standing in the way of economic and social change.[48] He was leading a reform movement from below against the political and economic establishment at which he was the head[49]—thus, as Soviet commentators observed, "trying to be Luther and the Pope at the

[41]Ibid., p. 67.

[42]Wharton Econometric Forecasting Associates, "Centrally Planned Economies Outlook for Foreign Trade and Finance," in U.S. House of Representatives, Committee on Banking, Finance, and Urban Affairs, Subcommittee on International Finance Trade and Monetary Policy, *Bank Lending to Warsaw Pact Nations*, Hearings, September 22, 1988 (Washington, D.C.: GPO, 1988), p. 230.

[43]Karen Dawisha, *Eastern Europe, Gorbachev, and Reform*, 2nd ed. (Cambridge: Cambridge University Press, 1990), p. 169.

[44]Ibid., p. 170.

[45]Ibid., p. 118.

[46]International Monetary Fund, *World Economic Outlook, May 1990*, pp. 66–67.

[47]In 1988, East European states directed 61 percent of their trade within CMEA, while just over half of the Soviet trade went to East Europe. See International Monetary Fund, *World Economic Outlook, May 1990*, p. 65.

[48]Aurel Braun and Richard Day, "Gorbachevian Contradictions," *Problems of Communism*, 39, no. 2 (May–June 1990), 38.

[49]Ibid.

same time."[50] This inherently incompatible position led Gorbachev to lurch back and forth between bold efforts to change the USSR's political-economic system and repression of such changes in the name of preserving order. In the process, he unleashed forces in the USSR and in Eastern Europe that undoubtedly went well beyond his intentions and which, by 1991, threatened not only his position of leadership but also the cohesion of the Soviet Union.

The process of *Glasnost*, which began as criticism of entrenched state and party bureaucracies in 1985 and 1986, expanded to broader attacks on the Communist party itself, on its monopoly of power in the USSR, and upon Gorbachev's leadership. By 1987, Gorbachev moved to a democratization policy of multiple candidate elections to party and state posts and fixed terms in office for state and party officials.[51] By 1989–1990, political reforms in the USSR had carried Gorbachev to the point of restructuring party and state institutions including, among other things: the contested election of a Congress of Deputies to select a Supreme Soviet with enhanced legislative powers; the creation of a presidency with strong executive powers to which Gorbachev was elected, enabling him to expand his political base beyond the CPSU; the removal of the constitutional prerogatives of the CPSU as the leading force in Soviet society; the legalization of parties to compete with the CPSU in national, regional, and local elections—with notable success in winning these contests; and an unprecedented liberalization of political expression as evidenced by frequent demonstrations and greater openness in the press.

Gorbachev's domestic reforms were, of course, accompanied by a redefinition of Soviet foreign policy. Significant economic change in the USSR required the redirection of resources to consumer-oriented production from heavy industry and military output, long the priorities of its command economy. This, in turn, meant reducing Cold War tensions with the West to permit reductions in defense spending and the release of resources for economic reforms. Moreover, improved relations with the West offered potential access to foreign capital and technology, desperately needed to revitalize the moribund Soviet economy. Gorbachev was remarkably successful in these foreign policy transformations during the first five years of his leadership.

Alterations in military doctrine and in the force posture of Warsaw Pact troops provided the Western states with evidence of Soviet emphasis on defensive, rather than an offensive, conventional war strategy in Europe.[52] This, combined with the continuation of political and economic reforms in the USSR and in East Europe (to be discussed below) between 1987 and 1990, opened an unprecedented era of arms control negotiations between the United States and the USSR. In 1987, an agreement was

---

[50]Z, "To the Stalin Mausoleum," in *At Issue: Politics in the World Arena*, 6th ed., ed. Steven Spiegel (New York: St. Martin's Press, 1991), p. 477.

[51]Ibid., p. 471.

[52]Dawisha, *Eastern Europe*, pp. 210–13.

reached to remove intermediate and short-range missiles from Europe.[53] The USSR agreed to asymmetrical reductions in conventional arms, making possible an agreement in 1990 to reduce conventional forces in Europe. President Bush and Gorbachev were pressing forward at the same time to negotiate deep cuts in strategic nuclear weapons under the auspices of the Strategic Arms Reduction Talks (START) begun during President Reagan's administration. So stunning was the improvement in East-West relations made possible by these other Soviet initiatives, that Gorbachev was awarded the Nobel Peace Prize in 1990.

These moves were accompanied by changes in the USSR's foreign economic policies. In the late 1980s the USSR was considerably behind China and most of the East European states in forming links with the key international economic institutions.[54] Yet, the USSR began seeking an observer status in the GATT in 1986, and was finally successful four years later.[55] New trade pacts were negotiated with the EEC[56] and the United States.[57] Western nations relaxed COCOM controls on numerous technology exports to the USSR and countries in East Europe.[58] To help deal with food shortages due to hoarding and distribution problems in association with Soviet economic reforms in late 1990, the United States offered financial aid to the USSR and "proposed that the World Bank and the International Monetary Fund give Moscow a 'special association' to provide assistance and advice in transforming the Soviet command economy into a market-driven system"[59]—opening an avenue for possible future Soviet participation in the key financial institutions in the global economy. In these and other ways, the USSR made dramatic, if limited, progress during the second half the decade in forging economic ties with the leading capitalist states and the international economy which they anchor.

The political and economic reforms initiated by Gorbachev in the USSR, and the dismantling of its Cold War posture vis-à-vis the West, were closely watched by the population in East European states, long restive under Soviet domination and national Communist leadership. Much like the linkage between the Polish and Hungarian uprisings and Khrushchev's de-Stalinization campaign in 1956, the USSR's domestic reforms in the late 1980s invited political and economic challenges to Communist regimes in East European states. When Gorbachev made it clear that the USSR would

[53]"Text of Treaty on Intermediate-Range Missiles," *Congressional Quarterly*, December 12, 1987, pp. 3070–85.

[54]For a survey of Soviet and East European relations with the IMF and the IBRD, see Valerie Assetto, *The Soviet Bloc in the IMF and the IBRD* (Boulder: Westview Press, 1988).

[55]"GATT Grants Observer Status to the Soviet Union," *Focus, GATT Newsletter*, No. 71 (May–June 1990), 1.

[56]"Trade Pact for Soviets and Europe," *The New York Times*, November 28, 1989, pp. 29, 33.

[57]"Negotiations Concluded Over U.S.–Soviet Trade," *The New York Times*, May 29, 1990, p. A6.

[58]"The Dismantling of a Cold-War Icon," *Business Week*, June 25, 1990, p. 41.

[59]"Bush, Lifting 15-Year-Old Ban, Approves Loans for Kremlin to Help Ease Food Shortages," *The New York Times*, December 13, 1990, pp. A1, A6.

not use force to maintain its control over the region or to shore up national Communist regimes confronting popular unrest (i.e., renouncing the Brezhnev Doctrine),[60] the pace of political-economic change throughout East Europe made Soviet reforms look timid by comparison. Lacking both political legitimacy and the protection of Soviet power, the Communist regimes in one East European state after another cascaded into collapse during 1989[61]—highlighted by the removal of the Berlin Wall and the reunification of Germany in 1990.

Beyond its borders, the Soviet model of socialist, political, and economic development, on which all the East European regimes had been patterned, was spent. In its place emerged a wide array of political regimes with diverse economic systems and ties with the international economy. East Germany was absorbed by West Germany through unification, bringing it into a core state in the global economy with membership in the EEC. Poland, under the leadership of *Solidarity*, was the quickest to democratize and to leap toward a market economy in January 1990, with considerable support from Western states and the multilateral financial institutions with which it had negotiated traditional stabilization agreements. Czechoslovakia, under Václav Havel, was close behind on both counts—followed by Hungary. Rumanians overthrew and executed Ceaucescu, but the country faced repression and protracted political violence in the years following. In 1989 the Bulgarian Communist party ousted Zhivkov, its leader of thirty-five years but retained control over the political system.

With Germany a case apart, the most progressive efforts at democratization and movement toward a market economy in East Central Europe in the early 1990s were taking place in Poland, Czechoslovakia, and Hungary. Yet the challenges of a rapid transformation from centrally planned economies and authoritarian political systems to market economies and democracies are profound. Political and economic infrastructures must be completely rebuilt. Numerous parties suddenly emerged to compete openly for political power, but it is not at all clear what they stand for, what elements of society they represent, or what capacities they have to guide wrenching social change. Communist rule since World War II repressed numerous territorial grievances, great ethnic diversity, and competing nationalist claims with which new, fragile democratic systems must now deal.[62] The transition to a market economy requires price decontrols and the elimination of extensive government subsidies to allow the emergence of prices reflecting scarcity, stimulating inflation in the short run. Currencies must be made convertible. Trade and capital movements must be liberalized to expand desperately needed commercial and financial ties with the inter-

---

[60]Dawisha, *Eastern Europe*, pp. 9, 218–22.

[61]See Grzegorz Ekiert, "Transition from State-Socialism in East Central Europe," and Andrew Walder, "Political Upheavals in the Communist Party States," *States and Social Structures Newsletter*, Social Science Research Council, No. 12 (Winter 1990), 1–9; Dawisha, *Eastern Europe*, pp. 152–96. For a chronology of 1989 events in the USSR and East Europe, see "America and the World, 1989/90," *Foreign Affairs*, 69, no. 1 (1990), 213–30.

[62]See Zbigniew Brzezinski, "Religious and Ethnic Nationalism: Post-Communist Nationalism," *Foreign Affairs*, 68, no. 5 (Winter 1989–90), 1–25.

national economy. State enterprises must be privatized on a scale never before attempted. (Poland, for example, had over 7,000 state enterprises that were candidates for privatization in 1990. Over the entire decade of the 1980s, Margaret Thatcher as an aggressive advocate of privatization in Britain, moved only two dozen public firms into the private sector.)[63] New legal systems defining property rights, labor law, and company law must be put in place, as well as social safety nets. Modern banking, management, and accounting practices must be imported.[64]

The seductive appeal of democracy and markets in East Central Europe is tempered by the realization that the transformation itself will witness political turmoil, inflation, company failures, bankruptcies, unemployment, increases in income inequalities, elimination of subsidies, lost access to housing, and so forth.[65] Fears of such developments have inhibited the pace of political and economic reforms in some countries, such as Hungary.[66] Dealing with such developments will require substantial assistance for East European states from the advanced industrial states of the West and multilateral trade and lending agencies.[67] East European states pushing boldly toward implementing a market system received substantial Western encouragement and support during 1990. A European Bank for Reconstruction and Development capitalized at $12 billion was established by forty-two states, including the United States, to promote the private sector in East European states as a means of implementing market-oriented, structural economic reforms.[68] Poland, Hungary, and Czechoslovakia received loans from the IMF to assist early economic reform efforts.[69] Besides the value of the IMF loans, themselves, these agreements are essential for gaining access to finance from other private and public lending sources in the West—as noted in Chapter 3.

Western Europe has taken a leading role in forging economic relations with the states in East Central Europe. Developing some type of association for countries in East Europe will constitute a major challenge to the EEC during the 1990s.[70] Given geographical proximity and historical economic

[63] Jeffrey Sachs and David Lipton, "Poland's Economic Reform," *Foreign Affairs*, 69, no. 3 (Summer 1990), 61.

[64] For an analysis of Poland's "jump to the market" begun in 1990, see ibid. For a more general overview of the problems accompanying such transitions, see International Monetary Fund, *World Economic Outlook, May 1990*, pp. 68–93.

[65] See, for example, "For Eastern Europe Now, a New Disillusion," *The New York Times*, November 9, 1990, pp. A1, A7; "Year of Economic Tumult Looms for Eastern Europe," *The New York Times*, December 31, 1990, pp. 1, 24; and "Slow Pace for Reform in East Bloc," *The New York Times*, January 29, 1990, pp. C1, C4.

[66] "Year of Economic Tumult Looms in Eastern Europe," p. 24.

[67] See Sachs and Lipton, "Poland's Economic Reform," pp. 64–66.

[68] "Countries Reach Terms on East Europe Bank," *Congressional Quarterly*, April 14, 1990, p. 1129; "A New Bank Plans East European Aid," *The New York Times*, May 30, 1990, p. A8.

[69] "Czechoslovakia Gets $1.8 Billion I.M.F. Loan," *The New York Times*, January 8, 1991, p. A8.

[70] See Alfred Van Staden, "Perestroika and the Response by Western Europe: The Role of the European Community," Paper delivered at the American Political Science Association, San Francisco, August–September 1990.

ties between East and West Europe, the EEC will be a pivotal receiving structure for helping to integrate these countries into the global economy. This will pose a formidable challenge to the EEC, which is preoccupied with creating a single market among its twelve members in 1992. Moreover, trade growth for East European states will turn importantly on securing access to the EEC for their agricultural exports—further complicating agricultural trade issues in commercial relations between the European Community and the rest of the world.

At the outset of the 1990s, political-economic reforms in East Europe unleashed by Gorbachev's earlier domestic and foreign policy initiatives had assumed a momentum no one had imagined possible a few years before. The chain reaction of reformist thought and political events in East Europe during 1989 helped embolden political dissent in the Soviet Union itself. This took its most dramatic form in the 1990 declarations of intentions to secede from the USSR by newly elected non-Communist governments in Lithuania, Latvia, and Estonia—reasserting the independence they achieved during the period between World Wars I and II. But the Baltic Republics of the USSR were only the most salient manifestations of ethnic and regional challenges to Moscow's authority arising across the country in the Ukraine, Byelorussia, Russia, Georgia, Kazakhstan, Armenia, Azerbaijan, and Uzbekistan.[71] Similarly, the aggressiveness of Poland and Czechoslovakia's moves to achieve market-oriented economies served to underline the timidity of the half-measures at economic reform that Gorbachev found himself willing to support as the Soviet economy continued in a tailspin.[72]

Gorbachev by 1991 had assumed great formal presidential powers to direct the economy and the political system. Yet, having discredited the Communist party and central economic planning, he lacked political legitimacy and economic alternatives to central planning. It was unclear what institutional mechanisms existed to implement whatever policies he might decree in Moscow.[73] After leading political and economic reforms for his first five years of leadership, Gorbachev surrounded himself with conservative political operatives, and he turned increasingly to the KGB and to the military to maintain domestic social order. The USSR found itself in a "race between the forces of pluralism and those of repression,"[74] with Gorbachev vacillating between them. Soviet military forces would be used one day to repress separatists in the Baltic.[75] The next day, Gorbachev would deny his responsibility in issuing the orders, raising grave questions about political authority in Moscow. In 1991, Gorbachev's reliance on the military seemed to be placing them in a position to interfere with progress on

[71]See Brzezinski, "Post-Communist Nationlism," pp. 5–16; and Paul Goble, "Ethnic Politics in the USSR," *Problems of Communism*, 38, no. 4 (July–August 1989), 1–14.

[72]"Gorbachev Offers His Plan to Remake Soviet Economy," *The New York Times*, October 17, 1990, pp. A1, A9.

[73]Braun and Day, "Gorbachevian Contradictions," p. 36.

[74]Ibid., p. 49.

[75]"Soviet Loyalists in Charge After Attack in Lithuania," *The New York Times*, January 14, 1991, pp. A1, A6.

finalizing conventional and strategic arms control agreements, a corner-stone of his opening to the West. At the same time, disclosures about the state of the Soviet economy became ever more ominous, giving rise to desperate Soviet appeals for foreign economic assistance. Gorbachev's lead-ership seemed to be sustained by timely flip-flops in his association with reformist and conservative elements in Soviet society. He took the country to a major turning point in its domestic and foreign policies by unleashing powerful domestic political and economic forces, but Gorbachev seemed unable to channel them toward any predictable outcome.

To the country and the world's dismay, Gorbachev was removed from power on August 19, 1991 in a coup engineered by conservatives in the Party, the KGB, and the military. They were attempting to recentralize economic and political power in the hands of the CPSU and traditional Soviet ministries in Moscow on the eve of Gorbachev's signing a new union treaty which would surrender vast new political and economic powers to elected leaders in the union republics—signalling the demise of the old Soviet order. Thousands of Soviet citizens responded to appeals by Boris Yeltsin, the freely elected president of the Russian Republic, to oppose the coup and to demand Gorbachev's return to power. They surrounded and barricaded the Russian Parliament, where Yeltsin led the democratic op-position, and were joined by some defecting armored units of the Red Army. The stand-off and defiance of the coup leaders' authority by the Moscow population, as well as key elements of the KGB and of the military, combined with Western leaders' refusal to recognize the new government, led to its collapse. Gorbachev was released from house arrest to reassume his position of leadership in just three days time; but in a radically trans-formed domestic political environment.

After years of vacillation Gorbachev would be expected to forge ahead decisively with political and economic reforms in the Soviet Union. Con-servative opposition to rapid democratization and the introduction of mar-ket mechanisms should no longer inhibit action, having been discredited by the abortive coup. The forces for democracy, now led by Yeltsin, had found new strength through the public's exhilarating role in defying a return to authoritarianism. Political and economic power would certainly move even more decisively from Moscow to the union republics, embol-dened by the revealed weakness of the central government.

The challenges of governing the USSR and transforming its economy were even more formidable after August 1991 than before. Expectations and demands on Gorbachev had increased dramatically as his power was diminished by political events. The forces of change he set in motion after 1985 had clearly outrun him. The question was whether Gorbachev could catch up to them after his return to power on August 21, 1991 as the political institutions of the center, including the Communist Party, collapsed and as assertions of independence by numerous union republics threatened the disintegration of the USSR. At the same time, the Soviet economy was in a condition of free-fall more severe than the Great Depression of the 1930s. The political economic system of the USSR had imploded. No one in 1991 could sensibly predict its future course.

Predictions about the future political-economic course of the USSR and countries in East Central Europe are necessarily uncertain. It is important to note, however, that all link renewed economic vitality to greater reliance on market processes and to reintegration with the global economy for trade, finance, investment, and technology critical for competitiveness and growth. This process is likely to be carefully managed with a larger role for the state and more constraints on market forces than Western liberal economists would prescribe. Yet, continued need for access to Western trade and finance as well as a strong desire to rejoin Europe will give most states in East Central Europe strong incentives to seek closer association with the European Community and key international economic institutions. Greater conformity with the policy prescriptions of the IMF, the IBRD, and the GATT is likely to provide important signals about the direction of their domestic economic development and the reordering of their societies. Accordingly, international forces will play an important role in reshaping state-society relations as the political-economic transformations from centrally planned economies in East Europe unfold. If momentum for the reform process can be recovered, similar expectations should apply to the Soviet Union—albeit to a lesser degree, given its immense size and greater political distance from Europe. If, on the other hand, Soviet political leaders find it necessary to use force to maintain social order and to resolve the constitutional crisis between Moscow and the Union Republics, the USSR might well retreat to a much more insular, autarkic stance than that of most East European states.

Considerable uncertainty also surrounds assessments of the world order implications of recent developments in the Soviet Union and in East European states. Political realists, such as John Mearsheimer, envision the emergence of politically and economically fragile, hyper-nationalistic states in East Europe giving rise to a highly unstable, multipolar balance of power in the region. They fear that domestic disorder in the USSR and in East Europe could introduce much greater potential for international conflict and war than the earlier bipolar, Cold War confrontation between a strong United States and USSR, each having great influence over allies within their respective spheres of influence.[76] Liberals view the transformation of East European states into market-oriented economies with democratic political systems as likely to make the European political order more peaceful.[77] This is especially likely if they are vigorously assisted by, and absorbed within, the existing framework of liberal international political and economic institutions—the EEC, most importantly.[78] Neo-Marxists are likely to view the same political and economic process as resulting in East European states being connected to the international economy in a highly

[76]John Mearsheimer, "Why We Will Soon Miss the Cold War," *Atlantic Monthly*, August 1990, pp. 35–50.

[77]On this point see Jack Snyder, "Averting Anarchy in the New Europe," *International Security*, 14, no. 4 (Spring 1990), 7–9.

[78]Ibid., pp. 30–41.

dependent fashion, not unlike that of Latin American states—low-value-added industrial production, heavy reliance on commodity exports, large foreign debts, repeated exposure of domestic policies to the dictates of the IMF and other foreign creditors, extensive penetration of their economies by multinational firms, and so forth.

These contradictory speculations cannot predict the future for us. Yet they do indicate how profound the recent transformations in the Communist world have been. We now think of these states in terms of the same political, economic, and security forces and the same models typically used to understand developments in the rest of the world. Whatever their future course, the USSR, China, and the states of East Europe have become (in varying degrees) an integral part of the global political economy during the 1980s, rather than a subsystem of states largely separated from it.

THE GLOBAL ECONOMY AND DOMESTIC POLITICAL-ECONOMIC CHANGE

The world has experienced a dramatic internationalization of production and finance in recent decades. Beyond this increasing international economic interdependence, a noted political economist observes the emergence of an ideological framework based on an open international economy that transcends states with divergent political economic philosophies.[79] He goes on to argue that this has given rise to an "internationalization of the state." The state used to act as a "buffer between the external economic environment and the domestic economy."[80] Its political accountability was to domestic forces, and its main task was to defend domestic interests from disturbances emanating from abroad. The "internationalization of the state" describes "a global process whereby national policies and practices have been adjusted to the exigencies of the world economy of international production [and finance]."[81] The primary role of the state, therefore, becomes that of accommodating the structure of the domestic economy to the imperatives of international economic developments, rather than defending domestic interests from international economic disturbances.

This is an emerging tendency, not a universal law of behavior—states still exhibit neo-mercantilist behavior in all varieties of economic relations designed to buffer domestic interests from foreign interests, and they definitely remain accountable to domestic forces. Yet in broad terms Cox is identifying a pattern of behavior by states that we do witness the world over. The imperative of accommodating international economic processes and change, or falling further behind, has been an important component in the drive for economic and political reforms reintegrating China, the Soviet Union, and the East European states with the global economy. Those

[79]Robert Cox, *Production, Power and World Order* (New York: Columbia University Press, 1987).

[80]Ibid., p. 254.

[81]Ibid., p. 253.

former Communist states that transform themselves into market-oriented systems will have to redefine their domestic social order and state-society relations in a manner that conforms generally to the expectations of international sources of capital, trade, and technology (public and private, bilateral and multilateral). Domestic interests and forces will *not* be buffered by the state in this process. To the contrary, effective transformation processes are expected to undermine established domestic, political, and economic interests and coalitions—the quicker the better.[82]

What is true for the former Communist states is true of most others as well. Less developed country debtors must undertake stringent austerity programs to secure IMF stand-by agreements and to maintain access to finance from other sources abroad. Even if these programs bring positive results over the long term, they have, in the short term, imposed great hardships on the domestic population, undermined long-standing political coalitions, destabilized the order of society, and toppled governments. These domestic societies find it imperative to accommodate international forces.

Among the advanced industrial states of the West, we see European prosperity being linked to the success of efforts to remove all remaining barriers to a single internal market in the EEC. Community economic and social policies are being driven as much by the requirements of retaining competitiveness in international production, service delivery, and finance as by demands for protection of domestic interests and forces. In the United States, sustaining flows of foreign capital to finance yawning government budget deficits in a major consideration in managing interest rates, the exchange rate of the dollar, and macroeconomic policies. In fundamental respects, foreign capital flows dictate American domestic economic policies contrary to the political preferences of the White House, Congress, or organized domestic economic interests. Finally, the emergence of Japan as the world's leading creditor and the appreciation of the yen as an international currency are straining the social bargains and state-society relations associated with its economic miracle in the postwar years. The global interests of Japans' leading multinational firms and financial institutions, for example, complicate the practice of lifetime employment for their Japanese work force, as well as effective administrative guidance of the leading firms and banks by economic ministries of the Japanese state.

The internationalization of production and finance may not have fully internationalized the state to the extent that Cox suggests, but he has placed his finger on an extremely important pattern in the contemporary international political economy. The challenges of managing a national economy in more highly integrated international markets is forcing states everywhere to reposition themselves in relation to their domestic societies and to foreign economic interests. Centrally planned economies search for ways to reorder society by greater use of markets. States in market economies with institutional and historical traditions of noninterference in the private sector (such as the United States), search for acceptable forms of market inter-

---

[82]International Monetary Fund, *World Economic Outlook, May 1990*, p. 71.

vention to remain more competitive with industrial powers having strong state traditions (such as Japan).[83]

The most significant consequence of increased international economic interdependence is its role in reordering domestic societies. Small states and less developed countries have long appreciated this fact. The United States, however, is only now coming to fully appreciate it. Until recently in the postwar period, the United States was in the paradoxical position of occupying the center of the global political economy, while having such a large and comparatively self-sufficient domestic market that foreign economic policies were derivatives of its domestic political-economic concerns. As we approach the turn of the century, the changing character of international economic relations will increasingly define America's domestic economic agenda and policies. To comprehend and to address internal social, political, and economic challenges, we all have to increase our knowledge of international political-economic developments. This examination of the politics of global economic relations offers only a small step in this direction.

---

[83]For a classic comparison of state-society relations as they affect foreign economic policy among the leading industrial states, see Peter Katzenstein, *Between Power and Plenty* (Madison: University of Wisconsin Press, 1978). For a recent analysis of the manner in which the character of state-society relations in the United States has changed, see John Ikenberry, David Lake, and Michael Mastanduno, eds., *The State and American Foreign Economic Policy* (Ithaca: Cornell University Press, 1988).

INDEX